JORGE LUIS BORGES IN CONTEXT

Jorge Luis Borges (1899–1986) is Argentina's most celebrated author. This volume brings together for the first time the numerous contexts in which he lived and worked; from the history of the Borges family and that of modern Argentina including his fascination with the Banda Oriental, through two World Wars, to events including the Cuban Revolution, military dictatorship, and the Falklands War. Borges's distinctive responses to the Western tradition, Cervantes and Shakespeare, Kafka, and the European Avant-Garde are explored, along with his appraisals of Sarmiento, gauchesque literature and other strands of the Argentine cultural tradition. Borges's polemical stance on Catholic Integralism in early twentieth-century Argentina is accounted for, whilst chapters on Buddhism, Judaism, and landmarks of Persian literature illustrate Borges's engagement with the East. Finally, his legacy is visible in the literatures of the Americas, in European countries such as Italy and Portugal, and in the novels of J. M. Coetzee representing the Global South.

ROBIN FIDDIAN is Emeritus Fellow of Wadham College, Oxford and the author of eight books and over 50 articles. The majority of his publications are on topics in Spanish American literature, including the novels of Fernando del Paso (2000) and short fictions of Gabriel García Márquez (2007). His most recent book is *Postcolonial Borges. Argument and Artistry* (2017).

JORGE LUIS BORGES
IN CONTEXT

EDITED BY

ROBIN FIDDIAN

University of Oxford

CAMBRIDGE
UNIVERSITY PRESS

CAMBRIDGE
UNIVERSITY PRESS

University Printing House, Cambridge CB2 8BS, United Kingdom

One Liberty Plaza, 20th Floor, New York, NY 10006, USA

477 Williamstown Road, Port Melbourne, VIC 3207, Australia

314-321, 3rd Floor, Plot 3, Splendor Forum, Jasola District Centre, New Delhi - 110025, India

103 Penang Road, #05-06/07, Visioncrest Commercial, Singapore 238467

Cambridge University Press is part of the University of Cambridge.

It furthers the University's mission by disseminating knowledge in the pursuit of
education, learning and research at the highest international levels of excellence.

www.cambridge.org
Information on this title: www.cambridge.org/9781108456050
DOI: 10.1017/9781108635981

First published 2020
First paperback edition 2022

A catalogue record for this publication is available from the British Library

Library of Congress Cataloging in Publication data
NAMES: Fiddian, Robin W., editor.
TITLE: Jorge Luis Borges in context / edited by Robin Fiddian.
DESCRIPTION: Cambridge, United Kingdom ; New York, NY : Cambridge University Press,
2020. | SERIES: Literature in context | Includes bibliographical references and index.
IDENTIFIERS: LCCN 2019038148 (print) | LCCN 2019038149 (ebook) | ISBN 9781108470445
(hardback) | ISBN 9781108635981 (epub)
SUBJECTS: LCSH: Borges, Jorge Luis, 1899–1986 – Criticism and interpretation. | Argentina –
Intellectual life – 20th century.
CLASSIFICATION: LCC PQ7797.B635 Z7484 2020 (print) | LCC PQ7797.B635 (ebook) |
DDC 868/.6209–dc23
LC record available at https://lccn.loc.gov/2019038148
LC ebook record available at https://lccn.loc.gov/2019038149

ISBN 978-1-108-47044-5 Hardback
ISBN 978-1-108-45605-0 Paperback

Contents

Illustrations

Contributors

LUCAS ADUR is Professor of Latin American Literature at University of Buenos Aires.

ALFREDO ALONSO ESTENOZ is Associate Professor of Spanish at Luther College, Iowa.

MARIELA BLANCO is Jefe de Trabajos Prácticos de Literatura Argentina, Universidad Nacional de Mar del Plata and Investigadora Adjunta de CONICET.

BEN BOLLIG is Professor of Spanish American Literature, University of Oxford, and Fellow of St Catherine's College.

ANA C. CARA is Professor of Hispanic Studies, Oberlin College, Ohio.

SANDRA CONTRERAS is Profesora Titular de Literatura Argentina, Universidad Nacional de Rosario and Investigadora Independiente de CONICET.

CORINNA DEPPNER currently holds a Postdoctoral position at University of Erfurt.

XON DE ROS is Professor of Modern Spanish Studies, University of Oxford, and Fellow of Lady Margaret Hall.

ROBIN FIDDIAN was Professor of Spanish and Spanish American Literature at the University of Oxford until his retirement in 2015. He is now Emeritus Fellow of Wadham College.

EVELYN FISHBURN is Honorary Professor at University College, London and Emeritus Professor, Metropolitan University of London.

FERNANDO GALVÁN is Professor of English Literature at the University of Alcalá, Madrid.

NIALL H D GERAGHTY is Lecturer in Latin American Cultural Studies and Leverhulme Early Career Fellow at University College London.

ROBERTO GONZÁLEZ ECHEVARRÍA is Sterling Professor of Hispanic and Comparative Literatures at Yale University and a Member of the American Academy of Arts and Sciences.

ROBERT S. C. GORDON is Serena Professor of Italian and Fellow of Gonville and Caius College, Cambridge.

ELENI KEFALA is Senior Lecturer in Latin American Literature and Culture at University of St Andrews.

EFRAIN KRISTAL is Distinguished Professor of Comparative Literature at the University of California Los Angeles and a Fellow at the Institute for Advanced Study in Berlin.

ANNICK LOUIS is Maître de Conférences Habilité, Université de Reims-Champagne-Ardennes and Membre de l'équipe pédagogique de l'EHESS Paris–CRAL.

MARINA MARTÍN is Professor of Hispanic Studies, College of Saint Benedict, Saint John's University, Minnesota.

EAMON MCCARTHY is Lecturer in Hispanic Studies, University of Glasgow.

DOMINIC MORAN is Faculty Lecturer in Spanish and Student of Christ Church, Oxford.

PATRICIA NOVILLO-CORVALÁN is Senior Lecturer in Comparative Literature, University of Kent.

HUMBERTO NÚÑEZ-FARACO is Senior Lecturer in Spanish and Latin American Studies, University College, London.

SHAAHIN PISHBIN is pursuing doctoral studies at University of Chicago.

SARAH ROGER is an assistant professor of English and Cultural Studies at McMaster University in Canada.

PHILLIP ROTHWELL holds the King John II Professorship of Portuguese Studies at the University of Oxford, where he is a Fellow of St Peter's College.

GUSTAVO SAN ROMÁN is Professor of Spanish at University of St Andrews.

PHILIP SWANSON is Hughes Professor of Spanish, University of Sheffield.

EDWIN WILLIAMSON is King Alfonso XIII Professor Emeritus in Spanish Studies, University of Oxford and Emeritus Fellow, Exeter College, Oxford.

JASON WILSON is Emeritus Professor at University College, London.

Acknowledgements

This volume could not have come into being nor reached completion without the input of several colleagues. The authors involved in the project have been unfailingly helpful, responsive, and generous with their time. At the stage of design, I was aided in particular by Edwin Williamson and Dan Balderston, whose thoughtful suggestions re topics and contributors epitomized the collaborative spirit of Borges studies at its best. Joanna Page and Evi Fishburn were also supportive at key moments, as were Joanne Edwards of the Taylor Library, University of Oxford, and the 'dream-team' at the Library of Wadham College, Oxford. My thanks go especially to Maria Donapetry, for her incisive comments and criticism and her matchless sense of visual decorum. And to Sarah Roger, for her impeccable work compiling the Index of this volume.

Permissions

On behalf of Cambridge University Press, the Editor thanks the following institutions for granting permission to reproduce material included in the chapter entitled '1920s Buenos Aires': Fundación Pan Klub-Museo Xul Solar, for *Buenos Aires*, 1929, and Dirección General de Estadística y Censos – Ministerio de Economía y Finanzas – Gobierno de la Ciudad de Buenos Aires. República Argentina, for 'Crecimiento de Buenos Aires comparado con el de otras importantes ciudades en la década 1893–1902', originally published in *Anuario Estadístico de la Ciudad de Buenos Aires. Año XIII–1903.*

Note on Primary Sources and Editions Used

Throughout this volume, where reference is made to Borges's works in the original Spanish the preferred source is *Obras completas* (Barcelona and Buenos Aires: María Kodama and Emecé Editores, 1989), 3 vols. In the instances where contributors have used another source, they make this clear in the notes to the chapters concerned. The following works not included in the *Obras completas* are also cited: *Inquisiciones* (1925) (Barcelona: Seix Barral, 1994); *Textos cautivos. Ensayos y reseñas en 'El Hogar'* (Barcelona: Tusquets, 1986); *Textos recobrados, 1919–1929* (Buenos Aires: Emecé, 1997) and *Textos recobrados, 1931–1955* (Buenos Aires: Emecé, 2002).

Chronology

Note: Besides recording significant moments in the life and career of Jorge Luis Borges, this chronology lists events from the public sphere, including cultural landmarks, where they are relevant to a contextual understanding of the writer's life and works. The Chronology draws on previous scholarship including *The Cambridge Companion to Jorge Luis Borges* (2013), the diary-format of Adolfo Bioy Casares, *Borges* (2006), and the archives of the *Borges Center*, University of Pittsburgh (www.borges.pitt.edu).

1776	Viceroyalty of the Río de la Plata established with its capital in Buenos Aires.
1810 25 May.	The city of Buenos Aires forms its own ruling council ('junta'), which breaks with Spain.
1816 9 July.	An assembly of the members of the Viceroyalty meeting in San Miguel de Tucumán declares Argentina formally independent under the name 'United Provinces of the Río de la Plata'.
1824 6 August.	Battle of Junín, in the Andes, where Borges's great-grandfather, Isidoro Suárez distinguishes himself in the closing stages of the fight for South American independence from Spanish rule.
1829	Juan Manuel de Rosas becomes governor of the province of Buenos Aires.
1835	Rosas begins 17-year-long rule over Argentina.
1838–1840	Esteban Echeverría writes 'The Slaughterhouse', which will not be published until 1871.
1845	Domingo Faustino Sarmiento, *Facundo, or Civilisation and Barbarism*.
1850	Domingo F. Sarmiento, *Recollections of a Provincial Past*.

1872	José Hernández, *The Gaucho Martín Fierro* (*Part One; Part Two* follows in 1879).
1874	Paternal grandfather Colonel Francisco Borges dies in action in the final stages of the Conquest of the Desert.
1899 24 August.	Jorge Luis Borges is born in Buenos Aires to Jorge Guillermo Borges, a half-English lawyer and aspiring writer, and Leonor Acevedo Suárez.
1914–1918	The Borges family spends the bulk of the years of the First World War in Geneva, Switzerland, where the young Jorge Luis attends school.
1916	Leopoldo Lugones publishes *El Payador*. Tercentenary of deaths of Miguel de Cervantes and William Shakespeare.
1918–1920	The Borges family moves to Madrid, where Jorge Luis works closely with the Ultraist group. In 1920, he publishes 'Expressionist Lyric: A Synthesis', which is an essay on German Expressionist poetry, and more than a dozen other essays and translations, all in *Grecia* (Madrid).
1921	Family returns to Buenos Aires. Borges collaborates in the 'mural magazine', *Prisma*, which lasts two issues.
1922	James Joyce, *Ulysses*. Borges launches the magazine, *Proa*; he also writes 'The Nothingness of Personality'.
1923	Publishes *Fervour of Buenos Aires* (poetry). Makes a second trip to Europe.
1924	Returns to Buenos Aires, where he re-launches *Proa* and promotes a type of cultural nationalism called 'criollismo'.
1925	Publishes *Moon Across the Way* (poetry) and *Inquisitions*, a volume of essays including 'The Complaint of Every *criollo*'. Publishes a short review-essay, 'Joyce's *Ulysses*', in *Proa*.
1926	Ricardo Güiraldes publishes *Don Segundo Sombra*. Borges publishes *The Full Extent of My Hope* (essays).

1927	Undergoes operation for cataracts. Campaigns for the re-election to the Argentine presidency of Hipólito Irigoyen.
1928	*The Language of the Argentines* (essays). Irigoyen elected President in April.
1929	William Faulkner, *The Sound and the Fury*. Borges publishes *San Martín Notebook*, which is a set of poems. 'Paul Groussac' is an obituary for the French-born emigré who would become a literary critic, polemicist and, eventually, Director of the National Library in Buenos Aires from 1885 until his death.
1930	General José F. Uriburu leads a coup d'état against President Irigoyen. Borges publishes *Evaristo Carriego* – a prose biography of a local poet (1883–1912), supplemented by writings on themes of popular culture.
1932	Publishes *Discussion* – a volume of essays containing 'Gauchesque Poetry', 'Films', 'A Defence of the Cabbala', 'Our Inabilities', and others.
1933	Co-Editor of the 'Saturday Colour Magazine' of the tabloid newspaper *Crítica*, where he publishes stories, essays, reviews, and sketches.
1935	*A Universal History of Infamy*.
1936	William Faulkner, *Absalon, Absalon*. Borges publishes *A History of Eternity* (essays). Begins regular contributions to *Home* weekly magazine (*El Hogar*), for which he writes reviews and capsule biographies of writers such as Benedetto Croce and Virginia Woolf. Founds the magazine *Destiempo* with Adolfo Bioy Casares.
1938	In February, Jorge Guillermo Borges dies. Borges himself suffers a freak accident on Christmas Eve which leads to life-threatening septicaemia.
1939	Loses job at *Home*. Publishes 'Pierre Menard, Author of the *Quixote*' and 'An Essay on Neutrality', which is followed by other writings on the War. 'Joyce's Latest Novel' is a short note on *Finnegans Wake*.

1940   Begins literary collaborations with Bioy Casares.
        Contributes regularly to *Sur*, the cultural periodical
        founded by Victoria Ocampo in 1931.

1941   *The Garden of Forking Paths* (fiction). Publishes 'A
        Fragment on Joyce', in the February number of *Sur*.
        1941 sees the publication, in Buenos Aires, of
        Américo Castro's provocative essay, *La peculiaridad
        lingüística rioplatense y su sentido histórico*.

1942   Borges is overlooked by the panel awarding the
        National Literary Prize. *Six Problems for Don Isidro
        Parodi* is a collection of detective stories co-written
        with Bioy Casares.

1943   Military coup by Argentinian officers sympathetic to
        Mussolini. *Los mejores cuentos policiales*, with Bioy
        Casares.

1944   *Fictions*. Publishes 'A Comment on August 23, 1944',
        which is prompted by the liberation of Paris from
        German occupation.

1946   Juan Domingo Perón officially elected President of
        Argentina. Borges takes over the editorship of a
        literary and cultural review, *Los Anales de Buenos
        Aires*.

1947   Fourth centenary of the birth of Miguel de
        Cervantes. Borges writes 'La fiesta del Monstruo',
        with Bioy Casares.

1948   Writes 'The Simurgh and the Eagle', which will
        subsequently be collected in *Nine Dantesque Essays*
        (1982). With Bioy Casares, *Prosa y verso de Francisco
        de Quevedo*.

1949   *The Aleph* (fiction).

1950   'Personality and the Buddha' appears in *Sur*, nos.
        192–194 (Oct.–Dec.) and will never be reprinted.

1951   Delivers lecture, 'The Argentine Writer and
        Tradition', on 19 December at the Colegio Libre
        de Estudios Superiores. Publishes 'Kafka and His
        Precursors', which will be included in *Other
        Inquisitions* (1952), along with 'Keats' Nightingale'
        and others.

1954   The year when, according to Borges, he lost his
        sight.

1955	Perón is overthrown in a military coup. 'A History of the Tango' is printed in its entirety in the 1955 edition of *Evaristo Carriego*. Borges writes 'Parable of Cervantes and Don Quixote'. With Betina Edelberg, he co-authors *Leopoldo Lugones*, which is an essay on the older poet and essayist. Appointed Director of the National Library in Buenos Aires.
1959 1 January.	The forces of the Cuban Revolution oust the régime of Fulgencio Batista.
1960	*The Maker* is a collection of prose and poems, including 'The Simulacrum', 'Parable of Cervantes and Don Quixote', 'Everything and Nothing', 'The Borgeses', and 'To Luis de Camóes', amongst others.
1961	Awarded International Publishers' Prize, shared with Samuel Beckett.
1961–1962	Spends semester as Visiting Professor at University of Texas at Austin.
1964	*The Self and the Other* is a collection of poems including 'Sarmiento', 'The Golem', and 'Junín', amongst others.
1965	*For Six Strings* contains lyrics for *milongas*.
1967	With Bioy Casares, *Chronicles of Bustos Domecq*.
1968	Uprising of workers and intellectuals in cities including Córdoba (the *Cordobazo*).
1969	*In Praise of Darkness* (poems).
1970	*Brodie's Report* is a collection of stories mostly on Argentine themes.
1973	Under pressure from the new Peronist government, Borges resigns his post as Director of the National Library as a political act to express his disgust with the re-election of Perón as president.
1974	First edition of *Obras completas*.
1975	In July, his mother, Leonor Acevedo Suárez, dies, aged 99. *The Book of Sand* (fiction) and *The Unending Rose* (poems); *Prólogos, con un prólogo de prólogos* is a compendium.
1976	*The Iron Coin* (poems).
1977	*New Stories by Bustos Domecq*, with Bioy Casares.

1979	Visits Japan in the company of Maria Kodama. Publishes 'Franz Kafka: *The Vulture*' in *The Library of Babel*, which is a series of short volumes of fantastic tales, each selected and introduced by Borges, and published in Spain from 1978 to 1986.
1980	Awarded the *Premio Cervantes* (*ex aequo* with Gerardo Diego).
1981	*La cifra/The Limit*, for the most part, poetry.
1982	*Nine Dantesque Essays.*
1983	*La memoria de Shakespeare* comprises four stories.
1985	*Los conjurados* is a miscellany of writings on essential themes.
1986	Dies in Geneva, Switzerland, on 14 June.

Note on Translations and Abbreviations

Quotations in English from the works of Jorge Luis Borges derive from a number of different sources, identified as follows:

CF   *Collected Fictions* by Jorge Luis Borges, trans. Andrew Hurley (New York/London: Penguin, 2000).

Lab   *Labyrinths*, trans. Donald Yates and James E. Irby (London/ New York: Penguin 1970).

OA   Jorge Luis Borges. *On Argentina*, trans. Alfred Mac Adam (New York: Penguin, 2000).

SN-F   Jorge Luis Borges. *Selected Non-Fictions*, ed. Eliot Weinberger (New York: Viking, 1999; also, Penguin, 2000).

TTL   Jorge Luis Borges. *The Total Library: Non-Fiction, 1922–1986*, ed. Eliot Weinberger (London: Allen Lane/Penguin Press, 2000). In essentials, identical to *SN-F*.

Where contributors have worked with other sources, and where they are responsible for their own translations, they indicate so in the notes to the chapters concerned.

Borges in Context, Context in Borges

Robin Fiddian

The award of the inaugural International Publishers' Prize for literary excellence, in 1961, jointly to Samuel Beckett and Jorge Luis Borges for *Trilogy* and *Fictions* respectively, signals a milestone in Borges's accession to the rank of world author. Born in Buenos Aires in 1899, Borges had published the twin collections, *Ficciones* and *Artificios*, in the early-to-mid-1940s and, as the 1950s came to a close, was better known in France and Italy, and latterly, Germany, than in Spain, the United Kingdom, or the USA. Within a couple of years, the picture had changed dramatically: around the time of the announcement of the award of the International Publishers' Prize, Borges would receive an invitation to take up a visiting position at the University of Texas at Austin – the first of many such invitations and acts of recognition, by a major university in the USA, of his stature as a creative writer. Meanwhile, in the Hispano-phone world, the peculiar, hybrid narratives of *Fictions* had elaborated significantly on a long-established River Plate tradition and would provide the seeds, along with works by other contemporary authors from Argentina, Mexico, Uruguay, etc., for a flowering of narrative across Spanish America; this occurred, first, in the 1940s and 1950s (the decades of *la nueva narrativa*), and then, in the literary Boom of the 1960s, an explosion in the production and sales of prose fiction (mainly), that was accompanied by widespread critical acclaim. By the end of that heady decade, translations of works by Borges into several languages and the high-profile adaptation of one of his most enigmatic *ficciones* by Italian film director Bernardo Bertolucci in *The Spider's Stratagem* (1970), testified to Borges's undeniable status as an international cultural icon and source of inspiration for many.

On top of his reputation, Borges's claim on a place in a Writers in Context series is further cemented by the modelling, in one of his best known early fictions, of the very idea of 'context'. In 'Theme of the Traitor and the Hero', Borges analyses the multiple kinds of context that can shape a narrative subject, including its reception. As is well known, Borges, in this fiction, presents the reader, not with a complete and fully rounded story, but with the kernel or skeleton of one that he suggests he may develop at some point in the future. Essential to the story's intelligibility is the relation between historical particularities and multiple possible scenarios. Introducing his subject (one of the meanings of 'tema' in the Spanish language), the narrator, whom we shall call 'Borges', specifies the date of narration as 3 January 1944. A quotation from a section of *The Tower* by William Butler Yeats referring to the cycles of the 'Platonic Year' chimes in with the idea of renewal; the image, in the same verses, of men vividly dancing to 'the barbarous clangour of a gong' evokes a scene of irrationality redolent, to the contemporary reader in Buenos Aires and beyond, of the barbarism of the Second World War. Through the date, 3 January 1944, Borges inscribes his work in a historical context that is immediate and charged with significance.

Moving into retrospective mode, although still writing in the present tense, the narrative entertains a multiplicity of historical moments and locations as potentially suitable for its story, which consequently takes on a speculative air: 'The action takes place in an oppressed and tenacious country: Poland, Ireland, the Venetian Republic, some South American or Balkan state.' After some suspended points (which heighten the sense of imprecision), the narrator elaborates: 'Or rather, it has taken place, since, though the narrator is contemporary, his story occurred towards the middle or the beginning of the nineteenth century' (*Lab*, p. 102). There is considerable slippage and ambiguity in this formulation. First, it is difficult to dissociate the narrator Borges from the second-order narrator inside his blueprint of a fiction; the qualification of that narrator as 'contemporary' begs the question as to whether his function is contemporary with events or with the moment of narration – a question which by implication also attaches to the primary narrator of 'Theme of the Traitor and the Hero': the Argentinian author, Jorge Luis Borges.

The ambiguities inherent in the use of the term 'contemporary' are compounded by the inexactness of the temporal markers 'towards the middle or the beginning of the nineteenth century'. Borges abandons the precise historical grounding of the narrative frame in favour of a formulation that is both accommodating and strange, inasmuch as it inverts the normal chronological order of the beginning and later points of a century. The temporal coordinates of his story-to-be match, in their vagueness, those of its geography, which freely accommodate northern Europe, Eastern and Central Europe, and South America.

Sensitive, no doubt, to the requirement that his – and any – historical story or subject should have a precise temporal and geographical location, Borges now pinpoints Ireland, in 1824; yet the reason for this, he adds, is 'narrative convenience'. A spirit of playfulness is at work here, but a no less important factor is what we might call the dialectic of the One and the Many. By settling on Ireland in 1824 as the setting for his story, Borges certainly complies with some readers' expectations. However, the choice of one out of many possible scenarios is not intended to erase the others; it actually keeps them all in play. Poland, the Venetian Republic, or a Balkan state such as Greece are equally suited to the design and purpose of Borges's story. In philosophical terms, he interleaves Aristotle with Plato, the individual case (here, Ireland in 1824) with the type, of which he cites several instances.

The type to which I allude is the political and cultural phenomenon of early nineteenth-century Romantic nationalism. Associated with writers and political activists such as Adam Bernard Mickiewicz (Lithuania 1798–1855), Johann Wolfgang von Goethe (1749–1832), Lord Byron (1788–1824), and Victor Hugo (1802–1885), Romantic nationalism is common to all the locations in Borges's roster of 'oppressed and tenacious countries' at the start of the nineteenth century. Although they are not named in Borges's story, Wolfe Tone (1763–1798) and Daniel O'Connell (1775–1847) are emblematic figures in modern Irish history who instigated rebellion against British rule at the end of the eighteenth century – with Wolfe Tone leading the Irish Rebellion of 1798 and O'Connell inheriting his mantle and, with it, the sobriquets of 'The Emancipator' and 'The Liberator'. Passed off deceptively as a tool of 'narrative convenience', Ireland in fact stands out at one and the same time as a unique instance of a people's historical aspirations and an example of a wider phenomenon consisting in the break-up of the geopolitical order of imperial Europe.

Within these coordinates, Borges fleshes out the contextual details of the narrative that he imagines writing one day. In 'Theme of the Traitor and the Hero' he sketches a two-tiered trans-historical plot involving two Irishmen, who are blood relatives. One, Ryan, is a writer and the narrator's mid-twentieth-century contemporary; the other is his great-grandfather, Fergus Kilpatrick, a much-revered man and leader in the struggle against the British, who was assassinated in Dublin in 1824. As he researches Kilpatrick's death, Ryan stumbles across inconsistencies in the historical record which bring him to the realization that, far from acting as a true patriot, his great-grandfather actually betrayed the Irish cause and was assassinated by his fellow-conspirators in a cover-up. Borges goes so far as to imagine a date and a location for Kilpatrick's execution, which is scripted and stage-managed as a theatrical event that takes place in Dublin on 6 August. The circumstances of Kilpatrick's death are seen as prefiguring those of Abraham Lincoln, who would be assassinated, likewise, in a theatre, in Washington DC on 14 April 1865 – suggesting an archetypal connection between the two deaths.

Cast in a melodramatic mould, Kilpatrick's story is over-determined and somewhat blasé about the protocols of historical realism (most importantly – and curiously–, Ireland experienced no 'victorious revolt' or definitive liberation from the British in 1824 . . .). However, the choice of date for the evidently fictional and pun-named Kilpatrick's execution, in a Dublin theatre, has resounding relevance for South America, since it was on 6 August 1824 that the Battle of Junín was fought and won, high up in the Andes, by an army of loyalists under the joint command of Venezuela's General Simón Bolívar and General José Sucre of Peru. Followed shortly by the Battle of Ayacucho, the Battle of Junín precipitated the end of Spanish rule in South America and prepared the way for the emergence, throughout the sub-continent, of a number of budding nation-states, starting with Colombia and Venezuela in the north and going all the way down to Chile and Argentina in the south. Although Borges situates his kernel of a story in colonial Ireland, he calls up the crucial moment in Argentine (and Peruvian) history when those two countries acceded to modernity, breaking with the vice-regal structures of Spain. Contextual detail thereby does double duty, operating at one and the same time through entirely plausible (but inexact) reference to early nineteenth-century Ireland, and by analogy to a roster of countries that in fact experienced political upheaval in South America and beyond.

As the mention of Victor Hugo, W.B. Yeats and others illustrates, Borges's story draws on a cultural matrix comprising not only the history of ideas (Romantic nationalism, Condorcet, Vico . . .) but also genres of literature and forms of art. Of these, poetry and drama are woven most conspicuously into the fabric of 'Theme of the Traitor and the Hero', where Robert Browning and Victor Hugo are credited with authorship of some verses celebrating Kilpatrick's status as Romantic hero. However, it is the works of Shakespeare, especially *Julius Caesar* and *Macbeth*, that provide the scaffolding for the theatrical performance in which Kilpatrick, whose treachery has been exposed, is dealt with by his peers. In the course of his investigations, Ryan recognizes certain words uttered by a beggar in conversation with Kilpatrick on the day he dies, as having been copied from a passage in *Macbeth*. For his part, the narrator informs us that James Alexander Nolan, the patriot who masterminds Kilpatrick's demise, freely plagiarized 'the English enemy, William Shakespeare' (*Lab*, p. 105) in scripting the scenario of Kilpatrick's death, while preserving intact both his public reputation as a hero, and the cause of Irish freedom. Through these extravagances of plot, Borges acknowledges the power of a tradition of political tragedy epitomized by Shakespeare; at the same time, he sets his own story of rebellion and betrayal within the context of Romantic drama as exemplified by Victor Hugo, Adam Bernard Mickiewicz, and Spain's Duke of Rivas: all of them, recognized champions of freedom in their politics and creative writing.

The blueprint of a story set in the period of Romantic nationalism in Ireland and elsewhere reveals a connection with Borges's own family history – which is a further context that informs 'Theme of the Traitor and the Hero'. In casting the relationship between Ryan and Kilpatrick as one between a great-grandson and his great-grandfather, Borges brings his own ancestor, Colonel Isidoro Suárez, into the frame, with himself, a writer in his early forties, in the roles of sleuth and scion of a family that distinguished itself in the wars of independence from imperial Spain. The analogy goes only so far: the historical archive includes no mention of any act of betrayal or cowardice on the part of Isidoro Suárez, who consequently emerges every inch a hero from a comparison with Fergus Kilpatrick; nor is any cause given for his great-grandson to feel anything but pride and admiration towards him. A parallel exists, certainly, between Borges and Isidoro Suárez and Ryan and Kilpatrick, the ultimate motivation of which, I suggest, is Borges's desire to inscribe the history of both his family and his country in a grand narrative: one which asserts the heroic foundations of modern nation-states such as Poland, Greece, Argentina, and Peru, and (a full century later) Ireland.

A further context that is embedded in 'Theme of the Traitor and the Hero' concerns the afterlife of an author and the impact his or her narrative may have on readers at some point in future time. At the end of Borges's story, Ryan comes to picture Nolan as a spider-like figure who in 1824 set a trap, not only for the traitor, Kilpatrick, but also for the person who subsequently would take it upon himself to investigate the story of the traitor and the hero. More than a century after the revelations concerning his great-grandfather, Ryan feels disinclined to divulge the truth about his treachery, and he effectively acquiesces in Nolan's scheme. This is clearly problematic and raises thorny ethical questions: was Ryan really bound to silence the truth? Could he not have acted differently? Did he have to publish a book dedicated to the glorious memory of an inglorious man?

The text leaves these and other questions hanging in mid-air . . . Putting judgement of Ryan to one side, we have to acknowledge the scale and cunning of Nolan's master-plot, including the anticipation of a moment when someone, somewhere, will come face to face with the disquieting truth about Kilpatrick and his fellow-conspirators. The context of reception is thus an integral part of Kilpatrick, Nolan, and Ryan's stories, and one that is destined to remain a source of puzzlement, and vicarious embarrassment, for generations of readers to come.

The history of the world and of the Argentine nation; family history and specific cultural matrices; the afterlife of a text and the conditions of its reception: these are the principal building blocks of *context* as modelled in 'Theme of the Traitor and the Hero' by Jorge Luis Borges. Acknowledging their value and usefulness, I adopt them here as a framework and rationale for the 32 chapters of *Jorge Luis Borges in Context*, which I divide into two, roughly symmetrical, parts.

Part One of *Jorge Luis Borges in Context* comprises 16 essays, arranged in two groups. The essays in the first group (Chapters 1–7) focus on family and personal history, the history of the River Plate, and that of the wider world, as Borges engaged with, and was shaped by, it over the nine decades of his life. The development of modern Argentina runs like a thread through these opening essays, which range from the early nineteenth century to the War of the Falklands/Malvinas in 1982. The Battle of Junín in 1824, the years of terror of Juan Manuel Rosas, relations between modern Argentina and Uruguay, and the effects of two World Wars, frame some of the most dramatic experiences in the lives of the Borges family and their famous son.

The essays in the second group (Chapters 8–16) centre on the cultural context of Argentina, from the mid-nineteenth century (with particular reference to works by Sarmiento and *The Gaucho Martín Fierro*), until the end of the twentieth century. This context embraces writing, art, music, social and political affairs, and popular culture. An essay on the responses to Borges of a pair of late twentieth-century Argentine writers moves beyond his lifetime, at the same time as it anticipates further studies of the topic of reception included in Part Two.

The essays in Part Two divide, once more, into two groups, the first of which (Chapters 17–24) acknowledge the impact, on Borges, of the Western literary canon. Starting with Cervantes and Shakespeare (for Dante, see the later chapter, 'Borges in Italy'), the essays proceed via the English Romantics and the early Avant Garde in Spain to Borges's contemporaries, James Joyce and Kafka. The philosophical tradition of

Idealism receives attention on account of its centrality in modern Western thought and its intrinsic importance to Borges. The topic of 'Borges and the Bible' also features, as a reflection of Judeo-Christianity's prominence within the Western tradition, its relationships with other belief systems, and Borges's post-Orientalist deconstruction of the Bible in the context of East-West relations.

Chapters 25–27 address the topics of Borges and Judaism, Borges and Buddhism, and his engagement with Persian literature. The triplet elaborates on the theme of the Middle East and its manifold cultural heritage. Some readers will regret the absence of an essay on Borges and Islam, which would have been a natural complement to those on Judaism, the Bible, and Buddhism; recent work by Luce Baralt and Ian Almond, amongst others, goes some way towards compensating for this lack (see Further Reading).

Rounding off the volume, contexts of reception and 'afterlife' are illuminated in a set of five essays (Chapters 28–32) which document the depth and breadth of Borges's influence on writing and society. The principal authors of the Latin American 'Boom' acknowledged a debt to Borges; his reception in Cuba and in Argentina around the time of the Cuban Revolution is the subject of a valuable new study here. From the 1980s, younger generations of writers and critics construct a 'Borges' more in tune with their poetics and politics – be they Argentine (cf. the essay by Geraghty referred to above) or non-Argentine. In this latter category, Borges appeals once more to contemporary writers of Italy and Portugal (he had first made an impact there in the 1960s) and to Anglophone writers from both hemispheres: see, for example, Paul Auster, whose novel, *4,3,2,1* (2017) is conspicuously Borgesian in conception, and J.M. Coetzee representing the Global South (see Chapter 30). In the chapters on Portugal and Italy, Borges's contemporary impact is set against the history of his prior engagement, as a reader, with Dante, Camões, and other landmarks of the literary traditions of Portugal and Italy.

Without doubt, the biggest challenge of this compendium has been to provide coverage of the various contexts surrounding a major world author, while ensuring a sharpness of focus in each of the essays included here. Inevitably, there are some gaps in coverage: Homer, Anglo-Saxon literature, Quevedo, Pascal, and Hawthorne are notable absentees. Fans of Bolaño may justifiably argue that he is no less worthy of mention than Piglia, for example; or, that the topic of Borges and film is intrinsically less interesting than the Argentine author's thoughts about Paul Groussac or G.K. Chesterton ... Considering the topics that *are* dealt with, I would argue that they have an incontestable bearing on the core subject, which they illuminate in a variety of ways. In spite of their considerable number, all 32 essays adhere with remarkable closeness to one or more aspects of the model of *context* outlined in 'Theme of the Traitor and the Hero'. Individually and collectively, they thereby justify their place in the volume's design. Suggestions for further study can be found in the concluding section of *Jorge Luis Borges in Context*.

PART I

Self, Family, and the Argentine Nation

CHAPTER I

Borges and the Question of Argentine Identity

Edwin Williamson

Borges conceived the War of Independence as 'an act of faith' in the possibility of creating a national identity distinct from that of Spain.[1] But the nature of that identity was a contentious issue which had come to be associated with the figure of the gaucho thanks to two foundational texts of Argentine literature – *Facundo, or Civilization and Barbarism* (1845), by Domingo Sarmiento, and José Hernández's narrative poem *The Gaucho Martín Fierro* (Part 1, 1872; Part 2, 1879).

Facundo was the biography of a blood-thirsty *caudillo* who was active in the turbulent aftermath of independence. Sarmiento argued that the country could only be saved from this 'barbarism' by adopting the Enlightenment values of European 'civilization', championed by the liberal elite of Buenos Aires, who had given intellectual and political leadership to the independence movement. Barbarism, he believed, was rooted in the underpopulated pampas because the gauchos lacked the 'sociability' required for a law-abiding society. He epitomized the plight of Argentina in the image of a gaucho's dagger stuck in the heart of liberal Buenos Aires, for *caudillos* like Facundo had used the gaucho as a tool in the power-struggles which had brought endemic lawlessness to the young republic. Even so, Sarmiento betrayed a certain admiration for the gaucho's skills as a horseman, tracker, and wandering troubadour but he nevertheless rejected his way of life as a pattern for modern Argentina. This was 'a missed ideological opportunity' because the gaucho's rugged individualism could have been portrayed as the cornerstone of a liberal society, as would occur in the case of the cowboy in the USA.[2] The gaucho thus became an ambivalent figure in Argentine culture, for he may well have been a 'barbarian' but he was also a son of the native soil who represented whatever distinctive identity the young republic could claim to possess in relation to Spain.

The ambivalence of the gaucho is evident in Hernández's *Martín Fierro*, which crystallized an anxiety about progress, a fear that the country might sell its soul to the devil of new ideas and foreign commerce. Fierro is an innocent victim of a liberal government in Buenos Aires: he is conscripted to serve in a frontier garrison but he is exploited by the army, so he deserts and roams the pampas as an outlaw, killing a man in a brawl and later claiming another victim; he seeks refuge with the Indians but is eventually horrified by their 'barbarism' and tries to return to 'civilization'. Unable to settle down, he ends up a rootless outlaw once more.

The question of national identity resurfaced in the early decades of the twentieth century, by which time Argentina's economic success had attracted a huge influx of foreigners, to the point where immigration was widely felt to be a threat to the national identity. What did it mean to be an Argentine? The famous poet, Leopoldo Lugones, addressed this question in 1913, in a series of lectures attended by the President of the Republic. He argued that the gauchos, who had formed the backbone of the armed forces which had won independence, provided the foundation of Argentine identity; he called *Martín Fierro* the 'epic' of the *criollos* – Argentines of Spanish descent – because it expressed 'the soul of the race, the key to its destiny'.[3] But troubling questions remained: what about the status of the millions of immigrants who had come to Argentina, and how could city-dwellers identify with the gaucho's wild life on the pampas?

The Mythologizing of Buenos Aires

Shortly after his return to Argentina from Europe in 1921, the young Borges wrote a 'Complaint of All *Criollos*' which echoed the cultural anxiety expressed by Lugones (*OA* 25–30). The 'tragedy' of the *criollos* had been caused by economic progress: the advent of the railway, the replacement of ranching by 'profit-seeking' agriculture, the 'imprisonment' of the pampas by barbed wire, the 'subjugation' of the gauchos, all had conspired to turn the *criollo* into a stranger in his native land and Buenos Aires into a veritable Babel. By 1924 Lugones was urging the armed forces to arrest the rise of what he regarded as demagogy, collectivism, and other alien influences. Argentina, he asserted, should remain a society in which the *criollos* were accorded a cultural pre-eminence over the immigrants, a privilege guaranteed by military force, if necessary.

At around this time, however, Borges's views began to change. He had become smitten with Norah Lange, a girl of Norwegian descent and a budding poet whom he adopted as his protégée.[4] She lived in the far north-west of the city, not far from Palermo, where Borges had lived as a boy. Neighbourhoods like these, bordering the great plains, were known as the *orillas* or 'shores' of Buenos Aires, and they had produced a vibrant plebeian subculture: rustic speech had become inflected with new words to create dialects like *lunfardo*; the music of the gauchos had evolved into the *tango* played in brothels and dance-halls; gaucho outlaws like Juan Moreira and urban *cuchilleros* (knife-fighters) like Juan Muraña were celebrated in song and legend. Borges saw a heroic quality in the brutal knife-fights of the *cuchilleros*, whom he regarded as heirs of the gauchos, and he would celebrate this 'cult of courage' in poems, stories, and essays.

It was this intermingling of country folk and immigrants in the *orillas* that led him to overcome his negative view of Argentine history. The catalyst in this transformation was his fascination with Norah, his Scandinavian muse, who, being the daughter of an immigrant family herself, would inspire him to break out of his dead-end belief in the 'tragedy' of the *criollos* and develop an intensely optimistic vision of the destiny of Argentina. It occurred to him that the *orillas* represented a continuity between the rural past of the *criollos* and the present-day melting-pot of the city. It was natural, he wrote, that the pampas and the gaucho should be revered as 'archetypes' or 'totems' in a pastoral country like Argentina but the peripheral suburbs had also acquired totemic status, for even though Buenos Aires was a 'Babel-like' city which had attracted immigrants 'from the four corners of the world', the *orillas* were still permeated by the influence of the great plains (*OA* 49–52).

In this idea of 'continuity' Borges saw the possibility of creating a new Argentine identity centred on Buenos Aires. Far from believing that the *criollos* had been condemned by progress to cultural extinction, he now urged them to forget their pride in their lineage and become 'confederates' (*conjurados*) with the immigrants in order to create what he termed a 'new man', a new kind of Argentine, in a country where people of diverse backgrounds might find a common home:

> In this house which is America, my friends, men from various nations of the world have conspired together in order to disappear in a new man, a man who is not yet embodied in any one of us but whom we shall already call an 'Argentine' so as to raise our hopes. This is a confederacy without precedent, a generous adventure by men of different bloodlines whose aim is not to persevere in their lineages but to forget those lineages in the end: these are bloodlines that seek the night. The *criollo* is one of the confederates. The *criollo*, who was responsible for creating the nation as such, has now chosen to be one among many.[5]

Borges aspired to create a *criollismo* which was democratic and progressive, unlike Lugones's nostalgic and reactionary version. The latter had argued that *Martín Fierro* was the national epic, but Borges believed Buenos Aires should become the symbolic locus of a new urban *criollismo* shaped by immigration and based on the culture of the common people of the *orillas*. He began to see glorious literary and cultural potential in the Argentine capital: 'Nothing has happened yet in Buenos Aires, whose grandeur has not been validated by a symbol, a surprising fable, or even an individual destiny comparable to Martín Fierro's.'[6] His poem, 'The Mythical Founding of Buenos Aires', played with the conceit that the Spanish had founded the city in the barrio of Palermo, and specifically in the very block where he had been raised as a boy (*OA* 16–17), for he had conceived the possibility of writing an epic – in either prose or verse, he said – which would make the knife-fighter of the *orillas* as much an archetypical figure of the city as Martín Fierro was of the pampas.[7] And he went so far as to call on writers and artists to help him 'incarnate' a new culture no less:

> More than a city, Buenos Aires is a country, and we must find for it the poetry, the music, the painting, the religion, and the metaphysics appropriate to its grandeur. This is the full extent of my hope, which invites all of us to be gods and to work toward its incarnation. (*OA* 47)

Borges thought he had found a political champion for his new *criollismo* in Hipólito Irigoyen, the Radical party candidate in the approaching presidential election. Irigoyen, he wrote, 'represents Argentine *continuity* . . . he represents the present which, without forgetting the past and finding honour in it, turns itself into the future' (my italics). And the future Borges envisaged was of an Argentina free at last of the scourge of *caudillismo*: 'He [Irigoyen] is the *caudillo* who has decreed, with all the authority of a *caudillo*, the death without appeal to all forms of *caudillismo*.'[8] In October 1927, Borges founded a 'Committee of Young Intellectuals for Irigoyen' which would play a very active part in the election campaign. But Irigoyen was a divisive figure: during his first presidential term (1916–1922) high public spending had resulted in soaring inflation and violent industrial unrest. The young writers of Buenos Aires split over Irigoyen, and those of a *nacionalista* persuasion, inspired by Lugones, began urging the army to seize power and establish a corporate society led by a supreme *caudillo*, whose guiding principles would be derived from Catholic social doctrine and traditional *criollo* values.

   Although Irigoyen was elected president in April 1928, Borges's fervent hopes for a future without *caudillos* would not prosper. His first disappointment came around February 1929, when Norah Lange finally rejected him in favour of a rival poet; this plunged him into a long period of depression that sapped his creative energies.[9] Then, in September 1930, after months of agitation by right-wing *nacionalistas*, Irigoyen was overthrown in a military coup d'état. The fact that his hero's downfall was greeted by widespread popular rejoicing made Borges lose heart in the project of mythologizing his native city. The cornerstone of his *criollismo* – the 'continuity' between pampas and *orillas* – now seemed impossibly fanciful: the gaucho belonged to mere folklore, he wrote, and an authentic *criollo* was to be found only in remote places like northern Uruguay, where he had not yet been 'falsified'.[10] Even so, he would remain a public intellectual, and as a semi-fascist, authoritarian *nacionalismo* came to dominate Argentine politics, he would defend the cause of the freedom of the individual.

Borges Against Perón

In 1943, a group of *nacionalista* army officers, admirers of Mussolini and Hitler, seized power. The new junta resolved to preserve 'the sacred interests of the nation' and to resist any attempts to subvert the foundations of 'national identity'.[11] Its dominant figure, Juan Domingo Perón, was elected president in 1946. Shortly afterwards, having resigned his job in a municipal library after claiming to have been humiliatingly 'promoted' by the Peronist authorities to a post as an inspector of chickens, Borges wrote: 'The most urgent problem of our time . . . is the gradual interference of the State into the acts of the individual' (*OA* 133). Argentines, he claimed, did not identify with the State: 'An Argentine is an individual, not a citizen' (*OA* 131). He cited in evidence the scene in *Martín Fierro* in which the police sergeant Cruz, an agent of the State, is so impressed with Fierro's bravery that he decides to join the outlaw and fight against his own men. Borges was playing the *nacionalistas* at their own game: he appeared to concede that the gaucho did indeed represent 'the soul of the race', as Lugones had claimed, but the actual spirit he embodied was precisely the anarchic 'barbarism' that Sarmiento had rejected in *Facundo* but which Borges now characterized as a primitive version of the individual freedom which formed the basis of a liberal society. He returned to this theme in 'The Argentine Writer and Tradition', where he again rejected Lugones's definition of *Martín Fierro* as an epic – Fierro was a killer, brawler and drunk, and exemplary only in so far as he lived by an ethic of courage and personal freedom (*OA* 134–142). Likewise, Argentine writers should not feel constrained by a national 'tradition' defined by the State; they were heirs to the whole of Western culture, which they, as individuals, were free to develop as they pleased.

The young Borges had hoped that Irigoyen would 'decree the death' of 'all forms of *caudillismo*', but Perón threatened to further entrench *caudillismo* in the political culture of Argentina. Borges therefore became an implacable opponent, even justifying the military coup which overthrew Perón in 1955 as a necessary step towards the reconstruction of a genuinely democratic system.[12] Perón, however, would continue to exert enormous influence from his exile abroad, and Borges had to struggle with the fact that a majority of his fellow citizens would at every opportunity vote for supporters of a *caudillo* who was hostile to liberal democracy. He came to doubt the wisdom of 'the people', and briefly joined the Conservative party in 1963. When Perón was re-elected president in 1974, he resigned as Director of the National Library. As it turned out, Perón died after only a year in office, yet his posthumous influence remained so great that no government was able to manage the economy without the acquiescence of the Peronists: 'Argentina would therefore experience periodic convulsions in an otherwise paralysed system, convulsions that would become progressively more violent, as industrial unrest gave rise to guerrilla terror, which would in turn be met by military counter-terror to the point where the nation would all but tear itself apart.'[13]

The Final Years

It is in this context of spiralling conflicts that one must set Borges's notorious declarations in support of the military coup of 1976.[14] As had occurred when Perón was ousted in 1955, he again mistakenly believed that the military junta would prepare the ground for the eventual institution of a genuine liberal democracy, but he soon became disillusioned with the aggressive nationalism and economic incompetence of the dictatorship; subsequent military juntas would prove no better. When reports of torture and 'disappearances' came to light after the restoration of democracy in 1983, he called for the punishment of the military officers responsible for those atrocities.[15]

Such painful realities led to his political radicalization towards the end of his life. His last book, *Los conjurados*, took its title from a poem in which he praised the confederation of Swiss cantons as 'a tower of reason and solid faith' created by 'men of diverse races, who profess diverse religions and speak diverse tongues', and who have 'taken the odd decision . . . to forget their differences and accentuate their affinities'.[16] The term *conjurados* harks back to 1928, when he had urged the *criollos* to become 'confederates' (*conjurados*) with the immigrants in the creation of a new Argentine identity (see p. 13 above). The poem implicitly vindicated the democratic *criollismo* of his youth but it transcended nationalism altogether in its final utopian vision of the entire planet becoming a Swiss-like confederation of cantons too. In November 1985, knowing he was terminally ill with cancer, he departed for Geneva, where he had lived for six years as an adolescent and to which he frequently returned in old age.[17] It was there, a city he had taken to calling 'one of my *patrias*', that he chose to meet his end instead of in his native Buenos Aires.[18] Given Argentina's blood-soaked history, this surprising decision may be regarded as the final act of Borges the public intellectual – he was pointing to the Swiss Confederation as an ideal model for his tragically divided native land.

Notes

1. E. Williamson, *Borges: A Life* (New York: Viking, 2004), p. 4. Translations into English are my own unless otherwise indicated.
2. E. Williamson, *The Penguin History of Latin America* (London: Penguin Books, 2009), pp. 291 and 289–293.
3. Lugones, *El payador* [1916] (Buenos Aires: Centurión, 1961), p. 16.
4. Williamson, *Borges: a Life*, pp. 124–129 and 142–146.
5. 'Página relativa a Figari', in *Jorge Luis Borges: Textos recobrados, 1919–1929*, p. 362.
6. 'After Images', in S.J. Levine (ed.), Jorge Luis Borges, *On Writing* (New York: Penguin, 2010), p. 9.
7. 'Invectiva contra el arrabalero', in *El tamaño de mi esperanza* (Buenos Aires: Espasa Calpe/Seix Barral, 1993), pp. 125–126, and Williamson, *Borges: A Life*, pp. 137–142.
8. Unpublished letter. See Williamson, *Borges: A Life*, pp. 164–165.
9. *Ibid.*, pp. 123–159 and 167–168.
10. 'Our Inabilities', in *On Argentina*, pp. 117–121, and Williamson, *Borges: A Life*, p. 174.
11. David Rock, *Authoritarian Argentina* (Berkeley: University of California Press, 1993), p. 135.
12. Williamson, *Borges: A Life*, pp. 334–335.
13. *Ibid.*, p. 339, and *The Penguin History of Latin America*, pp. 471–479.
14. Williamson, *Borges: A Life*, pp. 422 and 424–425.
15. *Ibid.*, pp. 458–459 and 474.
16. *Ibid.*, p. 465.
17. *Ibid.*
18. For his last days, *ibid.*, pp. 475–489.

CHAPTER 2

Borges and the Banda Oriental

Gustavo San Román

The Banda Oriental is the ancestral name of Uruguay, but the two terms have different associations. 'Uruguay' tends to denote a modern country which has enjoyed a generally stable and progressive democracy since the beginning of the twentieth century. By contrast, 'Banda Oriental' designates the same territory and community during colonial times, some of whose characteristics continued to prevail until the end of the nineteenth century. Whilst the area was part of the Viceroyalty of the River Plate, with Buenos Aires as its capital, the name Banda Oriental signified its geographical situation to the east of the Uruguay River, where the main urban centre was Montevideo.

After the declaration of independence from the Napoleonic government of Spain by the Buenos Aires leaders in May 1810, the Banda Oriental became a member of the United Provinces of the River Plate (1810–1817) and assumed the name of Provincia Oriental. It was during this time that the figure of José Artigas, the leader of the *Orientales* who demanded a proper confederation of autonomous provinces, rose to prominence and became a thorn in the side of the Buenos Aires elite and its centralizing aspirations. Following an invasion of the area from the east, to which Buenos Aires turned a blind eye because it helped restrain Artigas's exigencies, the region fell under the jurisdiction of the Empire of Portugal and, from 1822, of independent Brazil; during this period it became known as the Provincia Cisplatina (1817–1828).

The geographical reference in relation to the river border remained when the province – following a revolution started in 1825 by the legendary Thirty-Three Orientales led by Antonio Lavalleja, but ultimately as a decision by the governments of the United Provinces, Brazil, and Great Britain – turned into the Estado (later República) Oriental del Uruguay in 1828. The new nation, created as a buffer state between the two giants, experienced political and social instability for the rest of the century as a result of internecine conflict between two caudillo-led forces and later political parties: the Blancos (roughly, traditionalists, Americanists and with a stronger rural base), who were close to the Argentinian Federalists, and the Colorados (cosmopolitanists with support from urban elites), generally allied to the Unitarians across the Plate. The local discord became entangled in transnational tensions involving Argentina, under the Federalist Juan Manuel de Rosas, Brazil, and indirectly France and Britain; major confrontations during this period were the Guerra Grande (Great War) (1838–1851) and the infamous War of the Triple Alliance against Paraguay (1864–1870).

'The Banda Oriental' therefore designates, first of all, a space that twice progressed from colonial region to province (under a confederation in name rather than in fact; and as a dominion of empire), neither of which satisfied most of its population, as shown by the great popular support for Artigas, until finally, and contrary to Artigas's and Lavalleja's wishes, it became an autonomous nation.

In a complementary sense, the label indicates a more primitive and traditional world marked by post-independence discord where the elemental values of the gauchos and rural caudillos threatened the aspirations of a weak urban elite struggling to move the country towards modernity. Domingo F. Sarmiento's famous opposition of civilization versus barbarism certainly comes to mind. The transition between the old Banda Oriental and a new, progressive Uruguay culminated with the last civil war in the country, which pitted the Colorados, led by the great visionary president José Batlle y Ordóñez, and the Blancos, commanded by the legendary rural caudillo, Aparicio Saravia. The war was won by Batlle, and the modern nation was born. The date was 1 September 1904 and the event the Battle of Masoller, at a site on the north-eastern border with Brazil, when Saravia was fatally wounded.

The turmoil as well as the attraction of the Banda Oriental was captured by the Anglo-Argentinian writer and naturalist, W.H. Hudson, in his 1885 novel, *The Purple Land that England Lost*. The protagonist, Richard Lamb, moves from despising the country for its primitive nature to celebrating its dignity and freedom from the shackles of class. Jorge Luis Borges, an admirer of Hudson, also provides an imagined vision of the region to the east of the Uruguay river. Indeed, it could be argued that both writers shared a perspective that is in fact not uncommon amongst their countrymen, especially *porteños* (Buenos Aires dwellers), which we might call the cultural phantom limb syndrome, as it involves deep dissatisfaction with the secession of the Banda Oriental in 1828 and, symbolically, its denial. One rather colourful expression of the syndrome occurred in a speech by

President Cristina Fernández de Kirchner during 2013, the bicentenary of
the 'Instructions' sent by José Artigas to the Buenos Aires Junta demanding
a confederation of autonomous provinces. Before a large audience in Entre
Ríos, an Artiguista stronghold during the caudillo's rule, Mrs Fernández
regretted the Junta's rejection of the proposals and her heartfelt position
came out spontaneously in a broadside: 'Artigas wanted to be Argentinian
and we did not let him, damn it!!'[1]

Other versions of the condition have occurred in literature. One, also
fairly candid, is by the writer and blogger Hernán Casciari, who roundly
claimed that he was a Uruguayan trapped within the body of an
Argentinian.[2] For his part, Julio Cortázar in his great novel *Hopscotch*
(1963) chose a Uruguayan girlfriend for his male protagonist and alter
ego, Horacio Oliveira. La Maga represents a sensual and telluric force that
is beyond the rational understanding of the porteño intellectual Oliveira,
who moved to Paris to seek (but failed to find) European answers to the
meaning of life. But probably the writer who engaged in the most thorough
display of phantom limb syndrome amongst his compatriots is Borges,
who claimed in one of his stories, 'The Other Death', which is precisely
about a man who fought at Masoller, that 'Uruguay is more elemental than
our own country, and therefore wilder' (*CF* 225).

Borges had family links with the country on both maternal and paternal
lines, since his grandfather, Colonel Francisco Borges Lafinur, was born in
Montevideo and his grandmother, Leonor Suárez Haedo, in Mercedes, in
the department of Soriano.[3] He also declared in interviews that he could be
considered an Oriental, as he was probably conceived in an estancia near
Fray Bentos, a location which his parents and later Borges himself often
visited on holiday (it is also the original site of the factory which produced
and exported the famed corned beef and pies).[4] The Banda Oriental/
Uruguay figures in a number of his works, as exemplified by two poems
and two stories. 'Montevideo' is a short celebration of the capital, described
as the Buenos Aires 'which we used to have'.[5] A more substantial poem is
'Milonga for the Orientales', the term *milonga* stressing nostalgia as it
denotes an earlier version of the tango genre.[6] It begins with the poet
identifying himself as a porteño and addressing his neighbours as
Orientales and moves on to speak of the entanglement ('entreverar'
means mixing together in a such a way that the original parts are difficult
to distinguish) of the histories of the two countries and of his own family
across the border. The bond is expressed through battles (Cagancha,
December 1839, during the Guerra Grande, when forces sent by Rosas
from Argentina were defeated after a close fight by those of the Colorado

General Rivera; and the notorious siege of Blanco-held Paysandú by the Colorados, December 1864–January 1865, whose defenders included Rafael Hernández, brother of the author of *Martín Fierro*); places which Borges knew well (Paso Molino in Montevideo, Cuchilla de Haedo, named after one side of his family, in the north-west of the country); streets in Buenos Aires and Montevideo where tango was born (Junín and Yerbal, the latter no longer in existence after redevelopment); and caudillos (Ramírez and Artigas, the former once Artigas's lieutenant in Entre Ríos, until he signed a peace agreement with Buenos Aires; this was the last straw for the leader of the Orientales, who went into permanent exile in Paraguay). The poem's last stanza rather wistfully stresses similarity beyond the subtle differences, hoping that time will 'erase borders' because the two flags share the same colours.

Borges's prose writings include essays and short fiction about paradoxical arguments in philosophy and intricate storylines where impossible events intrude in normal reality; in both cases he pokes fun at human attempts at explaining the universe. But there is also a more serious streak in his work which engages with intense experiences, enigmatic characters and matters of elemental honour and morality. It is proposed here that the setting par excellence for this dimension in Borges's work is the Banda Oriental.

In his biography of the author, Edwin Williamson recalls an encounter Borges had in the Uruguayan countryside in November 1934 during a holiday with his friend and fellow writer Enrique Amorím. They were travelling through Tacuarembó, which is very much Uruguay *profond*, as it is the only department with an indigenous name (from Guaraní *caña tacuara*, a kind of bamboo) as well as being located in the centre of the northern half of the country. Traditionally called 'the desert', this area is still much less populated than the region below the Negro River. As they were driving on country roads, Borges and Amorím saw a large group of gauchos. Borges was amazed, exclaiming 'Good Lord! Three hundred gauchos!' The experience of this elemental world impressed him deeply: 'Everything I then witnessed – the stone fences, the longhorn cattle, the horses' silver trappings, the bearded gauchos, the hitching posts, the ostriches – was so primitive, and even barbarous, as to make it more a journey into the past than a journey through space.'[7] Tacuarembó is the scene for 'The Shape of the Sword' (1942), about an Irish political rebel who, at the end, confesses he had been a traitor and asks Borges to despise him. The department is therefore a locus of redemption.

Two other stories further illustrate the power and fascination of the Banda Oriental for Borges. 'Funes, His Memory' (1944) is about a young gaucho from Fray Bentos. The first-person narrator makes autobiographical references, including to his cousin Bernardo Haedo, brother of Borges's childhood love, Esther Haedo, who married the aforementioned Enrique Amorím, as well as to a number of figures of Uruguayan history, such as the soldier and politician Máximo Pérez, the liberal intellectual Agustín de Vedia, the avant-garde poet Pedro Leandro Ipuche, and Luis Melián Lafinur, a lawyer and politician and a relative of Borges's.

The story illustrates what would happen if the theory of empiricism, as proposed by John Locke, who is mentioned in the text, were to apply. If all our knowledge of the world came exclusively from sense data, Borges is saying, we would not be able to think, as thinking involves abstract ideas. But if we leave this philosophical proposition aside, the setting of the story and the protagonist's nationality add further significance to the tale.

There are at least three instances which demonstrate that Funes occupies a superior position to the narrator, and they are all related to the fact that one is an illiterate gaucho whilst the other is an urban intellectual. The first involves the key theme of memory and reliability: the opening sentence declares that whilst Funes is truly able to remember, the narrator's own memory is untrustworthy. The second places the gaucho in a bygone world which seems more attractive than the contemporary habits of Borges's own cosmopolitan city: the gaucho's speech is in 'the slow, resentful, nasal voice of the toughs of those days, without the Italian sibilants one hears today' (*CF* 131). More explicitly, Funes and his countrymen stand for solid values as against the superficiality of Buenos Aires: the narrator's identity as a porteño intellectual is bound to inspire prejudice in Funes, even though the gaucho, who is typically cautious with words, does not declare it: '*Highbrow, dandy, city slicker* – Funes did not utter those insulting words, but I know [...] that to him I represented those misfortunes' (*Ibid.*). A third area of contrast builds on this ethical dimension as it represents the narrator in dubious terms that contrast with Funes's stoical dignity. This happens at least twice. The first time is when Borges, on hearing the news of his father's serious illness, allowed his filial duty to be overruled by the 'prestige' of receiving a telegram and the impulse to 'dramatize my grief by feigning a virile stoicism' (*CF* 133): he therefore appears dishonest and unfeeling (as well as insufficiently masculine). The second moment is the closing portrait of Funes, when Borges describes the gaucho as 'monumental' (*CF* 137).

The second story is 'Avelino Arredondo' (1975), who committed the only assassination of a president in Uruguayan history. The victim, Juan Idiarte Borda, was shot at point-blank range as he was leaving Montevideo's cathedral after a *Te Deum* on 25 August 1897, the national day. The story elaborates on the few facts that are known about the killer and on the brilliantly argued case for the defence by none other than Borges's aforementioned relative, Luis Melián Lafinur, to provide a portrait of Arredondo's character that is consistent with the vision of Uruguay that we have been cataloguing.[8]

Arredondo is friendly with a group of other young men who are also critical of the president, but he is not like them. The first difference is that whilst they are all Montevideans, the eponymous hero, like Funes, is 'from the interior' (literally, 'from deep in the country') (*CF* 472). A second contrast is that the men condemned the undemocratic actions of the president but did nothing about it; for his part, Arredondo kept emotions to himself and 'remained silent' (*Ibid.*): he is a man of action, not of words. The fact that he is resolutely not an intellectual is the third significant feature of his character.

Avelino 'was not a thinking man, or one much given to meditation' (*CF* 474) and he was a student of law 'in his spare time' (*CF* 472), which suggests that he was not convinced about the usefulness of the discipline. When he retires to prepare for the assassination, Avelino disposes of his library, keeping only the Bible. From it he read especially, and memorized, two significant books (Funes also learned books by heart). The first is Exodus, which echoes the 1811 epic journey, led by Artigas, of the people of the Banda Oriental after Buenos Aires refused to support his siege of royalist Montevideo; the second book is Ecclesiastes, arguably the greatest book of wisdom in Western culture, which challenges all human aspirations to happiness and instead recommends leading a simple life with stoicism.

Arredondo's association with the grassroots democratic clamour that characterized the Banda Oriental since its beginnings is evident in his recollections as he prepares for his action. Notable images are a stagecoach travelling from Fray Bentos (the land of Funes); the nearby beach at Agraciada where the Thirty-Three Orientales arrived from Buenos Aires; and Hervidero, the location of Artigas's headquarters. A further echo of 'Funes' is the use of the verb 'recordar' (remember) here in its sense of 'wake up' ('He would have liked to wake up when the sun was high' (*CF* 474)). Finally, it is Avelino's deep moral conviction that drives him to the murder, as he declares, after the deed, that it was an 'act of justice' and that he had worked alone (*CF* 476).

The Banda Oriental, as we have seen, is strongly associated in Borges's work with certain powerful, primordial values. His poetry on the subject highlights a shared origin, regrets the separation and muses on what still connects the two nations either side of the River Uruguay. Funes represents elemental principles of humility and stoicism; similarly impassive, Avelino stands for righteousness in a context of ineffectual criticism of corrupt government.

The closing sentence of 'Avelino Arredondo' expresses the ability of fiction to provide missing information: 'This is how the events might have taken place [. . .]; this is how I can dream they happened' (*CF* 476)). The statement can be interpreted more broadly to include the role of the Banda Oriental in Borges's work as the expression of the phantom limb syndrome. His stance is nuanced and ironic; but ultimately it is not inconsistent with the more vivid articulation by Cristina Fernández, who could very well have proclaimed, in that speech of June 2013: 'Why did we lose the Banda Oriental, damn it?'

There is a curious autobiographical echo to his position, as Borges was born on 24 August 1899, that is, on the eve of one of the two national days of Uruguay (the other is 18 July, marking the people's approval of the constitution of 1830). August 25th (the date of Arredondo's action in 1897) commemorates the declaration of independence from Brazil by the Thirty-Three Orientales. That document (surely being formulated still the day before) explicitly states the patriots' wish to remain part of the United Provinces; the fact that the latter became Argentina and their own province an independent state was not the outcome they sought.[9] The coincidence in dates makes it a most appropriate birthday for someone who lamented the loss of the Banda Oriental.

Notes

1. 'CFK: "Artigas quería ser argentino y no lo dejamos, carajo"', *El Observador* (Montevideo), 26 June 2013. The video can be found online.
2. Hernán Casciari, 'Nacer a 340 kilómetros de la cuna', *La Nación* (Buenos Aires), 6 December 2009. Online.
3. Jorge Oscar Pickenhayn, *Borges a través de sus libros* (Buenos Aires: Plus Ultra, 1979), p. 229.
4. Ana Inés Larre Borges, 'La orilla oriental de Borges, una puerta falsa a la alegría', *Actas de las Jornadas Borges y el Uruguay*, ed. Sylvia Lago (Montevideo: Universidad de la República, 2001), p. 99.
5. 'Montevideo' is included in *Luna de enfrente* of 1925; translation my own.
6. 'Milonga de los Orientales', in *Para las seis cuerdas* (1965), *OC* II, pp. 345–346.

7. E. Williamson, *Borges: A Life* (London: Viking Penguin, 2004), p. 210.

8. Luis Melián Lafinur, *Causa política de Avelino Arredondo acusado de homicidio en la persona del Presidente de la República* (Montevideo: Impr. Latina, 1898).

9. See Eduardo Acevedo, *Anales históricos del Uruguay*, Vol. 1 (Montevideo: Barreiro y Ramos, 1933), pp. 292–295.

CHAPTER 3

Borges in Person: Family, Love, and Sex

Edwin Williamson

Borges's mother and father crucially influenced the kind of writer he was to become. Leonor Acevedo was a strong, domineering woman and a strict Catholic who came from a middle-class *criollo* family, but she instilled in her son 'Georgie' and daughter Norah a fierce pride in the patrician status their line of noble warriors had bestowed upon them all. One of their ancestors had taken part in the conquest of Peru, another won Paraguay for the Spanish Crown, a third founded the city of Córdoba, while Juan de Garay secured the settlement of Buenos Aires. Their forebears also fought to create the Argentine nation: Francisco de Laprida was president of the congress which declared independence; Miguel Estanislao Soler commanded a division in San Martín's army of liberation; and Isidoro Suárez led the cavalry charge which turned the tide of battle at Junín, winning praise from Simón Bolívar himself.

The Borges lineage, though comparatively modest, had honourable ancestors too: Juan Crisóstomo Lafinur was among the first poets of Argentina, while Colonel Francisco Borges distinguished himself in the Indian wars. He met an early death in combat, however, and his English widow would bring up her two sons in straitened circumstances. One son, Jorge Guillermo, Borges's father, became a reluctant lawyer by profession, a free-thinking anarchist, and a compulsive philanderer, who kept trying and failing to become a writer. He settled the family in Palermo, a barrio bordering the pampas once notorious for its *cuchilleros* (knife-fighters) but then becoming gentrified. He had his son 'Georgie' tutored at home until about the age of 11, allowing him also free access to his library of over a thousand volumes, where the boy would spend hours devouring tales of fantasy and adventure. Cut off as he was from other children (other than his sister Norah), Father's library, in effect, became his playground, a place of dreams and terrors, but for all the thrills of reading, books offered a second-hand picture of the world, a kind of 'unreality', and Georgie was drawn to the world outside the confines of the home, especially the

exciting world of gauchos and *cuchilleros* celebrated in poems extolling the
'cult of courage' which Evaristo Carriego, one of Father's bohemian
friends, often recited at the family house. Father's library, then, was
a mixed blessing: 'As most of my people had been soldiers [...] I felt
ashamed, quite early, to be a bookish kind of person and not a man of
action.'[1]

Poles apart though they were, Mother and Father agreed on one thing:
'From the time I was a boy, it was tacitly understood that I had to fulfil the
literary destiny that circumstances had denied my father.'[2] This expectation fostered an idea which long endured in Borges's imagination: the man
of action, whether hero or outlaw, was capable of clinching in combat
a defining sense of true being: 'Any life however long and complicated it
may be, actually consists of a single moment – the moment when a man
knows forever more who he is' ('A Biography of Tadeo Isidoro Cruz
(1829–1874)', *CF* 213). Likewise, a writer might find his destiny by creating
a single, self-defining work: 'I have already written more than one book in
order to write, perhaps, one page. The page that justifies me, that summarizes my destiny' ('A Profession of Literary Faith', *SN-F* 27). This quest
to fulfil a 'literary destiny' provides a thread that runs through Borges's
manifold writings from beginning to end.

In 1914 Dr Borges took the family to Europe, where they were surprised
by the outbreak of the First World War and took refuge in neutral Geneva
for the duration. One of Georgie's earliest texts was an impassioned fantasy
about making love to his sweetheart, a Swiss girl called Emilie:

> Oh Beloved, our kisses will light up the Night! (Oh Adamic phallus!).
> Throw open the Windows, for I want to invite the Universe to my
> Nuptials. Kiss me. Kiss me ... Already my woes have died, and with you
> by my side I feel strong as a God. I am a God. I can create life.[3]

Here we find already two abiding themes: the aspiration to experience
a mystical (and highly eroticized) union of self and world in a rapturous
totality, and the muse who will inspire him to realize that union in
a literary work. Shortly after Georgie fell in love, however, Dr Borges
sent his son to be initiated by a prostitute, an experience that caused
a nervous breakdown and contributed to life-long difficulties with
women.[4] This, and his father's decision to take the family to Spain, put
paid to Georgie's first romance.

In Seville, and then Madrid, both he and his sister Norah, who was by
now an accomplished painter and maker of woodcuts, befriended several
young Spanish writers and artists. Brother and sister became active in the

nascent Spanish avant-garde. Norah would eventually marry the poet and
critic Guillermo de Torre, one of her brother's closest associates at the
time. Jorge Luis wrote several poetic manifestos with the aim of steering the
Hispanic avant-garde in the direction of the expressionism he espoused.
He valued originality above all else: each poet should strive to be different
from all the others; he must 'throw overboard the whole of the past' in
order to achieve 'a naked vision of the world, purified of ancestral stigmas'.[5]
A poem should not be a 'passive mirror' of reality but should refract
experience through the 'active prism' of feeling and imagination in order
to rise above contingent circumstances and 'convey naked emotion'.[6]
Nevertheless, on his return to Buenos Aires in 1921, and despite leading
an avant-garde revolt against the Argentine literary establishment, he felt
haunted by the 'anguished' voices of the dead heroes whose portraits hung
in the family drawing room.[7] He took to writing about the 'nothingness of
personality',[8] but gradually, as is evident in many of the poems in his first
published book *Fervor de Buenos Aires*, he overcame these feelings of
alienation when he fell in love with Concepción Guerrero, for love, he
believed, could connect one's self to another, and through the lover, to the
essential reality of the world. ('Throw open the windows, for I want to
invite the Universe to my Nuptials.') Doña Leonor, however, thought
otherwise: Concepción, the daughter of humble Spanish immigrants,
would never do for the scion of a patrician *criollo* family, so she engineered
a year-long trip to Europe (1923–1924) which resulted in the break-up of
Georgie's second romance.[9]

    Not long after his return to Buenos Aires, Borges became infatuated
with a tall, fair-skinned girl of Norwegian descent boasting a glorious mane
of red hair.[10] Norah Lange, he wrote, was 'illustrious for the double
brilliance of her hair and her haughty youth', she was 'light and haughty
and passionate like a banner unfolding in the breeze'. What is more, she
was a budding poet, so he adopted her as his protégée, seeing her first book
into print and welcoming her to his circle of avant-garde poets. The group
would meet every Saturday at the Lange family villa on Calle Tronador to
recite and discuss their poems and then dance to tangos that Norah played
on the piano. Inspired by his dazzling Nordic muse, Borges conceived the
project of 'mythologizing' Buenos Aires, which he expanded into an
ambitious vision of creating a new Argentine cultural identity no less (see
Chapter 1, above). But in November 1926, Norah fell head over heels in
love with Oliverio Girondo, Borges's most hated rival for the leadership of
the avant-garde. For over two years she would oscillate between Girondo
and Borges, creating a love-triangle which brought great anguish to all

three.[11] While waiting for Norah to choose between her two suitors, Borges wrote: 'For love unsatisfied the world is a mystery, a mystery that satisfied love appears to understand.'[12]

After Norah finally rejected him around February 1929, he abandoned forever the project of creating a new Argentine identity and culture based on his native city. He recorded a dream about waking up in a strange room: 'I thought fearfully, "Where am I?" and I realized I didn't know. I thought, "Who am I?" and I couldn't recognize myself ... Then I really woke up, trembling' ('The Duration of Hell', *SN-F* 51). Gone were the ties that bound him to a familiar world, gone the dream of the realized self, the promise of love had vanished, and Hell was a room in the middle of nowhere in which you had lost all sense of who you were.

Many years later, Borges cryptically evoked the loss of Norah Lange in 'The Aleph', which dwelt on the notion of love as the key to 'understanding' the world by describing the extreme obsession of a character called 'Borges' with Beatriz Viterbo – even after she dies (nb. in *February* 1929, *OC* I: 617–618), he brings a gift to her house every year on her birthday. The name Beatriz indicates that Borges took from Dante's *Divine Comedy* the theme that the poet's love of a woman may inspire the writing of a master-work describing the author's journey to salvation and a crowning vision of universal wholeness. But this Dantean aspiration is mocked through Carlos Argentino Daneri, a cousin and sometime lover of Beatriz, who is writing a laughably inept poem called *The Earth* in which he confidently expects to describe the entire globe. Daneri claims to be inspired by the Aleph, a magic orb set in the wall of a cellar in Beatriz's house in which all the myriad aspects of the universe instantly cohere. But, on contemplating the Aleph himself, 'Borges' realizes the futility of trying to capture the 'inconceivable universe' in human language, so he advises the lumpish Daneri to leave Buenos Aires for the country and allow Beatriz's house to be demolished.

In the 1930s, Borges was racked by insomnia, nightmares, depression, and even thoughts of suicide. He would scarcely write any poetry at all. His early promise seemed to have come to nothing and in 1938 he found a miserable job in a municipal library after his father became terminally ill. Dr Borges's published output amounted to a few poems and only one novel, *The Caudillo* (1921), but he could not resign himself to failure, so he asked his son to re-write *The Caudillo* 'in a straightforward way, with all the fine writing and purple patches left out', and the two of them would discuss ways of improving the work.[13] This strange request brought the question of fulfilling a literary destiny to a head, for how could Borges save his father from failure when he had himself been mired in failure for some ten years?

'Pierre Menard, Author of *Don Quixote*' was published in May 1939, just over a year after Dr Borges's death. It describes the attempt by a French author, recently deceased, to 'repeat' Cervantes's masterpiece by making his text coincide word for word and line by line with the Spanish author's. Had Menard's 're-writing' succeeded, it would have undermined Cervantes's unique status as the original author of the novel, but even though he managed to re-create two short passages, Menard found that time had changed their meaning anyway, which suggested that an author was not the indisputable source of meaning in a literary text but rather it was the reader who invented its meaning as he went along.

The story foreshadowed certain ideas later developed by French theorists, especially Roland Barthes's 'death of the author'. Nevertheless, a bitter irony pervades the narrative, for Menard's enterprise threatened to destroy Borges's own hopes of fulfilling his unique destiny with his pen. From the horror of that destruction Borges would derive some of the major themes of his *ficciones* – the merciless depredations of time, the elusiveness of reality, and the 'nothingness of personality': one man could be any man. Still, the desire for justification by writing would resurface from time to time. In 'The Secret Miracle', the Jewish writer Hladík, who is about to be shot by the Nazis, prays to God for the time to finish a play capable of 'rescuing' what was 'fundamental to his life': 'In order to complete that play, which can justify me and justify Thee as well, I need one more year' (*CF* 161).

Borges's hopes revived when he fell in love with a young writer called Estela Canto in 1944. He embarked on a turbulent relationship which, over its three main phases, was to last ten years (1944–1946; 1949–1950; 1955).[14] Already in the first phase he proposed marriage, and Estela agreed – but on condition they first had sexual relations. He went to a psychologist for help to overcome his inhibitions, but Estela came to resent what she saw as his fear of standing up to his interfering mother, who regarded her as a social inferior. In July 1946, she went off with another man. Her desertion provoked 'The Zahir', in which the protagonist, 'Borges', is in love with Teodelina Villar, who is indifferent to him. When she dies, he finds the Zahir, a coin which obsesses him to the point of madness. Borges would later describe this story as 'more or less "The Aleph" once again'.[15] And, indeed, the unforgettable coin is dated 1929, the year of Beatriz Viterbo's death in 'The Aleph', and also the year in which Borges himself had been rejected by Norah Lange.

The affair with Estela Canto came to an end in 1955, shortly after his appointment as Director of the National Library, a bittersweet honour, for a recent accident had left him unable to read or write, he had failed to find love, and here he was again, back in a library. But still he yearned to find his true self. In 'Borges and I', he split his intimate self from an inauthentic public 'Borges' who kept 'distorting and magnifying' the things they had in common:

> Years ago I tried to free myself from him, and I moved on from the mythologies of the slums and outskirts of the city to games with time and infinity, but those games belong to Borges now, and I shall have to think up other things. (*SN-F* 324)

In due course his amorous misfortunes would bring about a radical change of direction in his writing. Estela Canto had blamed Doña Leonor for her son's unhappiness in love, and Borges seemed to agree: 'Mother is very domineering, she only likes women whom she knows I don't like', he told his friend Bioy Casares.[16] He had attempted to rebel on various occasions, and when he fell for María Esther Vázquez, he knew Mother would disapprove. He proposed marriage nonetheless, but María Esther, a much younger woman, eventually married another man.[17] 'That's what my whole life is like,' Borges complained to Bioy, 'a chain of women' (p. 991).

Bioy surmised that his friend's relationships were invariably 'platonic' because he thought of sex as 'dirty': 'He sees obscenity as an atrocious flaw: a whore is not a woman who is paid, but a woman who goes to bed with a man' (p. 1458). This prudishness was the real obstacle: 'Without understanding the reality, he talks about his recurrent tragic destiny and about how, by some perverse fate, a man always appears and takes them from him' (p. 963). In 1967 Borges resigned himself to that 'tragic destiny' and agreed to marry a widow whom Mother had chosen to care for her blind son after her demise. The marriage lasted barely three years before he went back home to Doña Leonor.[18]

Meanwhile, a series of stories, later collected in *Brodie's Report*, reflected his inner struggle to be rid of psychological bonds forged within the family since childhood.[19] For instance, 'The Elderly Lady' is a portrait of a woman who clings to the memory of her illustrious ancestors in order to distinguish herself from the riff-raff of modern Buenos Aires. In 'Guayaquil' a patrician *criollo* historian cedes to his immigrant rival the privilege of studying letters written by Simón Bolívar. In 'The Story from Rosendo Juárez' a renowned *cuchillero* throws away his dagger because 'the seeming

coward' sees through 'the romantic nonsense and childish vanity of duel-
ling, and finally attains manhood and sanity'.[20]

During his unhappy marriage, Borges had struck up a friendship with
María Kodama, one of the students in his Anglo-Saxon class. Some time
after his marital separation, their relations blossomed into a love-affair,
even though María was about 40 years younger.[21] This was the first time
since the early 1920s that Borges would not be spurned by a woman, and
two stories of the 1970s show how the experience of mutuality freed him at
last from his mystification of romantic love as the key to understanding the
world. In 'Ulrica' an ageing South American professor befriends a young
Norwegian woman who reminds him of a girl who had denied him love in
his youth. But now Ulrica tells him: 'I shall be yours in the inn at
Thorgate.'[22] The term 'gate' derives from a Viking word for 'street', so
Thorgate means 'the street of Thor', or 'the street of the Thunderer', which
translates as 'Calle Tronador', the location of the villa where Borges had
once courted Norah Lange. At 'Thorgate', however, the professor is said to
have 'possessed the image' of Ulrica for 'the first and last time'. The story,
then, is not only a fantasy about finally possessing the muse, it is also about
letting go of that obsessive fantasy, and the related desire to 'fulfil the
literary destiny that circumstances had denied my father'.

'The Night of the Gifts' recalls 'first occasions that can't be forgotten',
and recounts the initiation of a boy in an Argentine brothel.[23] As a reward
for his 'cowardice' in fleeing upstairs from a gang of violent *cuchilleros*, he is
invited by a young prostitute to make love with her. Afterwards, he sees
a policeman killing Juan Moreira, the legendary outlaw revered by
Carriego as the supreme exemplar of the macho 'cult of courage'. In the
first story the woman is idealized as a golden Nordic maiden, in the second
she is a prostitute with half-Indian features, but when in each case she freely
offers herself to the man, the distinction between maiden and whore is
dissolved in 'the love wherein there is no possessor and no possessed, but
both surrender'.[24]

Borges's relationship with María Kodama, though discreet, had to be
conducted under the watchful and disapproving eyes of Mother and the
housekeeper Epifanía (Fani) Úveda de Robledo, who would conceive
a growing antipathy to her employer's 'literary secretary'. But after Doña
Leonor died in 1975 their romance became more widely known and soon
met with resentment from other family members and friends. These
strained relations, as well as the obsessive attention that Borges received
from the Argentine media, led to ever more frequent trips abroad with
María to speak at universities and literary events across the world.[25] And as

Argentina slid further into a vortex of political violence and economic chaos, the couple took to spending long periods together in Geneva, where he had lived for several years as an adolescent and which, having resumed his friendship with his former Swiss schoolmate Maurice Abramowicz, he now found particularly congenial;[26] so much so, indeed, that he would remark to a journalist that 'in a certain manner I am Swiss', and would even toy with the idea of adopting Swiss citizenship.[27] In 1985, he was diagnosed with terminal cancer, and in November of that year he secretly travelled with María to Geneva. There, he obtained a divorce from his estranged wife (by proxy in Paraguay since divorce was still illegal in Argentina), and married María in a civil ceremony. When news of the marriage eventually came out, it provoked a media sensation and aroused bitter hostility from family and friends.[28]

Borges died on 14 June 1986 and was buried in Geneva in the Cimetière de Plainpalais, a burial ground reserved for illustrious personalities. He had made a will in 1979 in which he named María Kodama as his sole heir, but left nothing to his sister Norah and her family, save for ceding his share of the family mausoleum in the Recoleta cemetery in Buenos Aires to Norah, and the gift of the several volumes of Richard Burton's *One Thousand and One Nights* to one of her sons, Miguel de Torre; to the housekeeper Fani he bequeathed half of whatever money he might possess at the time of his death. However, it transpired that in 1985 he had revised this will: María remained the sole heir on the same terms as in 1979, but the sum left to Fani was now fixed and much reduced. The validity of both wills would be challenged in the law-courts by members of the family, and also by an aggrieved Fani, who felt that her legacy in the revised will was an insufficient reward for many years of service.[29] These legal disputes would drag on for years in the glare of media publicity, but to no avail: Borges's will and María Kodama's right of inheritance were repeatedly upheld by the courts. Even so, public opinion was split between those sympathetic to Kodama and others who remained utterly opposed. From this latter camp would come occasional (and unsuccessful) calls for the 'repatriation' of Borges's remains from Geneva to Buenos Aires. The fact was that the actual motives and wishes of the private man had been all but eclipsed by that other public Borges, who, in that sly, rueful text 'Borges and I', was said to have a 'perverse way ... of distorting and magnifying everything' (*CF* 324). In the end, Jorge Luis Borges had become a *monstre sacré* brought into being by his compatriots' desire to find an anchor, some kind of reassurance, in the literary glory he had achieved at a time of tremendous political and economic turbulence in Argentina.

Notes

1. 'An Autobiographical Essay', *The Aleph and Other Stories* (London: Jonathan Cape, 1971), p. 211.
2. *Ibid.*
3. 'Paréntesis pasional' [1920], in *Jorge Luis Borges: textos recobrados, 1919–1929* (Buenos Aires: Emecé, 2001), pp. 32–33. Translations from Spanish are mine unless otherwise stated.
4. E. Williamson, *Borges: A Life* (New York: Viking Penguin, 2004), pp. 63–67.
5. *Ibid.*, pp. 86–87. For Borges and the Spanish avant-garde, see pp. 68–89.
6. 'Anatomía de mi Ultra' [1921], in *Jorge Luis Borges: textos recobrados, 1919–1929*, p. 95, and 'Ultra manifesto', in Jorge Luis Borges, *On Writing*, ed. Suzanne Jill Levine (New York: Penguin, 2010), pp. 3–4.
7. *Borges: A Life*, pp. 93–102 and 106. For Borges and the Buenos Aires avant-garde, pp. 99–114; 120–129; 130–148; 160–164.
8. *Ibid.*, pp. 96–98.
9. *Ibid.*, pp. 102–114 and 127–128.
10. *Ibid.*, pp. 124–148.
11. *Ibid.*, pp. 149–168.
12. Epigraph to *El idioma de los argentinos* [1928] (Buenos Aires: Espasa Calpe/ Seix Barral, 1994), p. 7.
13. 'An Autobiographical Essay', pp. 219–220.
14. *Borges: A Life*, pp. 275–332.
15. Carrizo, Antonio, *Borges el memorioso* (Mexico, D.F.: Fondo de Cultura Económica, 1983), p. 235.
16. Adolfo Bioy Casares, *Borges* (Barcelona: Destino, 2006), p. 1002. Subsequent page references are given in the text.
17. *Borges: A Life*, pp. 355–358.
18. *Ibid.*, pp. 369–381.
19. *Ibid.*, pp. 359–368.
20. 'Commentaries', *The Aleph and Other Stories*, p. 282.
21. *Borges: A Life*, pp. 379–396 and 416–424.
22. *Ibid.*, pp. 397–99.
23. *Ibid.*, pp. 399–401.
24. 'Happiness' ('La dicha'), *Selected Poems*, ed. Alexander Coleman (London: Penguin, 2000), p. 435.
25. *Borges: A Life*, pp. 416–451.
26. *Ibid.*, pp. 452–467 and 475–76.
27. *Ibid.*, pp. 476.
28. *Ibid.*, pp. 478–489.
29. *Ibid.*, pp. 477–478.

CHAPTER 4

Jorge Luis Borges's Fictions and the Two World Wars

Efraín Kristal

The European war contexts and subtexts of Borges's writings were obvious and poignant to his Argentine readers in the 1930s and 1940s. Not so to his readership in the 1970s, when he was the subject of international acclaim, and the two World Wars were no longer recent or current events. Borges scholarship has given pride of place to other deserving aspects of his writings, but it has not sufficiently noticed the extent to which the two World Wars were among his central concerns, and recurrent motifs in his fictional world.

A critical mass of Borges's signature tales take place in the context of the two World Wars, such as 'The Secret Miracle', set in Czechoslovakia during the Nazi invasion of 1939. There are also important Borges stories set in Argentina featuring European war exiles. In 'Guayaquil', for example, Eduardo Zimmermann, 'a foreign-born historian driven from his homeland by the Third Reich and now an Argentine citizen', loses his university position thanks to 'Martin Heidegger [...] who proved that Zimmerman was of Hebrew, not to say Jewish descent' (CF 391).

Passing references to the two World Wars that offer illuminating insights into characters and situations abound in Borges's fictions. 'The Utopia of a Weary Man', for example, addresses the legacy of Hitler and the extermination camps in a futuristic tale of time travel. And, in 'Shakespeare's Memory', Hermann Soergel, a trained philologist does research on Shakespeare during the First World War while his brother is fighting in the trenches and dies in 1917. Soergel translates *Macbeth* into German to try to forget the death of his brother. In the story, Borges comes up with a remarkable view of memory as a 'muddle of indefinite possibilities' ('un desorden de posibilidades indefinidas') (OC III: 397), in which what one would like to forget is as important as what one remembers. This view gains poignant undertones when one considers it in the context of the traumas of war.

35

Antecedents

Borges spent his formative years in Geneva as a teenager with his Argentine family from 1914 to 1919. In one of the last interviews he comments: 'We left for Europe in 1914. We were very "ignorant" and did not realize it was the first year of the First World War. We remained trapped in Geneva while the remainder of Europe was at war.'[1] Borges's first significant literary project was arguably his modest anthology of German expressionist poetry, featuring war poems. As he put it, 'The war did not create German expressionism, but justified it.'[2] The First World War also informed some of Borges's first published poems and pieces of narrative fiction, including 'The Fight', in which the survivor of hand-to-hand combat confuses his own identity with that of the man he killed.[3]

On Borges's return to Argentina after the First World War he published several book reviews about the war, including his assessments of Henri Barbusse's *Under Fire,* Erich Maria Remarque's *All Quiet on the Western Front,* and Ernst Jünger's *War as Interior Experience.*

Pierre Menard, Author of the Quixote

The end of the First World War, and the rise of Fascist and Nazi sympathies in Europe and in Argentina, are the contexts in which Borges wrote his first signature tale, 'Pierre Menard, Author of the Quixote', published in 1939, shortly before the outbreak of the Second World War. Most critics who have discussed this major story underscore its literary and philosophical aspects, its exploration of the relativity of readings and interpretations, and its blurring of the lines between the essay and the short story, and they are right to do so. But the war context is equally illuminating. Before he published the story, Borges wrote three pieces related in one way or another to Erich Ludendorff, the supreme commander of the German armed forces towards the end of the war; the mastermind, along with Adolf Hitler, of the Munich Beer Putsch of 1923; and the author of *Der Totale Krieg* (the total war), an ominous book published in 1935, in which he declares Germany's right to wage undeclared war, and to attack the civilian populations of its enemies.

In his review of the book, Borges quotes Ludendorff's main thesis: 'War is the highest expression of the will of the people. Therefore politics – the new totalitarian politics – must subordinate itself to a totalitarian war.'[4] Borges ends his review anticipating fears that came to pass, underscoring 'the killings of millions of which Ludendorff would like to be the prophet'.[5]

Borges also wrote a brief note on *Am heiligen Quell Deutscher Kraft* (On the sacred source of German might), a bi-monthly journal Ludendorff edited, with print runs of over 100,000 issues. In the pages of his journal, Ludendorff regularly called for the rebirth of German pagan religion while expressing contempt for other religions including Protestantism. One of Ludendorff's recurrent obsessions was the promotion of circumcision among Arian men, which he branded a ploy by enemies of Germany to Judaize its population. Borges makes the following assessment of the journal:

> Ludendorff's journal *On the Sacred Source of German Might* published in Munich wages a relentless, bi-monthly campaign against Jews, against Buddhists, against free masons, against theosophists, against the Society of Jesus, against communism, against doctor Martin Luther, against England, and against Goethe's memory.[6]

The first lines of 'Pierre Menard, Author of the Quixote' echo the polemical tone and some of the identical racist points of view Borges had noted in his journalistic articles on Ludendorff:

> The visible *oeuvre* left by this novelist is easily and briefly enumerated. Unpardonable, therefore, are the omissions and additions perpetrated by Mme. Henri Bachelier in a deceitful catalogue that a certain newspaper, whose Protestant leanings are surely no secret, has been so inconsiderate as to inflict upon that newspaper's deplorable readers–few and Calvinist (if not Masonic and circumcised) though they may be. (*CF* 88)

The narrator of the story is not Ludendorff, but his tone was clearly inspired by Borges's writings on Ludendorff. Borges's narrator, at least in the first few pages of the story, is an aggressive polemicist whose racism, misogyny, and anti-semitism go hand in hand with his admiration of aristocratic privileges and prerogatives, and his analysis of Menard's oeuvre is consistent with the dreadful positions he openly espouses.

The narrator argues that the Nietzschean underpinnings of Menard's *Don Quixote* are 'irrefutable' (*CF* 93). This interpretation is ostensibly based on the Nietzscheanesque notion that truth is a product of the will, something that emerges in history, something created rather than experienced, discovered, ascertained, or determined by evidence. The narrator's Nietzschean interpretation is not irrefutable, however. It is simply plausible when a text by Menard quoted in the story is read out of context:

> . . . truth, whose mother is history, rival of time, depository of deeds, witness of the past, exemplar and adviser to the present, and the future's counsellor. (*CF* 94)

The notion of truth as a creative act of the will, however, is consistent with Ludendorff's arguments about creating truths for the German people, as when he argues for the rebirth of the German nation through war:

> The saying of Fichte, that being German and having character are synonymous beyond controversy, must again become the truth. [...] May the nation now find men rejoicing in their responsibility like the generals in the front, to lead it, firm of will and tenacious of their aim, and to restore the sunken national life and inspire it with fresh and powerful enthusiasm. The men of the nation will unite all our creative forces in great creative action.[7]

In his essays Borges offered views that could be read as retorts:

> There is no end to the illusions of patriotism. [...] Fichte, at the beginning of the nineteenth century, declared that to have character and to be German are obviously one and the same thing. ('Our Poor Individualism', in *SN-F* 309)

One does not have to know that the narrator of Borges's story was inspired by Ludendorff to realize that he is racist, authoritarian, and churlish, or that his description of Menard's project does not square with that project itself. The narrator's reading of Menard's *Quixote* gives credence to a speech Borges delivered about ethics and literature:

> It may well be that no work of literature is intrinsically immoral, but there are readings of literary works that are clearly so, [and] to eliminate ethics from literature is to impoverish it.[8]

Putting the story in the context of Borges's writings about Ludendorff sheds light on Borges's proposal to shift the ethical focus from the condemnation of literary works to the condemnation of those who manipulate their literary interpretation for purposes that deserve condemnation.

Tlön, Uqbar, Orbis Tertius

When the Second World War broke out, Borges wrote essays condemning the Nazi war effort, and against his fellow-Argentines who expressed sympathy for the Third Reich. He wrote about his fears that a German victory would unleash latent fascist tendencies in his own country:

> A German victory would be the ruin and the degradation of the globe. And in what regards Argentina, I am not referring to the danger of a German colonial adventure; but to the local imitators, the resident Übermenschen, to whom we would be inexorably subject. I hope that in the years to come we will experience the destruction of Hitler, the atrocious son of Versailles.[9]

The first short story he wrote after the war broke out was 'Tlön, Uqbar, Orbis Tertius'. Without relinquishing any of its other complexities, it can be read as a loose literary allegory about the rise of Nazism. The narrator (and protagonist) unearths an extravagant conspiracy involving many individuals who have been fashioning an alternative universe over several generations. The conspirators have produced an encyclopaedia, in which a universe called Tlön behaves according to the philosophical idealism of Bishop Berkeley. The story moves from the outlandish to the fantastic when the universe, down to its physical laws, begins to transform itself according to the design of the conspirators. With bitter, understated irony the narrator explicitly compares the transformation of his universe to the rise of Nazism, anti-Semitism, and Stalinism: 'Ten years ago any symmetry with a semblance of order – dialectical materialism, anti-Semitism, Nazism – was sufficient to entrance the minds of men. How could one do other than to submit oneself to Tlön, to the minute and vast evidence of an orderly planet?'[10]

Borges published 'Tlön, Uqbar, Orbis Tertius' in 1940 after writing a newspaper article in which he publicly deplored the military objectives of National Socialism in Germany: 'The unbelievable, indisputable truth is that the directors of the Third Reich are procuring a universal empire and the conquest of the world' ('1941', in *SN-F* 206). In Borges's journalistic writings, he condemned Nazism with an argument paralleled by the plot of his story, namely that to grapple with perverse historical and political situations in the present, it is sometimes necessary to look to perverse ideas of the past, which might have been dismissed as passing fancies in their own time. In his commentary on 'Genealogy of Fascism' by Bertrand Russell, Borges makes the following point: 'Political events derive from much older theories, and that often a great deal of time may elapse between the formulation of a doctrine and its application. [. . .] Hitler, so horrendous with his public armies and secret spies, is a pleonasm of Carlyle (1795–1881) and even of J.G. Fichte (1762–1814)' (*SN-F* 209).

The Garden of Forking Paths

Another major story Borges wrote in this period was 'The Garden of Forking Paths'. In it, Yu Tsung, a Chinese spy based in England for Germany during the First World War, murders a man named Albert to let his minders in Berlin know that the German Air Force should target the French city of Albert for destruction. To his dismay and consternation, he learns that the man he needs to murder is a Sinologist familiar with his

family's past, and he kills him all the same. In the story's fantastic twist,
Albert lets Yu Tsung know that one of his ancestors wrote a book that
prefigures, or perhaps predetermines, the experiences they are now living,
as well as any number of other parallel universes, in which one or both or
none of them might kill or be killed.

The story begins with a historical note:

> On page 242 of *The History of the World War*, Liddell Hart writes that an
> Allied offensive against the Serre-Montauban line (to be mounted by thir-
> teen British divisions backed by one thousand four hundred artillery pieces)
> had been planned for July 24th, 1916, but had to be put off until the morning
> of July 29th. Torrential rains (notes Capt. Liddell Hart) were the cause of
> that delay – a delay that entailed no great consequences as it turns out.
> (*CF* 119)

Within the world of the story the note suggests that the Chinese spy's
murder was for naught. Anyone who reads the relevant sections of Liddell
Hart's book with care, or who is familiar with the battle of the Somme
(which began in July 1916), would have picked up on the fact that Borges's
account of the historical events does not correspond to the historical record.
Most of the preparations for the battle of the Somme 'were unconcealed',[11] as
Liddell Hart pointed out, and they were unconcealed on purpose because
the point of the battle of the Somme was to divert German troops from
Verdun, where the Germans were about to break through the military
impasse and capture Paris. Anyone familiar with the historical events
would know that if there was a battle for which espionage was hardly
necessary, it was the battle of the Somme, and they would also know that
bombing the city of Albert would make little difference to any military
outcome, as the city had already been bombed by the Germans, and British
military deployment to the area was no secret. The historical world of Yu
Tsung in the story is not that of the First World War as it is registered in the
historical record, but a variation of the First World War, as prefigured in his
ancestor's book. And the note with which the story begins is not about
Liddell Hart's famous book on the war, but on a variation of the same that is
also prefigured in the same fantastic book imagined in Borges's tale.

Deutsches Requiem

In the aftermath of the war, following the Nuremberg trials, Borges wrote
'Deutsches Requiem', a story about the nefarious consequences of fascism
and anti-Semitism even after Nazism was defeated. Its protagonist is an

unrepentant Nazi war criminal, the sub-commander of the Tarnowitz concentration camp, who writes about his life as he awaits execution. Otto Dietrich zur Linde is proud of his father who, according to his account, distinguished himself in the siege of Namur, a First World War campaign led by Erich Ludendorff, in which Germany attacked neutral Belgium in the hopes of quickly capturing Paris.

The most chilling aspect of his confession is not his lack of remorse with respect to crimes he openly committed, but his conviction that his world-view triumphed and will prevail even though he was on the side of those who lost the war. Zur Linde claims that he felt a sense of exhilaration in the aftermath of the defeat of the Nazis to whom he devoted his life, and that he needed to understand why. After testing several explanations he concludes that his elation comes from an intimate sense that his ideals, which were those of Hitler, have triumphed:

> Hitler thought he was fighting for *a* nation but he was fighting for *all* nations, even for those that he attacked and abominated. It does not matter that his ego was unaware of that; his blood, his will knew. [...] Now an implacable age looms over the world. We forged that age, we who are now its victim. (*CF* 234)

Borges's story is a cautionary tale about the survival of totalitarian impulses after the war, but it is also a commentary on *Mein Kampf*, in which Hitler discusses the First World War as a catastrophic military defeat for Germany that hastened the triumph of his ideals:

> For the German people we can almost regard it as a great fortune that the period of insidious disease was suddenly shortened by such a terrible catastrophe. [...] For this is not the first time that such a catastrophe has come down to this. It can then easily become the cause of a cure that sets to work with extreme resoluteness.[12]

One of the stated purposes of *Mein Kampf*, as Peter Sloterdijk has argued, was to give a perverse sense of meaning to the senselessness of war, and to stage Hitler's feelings of purposeful self-discovery in the light of a military defeat.[13] Along these lines, Borges's story offers a window into the cogitations of a criminal who takes pride in the fact that he has lost all compassion for his fellow-human beings in the name of a metaphysical approach to life that rationalizes injustice and murder.

Borges's gift as a writer of fiction is not to cast history overboard with his fantastic tales or philosophical abstractions. He could, for instance, draw on his experiences as an observer of the two World Wars – from the safety of neutral Switzerland during the first, or from distant Argentina during the second – to offer insights and aperçus that mere realism might not be able to provide. There are no contradictions between Borges's approach to fiction and his meditations on some of the most urgent issues of his time, and there are lessons to be drawn from the mechanism through which he tried to avoid the prejudices of nationalism and xenophobia in the construction of a literary world.

Notes

1. Jorge Luis Borges, 'Borges, Un tejedor de sueños', *Textos recobrados, 1956–1986* (Buenos Aires: Emecé, 2004), p. 332. (Note: All translations from Spanish sources are mine except quotations from the *Collected Fictions* and *Selected Non-Fictions*.)
2. Borges, 'Acerca del expresionismo', *Inquisiciones* (Barcelona: Seix Barral, 1994), p. 157.
3. Borges, 'La lucha', *Textos recobrados, 1919–1929*, p. 32.
4. Borges, 'Der Totale Krieg', *Textos cautivos. Ensayos y reseñas en 'El hogar' (1936–1939)* (Barcelona: Tusquets, 1990), p. 338.
5. Borges, 'Der Totale Krieg', *Textos cautivos*, p. 338.
6. Borges, 'De la vida literaria' (3 September 1937), *Textos cautivos*, p. 313.
7. Erich Ludendorff, *Ludendorff's Own Story*, Vol. II (New York: Harper, 1919), p. 434.
8. Jorge Luis Borges, 'Moral y literatura', *Borges en Sur* (1931–1980) (Buenos Aires: Emecé, 1999), p. 297.
9. 'La guerra. Ensayo de imparcialidad', *Borges en Sur*, p. 28.
10. Jorge Luis Borges, 'Tlön, Uqbar, Orbis Tertius' (trans. James E. Irby), *Labyrinths* (New York: New Directions, 1964), p. 17.
11. Liddell Hart, *A History of the First World War* (London: Pan Books, 1970), p. 250.
12. Adolf Hitler, *Mein Kampf* (Cambridge, MA: The Riverside Press, 1943), p. 413.
13. P. Sloterdijk, *Critique of Cynical Reason* (Minneapolis and London: University of Minnesota Press, 1987), pp. 412–413.

CHAPTER 5

Dictatorship and Writing (1976–1983)

Annick Louis

On the subject of Jorge Luis Borges and his position under the last Argentine military dictatorship, it is commonplace to refer to his enthusiastic support for the regime, as well as for other Latin American dictatorships (especially Chile) around the time. Nevertheless, not only did his attitude evolve during those years, but he constructed, in Argentine society, the complex persona of a writer in dialogue with his literary work, often expressing critical views about the regime and openly opposing it on several occasions.*

During the period of the dictatorship, Borges published 11 books, belonging to different genres. Collections of poems such as *La moneda de hierro* (1976), *Historia de la noche* (1977), and *La cifra* (1981) provided further evidence of his return to poetry; volumes of short stories, *Rosa y azul* (1977), *Un argumento* (1983), *Adrogué* (1977), *La memoria de Shakespeare* (1983), *Veinticinco de agosto de 1983 y otros cuentos* (1983); essays and lectures: *Siete noches* (1980), *Páginas de Jorge Luis Borges* (1982), *Nueve ensayos dantescos* (1982), *Qué es el budismo* (1976), and *Prólogos, con un prólogo de prólogos* (1977), and the anthologies *Libro de sueños* (1976) and *Breve antología anglosajona* (1978); finally, the collaborative work, *Nuevos cuentos de Bustos Domecq* (1977). Among the collections, we note the publication of 'La biblioteca de Babel' by Franco María Ricci, and among the interviews, *Borges oral* (1979), conversations with Osvaldo Ferrari. Many of the contents of these volumes had already been published in periodicals, and each volume's publication was widely relayed in the press.

On the global scale, the period is marked by burgeoning interest in Latin American literature and growth in Borges's fame worldwide, with tributes in his honour also finding echoes in the local press. This phenomenon reflected the complexity of the process leading to the canonization of Borges in Argentina, and the superimposition of his national and international celebrity; if internationally he was acclaimed for the quality of his writings, in

---

* I thank Alejandro Vaccaro, who provided the necessary material for this research.

Argentina, as he himself constantly repeated and as he suggested in his famous text 'Borges and I',[1] he embodied two different characters: the writer, renowned but little read, and the public figure famous for his opinions and wit, marking, by his physical presence, the city of Buenos Aires. Nevertheless, the prestige of the writer legitimized the public figure.

Give Us Each Day Our Daily Borges

The dictatorship years witnessed at first a continuity with the figure of the writer staged by Borges since the 1955 coup, which had turned him into an official writer whose presence was pervasive in the media. The phenomenon grew to such an extent that many newspaper articles took up the issue, often in a humorous tone, and proposed an explanation for the unsettling relationship between Borges's literary work and his public figure, often illustrated by his controversial political opinions.[2] Borges had become a national myth indulging in demystification through the means of caustic humour,[3] a *star*, who remained a contradictory character, funny and paradoxical, but also modest and approachable, an old man suffering from solitude and cultivating memory, for whom literature was everything, but who, at the same time, emphasized how crucial it is to be loved.[4] Although the press reported Borges's political remarks, they did not necessarily relate them to the contexts in which they had first appeared, thereby often failing to situate them thematically.

The variety of issues addressed by the media makes it necessary to distinguish different types of texts, which correspond to four categories: Borges's writings – essays, poems, narratives, generally published as collections later on; interviews about literature, politics, and culture, which often sparked controversy; articles concerning the editions and re-editions of his work, in Argentina and abroad, as well as film adaptations and films centred on him; finally, a series of notes and articles about his life and activities – travels, public lectures, tributes, participation in cultural activities, meetings with other writers or politicians, friends, family, and the women in his life. Harassed by the press and photographers, Borges often showed how tired he was growing of his celebrity.

The 'Enfant Terrible' of Argentine Society

For Borges, who was in the United States at the time of the coup, the event, above all, meant the end of Peronism,[5] and his support of the dictatorship may be partly explained by his visceral dislike of this movement, which he expressed in his public statements but rarely in his work, and which became more marked in the period of the banishing of Peronism (1955–1973). His initial statements echo his customary opinions – that Peronists are no more than thugs devoid of ethics or values – but he added that the new government was made up of gentlemen who would restore order in the country.[6] Notoriously on 20 May 1976, Borges had lunch with President Jorge Rafael Videla; other guests were Ernesto Sábato, Leonardo Castellani, and Horacio Ratti. The event was covered by the media, which demonstrates that the new government sought to present itself as an enlightened dictatorship. Leonardo Castellani took advantage of this lunch to inquire about two missing writers, Haroldo Conti and Alberto Costa.[7] Borges declared that he had intended to congratulate President Videla on 'saving the homeland' (from Peronism and communism),[8] but, after the event, seemed reluctant to make any statements. Pressed by the media, he reiterated his previous remarks but added that a writer's political opinions have no connection with his literary work, an opinion that seems to challenge the claims to legitimacy of the military government that was currying his favour. From then on, Borges never ceased to claim that politics was of no interest to him, and he advocated the autonomy of the writer vis-à-vis politics and all kinds of remuneration alike (and often reminded his interlocutors that he lived on his retirement pension).[9]

After this initial phase of enthusiasm, which caused him to overlook the violence of the new government, Borges would repeatedly criticize the policies and speeches of the armed forces, reinforcing his role as the 'enfant terrible' of Argentine society. But his remarks were not exclusively addressed to the government, they also gave voice to shared ideas about his country's literature and culture, to the extent that we may say that Borges continued the work of redefining Argentine culture that he had initiated in the 1920s. Regarding politics, there was controversy surrounding the border dispute between Argentina and Chile in 1978: Borges's statements ran counter to the propaganda of the military government, since he claimed that a war with Chile would be foolish.[10] His repudiation of any form of cultural policy was expressed in many situations, the most resounding being during the 1978 World Cup, when his statements acquired a particular anti-nationalist significance at the time when the country was overwhelmed by the delusion of living under a government that defended peace and civilization.[11] Among cultural issues, we may recall the numerous polemics about *tango*, which, in his view, is not Argentinian, and to which he opposes the form of the *milonga*, whose authenticity he emphasizes.[12] In his interviews and essays published in the press, he demystified the official Argentine literary history, for example, when he stated that the Argentine *avant-gardes* are an invention of the critics;[13] that Ricardo Güiraldes did not know anything about the rural world when he wrote *Don Segundo Sombra*;[14] or that Argentine history would have been different if the country had chosen as a classical work not José Hernández's *Martín Fierro* but Sarmiento's *Facundo* (while adding that Sarmiento was a 'montonero', a particularly embarrassing statement for a military government that aimed to eradicate the movement that bore this name in the twentieth century).[15]

These chronic polemics prompted renewed questions about Borges's 'true Argentine character'; it is common knowledge that it was when he started writing fiction in the 1940s that the image of a Borges alienated from his own country emerged, an image the press would take up again when he opposed the military government's policy, which led to him being accused either of being a European in exile, or of being anti-Argentinian.[16] We should also note that his attacks on cultural *doxa* were not limited to his country; he asserted that the English know nothing about whiskey,[17] and caused an uproar when he claimed, during a stay in France, that Latin America does not exist (as an entity); this latter declaration was understood as a denial of the subcontinent's culture.[18]

1980: The Turn of the Tide

At the political level, a radical change occurred in 1980. Now fully convinced that the 'rumours' about the disappearance of people and human rights violations were well-founded, Borges set out, gradually, to criticize the dictatorship's domestic policy. His rift with the government came to a head in the mid-1980s,[19] when he signed a request that the government clarify the fate of the missing persons on August 12,[20] and spoke out against clandestine justice: the military, he said, was fighting violence with violence; the country was caught between Peronism and the military. Reaching this conclusion plunged Borges into a form of desperation.[21] The attitude of the press was twofold, since it often celebrated his remarks, given that his prestige conferred on them a legitimacy quite impossible to dismiss,[22] but, at the same time, it printed articles and letters from readers who attacked him and defended the military government. The general tone of the articles was less lighthearted now.[23]

A particularly important issue during the period concerns the Nobel Prize for Literature. Every year, the press gave expression to the hopes of

Argentina, celebrated Borges as a national treasure, stressed how unfair and outrageous it was, in their view, that the Swedish Academy should ignore him every year, and offered explanations devoid of any political sense.[24] Borges adopted an attitude at once modest and ironic, claiming not to deserve the distinction, and reiterated the idea that he had not produced a coherent body of work, only a set of scattered writings or drafts,[25] while questioning the legitimacy of the prize. A particularly difficult moment for the dictatorship to manage was the award of the Nobel Prize for Peace to Adolfo Pérez Esquivel, a human rights activist, on 10 October 1980. The government was quite embarrassed. On that occasion, Borges declared that he did not know Pérez Esquivel but that he approved of the award, and seized the opportunity to condemn clandestine repression.[26]

From then on, Borges grew critical of his own attitude at the beginning of the dictatorship,[27] and expressed his concern over the levels of poverty, which increased with the aggravation of the economic crisis. Concurrently, he stated his support of the rule of law, and claimed that the military had no expertise to govern a country.[28] During the Falklands War (2 April–14 June 1982), he found himself in a delicate position: because he spoke out against the war, he was accused of supporting the British, at a time when nationalism flared in the country.[29] He also stated that the Argentine military confused the right to a territory with the right to invade it, and that they never really fought, properly.[30] When the military government lost the war and announced the restoration of democracy, Borges, who after the accession of Peronism to power in 1946 had expressed his scepticism about the democratic system – regularly stating that it is an abuse of statistics (one of the few political statements he includes in his writings, in the Prologue to *La moneda de hierro* of 1976) – declared anyhow that a democratic regime is nevertheless the best choice for the country, the only non-violent one, despite his fears of seeing Peronism regain power.[31] He also expressed his alarm at the prospect of a new coup, because of growing insecurity throughout the country.[32] Nevertheless, from the middle of 1983 he said he hoped democracy would be restored, while calling for a reduction in the presence and influence of the state.[33] This new stance echoed that of the majority of Argentines, which seemed to have played a significant role in this positive change. Raúl Alfonsín's election on 30 October 1983 surprised Borges, but he interpreted it as Argentines going back to common sense and ethics (we must not forget that he supported the Radical Party in the 1920s);[34] in 'The last Sunday of October', he claims he is pleased to see that the people of Argentina have proven to him how valuable democracy is, and that these elections show

the country transcending ideologies and parties.[35] At least three literary
texts of the period refer to the context: the poems 'Juan López and John
Ward' and 'A Soldier's *Milonga*',[36] and the short story 'An Argument'.[37] If
in the former the allusion to the Falklands War is blatant, the latter two can
be read, as Edwin Williamson suggests, as allegories of the military
government.[38]

Towards Democracy

During the Dictatorship, Borges's aura as a public figure grew more and
more appealing, but if his statements addressed political issues, his writings
at that time rarely referred to current affairs. Given that he claimed that
a writer must be judged on his production, and not on his political ideas,
there is a coherence between the literary conceptions expressed in his
writings and in his public statements, since the same themes inform both:
the idea that literature must be related to pleasure, like reading; his love of
literature and literary creation, and of travelling; the assertion that politics
and literature possess the same degree of reality;[39] the writer as creator of
genealogies, who communicates his personal tastes to the public, who gives
people the opportunity of discovering authors and books; dreaming and its
close relation to literary creation; his own tastes, his personal and family
history which is part of a literary tradition; blindness and shadow, his
memories, the spaces and people of his past, the writers he enjoys and
their works; loneliness and the expectation of death. It remains to explore
how this figure of a writer and his writings evolved after democracy was
restored.

Notes

1. Jorge Luis Borges, *El Hacedor* (Buenos Aires: Emecé, 1960), pp. 50–52. In the
   press, see 'Borges: The Other, to Whom Things Happen', *La Nación*, Buenos
   Aires, 19 May 1978; Requeni, Antonio: 'Jorge Luis Borges Talks About
   Leopoldo Lugones', *La Prensa*, Buenos Aires, 17 June 1979; 'Things of
   Borges', *La Razón*, Buenos Aires, 15 September 1982.
2. Louis Annick, 'El autor entre dictadura y democracia, fama nacional e inter-
   nacional. El caso de Jorge Luis Borges (1973–1986)', *Letral*, 14 (2015), pp. 17–32.
3. 'Menotti Interviews Borges', *VSD*, 1 December 1978.
4. 'I Will Die Being the "Future" Nobel Prize', *Popular*, Buenos Aires, 4 July 1976;
   Rocamora, Oberdón: 'Borges, the Terrible Child of Argentine Literature',
   Clarín, Buenos Aires, 15 June 1978.
5. 'Flowers for the Return of Borges', *La Opinión*, Buenos Aires, 13 May 1976.

6. 'Peronism Is the Absence of Ethics, the New Government Is Composed of Gentlemen', *La Mañana*, Montevideo, 24 April 1976.

7. 'A Frank Dialogue with Videla on Problems of Culture and the Spirit', *La Opinión*, Buenos Aires, 20 May 1976.

8. 'I Will Congratulate Videla for Saving the Country, Said Jorge Luis Borges', *El País*, Montevideo, 20 May 1976.

9. Jorge Luis Borges, 'I Am Not Sure that Writers Are a Guild . . .', *La Opinión*, Buenos Aires, 10 April 1977.

10. '1978: Borges and the Conflict in the Beagle: Borges, Jorge Luis Versus Manfred Schoenfeld, a Journalist from La Prensa', *Gente*, 686, Buenos Aires, 14 September 1978; Manfred Schönfeld, 'Borges and the Crime of War', *La Prensa*, Buenos Aires, 1 September 1978; Jorge Luis Borges, 'Men Cannot Be Measured by Maps', *La Prensa*, Buenos Aires, 6 September 1978.

11. 'The World Cup in the Opinion of Borges', *La Nación*, Buenos Aires, 9 May 1978; 'Borges Attacks the World Cup', *El Día*, Montevideo, 9 May 1978.

12. 'Gardel Never Loved Tango', *La Nación*, Buenos Aires, 18 April 1978; 'Borges, Gardel and Tango', *La Razón*, Buenos Aires, 18 April 1978.

13. M.E. Vázquez, 'The Love for Buenos Aires (A Dialogue Between Borges and Mujica Laínez)', *La Nación*, Buenos Aires, 30 April 1977.

14. 'Arguments about *Don Segundo Sombra* Refuted', *La Nación*, Buenos Aires, 9 August 1979.

15. 'Borges Spoke on Sarmiento and Education', *La Nación*, Buenos Aires, 13 November 1981. The 'montonera' was the collective name given to irregular armies that arose during the wars of independence; a century and a half later, the name was appropriated by an Argentinian armed organization made up of left-wing Peronist militants who took up arms and were pursued and murdered under the last Argentine military dictatorship.

16. 'Le Monde and a Note on Jorge L. Borges' ('An Englishman with the Wrong Passport'), *La Nación*, Buenos Aires, 17 December 1976.

17. 'The English Do Not Know What It Is to Drink Whiskey, Said Borges', *El País*, Montevideo, 16 February 1979.

18. 'Borges Compounded His Diatribes in France', *El Día*, Montevideo, 4 October 1980; 'Borges's Words Draw Reactions', *La Nación*, Buenos Aires, 7 October 1980.

19. 'Borges Affirms that He Cannot Understand Argentina and Sábato Shows His Concern for the Argentine Situation . . .', *La Razón*, Buenos Aires, 7 June 1980.

20. 'Request for the Disappeared', *Clarín*, Buenos Aires, 12 August 1980.

21. *Excelsior*, México, 21 August 1980; 'Tired of Living, but Dreaming of a Trip to China or Tahiti', *La Prensa*, Buenos Aires, 7 September 1980.

22. 'Here Borges Is Not Denied', *Crónica*, Buenos Aires, 13 March 1981; 'Political Synthesis, Martín Fierro or Borges', *Clarín*, Buenos Aires, 23 January 1983.

23. 'Borges Gives His Opinion', *La Nación*, Buenos Aires, 4 August 1981.

24. 'The Cover that We Would Have Liked to Give', *La Semana*, a. III, n. 156, Buenos Aires, 24 October 1979.
25. 'Borges: I'm Sorry I Wrote Those Drafts ... ', *El Día*, Montevideo, 8 November 1981.
26. 'I Don't Know Who He Is, but I Approve', *Buenos Aires Herald*, Buenos Aires, 15 October 1980.
27. Uky Goñi, 'Borges: Quiet Executions Have Replaced Loud Bombs', *Buenos Aires Herald*, Buenos Aires, 6 June 1981; 'Borges, the Nobel and Other Prizes', *La Nación*, Buenos Aires, 12 March 1981; 'Borges Is Sad for His Country', *Clarín*, Buenos Aires, 5 September 1983.
28. Roberto Alifano, 'Borges Between Politicians and Virtue', *Clarín*, Buenos Aires, 10 April 1981; 'Borges Spoke on Political Topics', *La Nación*, Buenos Aires, 18 January 1982.
29. 'Ironies of Sr. Borges', *Clarín*, Buenos Aires, 12 February 1982; 'The Whistle of the Bullets', *La Nación*, Buenos Aires, 30 May 1982.
30. 'A Postcript', *Clarín*, Buenos Aires, 24 September 1982; 'Skepticism and Irony in a Grand Old Man: Borges', *La Nación*, Buenos Aires, 16 January 1983.
31. 'Borges Believes that Elections Are a Solution', *Clarín*, Buenos Aires, 6 October 1982.
32. 'Borges's Skepticism', *La Razón*, Buenos Aires, 5 October 1982; 'Borges: The Shadow of the Army Is Behind the Polls', *La Prensa*, Buenos Aires, 16 October 1983.
33. José María Poirier, 'Electoral Fictions of Jorge Luis Borges', *Nuestro Tiempo*, Buenos Aires, 10/1983.
34. 'Borges: A Return to Soundness', *Buenos Aires Herald*, Buenos Aires, 7 November 1983; 'Borges Thinks About the Recent Elections', *La Nación*, Buenos Aires, 7 November 1983.
35. *Clarín*, Buenos Aires, 22 December 1983.
36. Published in *Clarín* on 26 August and 30 December 1982 respectively, both poems were included in *Los conjurados*, of 1985.
37. *Clarín*, 7 April 1983. Published in *Textos recobrados, 1956–1986* (2011), 204–205.
38. Edwin Williamson, *Borges: A Life* (New York and London: Viking, 2004), pp. 458, 461–462.
39. Luis J. Jalfen, 'The Heroism of Conscience', *La Nación*, Buenos Aires, 12 July 1981; 'Borges Meets Apprentice Writers', *Clarín*, Buenos Aires, 3 September 1981.

CHAPTER 6

The Public Author and Democracy (1984–1986)

Annick Louis

Borges's experience of Argentine democracy corresponds to what has been called 'the Alfonsinist spring', in the wake of the election to the presidency in October 1983 of Raúl Alfonsín. Between 1984 and 1987, the democratic and economic system entered a period of stability, society experienced a mood of optimism and renewal, and there was even an attempt to do justice to the victims of illegal repression. Under the democratic regime, Borges's presence in Argentine society made itself felt in the same areas as before, but with different connotations, whilst certain new aspects appeared: for the first time, the writer seemed to be in harmony with the Argentines (most of them at least); his private life, which had until then mainly consisted in recalling events from his past, became a controversial issue when he married María Kodama in April 1986 and chose to leave Buenos Aires and go and live (and die) in Geneva.

Few volumes were published during this last period of his life, which saw the start of the process of recovery of the work which he had refused to authorize for re-publication until then: *Atlas* (1984), in collaboration with María Kodama, depicted the poet as traveller; *Los conjurados* (1985) was a mixed collection of prose and poetry; the narrative diptych *La rosa de Paracelso*. *Tigres azules* (1986) recycled emblematic themes of former works; *Textos cautivos* (Barcelona: Tusquets, 1986) reproduced writings first published in *El Hogar* in the 1930s; several works made up of conversations were edited, the most famous being those with Osvaldo Ferrari, *Libro de diálogos* (Buenos Aires: Sudamericana, 1986), and Roberto Alifano, *Borges en diálogo* (Buenos Aires: Grijalbo, 1986). The collection 'Babel's library' proceeded, presenting works selected by Borges that he sometimes translated himself, along with his prologues; the publishing house Hyspamérica introduced 'The Personal Library' in March 1985, a very successful collection that helped to make Borges's literary preferences more widely known.

The Author in Democracy

The number of press articles dealing with Borges increased when democracy was restored, which led some people to claim that, like God, he was everywhere.[1] The tributes and the prizes, the editions, the popular repercussion of his words and the interest in his literature, the success of his books, continued to be widely covered in the Argentine press, which had already raised Borges to the rank of a national treasure. But the writer's support for the recently restored democracy, which he regarded as a miracle, differed somewhat from what was claimed in the press: for the first time, Borges appeared in harmony with Argentine society and his public declarations contributed to warrant that democracy was the only system that would enable the country to overcome the crisis. Given that under the military regime he had visited Pinochet and declared that the military were gentlemen, he undertook to meet some statesmen known for their commitment to democracy, such as Felipe González,[2] and he proclaimed that Alfonsín was a real *gentleman*. However, the similarity in attitude and words should not convey the idea that he supported the dictatorship and democracy in the same way: he insisted on his error of judgement concerning the military and, despite some occasional anti-Peronist declarations, he urged Argentines to settle their differences for the country's sake and reaffirmed his support for the rule of law. He toned down his declarations against Peronism and his jokes on that movement evidenced how he had failed to understand it as a historical and social phenomenon; the military and the Peronists were one and the same to him.[3] His opinions relied now on a first-hand knowledge of political developments; although he declared he would never have accepted to be part of the CONADEP commission (unlike fellow-author Ernesto Sábato), he attended a session of the military junta's Trial, which took place between 22 April and 9 December 1985. He met prosecutor Strassera, listened to one of the ghastliest testimonies, and declared that he had the impression that clandestine detention centres were some sort of hell where torture was routine, and that he felt he was facing an innocent form of evil;[4] those impressions made him call for the death penalty for some of the Argentine military.[5] At the time, Borges started to associate dictatorship with nationalism and with the historical period of Rosas (the Argentine dictator of the middle decades of the nineteenth century);[6] he showed he was concerned for the Argentine soldiers during the Falklands War, whom he considered innocent victims of the conflict.[7] He persisted in saying that Argentine history would have been different if its classical literary work had been *Facundo* by Sarmiento, as an illustration of the power and influence he assigned to literature over reality.[8]

Despite Borges's reconciliation with democracy and with the country, some newspaper articles attested that he was still considered a traitor by some Argentines, and an admirer of England for his attitude during the war, as well as his anti-Peronism.[9] Some polemics ensued, which show that the canonization process of Borges was slow and controversial. For instance, when he was awarded a doctorate Honoris Causa by Cambridge University, he observed that the University of Buenos Aires had never granted him such a distinction – because, he said, they knew him too well.[10] A debate followed the publication of an essay in which he studied some Argentine expressions as so many instances of Argentine hypocrisy, echoing the tone and stance of a famous fore-runner, 'Our impossibilities', published in *Discusión* in 1932, but suppressed in following editions.[11] On several occasions, he defined Argentine identity: Argentines are Europeans in exile, cosmopolitans who are fortunate not to be tied to tradition – the kind of definition he had already given in 'The Argentine writer and tradition' in the 1950s.[12] The question resurfaced when he was not awarded the Nobel Prize, and he seized the occasion to reiterate that the national character of Argentine literature is in the accent, and not in any local colour. The press grew impatient about the prize, for Borges's new political positions fostered hopes that he would eventually be rewarded; famous writers also declared that Borges deserved the prize.[13] When the news broke that he would not be the recipient, Borges again stated that it was because he did not have a proper body of work, and that the Swedish Academy was now committed to discovering literary values, as he did not know Claude Simon who received the prize in 1984, and that he wished he would be discovered too.[14]

Working with Democracy

As under the dictatorship, two kinds of interviews with Borges are to be found in the press at this time: on the one hand, those centred predominantly on literary subjects, like the conversations with Osvaldo Ferrari (*Tiempo argentino*[15]) or with María Esther Vázquez (*La Nación*[16]), which focused on Borges's creative process and his literary preferences, later to be edited and collected for publication by volume; on the other hand, interviews aimed at a wider public, published in magazines such as *Gente*[17] or in popular television programs such as Antonio Carrizo's, centred on Borges's life, his political opinions, his travels, rarely published as books. This second kind of interview is acclaimed by the press as a version of culture that is not boring.[18] Nevertheless, Borges's literary conceptions found their way into both kinds of interview: the aesthetic event takes place with the collaboration of the reader;[19] no writer should live exclusively off literature, if he wishes to enjoy total creative freedom;[20] all kinds of literature belong to the fantastic;[21] Buenos Aires is a city with no past, and this void is filled by literature;[22] short stories are superior to novels;[23] the American *western* is an epic genre;[24] lettered and popular culture are closely related, but not by hierarchical links;[25] literature is an addition to the world;[26] detective fiction is a major literary genre.[27]

Borges continued to propose his own interpretation of Argentine literary history, with its own classics and values, particularly in a series of prefaces.[28] Time made him one of the few surviving witnesses of the 1920s *avant-garde* and of the 1940s, conferring on him an authority that he displayed in interviews; his opinions competed with those of such contemporary critics as Ricardo Piglia or Beatriz Sarlo, who had found their niche in the institutions and the media since the restoration of democracy.[29] He also opposed reform of the curriculum at the Faculty of Letters, through which non-Argentine literatures became optional and their place could be taken by the sociology of literature, or by sociolinguistics.[30] A particularly intense conflict broke out when Carlos Hugo Christensen adapted the short story 'La intrusa', which Borges openly rejected.[31] Concurrently, there started the recovery of texts published in magazines and newspapers which Borges had refused to edit in book-form; just as he proclaimed that the *avant-gardes* were an invention of the critics,[32] the press published his *ultraist* poems;[33] his film criticism and his essays apropos the relationship between barbarism and literature were also republished.[34] The process got underway with the anthology *Páginas de Jorge Luis Borges seleccionadas por él mismo* (1982), a volume approved by Borges himself.

The writings of the period evidence Borges's intention of rereading his own works. *Tigres azules* is a narrative about the author's obsessions with tigers, considered by readers and critics alike as symbols of his work, also destined to come up at interview;[35] *Rosa de Paracelso* gave a disconcerting interpretation of the relationship between fame and craft, an issue also discussed in the interviews.[36] In *Atlas*, readers could encounter Borges's vision of the world, where literature shapes the places visited, and reality and literary text merge, in a volume that records the travels of the public figure; if global travel conveys the happiness that Borges experienced when he visited places around the world, *Atlas* also confirmed his lasting attachment to Buenos Aires, highlighted in such poems as 'The dreams' (*OC* III: 430).

Borges's Two Bodies

Borges's private life became a matter of national interest on two occasions: when he married María Kodama on 26 April 1986, and when he announced that he would settle down in Geneva, on 22 May 1986, which implied that he had chosen to die and be buried there, because, though the public at large was unaware of this, he knew he was terminally ill. The press was ignited by the two events, provoking a flood of comment and debate which all but engulfed his private life; he had often expressed his weariness at the constant attention of the press and people in public office, which verged on harassment.[37] The topics discussed were: the legality of the marriage, the situation of Fani/Fanny (who had been Borges's maid and suddenly found herself unemployed), his first marriage, his sexuality, and the fate of his inheritance.[38] Borges made few statements but publicly declared that he loved María Kodama, and gave an ironic version of his famous poem 'Remordimiento' (*La moneda de hierro*, 1976) : 'I committed the worst of sins: I got married.'[39] Although Ms Kodama had been his travelling companion since 1975, she was not often present at interviews or photographic sessions;[40] but Borges had dedicated *Historia de la noche* and *Los conjurados* to her. Besides, their intellectual partnership had been displayed in *Atlas*.

The marriage had not been officially announced, but Borges's decision to settle down in Geneva was made public on 22 May 1986. Borges had already expressed a wish to return to that city where nobody seemed to know him, and he justified his decision as a means of escaping from the press and the interest of people in the public domain; he added that his wish was to become H.G. Wells' invisible man, and that his Buenos Aires no longer existed.[41] In October 1984, he had already declared that he wanted to leave Argentina and go and settle in Japan;[42] his love and admiration for Switzerland, where he had lived as an adolescent, was expressed in 'Ginebra' (*Atlas*), where the city is associated with happiness, or in 'Los conjurados', where the country embodies a political ideal corresponding to his new ideas on the modern state.[43] Borges's private life was made of literary events; he often referred to his solitude, and to the death that awaited him; now his life was turned into a serial novel.[44] The tabloids described the marriage as the fulfilment of a love that had been growing for 20 years;[45] another part of the press was very critical of the countless intrusions into his private life, and yet another regretted the fact of Borges's exile.[46]

Nevertheless, it did not last, as Borges died from liver cancer on 14 June 1986. His death produced a radical shift of opinion: his marriage was then justified as a gift to the woman who had been his companion for several years. The issue became less important as tributes from writers and politicians followed, and the dispute around his inheritance began; Argentine newspapers attested to the impact of his death worldwide and remembered his career and work. The press proclaimed the Argentine character of his literature and, at the same time, its universality; the polemical aspects of his personality and popularity were evoked, as well as the numerous aspects of his work and career – from his relationship with his mother to his marriages, his conception of language, and his political ideas, humour and cynicism.[47] After his funeral in Geneva, the tributes continued, but the debates resumed too, particularly around his desire to be buried in that city and regarding his inheritance; at the Deliberative Council some Peronist representatives refused to pay him homage because of his political opinions.[48]

After Borges

After Borges's death, the process of recovery of his writings accelerated; if the press had started it, the management of his work entered a completely new phase when the writer authorized Rodríguez Monegal and Saceiro Garí to publish the chronicles of *El Hogar*, which met with huge success. At the same time, his manuscripts, original editions, and papers became valuable and started to be coveted by libraries and private collectors.[49] Borges's control over his printed works ended then; readers discovered unknown aspects of his production, but the *enfant terrible* and the polemicist, his physical presence in Buenos Aires, would remain vivid in memories and in the press.

Notes

1. María Esther Vázquez, 'Snapshots: Between Saintliness and Gastronomy' (Instantáneas: entre la santidad y la gastronomía), *La Nación*, 11 March 1984.
2. 'Borges Had Lunch Yesterday with Felipe González', *Clarín*, 4 June 1985.
3. 'A Ridiculous Country', *La Razón*, 12 August 1985.
4. 'Jorge Luis Borges Attended the Military Junta's Trial', *La Razón*, 22 July 1985; 'Borges at the Trials', *La Razón*, 22 July 1985; 'Borges with Strassera', *La Nación*, 23 July 1985.
5. 'Borges Said Some of the Commanders of the Army Should be Condemned to Death', *La Razón*, 11 November 1985.

6. 'Borges Continues His Fable: I and Journalism', *Tiempo Argentino*, 25 March 1984.
7. Vilma Colina, 'What Should We Do on April 2?' *Somos,* 391, Atlántida, 16 March 1984.
8. 'Conversations with Osvaldo Ferrari: The Classics and Borges', *Tiempo Argentino*, 29 August 1984.
9. Eduardo Gudiño Kieffer: 'Some Thoughts on an Insulting Stranger', *La Nación*, 21 December 1984; Susana Alonso, '"Who Is It? I Do Not Know Him" Said the Famous Author of *The Aleph*', *Tiempo Argentino*, 18 October 1985.
10. 'Distinction of the University of Cambridge: Borges, a Bridge of Reconciliation?' *Clarín*, 17 June 1984.
11. 'If There Is Hardship ['Miseria'], Let It Not Be Seen', *Clarín*, 8 March 1984.
12. *Discusión*, Buenos Aires, Emecé, 1953.
13. '[Rafael] Alberti Said that Borges Should Receive the Nobel Prize for 1984', *La Razón*, 1 August 1984.
14. Nilda Sosa: 'Today He Is 85, Borges Still on Stage', *Clarín*, 24 August 1984.
15. A Buenos Aires newspaper, founded by Raúl Horacio Burzaco and published between 1982 and 1986.
16. A traditional Argentine newspaper, founded in 1870 by Bartolomé Mitre, of conservative ideas.
17. Founded in 1965, this magazine specialized in international *jet-setters'* news, and was linked to the political right.
18. Aníbal M. Vinelli, 'Borges y esa cultura que no aburre', *Clarín*, 9 March 1984.
19. Amelia Barili, 'Thoughts of Jorge Luis Borges', *La Prensa*, 8 April 1984.
20. 'The Weight of Time', *Clarín*, 2 August 1984.
21. 'A Message from Borges to His Public, Filled with Hope', *Clarín*, 1 March 1985.
22. Carlos Ulanovski, 'I Was Never Beyond Good and Evil', *Clarín*, 17 March 1985.
23. 'The Short Story According to Borges', *Clarín*, 15 April 1985.
24. 'Conversations with Osvaldo Ferrari: How Hollywood and Its Cowboys Saved the Epic Genre', *Tiempo Argentino*, 26 June 1985.
25. 'Conversations with Osvaldo Ferrari: Carriego and Goethe: The Suburbs of the World', *Tiempo Argentino*, 3 July 1985.
26. 'Conversations with Osvaldo Ferrari: Poetry Does Not Correspond to an Emotion or a Theme: It Is an Object Added to the World', *Tiempo Argentino*, 1 August 1985.
27. 'Conversations with Osvaldo Ferrari: Short Detective Stories Are the Essence of Literature', *Tiempo Argentino*, 2 November 1985
28. Jorge Luis Borges, 'A Short Story by Eduardo Wilde', *Clarín*, Buenos Aires, 23 February 1984; 'Conversations with Osvaldo Ferrari: Past, Present and Future of His Country According to Borges', *Tiempo Argentino*, 13 June 1984.

29. Ricardo Piglia, 'The Chekhov Player', *Clarín*, 6 November 1986; Beatriz Sarlo, 'The Rise of Fiction', *Espacios de crítica y producción* (Universidad de Buenos Aires), 10 November 1987.
30. 'Borges's Criticism of Literary Studies. Acid Comments About Study Plans', *Clarín*, 24 February 1986.
31. 'Borges Criticizes "La Intrusa": The Film Is a Disgrace', *Clarín*, 29 July 1984.
32. 'Conversations with Osvaldo Ferrari: Boedo and Florida: Those Illusory Groups That Are Studied in Universities', *Tiempo Argentino*, 6 March 1985.
33. 'Borges's Prehistory (La Prehistoria de Borges)', *La Razón*, 16 December 1984.
34. 'Borges the Film Critic', *Magazine*, 19 April 1985; 'Rereading Sarmiento', *El Día*, Montevideo, 28 December 1985–03 January 1986.
35. 'Conversations with Osvaldo Ferrari: On Tigers, Labyrinths, Mirrors, Arms and Dreams', *Tiempo Argentino*, 27 June 1984.
36. 'Borges: The Poem Seeks Me Out', *La Nación*, 7 August 1985.
37. 'María Kodama Explains Why They Went to Geneva', *La Prensa*, 15 May 1986.
38. 'Family Lawsuit over the Borges Inheritance', *La Nación*, 15 May 1986; 'Legal Battle Because of Borges's Matrimony', *Tiempo Argentino*, Buenos Aires, 15 May 1986. See also observations by Edwin Williamson, in this volume (Chapter 3).
39. Jorge Luis Borges, 'I Committed the Worst of Sins. I Got Married'; 'Borges and María Kodama's Love Story', *Clarín*, 15 May 1986.
40. Alicia Barrios, 'I Am in Love and I Intend to Follow María Kodama to the End of the World", *Libre*, año 2, 67, 23 April 1985; 'Jorge Luis Borges Considers María Kodama as His Girlfriend and Is Desperate Because She Is Going to Japan on a Scholarship', *Semanario*, 24 April 1985.
41. 'Mis Libros', *La Nación*, 28 April 1985; 'Borges Stays in Geneva Because His Buenos Aires Does Not Exist Anymore', *Clarín*, 22 May 1986.
42. Esteban Peicovich, 'Borges: I Am Going to Live in Japan. They Promised Me I Will See Again', *Gente* 1005, Atlántida, 25 October 1984.
43. María Esther Vázquez, 'Our Duty Is the Credible Hope. An Interview with Jorge Luis Borges', *La Nación*, 19 August 1984.
44. Manuel Avelange, 'Borges, Master of the Soap-Opera (Borges, maestro del folletín)', *Tiempo Argentino*, 18 May 1986.
45. ' ... They Loved Each Other in Silence for 20 Years', *Para Tí*, 3333, 26 May 1986.
46. Carlos Martini: 'Borges's Exile', *Humor*, 175, June/1986.
47. 'Borges is Dead', *La Razón*, 14 June 1986; 'Jorge Luis Borges Died in Geneva', *Crónica*, 14 June 1986; 'Borges Died, María Kodama Was with Him', *La Gaceta de Hoy*, 14 June 1986.
48. 'Agitated Tribute to Borges in the Deliberative Council', *La Nación*, 21 June 1986.
49. 'Books, Manuscripts and Intimate Letters from Borges Will Be Auctioned in New York', *La Nación*, 20 September 1986.

CHAPTER 7

Borges and Las Islas Malvinas

Ben Bollig

In 1982, after massive demonstrations demanding a return to democracy, and having nearly gone to war with Chile over the Beagle Channel and islands in southern Patagonia, the Argentine military dictatorship under *de facto* president General Galtieri declared war on the United Kingdom and invaded the Malvinas/Falkland Islands and South Georgia and the South Sandwich Isles. This turned out to be a desperate miscalculation. Neither the UK government nor the international community, in particular the USA, reacted as they had hoped, if indeed any detailed strategic planning had informed the decision. The result was a short but bloody war, humiliation for the Argentine armed forces, and in some part the fall of the military *junta*.

From the early 1960s onwards, it became common for younger Argentine writers, especially those on the left, to dismiss Borges's writing on political grounds, despite his international literary renown. Ricardo Piglia, in a 1979 article in *Punto de vista*, spoke of Borges's politics in that period as a 'type of native fascism'.[1] Noé Jitrik reflected in 1981 on the problematic figure Borges had become for writers opposed to the Argentine dictatorship, in power since the coup of 1976. Jitrik asked, 'What would happen, I wonder, if Borges were on our side?'[2] 'What if he were not the "organic intellectual" of the dictatorship?' This was the role he seemed, to many, to occupy in the late 1970s and early 1980s.

The return to Argentina and subsequent election to the presidency of deposed former president General Juan Domingo Perón in 1973 inspired some of Borges's most controversial public interventions. The writer spoke out against democracy, calling it 'an abuse of statistics' in the prologue to the 1976 collection *La moneda de hierro* (*The Iron Coin*). In the wake of the putsch that toppled the technically legitimate but increasingly chaotic and indeed violent government of Perón's widow, María Estela ('Isabelita') Martínez de Perón, he met with the incoming military *junta* and announced to reporters that at last 'gentlemen' were running the country.

For many opposed to the dictatorship, such acts confirmed the impression that Borges was an oligarchic dinosaur. However, his engagement with the Malvinas/Falklands conflict offers an alternative possibility, of a more progressive politics in his work. Borges's poems on the Malvinas are of particular interest because, alongside his writings on the Six Days War (for example 'Israel, 1969'), and 'El simulacro' ('The Simulacrum', a fable about Peronism included in *El hacedor*), the Malvinas/Falklands War offers one of the very few occasions on which Borges commented directly in single-authored creative writing on contemporary political events. He said often that he did not hide his political opinions, including his anti-Nazism, his anti-Peronism, and his initial support for and later repudiation of the 1976–1983 military dictatorship. Conversely, he rarely opined openly in his creative writing. Borges wrote almost no overtly committed political works.

Borges had initially supported the military regime, but as evidence found its way to him of its crimes, in particular the disappearance of people and the widespread use of torture and extrajudicial killing, his opinion shifted. He also despaired of the military's increasing control of everyday life, and the economic crisis in the country. The declaration of war against the UK seems to have been the final straw for the staunchly Anglophone writer. In one interview, given in Dublin, Borges commented that the conflict was akin to two bald men fighting for a comb.[3] He suggested that the islands be given to Bolivia so the country could have a seaport. He was widely criticized in Argentina for this attitude.

Borges was one of a tiny number of writers and intellectuals who opposed the conflict. Julio Cortázar, for example, said that it was a war for 'some shitty islands full of penguins'. León Rozitchner, a prominent left-wing thinker exiled in Venezuela, criticized other left-wing intellectuals for supporting the military campaign. The poet, anthropologist, and gay rights activist Néstor Perlongher wrote a series of polemical articles condemning the left's support for the conflict. But these were lonely figures within Argentine intelligentsia, and even more solitary when compared to the waves of mass support for the conflict, including cross-party demonstrations in the Plaza de Mayo, or the backing of unions and even the exiled leader of the armed-left insurgent group Montoneros, Mario Firmenich.

The same could be said of poetry on the subject. There is a significant corpus of irredentist poems dating from before, during, and after the conflict. Many were collected in the 1983 collection *Nuestros poetas y las Malvinas* (*Our Poets and the Malvinas*).[4] Some are almost self-parodies of machismo and indignation, for example the poem 'A la isla ladrona' ('To the Robber Island') by José María Castiñeira de Dios, writing in 1954, which presents the islands as two testicles separated from the Argentine body, the visible symbol of a country bested in a contest of masculinity. Other poets in Müller's collection praise the war effort, for example Eduardo Carroll in his 'Soneto heroico' ('Heroic Sonnet', 1982); celebrate the victory as a result of which Argentina can finally call the islands 'Argentine'; and eulogize the dead as the basis for the nation's future, or as sowing the seeds for a new 'patria' (fatherland). Poems in the collection are, in general, neoclassical, and when read against contemporary poetry have an anachronistic feel, perhaps as writers seek established models for patriotic outpourings, either in the forms of national anthems or from other traditional poetic forms, including the sonnet in hendecasyllables.

In striking contrast to these stands Borges's 'Juan López and John Ward', first published in the important daily newspaper *Clarín*'s *Cultura y Nación* section on 26 August 1982. It is a very simple prose poem about two soldiers, one implicitly Argentine, and one implicitly English, who meet on a battlefield and kill each other. The poem describes encounters and missed encounters. One can observe the way, for example, that the two young men are brought together and separated throughout the poem: the title names them together and separately; but then the piece's first word, the pronoun 'they', unites them; similarly, in the penultimate line they are buried together.

Borges sets their encounter against a historical background, but one that lacks political details. We have, in the second paragraph, or stanza, a chaotic enumeration typical of Borges's poems and short stories, such as 'El Aleph', to give one example. Borges ironizes the 'no doubt' heroic pasts of the countries in conflict. A reference to dignitaries cast from bronze reminds us that Borges had earlier fallen out with relatives who wanted to erect an equestrian statue of one of their forefathers. That, for Borges, was the last thing anyone needed under a military dictatorship.[5] But Borges does not appear to blame any individuals for the war. Rather the fault is of a general situation characterized by borders and history, which lends itself to war.

Subsequent sections alternate between the two characters. This crossing has something of the chiasmus about it: López, then Ward; then Ward again; then the other (López). And their passions cross, too: the Argentine reads Conrad, the Englishman Cervantes. The effect is not unlike that of *rima abrazada,* or embraced rhyme, as one might find in some traditional Spanish verse. There follows something close to a *volta,* or turn, that we associate with the conclusion of a sonnet, stating that the two young men might have been friends. Finally, we read the brilliant, sad, synthesis: instead they become warring brothers, each Cain to the other's Abel, in another chiasmus. What finally brings them together is death, for they are buried together, and the snow and decay come to, in Borges's term, 'know' them. Borges often surprises the reader with his combinations of noun and adjective or verb and adverb. In this case, a mental verb presents the action of non-sentient objects – for decay is not a thing, but a process, which strictly cannot *know* anything. It might, perhaps, in the Biblical sense, in which snow and decay join the soldiers in a quasi-erotic intimacy.

The poem's final line is also intriguing. As in the opening, Borges makes no attempt to work out political specificities. But if one bears in mind that this poem was written and published only weeks after the end of hostilities, it generates chronological distance from the conflict. One might find a precedent in Esteban Echeverría's short story or chronicle 'El matadero' ('The Slaughterhouse', published in 1871 but most likely written in the late 1830s) which, although almost contemporary to the bloody regime of Juan Manuel de Rosas, sets the violent events described in a distant, historical past, as if looking back with bemusement on the horrors that had occurred. One might also find cause for optimism here: the poem suggests that we have moved on so quickly from the events of dictatorship and war, we almost cannot comprehend this 'other country' that is the recent past.

'Juan López and John Ward' is not an uncontroversial poem. It seems to want to strip the violence from its context, and to focus on the typical patterns – especially doublings – of Borges's fictions, without a sense of the political specifics. Julieta Vitullo, for example, argues that the poem presupposes an epic view of the homeland.[6] Martín Kohan, in a major study of war in Argentine literature, suggests that the poem relies on the cliché of mutual recognition to overcome the differences between the two countries.[7] Kohan's critique would be that a literary, or even archetypal solution, is just too simple, too easy, and lets those actually responsible for these boys' deaths off the hook.

Other commentators take a different approach. Jason Wilson includes this piece in his assessment of Borges's late poetry, calling it 'a prose poem which confronts both sides of Borges's identity as a patriot: the *criollo* and the Englishman, two sides of his literary persona meshing Buenos Aires and London'. Borges's position, 'contrary to countless patriots on both sides [...] is another sign of his valor'.[8] For Wilson, even as small a step as Borges was taking, to say that there might be something in common between British and Argentine fighters, was worthy in the context of post-war nationalism. A brief glance at official propaganda at the time, or even what some reputable writers wrote about the conflict, demonstrates the value of Borges's stance.

Bernard McGuirk reads Borges's poem in the wider context of writing about the conflict, linking it to a predecessor, Wilfred Owen's 'Strange Meeting'.[9] Borges follows Owen in presenting the irrational and inexplicable bloodshed of war. 'Strange Meeting', a poem written during and about the First World War, has the poem's speaker meet the German soldier he has not long earlier killed, in what we find out is a kind of hell. The soldier regrets both the loss and the incessant drive to further conflict and bloodshed. The voice of the German closes the poem:

> I am the enemy you killed, my friend.
> I knew you in this dark: for so you frowned
> Yesterday through me as you jabbed and killed.
> I parried; but my hands were loath and cold.
> Let us sleep now. . . .

Owen's poem is divided into what might be called 'half-rhyming' or 'pararhyme' couplets. That is to say, like Borges, we see a play between similarity and difference, between encounter and missed meetings, played out on the form of the poem. The suggested yet missed rhyme of Owen's poem is recalled in the various crossings of Borges's piece, in which characters miss each other or only meet in fatal circumstances: this is Borges's poetic, formal depiction of the shame of war.

Borges's second poem on the war, 'Milonga del muerto' ('Dead Man's *Milonga*') was first published in *Clarín* on 30 December 1982. Like 'Juan López and John Ward', 'Milonga . . . ' shifts our gaze away from nationalism or other more abstract notions, towards the fate of one of the combatants in the war. In this regard Borges was picking up on a growing sense in Argentina that those who had suffered most were the rank and file: conscripts, often from the poorest and more ethnically mixed or indigenous regions of the country, ill-equipped, barely trained, and badly fed. Stories emerged of mistreatment at the hands of officers, of racism (including anti-Semitism) and brutality against young soldiers. All of this is vividly recounted in novels such as Carlos Gamerro's *Las islas* (*The Islands,* 1998) or Rodolfo Fogwill's *Los pichiciegos* (*Malvinas Requiem,* 1983), or in films such as Tristán Bauer's *Iluminados por el fuego* (*Touched by Fire,* 2005). Borges's poem became a rallying cry for veterans and also for the anti-conscription movement, campaigning to end military service in Argentina.

The form is that of the *milonga*, an early version of the tango, which Borges enjoyed, and of which over the years he composed many examples, including the collection *Para las seis cuerdas* (*For the Six Strings*, 1965). In some respects, this is a simple poem. It is based on a dream about a conscript. It tells the story of a young man, from the interior, sent off to fight. In contrast to Borges's other *milongas*, here the lyric voice takes something of a backward step. It is not the lyric voice that does the fighting: rather it is the young soldier who is described. This is a far cry from the bravado and *braggadocio* of traditional *milongas*.

In the poem's third stanza we read an attack on government-backed propaganda, not least the lie that people do not die in war. During the campaign, the media in Argentina ran numerous fake stories about military victories. Thus for many Argentines, news of defeat came as a total shock. In the fourth stanza, one can see that the young soldier is little more than cannon-fodder. Stanza five is ironic, talking of prudence and care which is wholly out of keeping with what we know about the conflict and the poor preparations made by the Argentine top brass. The sixth stanza moves closer to pure invective, with its barbs against 'vain' military officials.

As the poem moves to a close, however, in the final three stanzas one encounters more ambivalence. Even if the situation is absurd, and the war repugnant, the young man himself is still brave. Bravery and a degree of stoicism are features of *milongas* (in contrast to the more sentimental tangos that followed them historically). The soldier cares not for politics; instead, he is testing himself. He passes the test, albeit fatally. The lyric voice accommodates mixed feelings, approving of his bravery but regretting his sacrifice: these mixed feelings are described as containing both envy and sorrow, or pity ('pena'), for a part of the lyric voice would welcome such a death.

Again, this is not an uncontroversial poem. Vitullo sees it as exemplary of Borges's individualism, reframing the soldier's death as a personal triumph.[10] For Carlos Gamero, there is an uncomfortable coexistence in the poem between criticism of the conflict and a celebration of bravery.[11] Indeed this is a poem that cannot, indeed does not attempt to, resolve its contradictions. The synthesis of López and Ward, above, is failed and lethal. They come together only in death. In the 'Milonga' we find no easy conclusion, as the poem's speaker and the reader are left with what Noé Jitrik called 'complex feelings'.

Balderston has said of Borges that

> His nasty turn to the right in reaction to a Peronism that he could only see as a homegrown fascism, should not obscure the fact that earlier in his career – and for that matter, also at the very end of his life, after the Malvinas war – his sympathies were those of a post-Enlightenment liberal intellectual.[12]

As Ana C. Cara points out, even someone on the very opposite end of the political spectrum to Borges, the poet Juan Gelman, whose son and daughter-in-law were murdered by the dictatorship, could speak of Borges's valour in admitting his errors, unlike many others who supported the military yet refused to recant or apologize.[13]

Importantly, in this poem, Borges creates a poor, working-class, and probably part-indigenous character with an inner life and a voice to express it; that is rather rare in the Argentine's work. His poem offers a plea for understanding and respect, similar to that found in 'Juan López and John Ward'. Late in life, Borges found himself attracted to Switzerland as a model of political organization, outlined in another late poem 'Los conjurados' ('The Plotters', or 'The Confederates'), a companion piece to his Malvinas poems in the collection of the same name. Here speaks the Borges who met the *Madres de la Plaza de Mayo*, the mothers of those 'disappeared' by the regime, bravely campaigning to discover the whereabouts of their loved ones; the Borges who in 1981 condemned the military;[14] the Borges of both individual rebellion and mutual tolerance.

Notes

1. Ricardo Piglia, 'Ideología y ficción en Borges', in Ana María Barrenechea et al., *Borges y la crítica* (Buenos Aires: CEAL, 1999), p. 93.
2. Noé Jitrik, 'Complex Feelings About Borges', in *The Noé Jitrik Reader* (Durham, NC: Duke University Press, 2005), p. 18.
3. Edwin Williamson, *Borges: A Life* (London: Penguin, 2004), p. 457.
4. Agueda Müller (ed.), *Nuestros poetas y las Malvinas* (Buenos Aires: Corregidor, 1999).
5. Williamson, *Borges: A Life*, p. 461.
6. Julieta Vitullo, 'Relatos de desertores en las ficciones de la guerra de Malvinas', *Hispamérica*, 35, 104 (2006), pp. 29–38.
7. Martín Kohan, *El país de la guerra* (Buenos Aires: Eterna Cadencia, 2014), pp. 270–271.
8. Jason Wilson, 'The Late Poetry (1969–1985)', in Edwin Williamson (ed.), *The Cambridge Companion to Jorge Luis Borges* (Cambridge: Cambridge University Press, 2013), p. 194.

9. Bernard McGuirk, 'Transcendental Echoes and the Snares of Intra-Colonialism: Falklands-Malvinas and the Poetry of War', in Diego F. García Quiroga and Mike Seear (eds.), *Hors de combat. The Falklands-Malvinas Conflict in Retrospect* (Nottingham: CCCP, 2009), pp. 121–132.
10. Vitullo, 'Relatos', p. 37.
11. Carlos Gamerro, *Facundo o Martín Fierro* (Buenos Aires: Sudamericana, 2015), p. 315.
12. Daniel Balderston, *Out of Context* (Durham, NC: Duke University Press, 1993), p. 136.
13. Ana C. Cara, 'Fighting Words, Disarming Music: Borges's "Milonga del muerto"', *Variaciones Borges*, 35 (2013), pp. 181–198.
14. Williamson, *Borges: A Life*, p. 454.

CHAPTER 8

Borges and Sarmiento

Sandra Contreras

The prologue that Jorge Luis Borges wrote for the 1974 edition of *Facundo*, published by Librería El Ateneo, is the only text he ever dedicated to that book, in which Domingo F. Sarmiento postulated, in 1845, the '*civilización-barbarie*' dichotomy as an interpretative framework for Argentine political reality. Borges's final statement could not be clearer: 'I will not say that *Facundo* is the first Argentine book. I will say that if we had canonized it as our exemplary book, our history would be different, and better.'[1] It is important to note that Borges is drawing attention to this classic book and its importance for the development of national culture in the precise context of the return to government of Juan Domingo Perón.[2] The fact also underscores, in retrospect, that it is always in the immediacy of specific historical junctures, which Borges construes each time as contexts of violence, that he writes about Sarmiento's texts and even brings them to bear on contemporary circumstance as weapons of combat. It is true that both the series of Borges's fictions shaped by the motif of courage (the tales of *cuchilleros* or knife-fighters and key stories such as 'The Biography of Tadeo Isidoro Cruz', 'The End', and 'The South') and the numerous essays in which he dealt with the poem *Martín Fierro,* even if to refute its place in the canon, show repeatedly that, when it comes to the two major classics of Argentine national literature, Borges's predilection always comes down on the side of José Hernández.

In contrast, the few texts that he dedicates to Sarmiento – barely two prologues, two brief notes on the author, two poems, no stories – would seem to indicate that perhaps in Sarmiento's works Borges did not find all that much symbolic capital for his own fiction. However, it is no less true that what he identifies as Sarmiento's incomparable clairvoyance, 'the feat of seeing the present day historically, of simplifying and grasping it as if it were already past' (*Prólogos*, 131), awakens in Borges a historical intuition of time. And it is precisely this experience that will find in Sarmiento's writing an extremely powerful tool for expressing its most controversial potential in discursive form: political intervention in the present. The war, then, or what Borges lives as a war, puts Sarmiento's interpretative formula to work once more and, whether against Nazism or Peronism, Borges will reactivate the dichotomy of *'civilización-barbarie'*.

1944

The prologue to Sarmiento's *Recuerdos de Provincia*, which Borges wrote for the 1944 Emecé edition, marks the beginning of this reactivation process. The decisive paragraph reads as follows:

> The course of time alters books. *Recuerdos*, re-read in 1943 is certainly not the book I experienced twenty years ago. The insipid world, at that time, seemed irreversibly distant from all violence. Ricardo Güiraldes evoked with nostalgia [...] the harshness of the life of *troperos*; we were happy imagining that in the high and war-stricken city of Chicago alcohol smugglers were fodder for the machine gun; with vain tenacity, with literary eagerness, I went looking for the last traces of the *cuchilleros* of the river banks. So tame, so irreparably peaceful did the world seem to us, that we played with fierce anecdotes and deplored the 'time of wolves, the time of swords' that other, more fortunate generations had merited. [...] The dangerous reality described by Sarmiento was, then, distant and inconceivable; now it is contemporary (European and Asian telegrams corroborate my assertion). The only difference is that barbarism, previously unpremeditated, instinctive, is now applied and conscious, and has at its disposal more coercive means than Quiroga's *montonera* spear or the jagged cutting edges of the *mazorca*. (*Prólogos*, 130)

The aestheticized violence of the 1920s (which Borges retrospectively recreates in the mythical world of his *cuchilleros* tales, or which he reads in the rural epic world of Ricardo Güiraldes's novel, *Don Segundo Sombra*) can be read as the avant-garde reinterpreting the intellectual climate that, at the turn of the century, had reversed the civilization-barbarism dichotomy (the countryside, barbarism, and primitive violence taking on the air of paradises lost). But the presence of the Second World War now eradicates any possibility of nostalgia and reverses the dichotomy once again: violence, now rational and immediate, means barbarism, and the more monstrous and the more horrific, the further it is from instinctive irrationality. The analogy is clear: the horror of rationalized barbarism is found now in Nazism in the same way Sarmiento found it in the tyranny of Juan Manuel de Rosas. In this sense, it is evident that one must read the prologue to *Recuerdos* together with 'A Comment on August 23, 1944', which Borges published in *Sur* on the occasion of the liberation of Paris, and which is part of the series of articles against Nazism that he wrote in those years.[3] Just as in 1938 Victoria Ocampo invoked Sarmiento in her defence of intelligence and freedom, that is, of Western civilization facing the threat of Nazism, so Borges in 1944, with the fall of the Axis imminent, recovers the terms of Sarmiento's dichotomy against the barbarism of totalitarianism.

Both texts also postulate hypotheses that, with variants, Borges will take up again in later interventions. One of them identifies political violence with nightmare and hallucination: 'Nazism suffers from unreality, like Erigena's hell. It is uninhabitable' ('A Comment'). The other one avers that only when the return of violence is unimaginable can nostalgia and aesthetic play take place: read in the 1920s, says Borges, '*Recuerdos de Provincia* was the document of an irrecoverable past and, therefore, of a pleasant one, since no one dreamed that its rigors could return and reach us.' And it was probably with the relief engendered by that nostalgia that the young Borges was able to transform the tension between fear and defiance that so fascinated Sarmiento in his chapter 'Barranca Yaco!' and to render in poetic language, in 1925, the festive recklessness of General Facundo Quiroga on the way to his fatal ambush: 'Ir en coche a la muerte ¡qué cosa más oronda!' (How grand, to ride to one's death by coach!) (in 'El general Quiroga va en coche al muere', *Moon Across the Way*, *OC* I: 61).

1957–1968

After 1955, that is, after what he experienced as 'the second dictatorship' and the consolidation of nationalist populism as a political and cultural identity, Borges resorts to Sarmiento for the second time and in a second sense.[4]

Two very brief interventions in 1961 reformulate the prologue of 1944: they historically re-contextualize Sarmiento's dichotomy, only to return it, now through Sarmiento's other classic book, to the field of what he understands as a national war: if in his childhood *Facundo* offered 'the same delectable taste of fable as the inventions of [Jules] Verne or the pirates of [Robert Louis] Stevenson', the 'recent dictatorship', Borges states in reference to Perón's two governments, 'has shown us that the barbarism denounced [by Sarmiento] is not, as we naively believed, a picturesque and bygone trait' but 'a current danger', 'a permanent risk'.[5] After the 'Revolución Libertadora' of September 1955, and once the regime he lived and recounted in terms of a civil war – and even as a war against himself – had ended, Borges returns to the civilization-barbarism formula to say that, in the mid-twentieth century (and after the naivety of childhood), it continues to be the best framework for interpreting Argentine reality. And, without nuances, in its exact terms.

However, this belligerent reprise of Sarmiento also coexists, in this period, with a series of prose writings from 1957 which, on the contrary, show how the conviction that Peronism is a thing of the past allows us to continue opting, aesthetically, for the world of courage. 'Dialogue of the dead' imagines an encounter between Rosas and Quiroga that includes a discussion about the value of a memorable death, clearly a 'romantic' theme in Sarmiento's lexicon. In 'The simulacrum', the 'incredible story' of the multiple representations of Eva Perón's wake (1952) in different villages in the interior of the country is seen by Borges as a 'farce' and the 'perfect figure for an unreal age'. And in 'Martín Fierro', while the battles of Independence and the confrontations registered during Rosism and, then, Peronism are, now, 'as if they had not been', the scene in Canto VII where Martín Fierro murders Moreno is the fight that, 'dreamed' by a man around 1872, 'returns infinitely' and becomes 'part of everyone's memory'.[6]

In 1957, then, while the unreality of nightmare remains reserved for wars and 'tyrannies', the most violent moment in the story of Martín Fierro is instead, for Borges, the material of that enduring dream that is the aesthetic phenomenon. And the three prologues he writes for different editions of the poem (two in 1962, the other in 1968) will return again and again to the idea of *Martín Fierro* as a book that successive generations 'will not resign themselves to forget'.[7] It is interesting to note that the recognition of this memorable character otherwise in the same terms that Borges used, in 1966, to reformulate his theory of a classic work, coexists peacefully with the fictional dialogue between Rosas and Quiroga that Borges composes, in the manner of a counterpoint between *cuchilleros*, with materials that he also finds memorable in Sarmiento's book. And that is interesting because in a short time Borges will discuss Martín Fierro's position in the Argentine canon, and Sarmiento's *Facundo* will be his tool to that end.

1974

Towards the end of the 1974 prologue, Borges enunciates for the first time the idea that Facundo, as crafted by Sarmiento, is 'the most memorable character in our literature'; even more than that, Borges states that Sarmiento's work as a whole has bequeathed 'to the memory of the Argentines' many 'imperishable images', including those of his

[Sarmiento's] mother and of Sarmiento himself, 'who lives on'. Immediately and by way of conclusion, he puts forward the controversial conjecture: if instead of canonizing *Martín Fierro* we had canonized *Facundo*, Argentine history would have been different, and it would be better. It is true that the last prologue that Borges wrote for the poem, in 1968, began by stating that 'After Sarmiento's *Facundo* or alongside it, *Martín Fierro* is the greatest work in Argentine literature', but the status of 'classic' was implicitly still aligned with Hernández's work, because it was the character of Fierro who, Borges said, had become 'the most vivid man our literature has ever dreamed'.

The 1974 return to Sarmiento is, then, twofold, in line with the two senses that Borges distinguished in his essays entitled 'On the Classics': on the one hand, the displacement of Fierro by Facundo in the realm of literary and cultural memory implies the idea that a classic, according to the version of 1965, is the result of its reading by successive generations; on the other hand, the hypothesis of its canonization as an exemplary book responds better to the idea of the classic as a canonical text invented and imposed by the 'pedagogues' of culture, an idea which Borges had rejected in the 1941 version of his essay.[8] When he insists on this second hypothesis in the 'Posdatas de 1974' added to the 1944 prologue to *Recuerdos* and to those of the 1960s to *Martín Fierro*, he will do so to show clearly that it is institutional pedagogy and its effects on the formation of cultural identity (now, he says, 'we are suffering the consequences' of having exalted a deserting gaucho as a national archetype) that need to be aired. At the political juncture of the 1970s, 'Sarmiento', Borges says, 'continues to formulate the alternative: civilization or barbarism' (*Prólogos*, 99 and 133).

The return of Perón, then, activates the recovery of Sarmiento, and, resuming his already long polemic with the cultural nationalism of the first decades of the century, Borges now engages – in an immediate political way – with what for him is its avatar in the Argentine present: Peronist populism.

As is well known, Borges repeatedly refuted what he considered to be exaggerated and erroneous readings of *Martín Fierro*: not only the profusion of critical errors that are condensed in *Historia de la literatura argentina* by Ricardo Rojas, but above all, the epic interpretation of the poem and its fighting drunkards found in Leopoldo Lugones's *El payador*. Borges contests that interpretation in his essays of the 1950s: 'Gauchesque poetry', 'The Argentine Writer and Tradition', and *El Martín Fierro*, and at the same time, from the 1930s, with his essay *Evaristo Carriego* and his tales of *cuchilleros*, he elaborates a fiction that

appeals to the minor tradition of *moreirismo* in order to demystify the
tradition of the *gaucho* that had been institutionalized by the nationalism of Rojas and Lugones. But in 1974, when nationalism and populism
have converged in the phenomenon of Peronism, when he understands
that its aesthetic, cultural, and political effects are colouring Argentine
reality once more, Borges introduces a variation to his refutation of the
national canon: he displaces Lugones's reading of *Martin Fierro*, not
with Eduardo Gutiérrez's *Juan Moreira* but with Sarmiento's *Facundo*.
And if the present, as Borges suggests, forces us to update the historical
question that had been posed in *Facundo*, the way in which the present
affects Borges himself is clearly shown in the transformation of the
dichotomy under consideration: what Sarmiento formulates in the
original title of the book as a tense articulation – civilization and
barbarism – Borges refashions as a stark opposition between mutually
exclusive terms: civilization or barbarism, Sarmiento or Hernández.

What is interesting, in this sense, is not so much the repetition of
a dichotomy that runs through Argentine thought – and one whose
inherent over-simplification is so alien to Borges's essayistic style – as
the virulence that the 1974 juncture re-awakens in Borges the man and
author: the imperceptible and at the same time violent torque through
which the essay modifies and even rectifies the immediately previous
readings of that classic book. In the three prologues he published in the
1960s, Borges insisted on an idea that he had not formulated before:
while it is true that Hernández's obvious purpose was to denounce the
War Ministry for fraudulently transforming the gauchos into deserters,
there is a moment – the 'mystery' of literature, Borges calls it – when the
character's voice prevails over the author's intentions, and it is this
unexpected twist that determined the emergence of 'the hard man
who we know to be a fugitive, deserter, singer, *cuchillero*, and, in the
estimation of some, champion' and who is 'one of the most vivid,
brutal, and convincing men that the history of literature records'. The
argument is noteworthy here for two reasons. First, because it is from
the value assigned to the 'hardness' of the character that Borges, who in
1931 refuted the 'national myth' argument, now, in 1962, concedes
a particular epic character to the poem. Second, because this preference,
this 'taste' for epic, not so much in terms of genre as in 'the after-taste of
destiny, adventure and courage that it leaves behind', continues to
operate, and powerfully so, even at the beginning of the 1970s. In
1970, Borges compiles and prefaces an anthology titled *El matrero* and
it is there that he formulates his choice of either-or for the first time.

Each country chooses its classic book, he postulates, and concludes: 'As far as we are concerned, I think that our history would be different, and it would be better, if we had chosen, from this century on, *Facundo* and not *Martín Fierro*' (*Prólogos*, 112). The formulation is the same as in 1974, and it can be argued that the popular insurrections that followed one another between 1969 and 1972 created the context of renewed violence that once again triggered Borges's 'reactive' preference for Sarmiento.[9] But here that hypothesis also coexists with an argument that Borges had been putting forward repeatedly, at least since 1946, when he published 'Our Poor Individualism': the idea that Argentines 'are attracted to the rebel, the individual, even uneducated or criminal, who opposes the State' (*Prólogos*, 113). And what is interesting is that this attraction to the individual – *matrero* or *peleador* – is linked not only with the idea that one of the virtues of this archetype is its 'belonging to the past' (which is why – he concludes – 'we can venerate it without risk'), but also with the pleasure that Borges himself continues to experience in imagining and contemplating it. An aesthetic pleasure that, in 1970, can eclipse all political and moral interpretation: 'This anthological book is not an apology of the *matrero*, nor an indictment of the State prosecutor. To compose it has been a pleasure; I hope this pleasure will be shared by those who turn its pages.'

Evidently, at the juncture of 1974, this pleasure recedes and the dichotomy – now entirely moral, entirely political – fills the centre-stage. If the prologue to *Facundo* closes with the same option that had first been formulated in 1970, the emphasis on an exclusive binary and its double re-inscription in 1974 shows to what extent Borges does not ignore the shift from the imaginary to the immediacy of political reality, and to what extent he is committed to reaffirming it. It also shows that the operation was never banal or simple. Each situation was structured around the relative anxiety produced by the remoteness or proximity of violence and, above all, by what he imagines as the improbable or the imminent return of its political expression.

A reading of 'Historias de jinetes' (Stories of horsemen) first published in 1954 (in the context of Borges's intense and complex work on the myth of courage and national tradition between 1951 and 1955), would at the same time show a disturbing surplus: a writing that, resorting to Sarmiento, intervenes politically in the context of the Peronist government while, in a typical Borgesian gesture, it avoids unmediated ideological reaction and reserves for Borges's essays and fictions the continuous movement of invention.[10]

Notes

1. This Prologue is included in Jorge Luis Borges, *Prólogos con un prólogo de prólogos* (Buenos Aires: Torres Agüero Editor, 1975). The quotation is taken from page 139. All translations from the original Spanish are the translator's.

2. After 18 years of proscription, in 1973 Juan Domingo Perón won the elections with 62% of the vote and began his third presidency. He died on 1 July 1974, and was succeeded by Vice-President María Isabel Martínez de Perón.

3. 'Ensayo de imparcialidad', *Sur* 61 (October 1939); 'Definición de germanófilo', *El Hogar*, 13 de diciembre de 1940; '1941', *Sur* 87 (December 1941); 'Nota sobre la paz', *Sur* 129 (July 1945); 'Anotación al 23 de agosto de 1944', *Sur* 120 (October 1944), later included in *Otras inquisiciones* (Buenos Aires: Sur, 1952). For an English translation of these texts, see *Selected Non-Fictions*, ed. Eliot Weinberger (New York: Viking, 1999), pp. 202–213.

4. In September 1955, the self-proclaimed 'Revolución Libertadora' overthrew the government of Juan Domingo Perón in a combined civilian-military coup d'état. Borges refers to Perón's first two mandates (1945–1951, 1951–1955) as a 'second dictatorship', considering, as did Sarmiento, that the first was that of Juan Manuel de Rosas between 1835 and 1852.

5. 'Sarmiento' (*La Nación*) [1961]; 'Sarmiento' (*Comentario*) [1961]; also collected in *Textos Recobrados, 1956–1986* (Buenos Aires: Emecé, 2003).

6. 'El simulacro', *La Biblioteca*, Segunda época, 9.1 (January–March 1957); 'Diálogo de muertos', *La Biblioteca*, Segunda época, 9.2 (April–June 1957); 'Martín Fierro', *Sur* 247 (July–August 1957), all later included in *El hacedor* (Buenos Aires: Emecé, 1960). *La Biblioteca* was the journal published by the National Library (Biblioteca Nacional) between 1957 and 1968, while Borges was the director of that institution (1955–1973).

7. The three prologues are contained in the cited edition of *Prólogos*.

8. 'Sobre los clásicos', *Sur* 85 (October 1941).

9. Between 1969 and 1972, cities of the interior of the country witnessed the famous 'puebladas' (for example the so-called 'Cordobazo' and two 'Rosariazos'). Together with workers' strikes and student unrest, the 'puebladas' protested against the civil-military dictatorship of 1966–1973 that styled itself 'Revolución Argentina'.

10. 'Historias de jinetes', *Comentario* 1.2 (January–February 1954); later included in the second edition of *Evaristo Carriego* (Buenos Aires: Emecé, 1955).

CHAPTER 9

Borges and the Gauchesque

Sarah Roger

Of his acquaintance with gauchos, Borges said,

> My first real experience of the pampa came around 1909 [...]. I remember that the nearest house was a kind of blur on the horizon. This endless distance, I found out, was called the pampa, and when I learned that the farmhands were gauchos, like the characters in Eduardo Gutiérrez, that gave them a certain glamour. I have always come to things after coming to books.[1]

Borges may have only ever caught passing glimpses of the pampas' nomadic, mixed-blood horse-riders on holidays, but stories of their exploits were a constant presence in his life thanks to gauchesque literature's pride of place in the Argentine canon.

According to Borges, gaucho literature (composed by and for gauchos) consists of poetry and folk songs about universal themes. By contrast, gauchesque literature is written in a pseudo-authentic gaucho style as imagined by often-patrician city-slickers:

> The popular poets of the countryside and the outskirts of the city versify general themes: the pain of love and absence, the sorrow of love, and they do so in a lexicon that is equally general; the *gauchesco* poets, on the contrary, cultivate a deliberately popular language that the popular poets do not even attempt [...]. In the *gauchesco* poets [...] there is a quest for native words, a profusion of local colour ('The Argentine Writer and Tradition', *TTL* 421).

A form of *costumbrismo* (an idealized portrayal of daily life and customs), gauchesque literature is characterized by local colour: exaggerated characters, stereotypical settings, and largely inauthentic ruralisms that conjure a romanticized version of the pampas. In the hands of some authors, the gauchesque is a parodic form that reduces the gaucho to a folksy stereotype for the entertainment of urban readers; as written by others, it is a populist style that elevates the gaucho to the status of archetype in a celebration of rural life.[2]

A Brief History of Gauchesque Literature

Throughout the nineteenth and into the first half of the twentieth century, the gauchesque was a major cultural influence in Argentina, used to promote views across the political spectrum by portraying gauchos as everything from outlaws to patriot-rebels. Bartolomé Hidalgo is often cited as the gauchesque's father, with his political poems that celebrate the gauchos as the embodiment of an independent Argentine spirit. Other notable early contributions include Eduardo Gutiérrez's novel *Juan Moreira* (serialized 1879–1880) and the comedic poems of Hilario Ascasubi and Estanislao del Campo. The latter's *Fausto* (1866) is a simultaneous send-up of rural gauchos and of urban gentlemen who were ignorant about the working man's life. Gauchesque theatre – with its roots in the itinerant circus-tent performances of Pablo Podestá – was immensely popular, especially Florencio Sánchez's and Ernesto Herrera's plays about the threat of modernization to the gaucho way of life. In his youth, Borges admired these writers of the gauchesque and others, including Rafael Obligado, Pedro Leandro Ipuche, and Fernán Silva Valdés.

Three works stand out as having had a lasting influence on Argentine literature in general and on Borges's thinking about the gauchesque in particular. First is Domingo Sarmiento's *Facundo, or Civilization and Barbarism* (1845), a biography-cum-polemic against the violent *caudillo* (authoritarian leader) Facundo Quiroga and a related attack on the Federalist dictator Juan Manuel de Rosas. The book is also Sarmiento's proposal to Europeanize Argentina through the civilizing influence of education. Although Sarmiento praises the gauchos for their horsemanship and traditional skills, he still casts them as illiterate barbarians, agents of Rosas's federalism, and obstacles to modern Argentina. Following *Facundo*, the dichotomy of civilization versus barbarism frequently featured in works that either asserted or challenged the place of the gaucho in contemporary Argentina, including Borges's 'Story of the Warrior and the Captive Maiden' (*The Aleph*, 1949) and 'The Gospel According to Mark' (*Brodie's Report*, 1970).

The second notable work that influenced Borges is José Hernández's *Martín Fierro* (1872, 1879). A poem in two parts, it responds to Sarmiento by raising the gaucho from barbarous threat to civilized archetype. Hernández wrote the epic at a time when political tensions, expanding railways, and an influx of immigrants endangered the gaucho's itinerant lifestyle. Hernández's populist *Martín Fierro* mythologized the gaucho's contributions to the nation and consequently became a favourite with gauchos themselves. In his youth,

Borges admired the sections of *Martín Fierro* that he felt accurately conveyed the gaucho's voice through an absence of local colour or slang. A mature Borges, however, found the poem simplistic; in *El Martín Fierro* (1953), Borges criticized Hernández for a reliance on stereotypes that betray the poem's inauthentic gauchesque origins. Perhaps because of this dual admiration for and disparagement of *Martín Fierro*, Borges reworked aspects of it in his own writing, memorably in 'A Biography of Tadeo Isidoro Cruz (1829–1874)' (*The Aleph*, 1949) and 'The End' (*Fictions*, 1944).

The third key gauchesque influence on Borges was Ricardo Güiraldes's *Don Segundo Sombra* (1926), which, Borges felt, presents a forward-looking version of the genre. Its archetypal wise old gaucho helps a young man navigate life on the plains while also equipping him with knowledge and skills for life in contemporary Argentina. Güiraldes's novel finds the middle ground between Sarmiento and Hernández: it enshrines the gaucho as a national and historical construct while also transforming him into an exemplar of international and contemporary values. Borges admired the novel's universality. He felt that Güiraldes privileged thematic clarity over nationalism and that his novel owed a debt not to gauchesque parody but rather to other coming-of-age stories such as Rudyard Kipling's *Kim* and Mark Twain's *Adventures of Huckleberry Finn*. Despite the international diversity of its precursors, Borges believed that *Don Segundo Sombra* was 'no less Argentine' – if anything, it was more so ('The Argentine Writer and Tradition', *TTL* 424). Borges expanded on this idea in his critical writing, where he emphasized the connection between the universal and the local.

Borges's Gauchesque Writing

Alongside reading gauchesque literature, Borges wrote about and in the gauchesque style. His interest in employing the genre can be traced to the 1920s, when he was looking for a way of writing that was distinctively *criollo* (historically Argentine but of European rather than indigenous descent). Newly returned from Europe, he wanted to capture his homeland's essence in his writing. As Borges explained in 'The Complaint of All Criollos' (1925), he aspired to modernize the gauchesque by transforming the gaucho into a *compadrito* (a street-corner thug) – the gaucho's urban knife-fighting heir. Borges was acquainted with these toughs from the slums around his childhood home; he idolized *compadritos* such as Evaristo Carriego and turned to them to provide local colour for his writing. Borges's earliest short story, 'Man on Pink Corner' (*A Universal History of Infamy*, 1935), with its dancehall violence and use of *lunfardo* (lower-class Buenos Aires slang), is an example of his modern gauchesque, as is his 1930 biography of Carriego himself.

As Borges opened himself to the mix of influences available to him, his determination to conjure something uniquely Argentine mellowed. He began to see parallels between gauchos, *compadritos*, and universal preoccupations such as bravery, honour, identity, and authenticity. He even started to question the very idea of a national literature. Borges's clearest expression of this view is 'The Argentine Writer and Tradition' (1951), often considered his authoritative statement about national identity. In this lecture, Borges concedes that he failed to create something distinctly Argentine in early texts such as 'Man on Pink Corner'. While these pieces overflowed with local colour and slang, they did not capture the essence of the nation. Borges says that it was only when he started writing works devoid of cultural specificity – stories that could be (and often were) set anywhere – that his readers finally found the flavour of Buenos Aires in his writing.

Borges goes on to suggest that it would be a mistake to require national literature to be replete with local colour. For Argentines to restrict themselves to portrayals of gauchos roaming the pampas would be to deny themselves the themes that represent their nation:

> We must believe that the universe is our birthright and try out every subject; we cannot confine ourselves to what is Argentine in order to be Argentine because either it is our inevitable destiny to be Argentine, in which case we will be Argentine whatever we do, or being Argentine is a mere affectation, a mask ('The Argentine Writer and Tradition', *TTL* 427).

This perspective is reinforced by a more mature Borges's conclusion on the gauchesque. He ultimately condemned *Martín Fierro* for its exaggerated inauthenticity and hyperbolic mythologization, while he celebrated *Don Segundo Sombra* for the universality of its themes and its parallels in international literature.

It is worth noting that Borges's ideas about national literature can be traced not only to his cultural interests and aesthetic preferences, but also to his family politics. He came from a long line of liberal, cosmopolitan *unitarios* who favoured the centralization of power in civilized Buenos Aires, and who opposed Rosas and Federalist thuggery more generally – a belief also at the core of Borges's opposition to Perón. Bookish and short-sighted, Borges would never be able to emulate the bravery of his *unitario* military ancestors; instead, the gauchesque provided him a way of using literature to represent an elusive but ideologically and personally desired masculinity.³ Perhaps this is why Borges wrote extensively about and in the gauchesque style even though he had some doubts about its relevance as a contemporary national genre. With Margarita Guerrero, he co-authored *El Martín Fierro*, a volume of literary criticism discussing not just Hernández's poem but also the gauchesque more generally. With Betina Edelberg, he co-authored *Leopoldo Lugones* (1955), a critical introduction to the works of the *modernista* writer who highlighted the importance of the gaucho to national identity in *El payador*, his 1913 lecture celebrating *Martín Fierro* as the founding myth of Argentina.⁴ Borges also penned a volume of gauchesque literary criticism, *Aspectos de la poesía gauchesca* (1950), and there are numerous pieces on the gauchesque throughout Borges's oeuvre, particularly in the *Textos recobrados* (a selection of which can also be found in the English-language collection *On Argentina*). Borges edited collections of gauchesque poetry with Adolfo Bioy Casares. He even tried writing in the gaucho and gauchesque forms, experimenting with everything from milonga lyrics to poems recounting pivotal moments in Argentine history.

Borges featured gauchos and aspects of their culture in stories that imagine the experience of glory-seeking outsiders, such as 'The Dead Man' (*The Aleph*, 1949), 'The Other Death' (*The Aleph*, 1949), and 'The Wait' (*The Aleph*, 1949); stories about individuals who reject or relinquish life in modern Argentina, such as 'The Captive' (*Dreamtigers*, 1960) and 'Story of the Warrior and the Captive Maiden'; and stories that build upon unknown or imaginary aspects of gaucho history and culture, such as 'A Dialogue Between Dead Men' (*Dreamtigers*, 1960), 'Martín Fierro' (*Dreamtigers*, 1960), and 'A Biography of Tadeo Isidoro Cruz (1829–1874)'. *Brodie's Report* (1970) contains a large number of stories featuring duels by gauchos, aspiring *compadritos*, and even men from the city playing at being gauchos. Stripped of Borges's youthful reverence for bravery and honour, these late stories consign the gaucho to Argentine mythology.

'The End' and 'The South'

Of Borges's many stories, 'The End' and 'The South' (both originally published in *La Nación* in 1953 and subsequently added to *Fictions* in 1956) are characteristic of his engagement with the gauchesque. They illustrate the creative ways Borges undermined the genre while also expanding it, embracing his literary past as a way of moving beyond it.

'The End' is an extension of and possible conclusion to *Martín Fierro*. It is told from the perspective of Recabarren, a paralysed barkeeper who watches the pampas through his window as he lies in bed. Into his field of vision, a poncho-wearing man arrives on horseback. This visitor approaches another man, described only as black and strumming a guitar, and the two exchange terse words. They have been waiting seven years for a duel that both view as undesirable yet unavoidable: the guitar-player wants to try to avenge the visiting gaucho's murder of his brother. Recabarren watches as they head onto the pampas. The guitar-player fulfils his obligations and kills the visitor, who is revealed in his final moments to be Fierro. The story concludes with the victor's departure.

'The End' is Borges's attempt to do away with an outdated archetype of Argentine national identity. By having Fierro's death narrated from the perspective of a paralysed man, Borges suggests that Argentina has been unable to overcome its monumental literary history: Recabarren was paralysed the day after witnessing the initial duel between Fierro and the guitar-player's brother (an event in *Martín Fierro* as well as the catalyst for the action in Borges's story). This implies that Argentine literature has been stalled since Hernández. In killing Fierro, Borges moves the nation's literature forward.

'The End' is also Borges's recognition that it is impossible for a nation to shed its literary precursors. The story concludes with a description of the guitar-player's return to the *arrabales* (the outskirts of the city), the home of Borges's modern *compadrito* Argentina and the terrain in which he tried to situate national identity in his youth. In the story's final line, the guitar-playing gaucho reflects that, having realized his destiny by murdering Fierro, he has become Fierro himself. He now must wait to be killed by someone seeking to avenge Fierro's death: 'His work of vengeance done, he was nobody now. Or rather, he was the other one: there was neither destination nor destiny on earth for him, and he had killed a man' (*CF* 170). The gaucho is caught in an endless cycle of national idolatry and erasure. Borges may have used 'The End' to kill off a literary precursor, but through his need to do so, he reinforces *Martín Fierro*'s canonical status. Like his guitar-playing gaucho, Borges recognizes that he cannot escape history.

While Borges's gaucho abandons the plains in 'The End' to await his death in the slums, the protagonist of 'The South' does the opposite, fleeing the city for a long-desired life (and death) on the pampas. After a head injury and hospital stay, Juan Dahlmann – the third generation of an increasingly assimilated *criollo*-immigrant family – leaves Buenos Aires for a dilapidated estancia. As he travels to the countryside, Dahlmann muses that it seems as though he is travelling into a fictionalized gauchesque past. Forced to alight from his train early, he visits an *almacén* (a hybrid general store, bar, and café typical of nineteenth-century Argentina) where he is challenged to a duel by a local tough. The two head out onto the pampas for a fight to the death; in his final moments, Dahlmann reflects that this is the honourable end he would have chosen for himself in the throes of his illness.

For Dahlmann, up until his trip to the pampas, the world of the gaucho existed only in fiction. When he finally encounters a gaucho at the *almacén* he feels as though he is seeing an archetype come to life:

> Dahlmann was warmed by the rightness of the man's hairband, the baize poncho he wore, his gaucho trousers, and the boots made out of the skin of a horse's leg, and he said to himself, recalling futile arguments with people from districts in the North or from Entre Ríos, that only in the South did gauchos like that exist anymore (*CF* 178).

Dahlmann's knowledge of the pampas has been drawn from reading rather than experience. For example, he notes an uncanny similarity between the *almacén* and an engraving he recalls seeing, possibly in the eighteenth-century French novel *Paul et Virginie* (a book that presents a romanticized view of an exotic land). Gaucho reality has become the gauchesque fiction coloured by an international literary heritage that Borges admired in *Don Segundo Sombra* and celebrated in 'The Argentine Writer and Tradition'.

'The South' is laced with hints that Dahlmann's experience is conjured out of his familiarity with gauchesque fiction. There are too many striking parallels between his literary knowledge and the pampas as he encounters them, which suggests that his journey is a fever dream. His death at the end of the story is not actually at the hands of a gaucho but rather imagined by Dahlmann as the one he would have chosen. 'The South', then, is Borges's acknowledgement that the gaucho now exists only in literature. In these respects, the story is an extension of the argument Borges puts forward in 'The Argentine Writer and Tradition'. It demonstrates the degree to which the cultural inheritance of Argentina has merged with that of the world – so much so that, as in Güiraldes's *Don Segundo Sombra*, Dahlmann's version of the pampas is intertwined with European literature.

While 'The End' demonstrates the impossibility of moving beyond the gauchesque, 'The South' shows that it is also impossible to return to it. Borges's version of the gauchesque is caught between the nation's past and its present, and between Borges's desire to write works that are distinctly Argentine but that also draw on an international literary heritage. These tensions are bequeathed by the genre itself, which – from its origins – has struggled with the divide between gaucho and gauchesque, civilization and barbarism, Argentine history and the nation's future.

Notes

1. Jorge Luis Borges, 'An Autobiographical Essay', *The Aleph and Other Stories: 1933–1969*, trans. and ed. Norman Thomas di Giovanni (London: Jonathan Cape, 1968), pp. 203–260 (pp. 212–213).
2. For more on the origins of gauchesque literature, see Nicholas Shumway, *The Invention of Argentina* (Berkeley: University of California Press, 1991), pp. 67–71.
3. For more on the gauchesque and masculinity, see Amy K. Kaminsky, *Argentina: Stories for a Nation* (Minneapolis: University of Minnesota Press, 2008), pp. 20, 56–57.
4. Jorge Luis Borges and Betina Edelberg, *Leopoldo Lugones*, 1955 (Buenos Aires: Emecé, 1998); Leopoldo Lugones, *El payador*, 1916 (Buenos Aires: Centurión, 1961).

CHAPTER 10

1920s Buenos Aires

Eleni Kefala*

'There are no legends in this land, and not a single ghost walks our streets', Borges wrote in 1926. The myth-deficient land he alluded to was not the vast stretch of the Pampa, which intellectuals of the Centennial (1910) had infused with national meanings, but what by then had become the largest city of the Spanish-speaking world and one of the fastest-growing urban centres on both sides of the Atlantic (fig. i).** 'More than a city, Buenos Aires is a country', claimed Borges, 'and we must find for it the poetry, the music, the painting, the religion, and the metaphysics appropriate to its grandeur. This is the full extent of my hope' ('The Full Extent of my Hope', *OA* 47).[1] Even though dressed in a future tense, the young poet's hope had in fact already materialized, and along with it his urge to carve a niche in the literary landscape of Argentina. His *Fervour of Buenos Aires* (1923), a collection of poems on his home city, did just that. Published soon after his return from Europe where he had spent seven years with his family, the book wove a mythology for a modern city in the making.

The Argentine capital's makeover from a *gran aldea* (large village) of 180,000 people in 1870 into a cosmopolitan metropolis of 1,300,000 by 1910 resulted from the country's spectacular economic burgeoning. The Pampean livestock industry, which took off in the late nineteenth century thanks to meat export made possible by the national railway system and transatlantic liners equipped with refrigerators, attracted an influx of immigrants, mainly from Spain and Italy, most of whom settled in or around the port city. In the period 1857–1914 alone, over 3,000,000 immigrants entered the country through the port of Buenos

* Luciano Miller *in memoriam*.
** I wish to thank the Dirección General de Estadística y Censos – Ministerio de Economía y Finanzas – Gobierno de la Ciudad de Buenos Aires – República Argentina and the Fundación Pan Klub-Museo Xul Solar for granting permission to reproduce images free of charge.

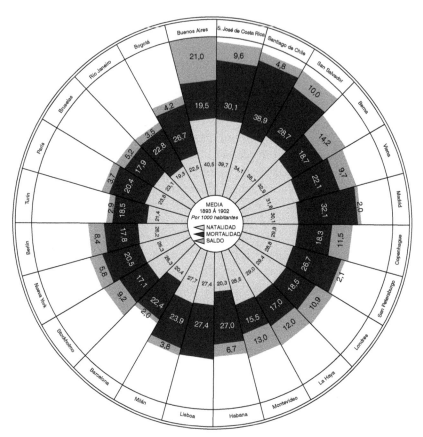

Fig. 1 Growth of Buenos Aires compared with that of other important cities in the decade 1893–1902, in *Anuario Estadístico de la Ciudad de Buenos Aires. Año XIII–1903*. Reproduced by permission of Dirección General de Estadística y Censos, Argentina.

Aires, while as late as 1930 40 per cent of the male population were foreign born.[2] At the turn of the century, lower tram fares allowed proletarian immigrants working in the city centre and the port to elude the precarious living conditions of downtown *conventillos* (tenements) and move to the outskirts, or *arrabales*, where they could afford cheaper housing. By the 1920s, the suburbs boasted the most culturally diverse and socially progressive areas of Buenos Aires.

Needless to say that the city Borges came back to on 24 March 1921 was not the one he had left behind as a teenager in 1914, nor was his childhood barrio, Palermo. When *Reina Victoria Eugenia* approached the port on that Thursday, the 22-year-old poet was already troubled by his homecoming. 'Don't abandon me in the exile of the gridded city and of the young men who speak of Argentineness ... Horror! Horror!',[3] he had pleaded in a letter to his Mallorcan friend Jacobo Sureda a few days earlier and while still on board the Spanish steamship. Borges's initial aversion to Buenos Aires and things Argentine was quickly swapped for a deep connection with his native city and an even deeper sense of nationalism. That his acquaintance with Macedonio Fernández, the eccentric author who initiated him into the marvels of idealism and whom Borges cherished throughout his life, acted as a catalyst for this change is well known. But Borges's 'Berkeleyan' 'rediscovery' of the 'almost endless city of low buildings with flat roofs, stretching west toward ... the pampa', and his celebration of 'the sunsets, solitary places ... unfamiliar corners ... and family history' were also coded in a double enterprise:[4] to revamp the aesthetic scene of Argentina, dominated by Leopoldo Lugones's outmoded *modernismo*, through the tenets of Ultraism that Borges had brought from Spain, and to yield an answer to the heated debates on national culture in an era of mass immigration and frenzied urbanization. While his theoretical attachment to Ultraism was scarcely consummated aesthetically – his literary work had little to do with the movement's precepts as set out by him in 1921[5] – the same is not true of his ideological project to which he remained loyal until the end of the decade. Introduced with *Fervour of Buenos Aires*, Borges's feverish *criollismo* would culminate in two further books of poetry – *Moon Across the Way* (1925) and *San Martín Notebook* (1929) – and three essay collections – *Inquisitions* (1925), *The Full Extent of my Hope* (1926), and *The Language of the Argentines* (1928) – as well as in the fictional biography *Evaristo Carriego* (1930).

Similar to the literati of the Centennial, who had railed at 'the overseas rabble' and the alleged 'anti-Argentine tendencies' of foreign schools in the country,[6] Borges read immigration and modernization, described as 'the garrulous energy of some downtown streets and the painful multinational mob in the ports' ('To the Reader', *FBA*),[7] against what he dubbed 'the *criollo* tragedy'. In a city 'called Babel', and a country where 'miserable and profitable agriculture impoverished easy cattle ranching', the criollo, he complained, had 'transformed into a foreigner in his own land' ('The

Complaint of All *Criollos*', *OA* 29). For the *criollista* neophyte, the city and
the Pampa were in captivity. But whereas a decade earlier Lugones's
generation had ventured into the Argentine plains to symbolically restore
criollismo away from the shocks and jolts of urban modernity, Borges
refused to depart from his home city. Between the Pampa and Buenos
Aires, in fact, he chose both. Neither the busy centre nor the buzzing port,
his Buenos Aires was the city of his childhood, the barrios and outskirts, the
orillas (edges or riverbanks) of the rural-urban fringe ('The Pampa and the
Suburbio Are Gods', *OA* 51). This liminal space, within which *criollismo*
and modernity figuratively converged, was also the backdrop against which
his romance with Concepción Guerrero played out in the early 1920s.
Borges's *arrabal*, most likely a borrowing from his fellow ultraist Rafael
Cansinos Asséns, was a canny manoeuvre that helped him shun both
immigration and Lugones's passé nationalism (or *gauchismo*), and a powerful ideologeme which persisted in his later work.[8]

Writing 'under the suburban stars' and not 'the energetic clarity of
streetlamps' ('Eduardo González Lanuza', *OA* 31) or the 'false lights' of
the neon signs downtown ('City', *FBA*), in *Fervour of Buenos Aires* the poet
set off to 'reconstruct', 'stone by stone' ('Absence', *FBA*), and 'recover', like
Benedict Anderson's solitary hero, his imagined criollo city.[9] The lyrical
subject strolls 'through the streets / like someone who traverses a recovered
country estate', we are told in 'Reconquered Neighbourhood' (*FBA*). The
book's opening poem leaves no doubt as to which streets the poet-flaneur
traverses in his mythopoeia: not the rowdy streets of the city centre, but the
'sweet' suburban streets as well as those edging the Pampa, where modest
'little houses' rise timidly under the 'great sky' ('Streets', *FBA*). Bursting
with immigrant life, the suburbs had little to do with Borges's solitary
experience. Emptied not just of foreigners but of people in general, the
urban periphery and its little houses, most of them actually immigrant
dwellings,[10] emerge as re-criollized metonymies for the nation: 'the streets
unfold like flags' and flutter in the poem's 'raised lines' (*Ibid.*). As streetscape and nationscape melt into a single plane, whoever navigates these
riverbanks navigates the fatherland. Through a rich repertoire of metonymies that includes streets, neighbourhoods, corner shops, hallways, cis-
terns, alleys, porches, grill windows, and patios, in short, all those 'sites'
where the poet's 'affection spreads' ('Outskirts', *FBA*), Borges renames the
nation from criollo to urban criollo. The play of metonymies is spelled out
for us in the essay 'Buenos Aires' (1925): 'Streets that approach silently with
the noble sadness of being *criollo*. Streets and houses of the homeland'
(*OA* 15).

Borges pits his mythical Buenos Aires against the actual city, which is de-realized as if turned into a criollo museum, by way of idealism, destined to nurture his craft beyond these years. The suburb, stripped of its cosmopolitan dimension (the immigrants), is conversely re-universalized via the same idealist principles. Treading upon 'the tremendous conjecture / of Schopenhauer and Berkeley' that reality exists in the perceiver's mind ('Dawn', *FBA*), the solitary flaneur fathers his street: 'if I stopped seeing it, it would die' ('Long Walk', *FBA*). The criollo city, having been disrupted by immigration and modernization, mockingly labelled 'progress' ('The Complaint of All *Criollos*', *OA* 29), is now recovered in the rehabilitated riverbanks and their temporal equivalents (twilight, sunset, dawn), which inundate Borges's writings in this decade. Not during daylight, nor in nighttime 'do we really see the city', he insists, but in the twilight. Neither day nor night, this ambiguous temporal crux beautifully complements his *orillas*, glossed as the 'indecisive part of the city' ('Buenos Aires', *OA* 13–14), which dithers between rural and urban, local and foreign, tradition and modernity. If Lugones turned Sarmiento's dichotomy of urban civilization and rural barbarism on its head, Borges strategically straddles its constituents by means of these spatial and temporal in-betweens. An army of symbols and references, among them swords, gauchos, marble statues, the card game *truco*, and guitars, parade in his pages, with *música patria* segueing into the background ('Music of the Homeland', *FBA*), while into the fabric of this intimate criollo mythology, the history of his homeland and that of his family are inextricably entwined. The national becomes personal and vice versa in the two poems with the title 'Inscription on the Tomb', both dealing with his heroic ancestors, Manuel Isidoro Suárez and Francisco Borges Lafinur (*FBA*), whereas indigenous, mestizo, and Afro-Argentines fade from the nation's horizon.

Borges's criollo fervour intensified in the second half of the 1920s, when his cultural revisionism was shaped by Argentinisms drawn from the lexicon, phonetics, and syntax of *porteño* Spanish. 'We would like a docile and felicitous Spanish that would be concordant with the impassioned condition of our sunsets, with the infinite sweetness of our neighborhoods', he explained in *The Language of the Argentines* ('The Language of the Argentines', *OA* 88). For all that the footprints of the quest for a criollo idiom to go with his urban mythopoeia were visible in his first poetry book, it was in this essay collection and in *Moon Across the Way* that his linguistic project was fully fleshed out. Besides, in the latter the contrast between past and present is striking: 'Then you were more sky and today you are mere facades' ('To Serrano Street', *LE* 27), the lyrical subject grumbles in his apostrophe to Serrano Street.[11] Unlike the evacuated and re-criollized streetscape of *Fervour of Buenos Aires*, the urban setting here is pregnant with its modern, immigrant present: the 'little Italian girls', the 'warm din of a pastry shop', and the gaudy ad which is 'red as an insult' (*Ibid.*).

On 2135 Serrano Street (currently Jorge Luis Borges Street) was where Borges's first family residence was located in Palermo. The destiny of the barrio did not differ from that of others and, by the time the Borges were packing for Europe, Palermo had expanded substantially. Within a decade, the number of houses had tripled (from 2,903 in 1904 to 8,206 in 1914) and continued to mushroom after the family's return in 1921.[12] The prologue to *Moon Across the Way* restates the poet's objects of affection: 'the sky-blue walls of the suburb and the little squares with their portion of sky' (*LE* 7), which, like the hallway, the patio, the cistern, and the balustrade, are synecdochically mobilized to rebuild the vanishing homeland ('Homelands', *LE* 33–34). But even if the subject matter remains the same as before – the city 'scattered in the suburbs like a gyronny flag' ('The Return to Buenos Aires', *LE* 24) – there is a pronounced realization now that the Argentine capital has ebbed in the face of immigration, generating a 'vision of painful streets' that plunge the poetic 'I' into grief (*Ibid.*).

Borges's urban fervour rounded off in *San Martín Notebook* and *Evaristo Carriego*. In the latter, he instilled the traditional horse-drawn cart, which was still in circulation together with modern modes of transport such as the motorcar and the tram, with a criollo temporality and a mythological quality. A stranger to fast-paced modernity and its progressive linearity, the slow-moving cart, argues Borges, enjoys a time that is almost synonymous with eternity. This 'temporal possession', he posits, 'is the infinite criollo capital'. Invested with timelessness, 'the cart persists', and so does the mythical criollo city, which the cart traverses in a way akin to that of the solitary poet (*OC* I: 148). Yet nowhere is that intimate city so unapologetically articulated than in 'The Mythological Foundation of Buenos Aires', a poem composed in 1926 and later incorporated in *San Martín Notebook*.[13] In defiance of existing narratives about the city's foundation, the poet places its mythical birth not near the Riachuelo River in San Telmo but, predictably, in his own barrio in Palermo. The first square block of 'the homeland', we learn, is the same we find in his neighbourhood: 'Guatemala, Serrano, Paraguay, Gurruchaga' (*CSM* 9–10). Home city and homeland once more overlap and are fixed in an archaic past. As nostalgia morphs into myth and childhood topography into national *geography* (gē, land + *graphein,* to write), Borges literally rewrites the nation, inscribing it, like the cart, into the sphere of eternity. 'I can hardly believe Buenos Aires ever had a beginning: / I consider it as eternal as water and air' (*CSM* 11), he concludes in the final two lines, essentially drawing his poetic nation-rebuilding to a close. The basic elements of Presocratic philosophy here lend *criollismo* a primal timelessness, as they did in the poem 'Outskirts' and the essay 'Buenos Aires', where the metonymical patio was 'founded' 'on the two most primordial things that exist: earth and sky' (*FBA* and *OA* 15).

By 1926 Borges's re-criollized fringes had become the flagship of the Argentine avant-garde. His nationalism may have been a cautious and conservative reaction to the 'juggernaut of modernity',[14] but it was not out of context. The painter Alejandro Xul Solar, the architect Alberto Prebisch, and the photographer Horacio Coppola were some of his fellow avant-gardists who responded to the ideological exigencies of the time with steadfast commitment. On the one hand, Borges's search for a criollo literary idiom in the 1920s was mirrored in Xul's *neocriollo* language (a fusion of Spanish and Portuguese), which was nevertheless not circumscribed by Argentina's borders but formed part of his Pan-American vision, fashioned after the Bolivarian ideal of 'our America ... the great Iberian America'[15] and executed in watercolours like *Mundo* (World) (1925), whose ethereal scene is teeming with Latin American flags.[16] Meanwhile, Xul's attention, unlike Borges's, was on cosmopolitan Buenos Aires, arrested in such paintings as *B.A. (Buenos Aires)* (1929) (fig. ii). In the 1930s, on the other hand, Prebisch stood on the same ideological terrain as Borges but looked in the opposite direction. With architectural undertakings like the white sky-piercing Obelisk (1936), he sought to recuperate not the periphery but the traditional centre of Buenos Aires. Similar to Borges's riverbanks, modern rationalist architecture was filled with criollo meanings through forged links with the long-lost colonial city of white pure lines. From suburb to downtown, Borges's and Prebisch's urban visions reflected the topological shift in the avant-garde penchant for a re-criollized modernity during the second and third decades of the twentieth century. Coppola's camera captured this ideological arc and somehow transcended it by shooting Borges's re-semanticized outskirts alongside Prebisch's reclaimed centre. In pictures like *Corner of Victoria and Bolívar* (1936),[17] where the mayhem of automobiles, tram rails, and trolley cars is offset by Borges's horse-drawn cart in the forefront, Coppola visually reconquered not the *porteño* neighbourhoods but the heart of the changing metropolis. In this high-angle shot of the surroundings of the presidential houses –

Fig. 2 Xul Solar, *B.A. Buenos Aires*, gouache and watercolour, 30 × 45 cm, 1929. Private Collection. Reproduced by permission of the Fundación Pan Klub-Museo Xul Solar.

Casa Rosada is a breath's distance away – the cart, contrary to the machinery stuck in the traffic jam, is embraced by the semicircle of the convex tram rails, advancing unhindered and, connotatively, circularly in the hub of modernity.

Borges's and Xul's criollo fervour waned in the 1930s, when their ideological projects gave way to the more philosophical and universal languages they are known for today. Throughout his lifetime, Borges redrafted those poetry books to eliminate their criollo excesses and never republished his essay collections. But it is because of those excesses that his Buenos Aires bears the marks of a nation in the remaking.

Notes

1. Jorge Luis Borges, *On Argentina*, ed. Alfred Mac Adam (New York: Penguin, 2010), p. 47 [*OA*].
2. José Ramón Navarro Vera, 'El Buenos Aires de Borges: paisaje interior versus paisaje construido', in José Carlos Rovira (ed.), *Escrituras de la ciudad* (Madrid: Palas Atenea, 1999), p. 132; James Scobie, *Buenos Aires: Plaza to Suburb, 1870–1910*

(New York: Oxford University Press, 1974); David Rock, 'Argentina 1930–1946', in Leslie Bethell (ed.), *Argentina Since Independence* (Cambridge: Cambridge University Press, 1993), p. 173.

3. Jorge Luis Borges, *Cartas del fervor: correspondencia con Maurice Abramowicz y Jacobo Sureda (1919–1928)*, ed. Cristóbal Pera (Barcelona: Galaxia Gutenberg/ Emecé, 1999), p. 194. Unless otherwise noted, all translations from Spanish are the author's.

4. Jorge Luis Borges, *The Aleph and Other Stories 1933–1969*, trans. Norman Thomas di Giovanni (London: Lowe and Brydone Printers, 1971), pp. 223–225.

5. Jorge Luis Borges, 'Ultraísmo', in Jorge Schwartz (ed.), *Las vanguardias latinoamericanas: textos programáticos y críticos* (Mexico, D.F.: Fondo de Cultura Económica, 2002), pp. 134–135.

6. Leopoldo Lugones, *El payador* (Buenos Aires: Otero, 1916), p. 15; Ricardo Rojas, *La restauración nacionalista* (Buenos Aires: Ministerio de Justicia e Instrucción Pública, 1909), p. 341.

7. Jorge Luis Borges, *Fervor de Buenos Aires* (Buenos Aires, 1923), np [*FBA*].

8. Beatriz Sarlo, *Jorge Luis Borges: A Writer on the Edge*, ed. John King (London: Verso, 2006), p. 20.

9. Benedict Anderson, *Imagined Communities: Reflections on the Origin and Spread of Nationalism* (New York: Verso, 2003), p. 30.

10. Adrián Gorelik, 'Horacio Coppola, 1929. Borges, Le Corbusier and the "Casitas" of Buenos Aires', in Jorge Schwartz (ed.), *Horacio Coppola: fotografía* (Madrid: Fundación Telefónica, 2008), ed. Jorge Schwartz, pp. 349–353.

11. Jorge Luis Borges, *Luna de enfrente* (Buenos Aires: Editorial Proa, 1925), p. 27.

12. Scobie, *Buenos Aires*, p. 261.

13. Jorge Luis Borges, *Cuaderno San Martín* (Buenos Aires: Editorial Proa, 1929), pp. 9–11 [*CSM*].

14. Anthony Giddens, *The Consequences of Modernity* (Cambridge: Polity Press, 1996), p. 139.

15. Alejandro Xul Solar, *Entrevistas, artículos y textos inéditos*, ed. Patricia Artundo (Buenos Aires: Corregidor, 2006), pp. 98–99.

16. In Mario Gradowczyk (ed.), *Alejandro Xul Solar* (Buenos Aires: Ediciones Alba, 1994), p. 125.

17. In Schwartz (ed.), *Horacio Coppola*, p. 143.

CHAPTER II

Borges and the Argentine Avant-Garde

Eamon McCarthy

The Borges family returned to Buenos Aires in 1921 after having spent the previous seven years in Switzerland and then Spain. They travelled to Europe again in July 1923, before returning definitively to Argentina in July 1924. By this time, Jorge Luis and his sister Norah had made significant contributions to *ultraísmo*, the nascent Spanish avant-garde movement, and both continued to send their work to Spain from Argentina. In addition to maintaining his links with Spain, Borges took the lead in trying to introduce avant-garde ideas to his native country. Drawing upon his experiences in Europe, in 1921 he created *Prisma*, which took the format of a large poster to be pasted on the walls of Buenos Aires, but it appeared only twice. It featured a manifesto, poetry, and prints by Norah Borges. The following year, he launched *Proa*, which ran for three issues and adopted a similar format to the Spanish magazine *Ultra*, to which both he and his sister had contributed. Again, the magazine contained a mix of poetry and images, as well as essays and a short note to the reader explaining *ultraísmo* in the first issue, which is one of the definitive explanations of the movement. Both these magazines show that Borges was keen to introduce avant-garde aesthetics to Argentina, although they were relatively limited in scope and did not have an immediate impact at the time because of the lack of openness to new ideas in the Argentine cultural sphere at that particular moment.

The return to his native Buenos Aires had a profound impact on the young Borges. The city he left in 1914 had undergone rapid expansion and the neighbourhoods of his childhood had given way to an expanding metropolis. Borges's first book of poetry, *Fervor de Buenos Aires* (1923) is a testament to the effect the Argentine capital had on him. The lyric speaker of 'Las calles' ('The streets'), the first poem in the collection, wanders along the streets away from the centre of the city to the *arrabal*, the outlying areas in which Borges constructed his poetic vision of Argentine culture. The poems in the collection were not markedly *ultraísta* and they showed influences of *modernismo* derived from Argentine poet Lugones. The collection shows that the young Borges learned that it would be impossible to import the principles of Spanish *ultraísmo* directly to Argentina. Instead, the young poet was aware of the need for the Argentine avant-garde to engage with the comparatively young literary traditions of the country that had gained independence just over a century earlier as well as set out a programme for aesthetic renewal. Just after the publication of his first book of poems, Borges returned to Europe for a year, spending most of his time in Spain.

In many ways both *Prisma* and the first iteration of *Proa* were forerunners to the more widely read magazines of the Argentine avant-garde. Upon his return to Buenos Aires in 1924 from his second trip to Europe, Borges found that like-minded individuals – such as Xul Solar – had come back after also having spent time in Europe. The magazine *Martín Fierro* had been launched in February 1924 and 'had the widest audience and the highest visibility' of the avant-garde publications circulating in Buenos Aires at the time.[1] Another important development was the founding of the *Asociación Amigos del Arte* in June 1924 and the opening of their exhibition space in July, the same month that the Borges family returned to Buenos Aires. The Association was set up and run by a group of mostly upper-class women and aimed to support young artists by showing and promoting their work. It was also a key organization in disseminating ideas about art and architecture. It maintained close links with *Martín Fierro* as the magazine held meetings in its premises and published favourable reviews of its exhibitions. Unlike the comparatively lacklustre artistic environment he found upon his return in 1921, Borges was greeted by and joined a vibrant group of writers and artists in 1924.

In August 1924, Borges, along with Brandan Caraffa, Ricardo Güiraldes, and Pablo Rojas Paz founded the second iteration of *Proa*, which was intended to open up a dialogue with his contemporaries about the nature of the avant-garde and create an open, less-fractious forum for such discussions.[2] Much valuable work has been done on the literary nature of Borges's contributions to both *Proa* and *Martín Fierro* and the poetry and essays he published in them are replete with themes he would continue to explore in his later work.[3] Yet, the magazines were not simply literary in nature and show that the historical avant-garde was an aesthetic project that explored the interactions between the verbal and visual. Beatriz Sarlo has begun to tease out some of the differences between the use of visuals in the two magazines, noting that because of the layout and vignettes used to fill blank spaces, *Proa* 'was thus seen in the same aesthetic frame in which it was read'.[4] Borges envisioned *Proa* as an aesthetic project in its own right, rather than a compendium of ideas. Yet, the eclectic nature of *Martín Fierro* would undoubtedly have appealed to the young man who collected literary and cultural references from across the world as he mused upon the nature of Argentine culture.

The first issue of this second iteration of *Proa* opens with a manifesto that explains the aim of the magazine, which is to introduce to Argentina some of the different ideas that the four editors have engaged with during their travels in Europe. The manifesto rejects barriers and any sense of division between groups; instead, it focuses on the importance of shared ideas. Artundo's work on the authorship of the text concludes that it is largely based on Caraffa's thoughts, which resonated with the other editors.[5] The two pages that follow the manifesto are dedicated to visual art. A print by Borges's sister Norah occupies an entire page and the following page contains a note on the artist by Caraffa, who was one of the editors. Norah Borges's print is stylistically indebted to German Expressionist woodcuts, which is very much in keeping with the intention of introducing European styles to an Argentine audience. The horse and rider in the background may well be a subtle nod to *Der Blaue Reiter*, a German Expressionist movement with which both siblings were familiar. This reference to the German context also points nicely to Borges's note on and translation of a text by Herwarth Walden, who is introduced as the director of the Expressionist magazine *Der Strum*. The essay itself focuses on visual art, particularly the ways in which different European avant-garde movements – Cubism, Futurism, and Expressionism – have built on and responded to each other. The overarching message is on the importance of innovation and of learning how to look at things anew. The inclusion of this piece in the first issue of the magazine shows that, at this time, Borges was engaging with the larger questions about the purpose of art that lay behind avant-garde movements and Walden's ideas echo sentiments he shared in a letter to his friend Maurice Abramowicz in 1920. Despite his interest in the overarching ideas of the avant-garde, Borges's review of González Lanuza's collection of poetry, *Prismas*, also published in the issue, appears to disentangle Argentine *ultraísmo* from its Spanish counterpart. Although, as Sarlo notes, 'the difference lay in the system of reading (which Borges, as usual, falsified), and in the place where the reading was done', which shows that Borges was aware of the importance of the audience to whom he was presenting these new ideas.[6] His creative distortions notwithstanding, this review and his translation of Walden show that Borges opened up a space through his work that stimulated new ideas about culture in his native Argentina.

The first issue of *Proa* contains more references to the visual arts than the issues that followed. In addition to the short piece on Norah Borges, it includes an unsigned note welcoming the foundation of the *Asociación Amigos del Arte*, proclaiming it fundamental to the development of the visual arts in the country. There is a short article by another of the editors, Pablo Rojas Paz on the Argentine artist Pedro Figari. In his one-page piece on Ricardo Passano, Brandan Caraffa mentions the Argentine actor's work as a visual artist and publishes two of his drawings along with the note. The issue also contains a longer article that compares the works of Spanish artists Ignacio Zuloaga and Joaquín Sorolla. The sheer volume of content on the visual arts in this issue of *Proa* shows the central role they played to the development of the avant-garde. Moreover, the issue contains a piece on Debussy as well as numerous poems and essays. It acts as a showcase of the most up to date thinking, eschewing specificities of genre, style, or movement as it attempts to inspire the reader. The subsequent 14 issues continue to engage with visual art, with reviews of some shows in Buenos Aires as well as a few short notes dedicated to specific artists. Visual images were reproduced in all issues of the magazines and included works by Europeans, as well as artists from other Latin American countries, yet the majority were by Norah Borges.

Martín Fierro was also founded in 1924 and published an eclectic range of writing and criticism relating to new cultural trends. The magazine is named after an epic poem by José Hernández, which was published in two parts, 'El gaucho Martín Fierro' (1872) and 'La vuelta de Martín Fierro' (1879). The significance of the poem in the national context and its status as the most important gauchesque poem were consolidated around the centenary celebrations in 1910, so it is no surprise that the name was adopted by a group intent on renewing Argentine culture. The reference back to the past and the insistence on developing a new aesthetic for the future marks a key difference between the European and Argentine avant-gardes. In the Argentine case, the past did not necessarily have to be overthrown, which is only logical in a country that had only gained its independence in 1810.

Whilst the magazine lacked the literary credentials of *Proa*, it 'was particularly strong in its consideration of the plastic arts and architecture' thanks to the presence of architect Alberto Prebisch on the editorial board.[7] The magazine was interested in all forms of new thought across a range of disciplines and from many countries. One key difference between the two is the distinctly pan-Latin American focus of the material published in *Martín Fierro*. The broader scope of the magazine was evident from the outset. The first issue contained a mix of short prose, poetry, letters, and many humorous pieces such as a set of comic funeral notices. The humorous tone is also evident in a note from the editors on the first page that addresses the name of the publication. It refers to the fact that there was an earlier magazine of the same name published in 1919 by using the title, 'La vuelta de "Martín Fierro"', itself a direct reference to the second part of Hernández's poem. It also states that this iteration of the magazine will continue the work of its predecessor. A manifesto was published in the fourth issue, which opens with six short paragraphs humorously criticizing the level of public debate around culture in Argentina. The subsequent ten paragraphs all outline the purpose of the magazine, which is essentially to focus on a new understanding of culture and to encourage people to look at culture from a new perspective. It closes with an open call for subscribers and collaborators. Borges himself was not an editor but he was a frequent contributor and often attended talks and gatherings organized under its auspices, which is documented in the photographs included in the magazine itself, under which the names of those appearing in the image are helpfully listed. The double issue 8–9, covering the months August and September 1924 is the first in which Borges appears. It contains a poem by him as well as a note on the publication of *Proa*, which is full of praise for the new magazine and is enthusiastic about the potential contribution it could make.

There are some important points of contact between *Proa* and *Martín Fierro*, particularly in the visual arts. Borges's sister Norah contributed a number of works to both magazines and published her own art manifesto anonymously in *Martín Fierro*. The artist Pedro Figari features significantly in both publications. In the August–September 1924 issue of *Martín Fierro*, there is an article about his recent exhibition with reproductions of four of his works. The September–October issue reproduces a speech given in his honour at a banquet, in which his contributions to both magazines are noted. Meanwhile, a short article on the artist appeared in the first issue of *Proa* in August. Four further articles were published about him in *Martín Fierro*, whilst another note was included in a later issue of *Proa*. The overlapping vision of the two magazines is again evident in the articles relating to an exhibition of Mexican art in Buenos Aires. The issues of both magazines that appeared in June 1925 report very favourably on the exhibition of the Mexican painters Manuel Rodríguez Lozano and Julio Castellanos in the Amigos del Arte. *Proa* addresses the question of an American style of art, whereas *Martín Fierro* centres instead on an accompanying exhibition of Mexican children's art. The difference in focus points to the slight divergence between the two magazines, with *Proa* taking up questions of a coherent aesthetic, whilst *Martín Fierro* opts to highlight innovation. Yet, ultimately, there is a shared focus between the two, which is seen most clearly in the visual arts. The two magazines were in dialogue with each other, with each choosing to highlight different ways of thinking about the same questions, which is hardly surprising as the same figures contributed to both publications.

In addition to his contributions to magazines in the 1920s, Borges published three collections of poetry and three volumes of essays, many of which had already appeared in *Proa* and to a lesser degree in *Martín Fierro*. In his early poetry, Borges 'constructed an ideologeme, the *orillas*: an indeterminate territory between the plains and the first house of the city, an urban-criollo frontier dividing and at the same time merging city and countryside' and he further theorized this space in essays.[8] In 'Leyenda policial', one of his earliest short stories published in *Martín Fierro* in February 1927, Borges introduced the figure of the *compadrito* or knife fighter from turn of the century Buenos Aires into the space he created. This early fascination with men of action would permeate many of his later stories and he re-wrote this particular story a number of times. The fact that he published what was an early draft of the story in the magazine shows that his focus on national identities and the ways in which he was writing about them at the time chimed with the wider avant-garde project in Argentina. Like the magazines with which he was associated, the space he created in his work at this time existed somewhere between tradition and modernity. The eclectic nature of the material he was seeing, reading, and publishing in avant-garde magazines had an impact on Borges. The spirit of questioning the old and seeking innovative ways to look at the world that permeated avant-garde movements can be seen in the ways in which the young Borges approached his writing and left its mark in his later works.

Notes

1. Beatriz Sarlo, *Jorge Luis Borges: A Writer on the Edge*, ed. John King (London and New York: Verso, 2006), p. 95.
2. Beatriz Sarlo, *Una modernidad periférica: Buenos Aires 1920 y 1930* (Buenos Aires: Ediciones Nueva Visión, 1999), pp. 107–109.

3. Sarlo, *A Writer on the Edge*, pp. 95–137.
4. *Ibid.*, p. 134.
5. Patricia Artundo, 'Punto de convergencia: Inicial y Proa en 1924', *Bibliografía y antología crítica de las vanguardias literarias. Argentina, Uruguay, Paraguay*, ed. Carlos García and Dieter Reichardt (Frankfurt: Vervuert, 2004), pp. 253–272 (p. 259).
6. Sarlo, *A Writer on the Edge*, p. 131.
7. Christopher Towne Leland, *The Last Happy Men. The Generation of 1922, Fiction, and the Argentine Reality* (New York: Syracuse University Press, 1986), p. 36.
8. Beatriz Sarlo, 'Borges: Tradition and the Avant-Garde', *Modernism and Its Margins. Reinscribing Cultural Modernity from Spain and Latin America*, ed. Anthony L. Geist and José B. Monleón (New York and London: Taylor and Francis, 1999), pp. 228–241 (p. 231).

CHAPTER 12

The Argentine Writer and Tradition

Humberto Núñez-Faraco

In a lecture delivered in 1951 at the Colegio Libre de Estudios Superiores in Buenos Aires, Jorge Luis Borges questioned the assumption that, in order to be authentic, Argentine writers should follow the stylistic and thematic norms exemplified in gauchesque literature. Argentine writers, he contended, have legitimate access to a multiplicity of traditions; therefore, they should not confine themselves to local or nationalistic themes.[1] This attitude, which may seem paradoxical when set against the linguistic and poetic tenets he held during the 1920s, reflects Borges's European kinship, a consequence not only of his heterodox family background but also of his school years in Switzerland and his broad humanist education. At the same time, the existence of a large library in the Borges household consolidated from an early age his enthusiasm for all sorts of books. British writers, including Stevenson, Chesterton, Kipling, and Shaw, figured among his favourite and most lasting influences. This circumstance enabled him to perceive world literature as 'an adventure into an endless variety of styles' in which the reader is free to create meaningful connections between distant authors and texts.[2] Borges reorganized the canon of Western literature not only by subverting the hierarchical conventions of literary history, which assigns fixed formal and genealogical characteristics to the works of the present in relation to those of the past, but also by bringing to the forefront a number of non-Western traditions (both secular and religious) with which he initiated challenging and innovative readings. Borges was eclectic in his conception of literary history just as he was sceptical about the formulation of a poetic creed that did not allow for change and renewal. As he put it: 'Literature is a game with tacit conventions; to violate them partially or entirely is one of the many joys (one of the many obligations) of a game of unknown limits.'[3] For him, reordering the library, placing Homer after Virgil or a French symbolist poet next to Cervantes is a form of literary criticism available to every reader.

In a wider historical perspective, Borges was aware of the fact that because of its international trade and commerce, its liberal economic policies, and its openness to European immigration since the second half of the nineteenth century, Argentine society at large had for more than a hundred years been receptive to Europe and the wider world. Rejecting the xenophobic tendency prevalent among nationalist circles throughout the 1930s and 1940s (which perceived non-Catholic and non-Romance-speaking immigrants as a threat to the survival of the country's core values and ethnic identity), Borges regarded modern Argentina as the product of a rich process of cultural miscegenation to which different ethnic and religious groups had made a positive contribution. Because of this, he argued, Argentine writers enjoy a privileged position vis-à-vis the European cultural legacy, one that allows them to interact with the Western literary tradition as a whole: 'I believe that our tradition is the whole of Western culture, and I also believe that we have a right to this tradition, a greater right than that which the inhabitants of one Western nation or another may have' (426). Although this premise is susceptible to criticism (On what basis can Argentinian intellectuals claim to have a greater right to the Western tradition than those who have forged it?), it reveals a logic of its own if read within the ideological context in which it was written: the Colegio Libre de Estudios Superiores where Borges delivered the talk was known for its liberal, anti-Peronist stance. Thus, Borges scorned a nationalist version of Argentine literature that sought to eliminate the notion of writing as a complex web of cultural influences. The formation of a writer, he suggests, requires the capacity to appreciate and assimilate different periods and styles, and this cannot exist – let alone flourish – without an adequate contact with other literatures and cultures.

Putting aside the issue of postcolonial cultural dependency that is at the centre of the confrontation between national and foreign literatures, a debate that was particularly intense in Argentina throughout the nine-teenth century, what is important to note here is Borges's defence of literary creation as a free and active engagement with the tradition (or traditions) within which a writer *chooses* to work. As he put it elsewhere, through the process of appropriation, each writer reinvents his or her own predecessors ('The fact is that each writer *creates* his precursors', *TTL* p. 365, italics in the original). Thus, by attacking the Argentine nationalists, Borges subverts the deterministic view of cultural heritage as the expression of a people's unique identity. Argentine writers – he suggests – should be characterized by their openness to a variety of influences, one that involves a dynamic process of interpretation, transformation, and subversion.

Nationalist ideologies, on the other hand, lead to the actions of intransigent regimes that end up building walls or burning books, as Borges eloquently illustrates in the essay 'The Wall and the Books' (1950) (included in *TTL* 344–346).

If artistic freedom has been shown to be an enriching factor in the development of the Western literary tradition, the idea of protecting specific aspects of a national literature against the corrosive effects of foreign influences (as maintained by cultural nationalists) is a limiting and ineffectual imposition that disempowers the capacity of Argentine writers to engage with broader aspects of human existence. Yet, if Borges defended the autonomy of the writer vis-à-vis the constraints of nationalist allegiances, this by no means implied in him a break with the Argentine literary tradition nor an aesthetic rejection of the vernacular models he always held in great esteem, for these, too, carry their own dimension of truth. For Borges, the works of the past constitute an endless source of creativity insofar as they remain open to a process of interpretation in which new meanings are generated. In the universal order of literary discourse imagined by him, what is borrowed and what is created anew become relative notions because of their interaction in the *interpretative* process: in Borges there is always an expansion rather than a limitation of creative freedom.

Borges's views on the question of a national literary tradition begin to take shape after his return to Argentina in the early 1920s, at a time in which the debate about language and identity in Argentine culture and society had acquired new impetus. Indeed, the concern in academic circles regarding the widespread neglect of Peninsular Spanish led to the creation, in 1922, of the Institute of Philology at the University of Buenos Aires. Its first director, Américo Castro, was a fierce advocate of linguistic orthodoxy. As a young writer with moderate nationalist sympathies, however, Borges promoted the defence of the vernacular in its capacity to supply the Argentine writer with a valuable set of linguistic tools. Thus, he rejected the adoption of standard Castilian together with the stylistic precepts of Spanish grammarians, although in his poetic practice Borges did not rule out their applicability. Indeed, because of his previous involvement with the Spanish Ultraist movement, it is possible to find in his early poetry a good number of verses conceived in a clear Castilian vein. Nevertheless, for the kind of cultural nationalism Borges was beginning to embrace at this time, it was evident that the rules and norms of Peninsular Spanish could not constitute the basis of a national literary praxis.

While discarding the value of marginal urban dialects to fulfil the requirements of a refined poetic expression (dialects such as the *lunfardo* and the *arrabalero* were by then making their way into popular music, poetry, and narrative under the disapproving gaze of the traditional creole elite), Borges finds in the nineteenth-century vernacular a firm basis upon which a true poetic tradition might be rooted. In contrast to the poverty of language and thought that, in his view, dominated the contemporary scene (he was particularly critical of the legacy of Nicaraguan poet, Rubén Darío), Borges discovers in the literary tradition of the Argentine creole – as manifested in writers such as Sarmiento, Echeverría, Mansilla, and others – the existence of a fertile ground which not only integrated but also dignified the dialect of its time. Borges's linguistic perspective during these years seems to indicate his desire to preserve a national character against the overwhelming cosmopolitanism of Buenos Aires through the consolidation of a unifying literary language. By drawing attention to the emotional transparency of the vernacular, Borges proclaimed his faith in the realization of a literary project that would bring to fruition its own mode of existence. And yet, despite his *criollista* standpoint Borges was far from supporting a literary practice that would do away with a reciprocal exchange of ideas and influences with other cultures around the world.

Notwithstanding his optimism about the expressive possibilities of the vernacular, Borges was soon to abandon the linguistic project he had forged during the 1920s in order to elaborate the highly artistic prose to which future generations of Spanish American writers are indebted. As he entered a new phase in his artistic development during the 1940s, his engagement with European languages and world literatures acquired a greater prominence; and when he returned to poetry in the 1960s, he put the study of Anglo-Saxon at the centre of his linguistic concerns. Nowhere is the passage from the particular to the universal made clearer than in Borges's interaction with language. In a talk on the theme of blindness delivered at the Teatro Coliseo in Buenos Aires in 1977, for example, he describes how the study of Anglo-Saxon facilitated a recuperation of his ancestral history. Elsewhere, he says (with Emerson) that 'all words are metaphors – or fossil poetry', by which he suggests the presence of an *archaic* poetic symbolism in language.[4] Inasmuch as metaphor lies at the heart of human discourse and indeed constitutes the primitive means of awareness and articulation, poetry becomes the space where man can recognize himself as part of a tradition that unfolds in and through the temporality of language. This view of poetry as a shared experience embedded in language rests on Borges's conviction that literary activity consists less in a capacity for invention than in the expression of a common reality for which the writer is simply an effective medium: 'A language is a tradition, a way of grasping reality, not an arbitrary assemblage of symbols.'[5]

As I have already mentioned, Borges believed that cultural diversity spreads the seeds of a fertile literary practice. Following Thorstein Veblen's postulate about the primacy of Jewish thought in Modern Europe, which hinges on the question of Jewish assimilation, Zionism, and multiculturalism ('It appears to be only when the gifted Jew escapes from the cultural environment created and fed by the particular genius of his own people ... that he comes into his own as a creative leader in the world's intellectual enterprise'),[6] Borges argues in 'The Argentine Writer and Tradition' that the contribution of the Jews to Western civilization has a socio-historical, rather than biological explanation due to the way in which Jewish scientists and intellectuals were able to create a hyphenate or interstitial status between their own ethnic and religious identity, and gentile society. That is to say, their peculiar place within the adopted culture allowed them to interact freely with different traditions and thus to contribute positively to the development of Western civilization. He also mentions the case of Shaw, Berkeley, and Swift (Joyce is, surprisingly, omitted from the list), who, as Irishmen, were able to make innovations in the English literary and philosophical tradition because of their intermediary position with respect to the dominant culture. According to Borges, Argentine writers are in a similar situation with regard to the West, a circumstance that allows them to take on all aspects of European thought and culture 'without superstition and with an irreverence that can have, and already has had, fortunate consequences' (426). However, in order to do this, he also perceived the need to overcome the cultural and psychological sense of inferiority created by the colonial experience, an issue that had already been denounced by prominent Latin American intellectuals from the 1920s onwards, so that Spanish American writers might approach the Western tradition without the inhibitions implanted by the dominant culture throughout four centuries of colonial rule; it was necessary, in short, to overcome the habit of servile imitation that had characterized Spanish American thought until then. The time to do so was ripe, given the moral crisis and socio-political divisions created in Europe by the rise of fascism, which forced Spanish American intellectuals to formulate their own ideological position both in the national and the international arenas. Thus, literature became the battlefield of a proxy war between antagonistic political factions, a struggle that in itself was beneficial for the awakening of the Latin American social conscience.

By way of conclusion: literary tradition, as a vital force, must feed on the past and, at the same time, aim towards the future. In doing so, it needs to keep a balance between those two poles. An excessive dependence on rules and norms erodes the tradition's vitality; an abrupt departure from its roots renders it meaningless. From this perspective, writers have a double responsibility: first, to assert their own voice in a way that is consistent with their literary tradition (or traditions), and, secondly, to be in control of the intellectual and expressive means that will guarantee the significance of their work. In his canonical story 'Death and the Compass' (1942), Borges signals the moment of tension between the past and the present in which a new artistic expression comes to life. What he had searched for in vain in his earlier work through the use and abuse of local colour had finally crystalized in a more authentic form. In it, I would argue, Borges found a metaphorical description for the kind of writing he had forged in *The Garden of Forking Paths*, his first ground-breaking collection of stories whose merits, nevertheless, failed to impress the pro-nationalist jury of the National Literary Prize to which he submitted the work in 1942. As Borges puts it in the story: 'the odious double-faced Janus *who gazes toward the twilights of dusk and dawn* terrorized my dreams and my waking'. Then he adds: 'I swore by the god who sees from two faces … to weave a labyrinth around the man who had imprisoned my brother. I have woven it, and it holds: the materials are a dead writer on heresies, a compass, an eighteenth-century sect, a Greek word, a dagger, the rhombs of a paint shop.'[7]

While the heterogeneous elements used in the creation of 'Death and the Compass' reveal the hybrid nature of its narrative – which, like a dream (one of Borges's preferred analogies for literary creation), is both deeply unsettling and strangely familiar – the Janus-faced figure reminds the reader of both the continuity and the innovation that are at play in the work. The essays, short stories, and poems written during the course of his life lend credence to the poetics of irreverence Borges so fervently upheld in the conference of 1951. However, far from requiring a mere parodic treatment of Western culture, Borges's own work bears witness to the fact that the notion of irreverence – which is akin to his interest in the eccentric and the unorthodox – does not merely entail mockery or derision but a critical posture that seeks to imprint the writer's own voice as the expression of artistic freedom and intellectual autonomy.

Notes

1. 'The Argentine Writer and Tradition', in Jorge Luis Borges, *The Total Library: Non-Fiction, 1922–1986*, pp. 420–427. Subsequent page references are cited in the text.
2. Seamus Heaney and Richard Kearney, 'Borges and the World of Fiction: An Interview with Jorge Luis Borges', *The Crane Bag*, 7 (1983), 71–78 (p. 73).
3. 'Preliminary note', in Thomas Carlyle: *Sartor Resartus* (Buenos Aires: Emecé, 1945), pp. 9–15 (p. 9); my translation.
4. Willis Barnstone, ed., *Borges at Eighty: Conversations* (Bloomington, IN: Indiana University Press, 1982), p. 165.
5. Jorge Luis Borges, *The Gold of the Tigers: Selected Later Poems*, ed. and trans. Alastair Reid (New York: E.P. Dutton, 1977), p. 8.
6. Thorsten Veblen, 'The Intellectual Pre-Eminence of Jews in Modern Europe', *Political Science Quarterly*, 34, 1 (1919), pp. 33–42 (p. 38).
7. Jorge Luis Borges, *A Personal Anthology*, ed. and trans. Anthony Kerrigan et al. (New York: Grove Press, 1967), pp. 1–14 (p. 11).

CHAPTER 13

Borges, Tangos, and Milongas

Ana C. Cara

Sparked in the 1920s, Borges's interest in tangos and milongas persisted for almost seven decades. Three key periods provide rich social, political, and literary contexts for the author's engagement with these vernacular forms: the 1920s, during which his early poetry and essays appeared; the 1960s, when he published *Para las seis cuerdas*; and the early 1980s, when he composed his later milongas.

Poet Norah Lange observed of the young Jorge Luis Borges: 'He can listen to a tango, on his feet, and in silence, as few others can.'[1] Surely, Norah would have known, for after his return from Europe in the early 1920s, it was in the Langes' home that Borges gathered with fellow writers, to discuss poetry, and to socialize and dance with friends. Dissonant with the Borges of our popular imaginary (hands resting on his cane), a youthful Borges not only listened but danced to tangos and milongas – most likely taught by Ricardo Güiraldes, his friend, co-founder of *Proa*, and author of *Don Segundo Sombra*.[2] Indeed, Victoria Ocampo, aristocratic doyen of the Buenos Aires intelligentsia at the time and editor of *Sur*, recalls Güiraldes as a *habitué* at those memorable encounters at her home, when, 'every Thursday, come rain or shine, the *"Pibe de la Paternal*,"[3] followed by his accompanists, came to the house' and 'we danced tango all afternoon'.[4]

Clearly, following its sensational reception in New York, Paris, and London, tango was no longer the exclusive property of the *orillas* (outskirts), the port cantinas, the brothels, the *sainetes* (popular plays), or the *conventillos* (tenements) of Buenos Aires, as it had been in prior decades. Tangos and milongas had filtered into most recesses of *porteño* (Buenos Aires) society, reaching '*el centro*' and upper- and middle-class audiences, who listened to tangos on their radios and Victrolas and consumed reams of scores and popular magazines featuring tango lyrics, photographs, and anecdotal accounts. Movies further captured tango's movements, and global popular culture appropriated the dance. By 1933, when the first full-length Argentine sound film, *¡Tango!*, appeared, the 1921 American silent film *The Four Horsemen of the Apocalypse* had turned Rudolf Valentino into an icon of the tango-dancing Latin Lover, inspiring a tango craze.

The 1920s was a 'golden age' of physical and demographic development for Buenos Aires, largely spurred by exports, foreign investments, and massive immigration. Borges, less interested in the city's growth or tango's international fame, was captivated instead by the tango and milonga worlds of Buenos Aires' *barrios*, and by the poetic capacity of these genres to voice 'criolledad', or 'creoleness'. Located in what was then the urban edge, many of these neighbourhoods bordered on empty lots that faded into the pampa, blurring the lines between city and countryside and creating the unique physical and cultural space around which, according to Beatriz Sarlo, Borges built his 'myth' of the *orillas*.[5] The on-the-ground reality, however, manifested a thriving tango-milonga cultural continuum throughout the city, and a dynamic exchange of expressive forms that cut across urban-rural, rich-poor, native-immigrant, popular-erudite, and oral-written divides.

The son of an immigrant laundress, singer Carlos Gardel (1890–1935) embodied this cultural multiplicity better than any other tango figure, becoming the *criollo* voice of Buenos Aires. An admirer of *payadores* (guitarist-singers of improvised lyrics) such as Afro-Argentine Gabino Ezeiza (1858–1916) and creolized-Italian José Betinotti[6] (1878–1915), Gardel acquired a significant folk repertoire – even as he incorporated techniques from Neapolitan canzonetta singers in *barrio* Abasto, and learned to vocalize from opera luminaries. His multifaceted self-presentation included performances in a top-hat and overcoat (evoking wealthy Argentines), in gaucho clothing (echoing Valentino), and in *compadrito* (ruffian/dandy) apparel wearing a neckerchief and cocked fedora. By performing all these identities, he reflected tango's appeal across social classes and cultural backgrounds.

Despite Gardel's charisma and celebrity, however, Borges and other avant-garde writers preferred the earlier, more jovial style of tango that brandished bravado rather than laments. In their critical writings, journalists and writers deliberated on the role of these vernacular forms in the nation's cultural history. In keeping with the Florida-Boedo literary divide, the Boedo group disregarded tango, considering it a distraction from more important concerns, whereas Florida writers celebrated the phenomenon, authoring (at times idealized) poetry and essays on tango aesthetics and related issues. In 1925, for example, Florida's *Martín Fierro* featured Sergio Piñero's 'Salvemos el tango' ('Let's Save the Tango'), followed just two years later by Boedo's *Claridad*, which circulated 'Síntomas de decadencia, el tango' ('Symptoms of Decadence, The Tango'). Straddling both groups, Borges declared in his 1928 essay, 'The Pointless Debate Regarding Boedo and Florida', his preference for a well-written milonga over a poorly-crafted sonnet (*Textos recobrados 1919–1929*, 366).

Notable among tango and milonga studies in this period is Vicente Rossi's *Cosas de negros* (1926), which Borges admired in a review published in *Valoraciones* (*Textos recobrados ...*, pp. 254–255). The following year Borges wrote his first essay on tango, 'Ascendencias del tango' ('Genealogy of the Tango'), and 'Apunte férvido sobre las tres vidas de la milonga' ('Fervid Note on the Three Lives of the Milonga'), both included in *The Language of Argentines* (1928). The second essay responds to Juan de Dios Filiberto's milonga classifications, establishing Borges's own assessment of the early milonga-tango relationship.

Popular magazines such as *El alma que canta*, which Alberto Vaccarezza claimed was read by the nation's president and the humblest farmer, published a cross-section of erudite and popular poets, including Evaristo Carriego, Rubén Darío, Leopoldo Lugones, José Betinotti, Almafuerte, Dante Linyera, Alfonsina Storni, and others – all eager for exposure through its wide readership.[7] In December 1925, the magazine organized a contest, announcing 'We're searching for the poet of tango.' The pursuit yielded Homero Manzi's 'Viejo ciego' lyrics, explicitly inspired by and dedicated to Evaristo Carriego.[8] Set to music by Cátulo Castillo and Sebastián Piana, the piece was first performed in 1926 (the same year Borges's 'Carriego y el sentido del arrabal' appeared in *La Prensa* and was subsequently included in *El tamaño de mi esperanza*). Both artists sought a model in this minor poet's capacity to portray his *barrio* and its characters. Borges published an entire volume titled *Evaristo Carriego* (1930), to which, in 1955, he added 'A History of the Tango'.

Clearly, cross-pollination among folk, popular, and erudite verbal artists was commonplace as tango lyricists and contemporary writers aimed to render Buenos Aires in verse. Tango lyrics betrayed inescapable literary influences, as seen in Manzi's 'Sur' and 'Monte criollo', which resonated, respectively, with Borges's 'Versos de catorce' and 'Truco'. Conversely, Borges, who had spoken with and come to know *payadores*, *milongueros*, tango musicians, and *compadres* (men from the outskirts), is said to have wittily written a Lunfardo-inflected tango (now lost) titled '*Biaba con caldo*'.[9] Moreover, he was well-versed in early tango lyrics and milonga quatrains. His nephew recalls Borges carrying him piggy-back, singing the anonymous '*Pejerrey con papa*' ('Fish and Potatoes') while dancing milonga steps.[10]

Politics as well as poetry offered common ground for writers and *tangueros*, many of whom supported Hipólito Yrigoyen, the twice-elected, middle-class president of Argentina, victim of a 1930 military coup. In fact, Borges headed the *Comité Yrigoyenista de Intelectuales Jóvenes* (with headquarters at his home), thus forging common cause with, among others, Manzi and Arturo Jáuretche, for whose book *Paso de los libres* (1934) Borges wrote the preface. And just as Enrique Maroni's tango 'Hipólito Yrigoyen' (recorded in 1927) sang Yrigoyen's praise, so too, though indirectly, did Borges's 'The Mythical Founding of Buenos Aires' (1929). In fact, Borges had already explicitly praised the populist Yrigoyen in an earlier essay, attributing to him criollo qualities comparable only to Juan Manuel de Rosas.[11]

It was this observation, perhaps, that in the early 1930s prompted a milonga dedicated (somewhat tongue-in-cheek) to Borges. Homero Manzi and Sebastián Piana's collaboration launched an important milonga revival, which featured variants to the traditional 'milonga campera'. The milonga repertoire now included '*milongas ciudadanas*' (citified milongas) and '*milongas-candombe*' or '*federales*'. An example of the latter was the milonga for Borges, titled 'Juan Manuel'.

Although a whiff of countryside air may still have lingered in early 1930s Buenos Aires with the milonga resurgences, old recordings of Gardel's folk repertoire, and tango lyrics with country themes, Argentina's urban tango predominated, reaching its 'Golden Age' between the late 1930s and early 1950s. Tango's rise, however, would lose pace in the 1960s.

Just as foreign immigration to Argentina began to wane in the mid-1930s, an emergent internal migration, spurred by industrialization, relocated rural residents from the provinces to urban Buenos Aires. With them travelled musical traditions generically termed *folclore* or 'folklore'. Before long, numerous local *peñas* (music clubs) cropped up in Buenos Aires, paving the way for what would become the '*boom del folklore*' of the 1950s and 1960s.

Radio had started broadcasting folk music along with tango in the late 1930s, and films further fostered these traditional genres. Television also later contributed to Argentina's folk boom, as did folk festivals such as the one in Cosquín (Córdoba, Argentina). Classical music, as well, began incorporating folk rhythms and native tonalities, including works by the internationally recognized composers Alberto Ginastera (1916–1983) and Carlos Guastavino (1912–2000). Moreover, it would be Guastavino who set Borges's first milonga to music in 1963.

Central to the promotion of folk music and musicians was the presidency of Juan Domingo Perón. A 1943 decree required that at least 50 per cent of artists at musical venues perform native music. Tango initially also prospered under the government's promotion of everything 'nacional y popular', though later enduring censorship of dissident lyrics. Following the 1955 coup, a period of 'desnacionalización cultural' ensued, generated by an influx of rock and pop music driven by external markets. In this emerging context, Argentine folk music joined other folk movements throughout the continent, becoming a liberal voice for the disempowered and (together with elements of 'rock nacional') part of the New Song Movement in the 1960s and 1970s. Tango, on the other hand, was increasingly associated with a former, older, more conservative Argentina.

While the nation's political scene indicated uncertainty after the fall of Perón, the country was nonetheless invigorated by foreign investments and new international cultural trends and influences, not only in music but in all the arts. Indeed, another 'Boom' was underway in Latin American literature, with Borges, who had soared to worldwide celebrity in the early 1960s, as its leading master. Though celebrated nationally, Borges was also criticized (harshly at times) for seeming 'un-Argentine' given his international reach and universal subject matter. Yet in 1965, perplexingly for some, Borges chose to publish a collection of milonga and tango poems, whose title, *Para las seis cuerdas*, referenced Argentina's traditional folk instrument, the guitar. Equally confounding was his collaboration with rising avant-garde tango composer Astor Piazzolla, who set a selection of these poems to music.

Piazzolla was a musical revolutionary eager to renovate tango and milonga by engaging them with Bartok, Stravinsky, and Baroque masters, and with genres ranging from Gregorian chant to contemporary jazz. This contrasted with Guastavino (born in the interior, versed in Argentine folk music, and sometimes called 'the Schubert of the Pampas'), whose musical setting of Borges's 'Milonga de dos hermanos' followed a rather traditional line. Conservative tango fans, ambivalent if not vehemently adverse to Piazzolla's 'New Tango', claimed he had destroyed its melody and made tango undanceable; and, as with Borges, many considered him un-Argentine. Piazzolla's followers – the intellectuals, professionals, university students, and middle-class young who listened to his music on television, cassettes, or at *tanguerías* – saw 'New Tango' as a revitalized fresh 'soundtrack' for Buenos Aires that contrasted with the old tango's outdated idiom. 'The street lamp, the neckerchief, the dagger, the sterile moanings' of old tangos, Piazzolla declared, no longer spoke to 1960s Buenos Aires.[12]

The Borges-Piazzolla LP titled 'El tango' was a provocative project, despite the prickly nature of the collaboration between them.[13] Although now a classic in the Piazzolla discography, the recording blends milonga musical innovations with lyrics that (while avoiding 'sterile moaning') speak of another era. As evident in his fiction and co-edited volume *El compadrito* (1945), Borges was intrigued by this marginal figure from the *orillas*, and with stories of knife fights. In contrast, the later Horacio Ferrer-Piazzolla collaborations were more successful at achieving a new '*música de Buenos Aires*'. While the 'Tango' LP gained recognition, and the Borges-Piazzolla milongas and tangos (and those set by others) were performed, recorded, and popularized through renditions by various artists, the original LP remains of interest primarily to scholars and collectors.

In Argentina, as elsewhere, the 1960s were a time of controversial creative exploration and 'high art' and 'low art' collaborations. It was also a time for listening more reflectively than nostalgically, and for theorizing and historicizing tango. Among the various studies that circulated was Ernesto Sábato's *Tango, discusión y clave* (1963). In its brief preface, while acknowledging their estrangement, Sábato addressed Borges: 'I would like to offer you these pages with my thoughts on tango. And it would please me greatly if you didn't dislike them. Believe me.'[14]

In four lectures on tango delivered in 1965,[15] Borges, too, contributed to the process of chronicling and reflection, offering insights regarding his experiences with *tangueros* and *compadritos*, assessing tango's history, and commenting on the creation of his own milongas.

The political turmoil of the 1960s, the return of Perón in 1973, his death in 1974, and the subsequent rule of his wife Isabelita culminated in the 1976 military coup. Calling itself the *Proceso de Reorganización Nacional*, the ensuing junta engaged in what some termed a 'Dirty War', imposing neoliberal policies and engaging in state terrorism against civilians (detention centres, torture, and 'disappearances'). Military rule lasted until defeat in the 1982 Falklands War, prompting the junta's demise in 1983 and a return to democracy.

With the notable exception of the demonstrations by the Mothers of the Plaza de Mayo, the regime banned public congregations during this period. Concerts, dances, and gatherings were viewed with suspicion, often ending in arrests. Consequently, tango venues diminished, and – despite the creation of the Día Nacional del Tango in 1977 – most *porteños* believed that, other than in select traditional locales, among older dancers, and in tourist venues, tango was dead.

Not just politics but a failing economy prompted many Argentines, among them intellectuals and artists, into exile. From Europe and Latin America, they voiced dissent as censorship annihilated almost all cultural manifestations at home. Albeit not exclusively, tango became associated with 'the generals', though only after their fall would the connection be explicitly articulated in memoirs, testimonials, and other venues, such as Spanish filmmaker Carlos Saura's *Tango* (1998), where the protagonist declares: 'The military played tangos at high volume during tortures to drown out the victims' screams.' Other films also reflected on this period, most notably Oscar-winning *La historia oficial* (1985), directed by Luis Puenzo and Aida Bortnik. Fernando Solanas's *El exilio de Gardel* (1985) and Marcos Zurinaga's *Tango Bar* (1987) employed tango imaginaries, interweaving a mythic past with recent realities.

Once fully aware of the *Proceso*'s activities, Borges distanced himself from his early notorious comments and readily expressed his abhorrence of the military and their actions. Crucial in this respect were the visits to Borges's apartment by members of the Mothers and Grandmothers of the Plaza de Mayo and testimonials from Falklands War veterans. Sent to war with minimal training and poor equipment, many of these conscripts were impoverished, indigenous or mestizo youths from the interior, unaccustomed to the cold, windblown climate of the South Atlantic.

Borges responded to these realities with a powerful milonga. Unlike his earlier milongas, where – despite their larger themes – Borges sang of *compadres*, knife fights, local neighbourhoods and characters, distanced by space and time, his 'Milonga del muerto' (originally titled 'Milonga de un soldado' (1982)) emerged organically from the immediacy of a sociohistorical moment. Signalling a shift in Borges's milonga production, this anti-war poem appeared in his last volume, significantly titled *Los conjurados* (1985), which also includes 'Milonga del infiel'. By referring to an earlier military conflict in the nation's history (the so-called 'Conquest of the Desert'), 'Milonga del infiel' implicitly lays bare the parallels between the brutal deaths of presumed '*bárbaros*' in the nineteenth century and of innocent conscripts in the deserted glacial islands of the twentieth. Yet another milonga, 'Milonga del puñal', published in *Atlas* (1984), corresponds in tenor with those in *Los conjurados*. Despite the more celebratory *Atlas* venture – featuring texts by Borges and photographs by María Kodama – 'Milonga del puñal' reveals the underlying anguish during this period and unequivocally presages a time of violence, reminiscent of yet another brutal era in Argentine history: the time of Rosas.

Sebastián Piana, who decades earlier had playfully dedicated the milonga 'Juan Manuel' to Borges, now composed the music for 'Milonga del muerto' in a more sombre spirit. Recorded by Sandra Mihanovich under its original title, Borges's 'Milonga de un soldado' was reportedly censored.[16] Once the military fell, Eduardo Falú, among others (including Mihanovich herself), recorded it as 'Milonga del muerto'.

By 1984, freedom of expression and artistic projects began to flourish again under democratic rule, and the highly publicized stage show 'Tango Argentino' circulated the globe, igniting renewed international interest in tango. Two years later, shortly before his death in Geneva, Borges spent his last days reciting his milongas and recalling those of others.[17] I had the pleasure of sharing those final hours with him and the privilege of witnessing the enduring conviction, expressed throughout his *oeuvre*, that *'Siempre el coraje es mejor / la esperanza nunca es vana'* ('Courage is always better / and hope is an absolute').[18]

Notes

1. Quoted in María Luisa Bastos, *Borges ante la crítica argentina 1923–1960* (Buenos Aires: Hispamérica, 1974), p. 80. All translations are mine unless otherwise indicated.
2. María Esther Vázquez, *Borges esplendor y derrota* (Barcelona: Tusquets, 1996), p. 103.
3. 'The kid from La Paternal' – nickname for Osvaldo Fresedo, songwriter and director of a tango orchestra.
4. Catalina Pantuso, 'Victoria Ocampo y su particular relación con el tango'. Available online at https://catalinapantuso.wordpress.com/2017/04/25/vic toria-ocampo-y-su-particular-relacion-con-el-tango/ (accessed 12 June 2018).
5. See Beatriz Sarlo, *Borges, a Writer on the Edge* (London: Verso, 1993).
6. Spelling varies: Betinotti, Bettinoti, Bettinotti.
7. Horacio Salas, *Homero Manzi y su tiempo* (Buenos Aires: Javier Vergara, 2001), p. 57.
8. Manzi was not the actual winner. For a full account, see Salas, pp. 148–149.
9. Roughly translated from Lunfardo as 'Bloody Skirmish'. See Vázquez, p. 103.
10. Miguel de Torre Borges, *Apuntes de familia* (Buenos Aires: Alberto Casares, 2004), p. 11.
11. Jorge Luis Borges, *Inquisiciones* (Buenos Aires: Editorial Proa, 1925), p. 132.
12. Quoted in María Susana Azzi and Simon Collier, *Le Grand Tango; The Life and Music of Astor Piazzolla* (New York: Oxford University Press, 2000), p. 80.

13. John Turci-Escobar, 'Rescatando al tango para una nueva música: Reconsidering the 1965 Collaboration Between Borges and Piazzolla', *Variaciones Borges*, 31 (2011), pp. 1–27.

14. E. Sábato, *Tango, discusión y clave* (Buenos Aires: Editorial Losada, 1963), p. 9.

15. Recently published as *El tango: cuatro conferencias* (Buenos Aires: Sudamericana, 2016).

16. Field interviews. Buenos Aires. Fall, 1984.

17. See Ana Cara-Walker, 'A Death in Geneva', *World Literature Today*, 62, 1 (Winter, 1988), pp. 5–9.

18. 'Milonga for Jacinto Chiclana', translation by David Young and Ana Cara-Walker, in 'A Death in Geneva', p. 9.

CHAPTER 14

Borges and Bioy Casares

Mariela Blanco

A Chronicle of Friendship and Writing

A significant proportion of Borges's work was done in collaboration with others. Among these varied projects, his writing partnership with Bioy Casares stands out. These friends and authors established one of the most fruitful and long-lasting working relationships in Argentine literature. Together, they moulded a discourse that is not inferior to the work each published individually, without resembling either's. Bioy's *Borges* (Buenos Aires, 2006), a diary of their conversations over nearly 50 years, paints a vivid portrait of their encounters as a laboratory of literary criticism, their distinctive brand of humour always to the fore in their impressions and reflections. Indeed, they gelled to such a degree that in the various masks they adopted, H. Bustos Domecq, B. Suárez Lynch, or just 'Borges and Bioy Casares', who came up with which line or idea loses all importance. Rather, traditional notions of authorship dissolve and a unique third voice emerges.

According to statements each made over the years, Borges and Bioy met either towards the close of 1931 or the beginning of 1932 at one of the many banquets hosted by Victoria Ocampo in honour of a visitor from abroad. Over the following years, they got together frequently, whether in Buenos Aires, Mar del Plata, or on the Bioys' estate in Pardo, in Buenos Aires province, where they wrote together for the first time.[1] Borges was earning his living principally as a journalist, and Bioy invited him to join him in a family venture for which they would be paid a not inconsiderable sum. An aunt of Bioy's had a dairy farm, La Martona, and to boost sales she hired the pair to produce advertising copy. Titled 'La Martona's Curdled Milk. A Dietary Study of Bitter Acids', they included recipes, captions, and descriptions where the scientific tone was undercut by purely subjective remarks. Although much of the irony may have been lost on the public, the leaflet was the first of a series of private jokes the pair would share in writing over the next few decades.

The text, along with a draft of a short story from the same era, 'El doctor Praetorius', appears in *Museo* (2002), a compilation of texts Borges and Bioy wrote together but which were not included in *Obras completas en colaboración* (Buenos Aires: Emecé, 1979). That title comes from the ragbag column of miscellanea they published in the magazines *Destiempo* (1936–1937) and *Los Anales de Buenos Aires* (1946–1948). Here they signed as B. Lynch Davis for the first time, 'B' as the initial each shared, and each surname coming from respective family members.

Pseudonyms and Literary Biographies

The most well-known pseudonym they wrote under was Honorio Bustos Domecq. From the first story they had published, 'The Twelve Figures of the World', in *Sur* 88 (January 1942), Borges and Bioy began to realize that Bustos Domecq was an autonomous creation with his own voice, and a second story, 'The Nights of Goliadkin', soon followed two months later, in *Sur* 90. This author of hard-boiled detective fiction would go on to enjoy some renown in Argentine literature partly in thanks to the official letter of introduction provided by his former primary school teacher, Adelia Puglione (later changed to Adelma Badoglio), which serves as the prologue to *Six Problems for Don Isidro Parodi* (Buenos Aires: Sur, 1942), the first book of short stories Borges and Bioy wrote together. This hoodwinking lent an air of credibility to an author who would also appear as a character. Indeed, there was nothing in the book to link Bustos Domecq with the authors responsible for his rambling, baroque style, and so it would stay for a long time. For the fictive author to gain sway over the public's imagination, however, an even higher authority was invoked, namely Gervasio Montenegro of the Argentine Academy. His 'Introductory Note' would bring even further veracity and vitality to Borges and Bioy's creation, were it not for his pompous absurdity and the fact he is also a character in the stories. This satirical element of the pair's collaborative work would become their trademark. Nevertheless, such artful hoaxes seem to have gone over the heads of the reading public as the stories never gained a widespread following.

Not to be deterred, in 1946, Borges and Bioy founded a press called Oportet y Haereses, which they used to publish *Dos fantasías memorables*, which includes the allegorical tales 'El testigo' and 'El signo', as well as *Un modelo para la muerte*, a short novel that resumes the Parodi saga. It is so replete with puns and private jokes as to render it opaque, which perhaps accounts for its going largely unnoticed. If in the previous volume the various prologues traced Bustos Domecq's literary biography, here Bustos himself prepares the way for his successor, B. Suárez Lynch. Indeed, genealogy is further emphasized here as Suárez was the name of one of Borges's grandparents, and Lynch one of Bioy's. Here Borges and Bioy carry the detective's deductive talents to an extreme as, between sips of the typical Argentine infusion *mate*, he has to solve mysteries from the confines of his cell, locked up as he is for a crime he did not commit. Albeit in the guise of fiction, the mise-en-scène is consistent with hypotheses that Borges ventured in several essays on the problematic relation between law and State in Argentina.

Borges and Bioy also worked together on several film scripts at this time. Although 'Los orilleros' and 'El paraíso de los creyentes' never made it to the screen, they were published in 1955 under their real names. The two writers had more success with the politically charged allegory *Invasión*, which was directed by Hugo Santiago in 1969. The fate of the movie would itself become an allegory of sorts, however. It was banned by the brutal dictatorship that took power in 1976, and two years later the original reels were stolen from the Alex laboratories in Buenos Aires, meaning it could not be shown even after democracy had been restored. Only in 2004 was a 35mm copy found in Paris, and the film was restored.[2]

This period also marked the return of an old friend in the 1967 collection, *Chronicles of Bustos Domecq*. With his name in the title, Bustos was now clearly part of the fiction, ceding authorship to Borges and Bioy. These stories abandon the detective genre, preferring to satirize Argentina's avant-garde, which, it must be said, had already fallen into some disrepute. By 1977 their creation was almost a household name, and *Nuevos cuentos de Bustos Domecq* brought the series to a close.

Readings, Commentaries, Translations

Though he was 15 years younger, Borges always insisted that Bioy influenced him greatly. Moreover, contrary to what might have been expected, in several interviews Borges claimed that the experience of working with Bioy lightened his own style considerably. While the influence was no doubt mutual, the difference in age and their respective positions in Argentine literature weighed most in Borges's public support for Bioy's writing, especially at the beginning of his career. In 1936, for example, Borges reviewed Bioy's first novel, *La estatua casera*, and in 1940 he wrote the prologue for *The Invention of Morel*, a text that has become famous in its own right for outlining the pair's aesthetic position. That same year saw the publication of one of Borges's most emblematic stories from this period, 'Tlön, Uqbar, Orbis Tertius'. Lest we forget, the plot begins with a conversation between Borges and Bioy about writing a story, and thereafter reality is eroded by a fiction.

In the real world, the pair had already been working towards reshaping the Argentine literary scene. In 1940, along with Silvina Ocampo, married to Bioy since the previous year, Borges published the famous *Book of Fantasy*, featuring translations by all three editors; and in 1941 the *Antología poética argentina* came out.[3] Two years later, Borges and Bioy were taken on as literary advisors for Emecé, an important publishing house, and they compiled another anthology, *Los mejores cuentos policiales* (The Best Detective Stories). Through these anthologies, prologues, translations, and their roles as judges of literary competitions, they consolidated a new space within Argentine narrative which championed plot as opposed to the social realism or psychological motifs of other literary trends. Their collection 'El séptimo círculo' (1945–1955) popularized detective fiction, and within a few years Borges and Bioy would become synonymous with this genre as well as with speculative tales of mystery. In this vein, in 1955 they were responsible for another memorable anthology, *Extraordinary Tales* (Buenos Aires: Raigal); and, in another area of interest, that same year they also issued a compilation of classic nineteenth-century Argentine poetry, *Poesía gauchesca* (México: FCE).

Among the diverse projects they undertook together, their glosses and textual commentaries are also significant. This area has yet to be sufficiently explored by critics but can be garnered from Bioy Casares's extensive diary of his friendship with Borges. For many years they dined together almost every day, and more often than not they would discuss and annotate texts – for publication or for pleasure – long into the night. Not all of these projects came to fruition, a notable case being the *Sumas* collection, which envisaged critical editions of classic texts; yet their glosses on contemporaries and forebears in these midnight sessions remain an invaluable resource for reappraising their roles as readers and commentators, not to mention the relation between these texts and their own writings, whether individual or as a pair.

Nationalism, Populism, and Popular Discourse

From its playful and recreational origins, writing as a pair afforded Borges and Bioy leeway to express themselves more directly than in their individual works. As they became more well-known and their roles as cultural mediators more involved, they reserved their work in collaboration for attacks on the nationalist and populist politics of Argentina at the time. What began as private jokes later took on a more aggressive tone.

If we consider Borges's writing before his collaborations with Bioy, it is clear he had already distanced himself considerably from his early *criollista* phase. Indeed, his essays insist frequently on the importance of literary autonomy in the face of burgeoning totalitarianism, a phenomenon that exacerbated his antipathy towards nationalist politics, especially after the outbreak of the Second World War. From 1936 on, however, he had warned of its dangers, and over the years this mistrust would give way to abhorrence for nationalist beliefs of any kind. Despite his similarly staunch defence of autonomy in the literary sphere, however, the texts written with Bioy Casares openly ridiculed proponents of nationalism, especially in the years 1942–1947.

One such text was 'La fiesta del monstruo', written in 1947, one year into General Perón's first government. Borges and Bioy publicly manifested their disapproval of the regime, and Borges's reluctant departure from the Miguel Cané library also attracted some public attention. Although satire had been their weapon of choice since the beginning, this story was their fiercest attack yet. Previously, they had condemned growing nationalist fervour among the elite, as well as the role of the military in state affairs, but 'La fiesta ... ' takes a working-class perspective in order to denounce the abuse of power, what they considered unacceptable state encroachment on the freedom of the individual. The nameless first-person narrator of this ferocious grotesque comes from a working-class neighbourhood on the outskirts of Buenos Aires, and is happily bullied and herded into a convoy so as to take part in a populist rally held by the 'monstruo' tyrant. Although never named as such, sufficient indications are given for the reader to identify the monster in question as Perón. Populism, violence, and allegory combine in a text where explicit political allusions are at odds with the rest of Borges and Bioy's work together. Having circulated clandestinely for several years, the text was finally published in the liberal Uruguayan magazine *Marcha* after Perón was overthrown in 1955.

The story pertains to an extensive tradition in Argentine literature concerning the representation of violence, which was inaugurated in the nineteenth century along the battle lines set out by Sarmiento in his famous essay-cum-novel *Facundo: Civilization and Barbarism* (1845). In particular, many critics have pointed out its resemblance to what is considered to be the first work of Argentine prose fiction, 'The Slaughter Yard', by Esteban Echeverría. The author's opposition to the regime of Juan Manuel de

Rosas limited its readership, and it was only published several decades later, in 1870, almost twenty years after the author's death, much as would happen with Borges and Bioy's story.[4] The debt due to Echeverría's story is especially evident in the portrayal of power and violence, for 'The Slaughter Yard' stages a series of scenes of mounting violence that culminate in the death of a Unitarian, who 'bursts with rage' at the hands of the gleeful Federalists just as they set about ceremoniously torturing him; while in 'La fiesta del monstruo' violence is visited upon a Jew whom the narrator's mob single out as they make their way to a political rally. Both victims' heroic, gruesome deaths are a result of their independent mind-sets and behaviour; both refuse to bow to the dictates imposed by the populist leader, who, according to these authors, typifies barbarism.

In terms of the spaces represented and the types of speech they give voice to, both stories are rooted in the world of the popular classes. Echeverría's takes place in Buenos Aires slaughter yard, where cattle are killed and meat prepared for sale, in other words where the city meets the countryside, and civilization meets barbarism. One century on, 'La fiesta del monstruo' is set not too far away on the southern limit of the city, among the factories and working-class neighbourhoods that so vociferously supported Perón in his rise to power. This is where the narrator's rowdy caravan sets out from as, with each leg of the journey carefully signposted, they head for the city's central Plaza de Mayo, the stage for many of Perón's most memorable speeches.

Another element common to both texts is the effective stylization of popular speech. This is particularly noteworthy since, on the one hand, it belongs to and enhances the tradition of portraying barbarism that Sarmiento began, while on the other, it takes up and makes a valuable contribution to one of the founding motivations of Argentine literature, namely a discursive representation of the nation's speech. Its importance can be seen from the fact that it featured in the title of one of Borges's first collections of essays, *El idioma de los argentinos* (1928), and it would continue to be a central concern in subsequent works. Later writers such as Julio Cortázar, Juan José Saer, and others carried on the tradition, thus constructing a vast tapestry of texts that focus on language as a way of exploring both the national question and the national imaginary, which became particularly pressing in the wake of the successive waves of mass immigration Argentina experienced from the end of the nineteenth century on.

Thus, realism and ironic distance are strategically deployed in defiance of the established authorities. The brutality of the descriptions of popular celebrations, evocative of the regime's oppressive co-opting of power, along with the allusive and elliptical ways of referring to Rosas and Perón respectively, are key to understanding how one story rewrites the other, and was no doubt clear to its first readers. By virtue of this homage, Borges and Bioy take their place in the liberal tradition, ever careful to defend the pre-eminence of the individual over and above the demands of the masses.

The language parodied in these texts takes in all social classes and a wide range of social actors. The chief target, however, are those writers whose language is contrived so as to impose reductionist and essentialist ideas of nationality; as a result, Borges and Bioy present diverse forms of speech and long-winded deliberations on the fine points of grammar. In these stories, those who assimilate the stereotypes of mass culture are mocked ruthlessly, while characters who assert their independence are celebrated. Popular discourse is thus one more way for Borges and Bioy to intervene in the contemporary polemics of Argentine literature, while also affording these two liberals the opportunity to censure totalitarianism or its local manifestation, in their view, Peronism. Borges had always defended Argentina´s liberal tradition, and his famous 1951 speech, 'The Argentine Writer and Tradition', makes the same arguments, only differing in tone.

The Borges-Bioy collaborations carry out an animated dialogue with the historical period in which they were written, whether literary or political; yet just as significant is the carnival atmosphere – also a setting in several stories – which sees roles inverted and absurd humour proliferate madly. Thus, the writings of this third author conform a discursive space characterized by deviancy and deflection, exploring both literary and social structures, prevailing aesthetic trends, and forms of speech. Over many years, their partnership helped define the contours of Argentine literature, just as the new voice they created shaped theirs.

Notes

1. An exact date has yet to be established. In different interviews, Bioy variously states that it was 1935, 1936 or 1937.
2. N. Schejtman, 'El camino de Santiago', *Página 12, Radar*, 8 April 2007. Available online at www.pagina12.com.ar/diario/suplementos/radar/9–3730-2 007–04-09.html (accessed 21 September 2018).
3. Both anthologies were published by Editorial Sudamericana.
4. The early years of the Argentine state were marked by a bitter and violent power struggle between Unitarians and Federalists over the political and cultural constitution of the republic. The *caudillo* Juan Manuel de Rosas governed

the key Province of Buenos Aires on two separate occasions and wielded enormous control among Federalists in the period 1829–1852. Echeverría and Sarmiento expressed their staunch opposition through their respective representations of what they saw as *barbarie*. Over a century later, Perón was seen as Rosas's heir by both supporters and detractors.

CHAPTER 15

*Borges and Popular Culture**

Philip Swanson

The 'greatness' of Jorge Luis Borges is something of an invention of the 1960s and after, based on the reception of a relatively small body of work from the 1940s. Then his works came out in English and other languages. He won a string of high-profile international prizes; he enjoyed a series of honours and invitations to speak at prestigious world universities and cultural gatherings, and he was profiled in a range of media outlets. It was in this decade that 'Borges' was created: the cosmopolitan, erudite, philosophical but ingeniously playful weaver of cerebral, labyrinthine, and slippery narrative puzzles. Yet the focus of much of Borges's life and work is the popular or even the vulgar: the gaucho code; the exploits of Buenos Aires hoodlums; pirates, cowboys and gangsters; detective stories and other genre works; classical Hollywood movies; tangos; and so forth.

Borges's engagement with what is called popular culture is selective and ambiguous. Borges is tantalizingly 'in-between' or, as Beatriz Sarlo would put it, 'on the edge', in the shady yet alluring territory of the *orillas*.[1] The *orillas* is both a literal and imagined space. It refers to the edge of Buenos Aires in the early twentieth century, the frontier between the city and the *pampa*, the open countryside. By the 1920s, the romanticized rural past of nomadic *gauchos* and vast open spaces was being overtaken by the reality of modernity. The city limits or *suburbios* were characterized by Borges as streets without pavements or sidewalks on the other side: that is, facing the grasslands of the interior. Instead of the gaucho, here one would find his urban successor, the figure of the *compadrito*, a sort of wise-guy whose toughness and prowess with a knife became the stuff of legend. Base, tawdry creatures were glorified in tangos and in Borges's own works. Moreover, they were figures of the imagination as much as reality, if not

---

* This is a shortened version of an essay published in Edwin Williamson (ed.), *The Cambridge Companion to Jorge Luis Borges* (Cambridge: Cambridge University Press, 2013), pp. 81–95. My thanks to the Press for their permission to produce this version.

123

quite vanished then probably largely subsumed into everyday urban life by the time they were being written about. On top of this, Borges's fascination with these men lies alongside his tendency towards *criollismo*, an admiration for the values associated with a line of longstanding Argentine families untainted by immigrant blood. The identity of the *compadrito* is in reality fractured along these lines of purity and contamination, while the supposedly *criollo* rural past is as threatening as it is seductive. And the chubbyish sedentary man of letters, Borges, is about as far away from both as it is possible for an admirer to get. His affected *criollismo* was tempered by his attraction to the underworld of the slums and their lurid inhabitants, while his championing (initially at least) of literary experimentation and, later and to a lesser extent, literariness was matched by a fascination with tradition, the popular, and economy of expression. As the writer of the *orillas*, Borges invented a sort of new cultural nationalist myth for Argentina, but one which was far from straightforward, combining as it did a deep populism with a patrician distance.

Two important early manifestations of Borges's fascination with the Buenos Aires subculture are his 'biography' of Evaristo Carriego (1930) and his first book of 'stories', *A Universal History of Iniquity* (1935). Carriego (1883–1912) was a dissolute poet who fancied himself a pal of the *compadritos* and the toughest of them, the *guapos*. A young Borges became taken by Carriego's association with the shady local underworld. The first chapter of *Evaristo Carriego* is a rather romanticized contextualization of the poet, concentrating on the history of the old neighbourhood of Palermo and the tales of *compadritos* and *cuchilleros* (knife-fighters); Borges's prologue to the 1955 edition alludes to the imaginary nature of this history. Carriego is lionized as 'the first observer of our poorer neighbourhoods', but as such is both 'the discoverer' and 'the inventor'.[2] The implication is that he (and Borges) are creating a myth as much as recreating a reality. But this myth has meaning. Carriego comes to embody a strain of earthy authenticity, yet one still channelled via poetic imagination. What Borges seemed to see in him was the chance to renovate *criollismo* by creating a new poetics of the city rather than one of rural tradition, a modern myth for the new Argentina, based not just on the land and its lost *gaucho* inhabitants but in the concept of the *orillas*.

Borges's own seminal contribution to the legend of the *compadrito* would be his first real short story published in a book, 'Man on Pink Corner' from *A Universal History of Iniquity*. A Northside tough known as the Yardmaster, Francisco Real, bursts into a bar outside his territory and challenges the *guapo* Rosendo Juárez to a knife fight. Juárez refuses to fight and his disgusted moll, La Lujanera, goes off instead with the interloper. Later that night Real is stabbed to death by a stranger. The macho fighter is much deflated in death. As a bystander comments: 'Man thought so highly of himself, and all he's good for now is to draw flies' (*CF* 51). There is a tension between heroic fantasy and grubby reality, probably because Borges's experience of the underworld is largely through other sources, often cultural products like stories, poems, or songs. Behind much of Borges's mythology of the *arrabales* lies a fascination with *gauchos* and tango. The *compadrito* or *guapo* is really a semi-urban version of the rural cowboy or *gaucho*, a figure equally famed for his manliness and prowess with a knife. Yet by the 1930s, the *gaucho* was most definitely a phenomenon of the past, now only truly alive in any pure sense in literature and the public imagination.

Many of Borges's stories from the 1940s onwards feature gauchos and references to the great national literary epic on this theme, *The Gaucho Martín Fierro* (by José Hernández, 1872 and 1879). The point is that the sources are literary rather than real. Juan Dahlmann, the protagonist of Borges's most famous story on this theme, 'The South', from *Fictions*, is a clear echo of the author: a bookish, sedentary city-dweller with an heroic Argentine family line and a penchant for a cultivated *criollismo*. His journey to the south is presented as a journey deep into Argentina's rural past, but Dahlmann is compelled to recognize that 'his direct knowledge of the country was considerably inferior to his nostalgic, literary knowledge' (*CF* 177). Indeed, when he enters the dangerous store-cum-bar where he will be challenged to a duel to the death by a local and egged on by an old gaucho who 'seemed to be outside time'(*CF* 178), he is rather affectedly struck by its resemblance to an engraving from an old edition of the 1788 novel *Paul et Virginie*! His romanticized (fundamentally literary) vision of the past, then, in which he appears to imagine in his mind a dramatic and deeply 'Argentine' death in a knife fight, is really masking a crude history of mindless violence.

Borges's liminal world of the *orilla* is also echoed in the cult of the tango. The customers of the bar on 'Pink Corner' are dancing to the tunes of tangos and their prototypes, *milongas*. The tango is generally associated by Borges with the evocation of the exploits of the *guapos*. The nostalgic tone is evident in a poem from *The Self and the Other*, entitled, 'The tango'.[3] This poem presents itself as 'an elegy' that asks 'of those who are no more': 'Where can they be?' Recalling the motiveless machismo of *guapo* knife-fighters, the poem complains that 'a mythology of daggers' has today been replaced by the sordid realities of crime reports. Yet these distant 'heroes' somehow survive:

Today, beyond time and fateful
death, those dead men live on in the tango.

They are in the music, in the strings
of the obstinate, labouring guitar,
which insinuates into a spirited milonga
the celebration of innocence and courage.

The tango transcends time and allows the reader the sensation of effectively experiencing the heroics of the *compadrito*:

... The tango creates a hazy
unreal past which is in some sense true,
the impossible memory of having died
fighting on a street corner in the slums.

This perhaps gets close to the crux of Borges's relationship with the popular. His tales of the *compadritos* are the compensatory fantasies of an everyday modern man: the pleasure lies in the momentary identification of the reader with a dramatic or exciting life that he (or maybe she) will never live in reality.

Gauchos and lowlife city slickers, however, are probably not what international readers of the cosmopolitan 'Borges' would associate with the author. If such readers were to see a link with popular culture, it would probably be with the detective story and his rather cerebral reinvention of the genre. Borges is clearly an admirer of the genre per se. He reviewed vast numbers of detective novels and, together with his friend and collaborator Adolfo Bioy Casares (1914–1999), founded and directed a crime series called *El Séptimo Círculo* (The Seventh Circle). The appeal of the detective story for Borges is in part its classical construction and sense of order. Those readers who characterize Borges as a 'difficult' high modernist might do well to remember this: his stories, while in many ways complex, are usually linguistically straightforward and formally very tightly constructed. Even so, Borges does seem to favour the analytic detective, distanced and detached. The model for this detective is, of course, C. Auguste Dupin, the protagonist of what is widely regarded as the first ever detective story, Edgar Allan Poe's 'The Murders in the Rue Morgue' (1841). Borges's most famous detective story, 'Death and the Compass' (from *Fictions*) features the ace gentleman-amateur sleuth Erik Lönnrot, 'who thought of himself as a reasoning machine, an Auguste Dupin'. However, the sentence continues: 'but there was something of the adventurer in him, even something of the gambler' (*CF* 147). Hence, the supposedly analytic detective gets his comeuppance. Lönnrot's Sherlock Holmes-like rationality actually leads him into an elaborately laid trap plotted by his arch enemy Red Scharlach. The story ends with the undermining of the analytical explanation of the mystery and the murder of the detective.

Together with Bioy Casares, Borges also created the detective Isidro Parodi, who appeared most famously in *Six Problems for Don Isidro Parodi* (1942) written under the pseudonym of H. (Honorio) Bustos Domecq (the characters from these stories would reappear in 1946 in the novella *Un modelo para la muerte* [*A Model for Death*], written by the pair under the nom de plume of B. [Benito] Suárez Lynch). The detective figure, as his surname implies, is a parody, and his character and adventures grew out of Borges's and Bioy's regular evenings of chatting and joking in the latter's home. Parodi, a former barber from Barracas in the Southside of Buenos Aires, languishes in the city penitentiary having been framed for the gang murder of an Italian butcher felled by a blow from a seltzer bottle. He sits in his prison room and solves, with thought alone (like a less salubrious August Dupin), the absurd mysteries told to him by a cavalcade of eccentric visitors to the now celebrated Cell Number 273. Nods to the foreign classic detective genre abound, but the stories are, in fact, exaggeratedly colourful and linguistically playful, offering the reader a gallery of rogues who unintentionally effect a pretty wide-ranging satire on contemporary Argentina. The resolution of the mysteries is really at the service of this humorous social satire, the apparently elaborate riddles all being reduced in the end to rather mundane examples of venal motivation. In the opening story, for instance, the baffling tale of a secret 'Druse' sect and their obsession with the signs of the zodiac turns out to be a prosaic case of embezzlement and arson (one red herring is an overheard discussion about books: rather than a literary debate, it transpires that it is an argument over a firm's ledger containing fiddled accounts!). However, Parodi's power as a character possibly lies in his unreal nature. Though his name and some other references might suggest immigrant roots, his values and comments link him, despite his humble background, to a species of Argentine tradition. It is through time in prison that Parodi 'had become an old established Argentine':[4] confined to his cell, he lives outside of time and inhabits another kind of *orilla*, therefore embodying a kind of ideal Borgesian Argentine identity aware of but relatively uncontaminated by the onward march of urban modernity.

One aspect of modernity and popular culture that Borges does seem to embrace from early on is the cinema. Borges and Bioy Casares collaborated on a number of screenplays, and Borges's career as a prolific film reviewer suggests a preference for westerns, gangster movies, and classical Hollywood cinema rather than the art-house variety. Borges appears to appreciate the formal simplicity of such movies. This is reflected in his own writing of fiction, which, albeit often subversively, uses genres, employs strict narrative forms, and even imitates the technique of cinematic montage. This cinematic style is probably most transparent in the early stories of *A Universal History of Iniquity*. What feels like a cut to the cat next to the protagonist's dead body in the final scene of 'Monk Eastman, Purveyor of Iniquities' is like a piece of classical editing for effect, while the opening of 'The Disinterested Killer Bill Harrigan' offers the reader-cum-viewer a pair of images in which the narrative cuts from an establishing shot of the arid Arizona landscape to one of Billy the Kid, the rider seated on his horse. But the technique is also present in the more technically complex mature stories: one has but to think, for instance, of the cuts, as in a montage sequence, that characterize the more dramatic moments of a tale like 'The Garden of Forking Paths' from *Fictions* or 'Emma Zunz' from *The Aleph*.

However, perhaps the most interesting aspect of Borges's relation to cinema is the question of his role in it, his 'influence' on it. There have been a number of Argentine and other Latin American adaptations of Borges's stories, though the best-received high-cultural translation to the screen is Bernardo Bertolucci's meditation on the fluidity of identity, *The Spider's Stratagem* (1970), based on 'Theme of the Traitor and the Hero' from *Fictions*. A particularly satisfying adaptation is Alex Cox's garish punk fantasy from 1996, *Death and the Compass*. Steeped in the imagery of 1980s pop culture, the movie, nonetheless, does not shirk complexity and shows considerable familiarity with Borges's literary universe. There are a series of clever embedded allusions to other stories and a cameo featuring a blind detective called Comandante Borges (played by Cox himself in a witty auteurist nod), whose actions are said to set in chain events that would come to envelop everyone – a fairly clear reference to Borges's concepts of interlinked destinies and intertextuality avant la lettre. Of note too is the notorious homage in Nicolas Roeg and Donald Cammell's dark, labyrinthine, swinging-sixties romp through identity crisis, *Performance* (made in 1968, but released in 1970), starring Mick Jagger and featuring various allusions to Borges, including a more-than-subliminal on-screen shot of him during a peculiar montage sequence. A cheekier insertion comes in Jean-Jacques Annaud's 1986 film, *The Name of the Rose* (after, of course, Umberto Eco's 1980 novel) in which the key to a very Borgesean murder mystery is revealed to lie with the blind old librarian, the venerable Jorge de Burgos! There is, moreover, almost certainly a surfeit of less clearly identifiable Borgesean connections in a whole range of popular as well as art-house movies. For example, Martin Scorsese's *Gangs of New York* (2002) echoes Borges's Monk Eastman story. One can surely also identify traces of Borges in a whole host of mainstream Hollywood movies. David Fincher's *Seven* (1995) or Bryan Singer's *The Usual Suspects* from the same year, with their twist-endings revealing the villain's secret scheme, are reminiscent of 'Death and the Compass', while Steven Spielberg's first feature, TV movie *Duel* (1971), with its story of a city man imperilled in an alluring yet terrifying landscape of the interior, complete with a tense scene involving urban visitor and rural folk in a roadside diner, is remarkably similar to 'The South'.

Such an intertextual understanding of cultural production would actually chime perfectly with Borges's own poetic creed. In his 'Ars Poetica', from *The Maker* (1960), he casts a poem in the light of, presumably, Heraclitus's river (always the same yet always different) and observes that poetry is 'immortal and poor'.[5] Originality is a form of reproduction, then, and identities and images repeat themselves endlessly throughout time and culture. 'Borges' continues to exist in culture in all sorts of seen and unseen ways and has even penetrated the everyday life of the popular. At the end of 'Death and the Compass', Lönnrot asks Scharlach to employ an alternative labyrinth with which to snare him 'when you hunt me down in another avatar of our lives' (*CF* 156). One suspects that, in another incarnation, Borges might not be just the purveyor of puzzling literary-philosophical abstractions, but perhaps a man of popular pleasures and actions, that Borges might be not just one of an elite, but a man of the people, one of the boys. In another life, Borges would be a *compadre*.

Notes

1. Beatriz Sarlo, *Jorge Luis Borges: A Writer on the Edge* (London: Verso, 1993).
2. Jorge Luis Borges, *Evaristo Carriego* (New York: Dutton, 1984), p. 105.
3. The translations of this poem are my own. For the original, see Jorge Luis Borges, *Obra poética 1923–1976* (Madrid: Alianza, 1979), pp. 209–211.
4. Jorge Luis Borges and Adolfo Bioy Casares, *Six Problems for Don Isidro Parodi* (London: Penguin, 1981), p. 109.
5. Jorge Luis Borges, *Selected Poems* (New York: Viking, 1999), p. 147.

CHAPTER 16

Argentine Responses: César Aira and Ricardo Piglia

Niall H D Geraghty

Anxiety, Tradition, and Argentine Talent

The other man dreamed me, but did not dream me rigorously.[1]

Jorge Luis Borges

When one considers twentieth-century Argentine literature post-1940, it is tempting to assert that all writers in this period have found themselves trapped in Borges's labyrinth. Certainly, the authors under discussion in this chapter, César Aira and Ricardo Piglia, seem to suffer from what Harold Bloom has denominated the 'anxiety of influence', that approach to literary tradition (based, in part, on Freud's conception of filial rivalry with the father) whereby a writer struggles to overcome their literary forebears.[2] For his part, Aira has specifically stated that Borges 'was a kind of paternal shadow that dominated all twentieth-century literature',[3] while Piglia (who engaged extensively with Borges throughout his literary and critical output) has even suggested that Borges was 'the best Argentine writer of the 19th Century'.[4] Moreover, where Bloom asserts that 'poetic influence [. . .] always proceeds by a misreading [. . .], an act of creative correction that is actually and necessarily a misinterpretation',[5] Piglia derives a similar theory from Borges's 'deliberate inclination to read badly',[6] and Aira also contends that 'misunderstanding is an important part of literature'.[7] As Piglia's argument suggests, this conception of Argentine literary tradition can be directly linked with Borges. As Bloom has argued, Borges 'is a great theorist of poetic influence' and 'the pattern of his tales betrays throughout an implicit dread of family-romance'.[8] More than this, however, in texts such as 'The Argentine Writer and Tradition' (1951), Borges consciously engages the work of T.S. Eliot to lay the foundation for a new Argentine literary tradition and ensure his place within it. In turn, I would suggest that both Aira and Piglia engage with Borges in a similar manner in order both to modify and write themselves into this same literary tradition.

While Aira and Piglia have become two of the most important figures in contemporary Argentine literature, it is important to note that their literary endeavours are frequently considered to be opposed and irreconcilable. This idea is largely derived from a critical essay written by Aira which declared that Piglia's *Artificial Respiration* (1980) was 'one of the worst novels of his generation' and that Piglia represented 'a lack of authentic passion for literature in contemporary Argentine fiction'.[9] The conflict between the two authors is also echoed in their relationship with Borges: both writers came to prominence while Borges was rejected by important sectors of the literary establishment, Piglia conscientiously attempted to counteract this tendency in the 1960s and 1970s, while Aira was one of its key advocates in the 1980s. Nonetheless Aira has recently suggested that all his work could be considered 'a footnote to Borges',[10] and I intend to demonstrate that each author's intentional misreading of Borges provides one way in which their work can be reconciled.[11]

Borges and Piglia

Intrapoetic relations are neither commerce nor theft, unless you can conceive of family romance as a politics of commerce.[12]

Harold Bloom

From the outset of his career Piglia conscientiously sought to re-write Argentine literary history by re-examining Borges's work. This is somewhat surprising given that, when Piglia first came to prominence in the 1960s, he was part of a new left-wing intellectual movement which derided Borges for his perceived conservatism, a situation which worsened in the 1970s when Borges publicly defended military governments in Chile and Argentina. Piglia's writings on Borges were composed over the breadth of his career, culminating in the four-part television series 'Borges by Piglia' (2013) which effectively synthesized his main arguments. It is remarkable, however, that Piglia defined these theses very early in his career and gradually refined them over the course of his life. For this reason, they can be most clearly seen by revisiting some of these early texts.

Although its title would suggest otherwise, one of Piglia's most important reappraisals of Borges's work is found in his short story 'Homage to Roberto Arlt' (1975). The text purports to be a critical introduction to a previously unpublished 'Arlt' story which Piglia claims to have discovered, but which is, in fact, a plagiarized copy of 'Darkness' by Leonid Andreyev. The subterfuge was so effective that for a time the story was catalogued as Arlt's in several international libraries. Crucially, the conception of plagiarism as a creative endeavour creates a strong link to Borges's story 'Pierre Menard, Author of the *Quixote*' (1939), in which the eponymous writer sets out exactly to reproduce Cervantes's text some 300 years after his demise. Just as Menard's act of plagiarism significantly alters the reception of Cervantes's text, so, too, Piglia's story radically altered the perception of Borges for his contemporary readers. Ellen McCracken succinctly captures this political reappropriation of Borges when she notes that, in 'Homage to Roberto Arlt', 'plagiarism is not a moral or literary problem but an economic one because it violates the laws of private property' which underpin contemporary capitalism.[13] In the essay 'Ideology and Fiction in Borges' (1979), Piglia extends this critique further still. In this text Piglia, much like Bloom, pays particular attention to the family drama which motivates Borges's literature. As Borges is the product of a union between a mother descended from the heroes of the conquest and foundation of Argentina and a father linked to English literature and culture, Piglia applies the conception of dialectical materialism to Borges's writing and proposes that its ideology is expressed through the tension between 'culture and class [that] are linked with inheritance and lineage'.[14] As Graciela Speranza notes, with these two texts Piglia thus 'definitively recovers Borges for the left'.[15] Furthermore, Piglia later uses this critique to redefine Argentine literary tradition.

In an essay comparing the work of Borges with that of Polish émigré Witold Gombrowicz, Piglia returns to Borges's argument in 'The Argentine Writer and Tradition' that writers within peripheral cultures are free to make irreverent use of European tradition, as exemplified by Irish and Jewish cultural history. For Piglia, Borges achieves this goal through 'the mechanisms of falsification, the temptation of theft, translation as plagiarism, mixing, the combination of registers [and] the confusion of affiliations', which he proposes are the essence of Argentine literary history.[16] When Piglia revisits the topic in his novel *Artificial Respiration*, he traces this conception of tradition to Domingo Faustino Sarmiento's erroneous attribution of the epigraph which opens *Facundo: Civilization and Barbarism* (1845).[17] Thus Piglia employs the same strategy as Borges in 'Kafka and His Precursors' (1951) to delineate his argument. Just as Borges proposed that Kafka redefined and thus created his own literary forebears, Piglia traces Borges's idiosyncrasy through the work of Arlt, Gombrowicz, and Sarmiento to redefine Argentine literary tradition. Moreover, Piglia utilizes this misreading of Borges to politicize his work and situate himself as Borges's true descendant.

Borges and Aira

To search for what you already are is the most benighted of quests, and the most fated.[18]

Harold Bloom

Unlike Piglia, Aira has openly admitted that he experienced a 'militantly anti-Borgesian phase'.[19] This antipathy is most fully expressed in his essay 'Exoticism' (1993) which specifically rejects the central thesis of 'The Argentine Writer and Tradition'. Where Borges famously cites the absence of camels in the Koran to argue against the use of 'local colour' in Argentine writing, Aira instead advocates the profusion of such elements and the adoption of a stereotypical style as a method through which 'a Brazilian becomes Brazilian, an Argentine, Argentine' and thus rediscovers their national identity.[20] As Bloom would recognize, an author who explicitly rejects another writer's work is paradoxically bound to their adversary. Indeed, as I will go on to argue, Aira's rejection of Borges may not be as absolute as it first appears.

In articulating his arguments against the inclusion of 'local colour' in Argentine literature, Borges first argues that the *gauchesco* literature prevalent in his time is not a tradition but rather a genre.[21] Within his essay, Aira situates the 'local colour' ubiquitous in *guachesco* literature within a wider analysis of what he calls the 'exotic' genre. From this simple opening, a rapprochement between Aira and Borges begins to crystallize. It is notable, for example, that Borges's praise of foreign elements in the work of Enrique Banchs, and his argument that Argentine writers 'can take on all the European subjects',[22] are readily identified in the work of Aira. In the first instance, Aira fills his historical novels such as *Ema, the Captive* (1981) and *The Hare* (1991) with exotic, foreign, and implausible elements. It is also inescapable that Aira consistently frames his wider literary process within the context of a largely international avant-garde, almost as if he directly takes up Borges's challenge. These simple parallels are the first indication that the use of stereotype advocated by Aira may not be entirely alien to Borges, and that his critique may be somewhat disingenuous. A review of an essay authored by Aira some 12 years prior to his denunciation of Borges, only deepens this suspicion.

In 'Who Is the Greatest Argentine Writer?' (1981) Aira reassesses Argentine literary history as a minor tradition. Not only does Aira argue that Borges is paradigmatic of this approach, but he also proposes that 'the Borgesian device may be the best tool to reactivate our literary history' and that Borges's biography of the minor poet Evaristo Carriego (1930) 'could serve as a manual for this revitalization'.[23] Not only is Carriego a poet of the typical Argentine *barrio* whose verse is filled with somewhat stereotypical 'local colour', but Borges's biography is most famous for its lack of discussion of the poet's life and work. Instead, Borges dedicates chapters to specific images of Argentine cultural tradition such as the history of tango, the card-game *truco*, the horsemen of the pampa and, that quintessential Borgesian object, the dagger. This is to say that Borges's work is replete with the romanticized 'local colour' which Borges later rejects and Aira recovers. Even Aira's paradoxical argument that stereotypical images can become the means by which an Argentine can become Argentine seems to be echoed in Borges's personification of the dagger which 'wants to kill, [. . .] wants to shed blood' and ultimately wants to becomes a dagger'.[24] This is to say that Aira redis-covers the techniques utilized by the youthful Borges as a means to overcome his more mature position and cement his own place in Argentine literary history. Moreover, Aira's reclamation provides a possible method of unifying his work with that of Piglia, as we shall now see.

The Transmigration of Borges's Soul

> To think is to ignore (or forget) differences, to generalize, to abstract.
> Jorge Luis Borges (*CF* 137)

Borges appears as the narrator of his short story 'The Other'. Ageing, almost blind, he sits on the banks of a river and encounters his younger self. The two men debate and disagree on various topics and the narrator laments that 'beneath our conversation, the conversation of two men of miscellaneous readings and diverse tastes, I realized that we would not find common ground. We were too different, yet too alike. [. . .] Each of us was almost a caricature of the other' (*CF* 416). The story concludes with the narrator's realization that he is the imprecise dream of his younger self. As we have already seen, in 'Kafka and His Precursors' Borges hypothesizes that a writer creates their own literary antecedents and thus rewrites literary history. This thesis is echoed by Bloom, who argues that a writer strives to 'achieve a style that captures and oddly retains priority over their precur-sors, so that the tyranny of time almost is overturned, and one can believe, for startled moments, that they are being *imitated by their ancestors*'.[25] Similarly, Eliot argues that within a given literary tradition the 'most individual parts' of a writer's work are 'those in which the dead poets, his ancestors, assert their immortality most vigorously'.[26] I would now suggest that these four texts constitute the cardinal points necessary to navigate the relationship between Borges, Aira, and Piglia.

As we have seen, in Aira's 'Exoticism' he positions himself as the precursor to the author of 'The Argentine Writer and Tradition' such that that later Borges becomes Aira's imperfect illusion, just as Aira becomes Borges's younger self. Thus Aira's misreading of Borges re-orientates the trajectory of Argentine literary tradition and situates Aira as both heir and antecessor of Borges's theory. Regarding Piglia, it is important to remember that in 'The Other', the young Borges discloses to his older self that he is composing a book of verse entitled *Red Anthems* which will 'be a hymn to the brotherhood of all mankind' and will 'address the great oppressed and outcast masses' (*CF* 416). These political views are derided by Borges the narrator, but it is this same legacy which Piglia strives to uncover in the writings of the mature Borges. Once more, Piglia follows the logic of 'Kafka and His Precursors' to re-create a political Borges, redirecting Argentine literary history and setting himself as both forebear and inheritor of Borges's legacy. Reflecting on Borges's story 'Shakespeare's Memory', in which the narrator literally receives the personal recollections of his illustrious predecessor, Piglia argues that 'literary tradition has the structure of a dream in which one receives the recollections of a dead poet'.[27] With this in mind, it seems that both Aira and Piglia receive the memory of a young Borges, use it to mark their difference from Borges himself, and thus claim their rightful place in Argentine literary history. And from this vantage point, further parallels between the work of Aira and Piglia begin to emerge. One is reminded, for example, that Aira specifically praises the poet Alejandra Pizarnik for her wilful plagiarism – the very basis of Piglia's misreading of Borges's conception of Argentine literary history – which is also echoed in Aira's consistent reference to the model of the *ready-made* in his theoretical writings.[28] And just as Piglia applies the Marxist conception of history to Borges's family ancestry, so, too, in his critique of Borges, Aira delineates the manner in which the 'exotic' genre has followed the history of capitalist expansion.[29] All this is to say that by viewing the relationship between Aira and Piglia through their respective misreading of Borges, they come rather to resemble each other, like two theologians debating the transmigration of souls.[30]

Notes

1. Jorge Luis Borges, 'The Other', in *Collected Fictions*, pp. 411–417 (p. 417).
2. Harold Bloom, *The Anxiety of Influence: A Theory of Poetry* (New York: Oxford University Press, 1997).

3. Carlos Alfieri and César Aira, *Conversaciones, entrevistas con César Aira, Guillermo Cabrera Infante, Roger Chartier, Antonio Muñoz Molina, Ricardo Piglia, y Fernando Savater* (Madrid: Katz, 2008), p. 30. Unless another work is cited, all translations are the author's own.
4. Ricardo Piglia, *Respiración artificial* (Barcelona: Anagrama, 2008), p. 130.
5. Bloom, *The Anxiety of Influence*, p. 30.
6. Ricardo Piglia, *El último lector* (Buenos Aires: Debolsillo, 2014), p. 25.
7. Luis Dapelo and César Aira, 'César Aira', *Hispamérica*, 36 (2007), pp. 41–53 (p. 49).
8. Harold Bloom, 'Introduction', in *Jorge Luis Borges*, ed. Harold Bloom (New York: Chelsea House, 1986), pp. 1–3 (pp. 2–3).
9. César Aira, 'Novela argentina, nada más que una idea', *Vigencia*, 51 (1981), pp. 55–58 (p. 58).
10. Alena Graedon, 'César Aira's Infinite Footnote to Borges', *The New Yorker* (27 January 2017).
11. Conscious of the phallocentric nature of Bloom's conception of literary history, I approach this task much as Deleuze approached the giants of the history of philosophy, from behind in the hope of a conception, monstrous, or immaculate as the reader prefers. Brian Massumi, *A User's Guide to Capitalism and Schizophrenia: Deviations from Deleuze and Guatarri* (Cambridge, MA: MIT Press, 1992), p. 2.
12. Bloom, *The Anxiety of Influence*, p. 78.
13. Ellen McCracken, 'Metaplagiarism and the Critic's Role as Detective, Ricardo Piglia's Reinvention of Roberto Arlt', *PMLA*, 106 (1991), pp. 1071–1082 (p. 1077).
14. Ricardo Piglia, 'Ideología y ficción en Borges', *Punto de Vista*, 2 (1979), pp. 3–6 (p. 5).
15. Graciela Speranza, *Fuera de campo: literatura y arte argentinos después de Duchamp* (Barcelona: Anagrama, 2006), p. 266.
16. Ricardo Piglia, 'La novela polaca', in *Formas breves* (Barcelona: Anagrama, 2000), pp. 69–80 (p. 73).
17. Piglia, *Respiración artificial*, p. 131.
18. Bloom, *The Anxiety of Influence*, p. 13.
19. Alfieri and Aira, *Conversaciones*, p. 31.
20. César Aira, 'Exotismo', *Boletín del grupo de estudios de teoría literaria*, 3 (1993), pp. 73–79 (p. 79).
21. Jorge Luis Borges, 'The Argentine Writer and Tradition', *TTL*, 420–427 (421).
22. *Ibid.*, pp. 423, 426.
23. César Aira, '¿Quién es el más grande de los escritores argentinos?', *Vigencia*, 53 (1981), pp. 84–85 (p. 85).
24. Jorge Luis Borges, *Evaristo Carriego, A Book About Old-Time Buenos Aires*, trans. Norman Thomas di Giovanni and Susan Ashe (New York: E.P. Dutton, 1984), pp. 126–127.
25. Bloom, *The Anxiety of Influence*, p. 141.

26. T.S. Eliot, 'Tradition and the Individual Talent', in *Selected Essays, 1917–1932* (New York: Harcourt, Brace and Company, 1932), pp. 3–11 (pp. 3–4).
27. Ricardo Piglia, 'El último cuento de Borges', in *Formas breves* (Barcelona: Anagrama, 2000), pp. 47–54 (p. 53).
28. César Aira, *Alejandra Pizarnik* (Rosario: Beatriz Viterbo, 1998), 53, pp. 79–80.
29. Aira, 'Exotismo', pp. 74–75.
30. Borges, 'The Theologians', in *Collected Fictions*, pp. 201–207.

PART II

The Western Canon, the East, Contexts of Reception

CHAPTER 17

Borges and Cervantes

Roberto González Echevarría

Miguel de Cervantes was a lifelong obsession for Borges. He wrote essays, stories, poems, and brief notes about the author of *Don Quijote* (who was born in 1547 and died in 1616) and about the novel (which was published in two parts, in 1605 and 1615) and its protagonist. I believe that this obsession was due to two factors. The first is that *Don Quijote* makes manifest issues about literary creation akin to those that Borges always returned to, and that Cervantes's novels took such questions as far as Borges himself would take them. In matters of literary speculation Borges could not get past or around Cervantes. This, it seems to me, vexed him in a productive way, as the essays, poems, notes, and particularly the story, 'Pierre Menard, autor del *Quijote*', reveal. The second factor is Borges's conflictive relationship with Spanish literature, about which he held, like many Latin Americans, a guarded opinion. His reservations were exacerbated by the presence of many Spaniards in Buenos Aires during his lifetime – everyday immigrants as well as writers and intellectuals. The crux of the matter would ultimately be rights over the Spanish language itself. Towards the end of his career and probably reflecting it, Cervantes and his novel serve Borges as a paradigm of literary creation, particularly his own, and he displays a more unabashedly romantic approach to the Spanish author and his own work than previously.

The indefinability of the author is a favourite topic of Borges, which was accompanied by a self-effacing Socratic posture of radical doubt that was disconcerting to others. It was an unsettling position that took the form of an engaging modesty but was really a subtle and effective form of self-assertion. Cervantes provided Borges with a ready-made formula for this ruse by the series of varied author figures that he includes in *Don Quijote*. This baffling strategy is introduced from the very beginning in the hilarious prologue to Part One (1605), where Cervantes claims to be at a loss about how to write it. He then tells a story about his conundrum in which a friend appears to help him overcome it. The friend allegedly tells him to stop fretting about precursors and antecedents, to make up a list of bogus sources for his book, and to dispense with previous traditions, as *Don Quijote* was heir to none. This is a claim of radical originality disguised as modesty. The telling of this tale becomes the prologue itself, which turns into a protracted speech act full of irony and good humour. Borges probably wished that he had written this stupendous piece of literary gamesmanship.

The layers of storytelling and their respective authors that Cervantes claims for his novel are themselves a considerable feat. He, the chief creator figure, avers not to be the author of *Don Quijote*, but rather an editor and transcriber. The original author was presumably one Cide Hamete Benengeli, a Moorish historian who wrote it, naturally, in his native tongue, and had a penchant for lying, the same as all Moors, according to the narrator. How the Cervantes in the novel got the text of the first eight chapters, presumably in Spanish, is never made clear. But in chapter 8 of *Don Quijote*, in the midst of a fierce battle between his protagonist and a Basque man, the narrator astonishingly alleges to have come to the end of the manuscript. In the next chapter of *Don Quijote*, he tells the story of how, by chance, he found some papers at a market in Toledo that, though in Arabic, which he could not read, he managed to glean contained the balance of Don Quijote's adventures. He secures the services of a *morisco*, a fellow of Moorish origin and bilingual, to translate it for him. This translation into Spanish is what we supposedly read, with occasional editorial comments by the original narrator, presumably Cervantes, and by the translator. In Part Two (1615), this situation is complicated when Don Quijote and Sancho meet other characters who have read Part One and expect them to act as they did in Part One. Several of these characters, particularly a university graduate called Sansón Carrasco, and the butler of a duke in whose country house Don Quijote and Sancho stay, script episodes for the pair, thus becoming internal authors of *Don Quijote*.

Other highly self-reflexive episodes in Part Two are Don Quijote's visit to a printing shop in Barcelona where an apocryphal *Don Quijote* is being produced, and Altisidora's dream, in which the young woman claims that while in hell, where she has gone after her (mock) death, she saw a number of devils playing a kind of tennis using books as balls, which they strike with flaming rackets. It is difficult to imagine a more outlandish representation of literature as something transformed into material objects, created independently of a given author. No modern writer even comes close, not even Borges.

This is where matters stood when Borges decided to write 'Pierre Menard, Author of *Don Quixote*', a dizzying story that is his principal reading of Cervantes's work as well as the most famous. Menard is a symbolist poet from Nîmes, author of modest works of both poetry and prose, who has recently died when the story begins. Borges's text is a kind of obituary and a corrective account of previous, incomplete versions of Menard's accomplishments written by one of his admirers; the narrator is an anti-Semitic intellectual of dubious standing. Among Menard's publications, other than poems that the narrator esteems, there are translations and literary games such as a rendition of Paul Valéry's 'Le cimitière marin' in alexandrine lines, as well as essays on chess and abstract philosophical questions. These predispositions explain Menard's most ambitious project, which constitutes the core of the story: to rewrite *Don Quijote*. It was never his aim to write a new *Don Quijote*, but to *rewrite*, word for word and line by line, the original. Menard was aware of the insurmountable difficulties of such a task: to become Cervantes he would have to master Golden Age Spanish, regain his Catholic faith, and forget European history between the end of the sixteenth and the beginning of the twentieth centuries. Menard is playing with the subversion of canonical literary history, by considering a deployment of works oblivious to chronology (the *Odyssey* after the *Aeneid*), anachronistic and erroneous attributions, like making *The Imitation of Christ* a book by Louis Ferdinand Céline. These are radical ideas about literary criticism that some enthusiasts have attributed to Borges; but he never practised any of them, and one must remember that they are evoked by the biased narrator.

Of the fragments of *Don Quijote* produced by Menard, Borges concentrates on one in which history is made out to be the 'mother of truth', a statement that he avers may have been acceptable in the seventeenth century but is ludicrous in the twentieth. It reads: 'la verdad, cuya madre es la historia, émula del tiempo, depósito de las acciones, testigo de lo pasado, ejemplo y aviso de lo presente, advertencia de lo por venir' (John Rutherford translates: 'truth, whose mother is history: the imitator of time, the storehouse of actions and the witness to the past, an example and a lesson to the present and a warning to the future').[1] The prank here is that the passage is quoted twice, the first as it appears in *Don Quijote*, and the second, verbatim, as (re)produced by Menard. But Borges or the narrator overlooks the fact that, in *Don Quijote*, this text is meant ironically, not as an expression of the truth or the beliefs of the author. And which author, anyway? It is part of a mock harangue by the narrator of *Don Quijote* to historians, urging them to be truthful while lamenting that Cide

Hamete Benengeli, who, being an Arab, was an enemy of Spain, probably played down Don Quijote's greatness for spite. It is indeed difficult to get around Cervantes's infinitely receding sequence of ironies.

A corollary to Menard's project is that the self of the author can be constructed because it is essentially made up of the texts handed down by tradition, which constitute an impersonal lot. This is a classical conception of the author contrary to a romantic one that would emphasize a creator's personal expression. Borges lays out this dichotomy in his essay, 'The Postulation of Reality' (*TTL* 59–64), in which he quotes a fragment of *Don Quijote* as an example of the classical style. We are dealing here with a favourite topic in Borges, who invokes it regarding himself most famously in 'Borges and I', in which he presumably dissolves behind a multiplicity of Borgeses, a highly ironic text that is essentially a sophisticated literary joke. Borges knew who and what he was. In 'Pierre Menard, Author of the *Quixote*' (and other writings), such a position leads to a contradiction. Menard's story, told posthumously by his admirer, is about a supreme effort to accomplish a task that the character knows to be impossible. Menard is an anguished romantic protagonist who dies from the strain of trying to become Cervantes. This romantic substratum, which Borges would have probably disavowed, is very evident throughout his entire work, however; Funes is another such tormented protagonist. Besides, there is no lack of authorial identification in Borges's invention of Menard, who is (to me) an obvious autobiographical character.

In 'Pierre Menard, Author of the *Quixote*', Borges does not miss the opportunity to mock Spanish celebrations of Cervantes. Although faced with the contemporary reality of a folkloric Spain as portrayed in the opera *Carmen*, Menard tries to represent the Spain of the time of Lepanto. Hence the narrator rejoices in that Menard did not allow himself the *españoladas* in which a Maurice Barrès or a Rodríguez Larreta would have certainly indulged.[2] (Barrès, a French writer, was a fervent nationalist, and Enrique Rodríguez Larreta, an Argentine, published *La Gloria de Don Ramiro*, a novel composed in imitation of Golden Age Spanish, a project that may have inspired Borges to write his story). We Latin Americans know well what these *españoladas* are like: kitschy self-serving exultations of 'Spanishness' that favour the folkloric – gypsies, castanets, and tambourines.

Argentina, a large, increasingly prosperous country to which many Spanish and other European immigrants had flocked during the nineteenth century, had by the time of Borges's birth in 1899, acquired an economic and cultural autonomy to which its geographic remoteness contributed no small measure. This situation led to cultural relations with Spain based on a shared past and a common language; but they were strained. As in the rest of Latin America, most recent Spanish immigrants were from the lower classes, not a few from regions of the Peninsula in which Spanish was not spoken, so they spoke it poorly. Besides the cultural conflict, there was a class prejudice in how everyday Argentinians (and Latin Americans in general) viewed Spaniards. To this must be added the condescending paternalism that Spanish institutions, created by the Madrid government to promote Spain, exhibited in their programmes. Argentine writers and intellectuals resented this, which is evident in the quip about *españoladas*.

Cervantes became a bone of contention in this conflict because the author of *Don Quijote* had figured prominently in formulations of Spanish identity from the beginning of the nineteenth century. Since Romanticism, Cervantes was promoted as the purest manifestation of the Spanish language and spirit. This nationalistic ideology intensified after Spain's crushing defeat by the United States in the Spanish American War. The Spanish writers of the so-called 'Generation of '98', who gained prominence in the wake of that event (Azorín, Unamuno, Maeztu, and others), devoted themselves to the exaltation and study of Cervantes and his works. Among their books we find Unamuno's *Vida de don Quijote y Sancho* (1905), Azorín's *La ruta de don Quijote* (1905), Maeztu's *Don Quijote, Don Juan y la Celestina* and, somewhat later, *Meditaciones del Quijote* (1914) by the philosopher José Ortega y Gasset. This trend increased as time went on, encouraged and subsidized by the Spanish government. Menard's story, as created by Borges, is in part a reaction to it.

Two events linked fortuitously to intensify Spanish interest and promotion of Cervantes during Borges's lifetime: Franco's victory in the Civil War and the 400th anniversary of Cervantes's birth in 1947. Franco's regime promoted *Hispanidad*, Spanishness, and what could be more Spanish than *Don Quijote*? But his policies found resistance in Buenos Aires, where many Republican exiles, writers and intellectuals among them, had found refuge. To complicate matters even more, the emerging Peronist regime in Argentina supported the Spanish dictatorship. This situation made for a lively kind of *cervantismo* in the River Plate. Borges was in the midst of it. A massive eleven-volume edition of the *Quijote* by Francisco Rodríguez Marín appeared in 1947–1949, and Joaquín Casalduero published his influential *Sentido y forma del Quijote* in 1949. Special issues of important Buenos Aires journals like *Sur* and *Realidad* were devoted to Cervantes. It would seem that a shared value would be found in *Don Quijote* to quell the discord. The only agreement, however, was about Cervantes's greatness and the tacit understanding that his novel represented the essence and very best of the Spanish language.

Borges threw a wet blanket over all of this. To begin with, he opposed both Franco and Perón, being a lifelong opponent of dictatorial regimes. He was also against the facile, nationalistic and ultimately fascistic linking of language, culture, and politics. He found the sycophantic commentaries on *Don Quijote* naive and self-serving, and he ridiculed the celebratory activities, including the 'obscenas ediciones de lujo' ('obscene deluxe editions' *OC*, 450) of the novel, as one reads in 'Pierre Menard, Author of the *Quixote*'. Borges did not find Cervantes's prose so perfect that it deserved imitation, and he considered the Spain that he depicted to be unworthy of praise. He writes, in a note prefacing an edition of the *Novelas ejemplares*: 'Juzgado por los preceptos de la retórica, no hay estilo más deficiente que el de Cervantes. Abunda en repeticiones, en languideces, en hiatos, en errores de construcción, en ociosos o perjudiciales epítetos, en cambio de propósito. A todos ellos los anula o los atempera cierto encanto esencial'[3] ('Judged by the standards of rhetoric, there is no style more deficient than Cervantes's. It is full of repetitions, listlessness, hiatuses, errors in grammar, useless or detrimental epithets, and deviations in purpose. They are all annulled or minimized by a certain essential charm'). Cervantes, Borges maintained, portrayed a provincial, sordid region of Spain that he contrasted to the idealized settings of the romances of chivalry that he was parodying. He thought it ludicrous that turn-of-the-century Spanish writers like those mentioned would long for such a country. It seemed to Borges that criticism that engaged in such nationalism overlooked the more important features of *Don Quijote*, which included its self-referential cast and the elusive figure of Cervantes himself.

A high point of this debate was the withering review that Borges published of a book by Américo Castro, a leading scholar of Spanish literature and of Cervantes who had also spent time in the 1920s in Argentina as the first director of the Instituto de Filología, an institution promoting the Spanish language that predated the Franco regime. Castro had dared to publish in 1941 a book, titled *La peculiaridad lingüística rioplatense y su sentido histórico* (Buenos Aires: Losada), in which – not without some paternalism – he examined and passed judgement on the way Argentines spoke and (some) wrote Spanish; Argentine Spanish is indeed unusual even to other Latin Americans, not just to Spaniards, we might add. This is not all there is to the book, which is a 159-page monograph that reflects a serious, if flawed, study of Argentine letters not without some merit. But Borges, in a review published in *Sur*, took exception to Castro's implicitly supercilious point of view, which seemed to suggest that Spaniards owned the Spanish language and were entitled to opine about how others spoke it. (The review appeared in *Sur*, 86, as 'Las alarmas del Dr. Américo Castro', November 1941, pp. 66–70, *OC*, pp. 653–657). Borges had a talent for invective, and he had his day with Castro, whom he mockingly referred to as 'Dr. Castro' to underline his narrow academicism. *Don Quijote*, though not the focus of *La peculiaridad lingüística rioplatense*, is mentioned and is clearly in the background. Borges did not want to let the Spaniards run away with one of his favourite books for reasons that he found objectionable.

Borges's admiration of Cervantes, and particularly *Don Quijote*, is somewhat surprising given his very guarded view on the novelistic genre as a whole and his preference for brief literary works. In his preface to Adolfo Bioy Casares's novel, *La invención de Morel*, he expressed his distaste for long prose fiction, especially of the realistic kind. He argued that it availed itself of well-worn conventions to represent its settings, and indulged in the elaboration of the deviant psychology of its characters, which he found bogus, lacking form or limits. The Russian novelists, for him, seemed to have exhausted all the odd character types. Borges goes so far as to say that there are pages of Proust that are as boring as life itself. Yet Borges found Cervantes's protagonists fascinating, perhaps because Alonso Quijano, who became the mad knight, was first and foremost a reader, and he was fixated on turning his humdrum life into literature. Borges's admiration was also due to the fact that Don Quijote possessed throughout both parts a quality that he valued highly: courage.

Borges found in *Don Quijote* a sophisticated game about authorship and the creation of literature beyond which it was impossible to go. This is his main appreciation of Cervantes. Towards the latter part of his life and career, however, Borges seemed to offer a view of the author of *Don Quijote* and his hero that is more romantic, comparing it to his own way of creation. He wrote a piece for the *Revista de la Universidad de Buenos Aires*, in 1956, about the last chapter of *Don Quijote* that deals essentially with the ending of the novel, but he is distressed by the offhand way in which Cervantes narrates the death of his hero. This is a new Borges who evinces pathos about the fate of Cervantes's protagonist and about Cervantes himself. In deeply sensitive poems, including a superb sonnet, 'Un soldado de Urbina', Borges evokes Cervantes as the tired soldier who, wearied by his empty life working at various jobs, delves into the fantastic

romances of chivalry and in a deep dream Don Quijote and Sancho appear
to him (*El otro, el mismo*, 1964, *OC* 878). In another poem from that same
book, 'Lectores', Borges conjectures that all of Don Quijote's adventures
were dreams of Alonso Quijano, who never really left his library, and he
remembers himself as a child, reading Cervantes's novel in a library (his
father's) (*OC* 892). In 'Sueña Alonso Quijano', from the book of poems *La
rosa profunda* (1975), Borges imagines Don Quijote awakening from
a dream, but he is himself, Cervantes's dream, Alonso Quijano, who in
turn dreams Don Quijote; the knight is the result of those two intertwined
dreams. And in 'El testigo', from that book too, a battered Don Quijote
will turn out to be the dream of the windmill that has knocked him off
Rocinante. Borges is seeking now the origin of literary invention. This is
the reason why he alludes to his own pursuit of imaginative freedom as
a child, which was to him not unlike that of Cervantes. In doing this,
Borges seems to be correcting his earlier view of literary creation, and
confessing to the romantic foundation of Pierre Menard's mission as well
as his own.

Notes

1. Miguel de Cervantes, *Don Quixote*, trans. John Rutherford, intro. Roberto
   González Echevarría (New York: Penguin Books, 2001), p. 76.
2. Jorge Luis Borges, *Obras completas* (Buenos Aires: Emecé, 1974), p. 448. Unless
   otherwise indicated, I refer here and in what follows to this edition of the
   Complete Works; translations into English are my own.
3. Jorge Luis Borges, 'Nota preliminar', Miguel de Cervantes, *Novelas ejemplares*
   (Buenos Aires: Emecé, 1946), pp. 9–11 (p. 10).

CHAPTER 18

Borges's Shakespeare

Patricia Novillo-Corvalán

In the year 1964, to mark the quatercentenary celebrations of Shakespeare's birth, the Buenos Aires literary magazine *Sur* (*South*) – founded in 1931 by the Argentine writer, publisher, and feminist Victoria Ocampo – joined worldwide celebrations by dedicating a special double issue to the Bard.[1] The issue featured an eclectic collection of essays ranging from contributions by Argentine authors such as Borges, Alicia Jurado, Jaime Rest, Manuel Mujica Láinez, and Ocampo (the latter in her role as editor of the compilation) to a miscellany of European authors including Aldous Huxley, John Wain, Yves Bonnefoy, Ivor Brown, Robert Donington, Edmund Tracey, and C.A. Lejeune.

The sheer eclecticism of the list of contributors was precisely what lent the special issue its cultural value: in typical *Sur* fashion, the aim was to pay tribute to Shakespeare by celebrating his art and life from a multiplicity of perspectives that combined local and international voices, thus emphasizing transnational exchange as its method, while also repositioning Argentina as the 'centre' shaping these meaningful encounters, an alternative geographical location from which Shakespeare's archive is complexly renegotiated. In addition, the special issue included a critical anthology selected by Borges himself that featured landmark seventeenth- and eighteenth-century essays on Shakespeare by renowned English authors such as Ben Jonson, John Dryden, and Alexander Pope, followed by eminent European Romantics such as Victor Hugo, Thomas de Quincey, and Goethe.[2] However, the final twist in the critical anthology lay in Borges's decision to counterbalance adulation with scorn by incorporating the voice of one of Shakespeare's most notable detractors, the Irish critic and playwright George Bernard Shaw, whose controversial denial of Shakespeare's genius is deliberately inserted at the end of the special issue.

Within the context of the anthology, Borges's own essay, entitled 'A Page on Shakespeare', immediately stands out as the shortest contribution

149

in the volume, irreverently implying that Shakespeare's 'greatness' can be negotiated through an exercise in 'lessness' and that the colossal magnitude of his works can be paradoxically summed up in a single page, thus expounding the aesthetics of brevity he had previously articulated in the prologue to *The Garden of Forking Paths* (1944). Borges's essay, in turn, functions as a *résumé* of his previous writings on Shakespeare, especially his super-concise parable 'Everything and Nothing' included in *The Maker* (1960), on one level, and as an anticipation of his last *ficción* and major story collection entitled *Shakespeare's Memory* (1983), on another. Similarly, the critical anthology operates as a multi-layered intertextual document that reveals the numerous sources that Borges repeatedly sifted through when composing his deeply idiosyncratic Shakespearean fictions.

In 'A Page on Shakespeare' Borges foregrounds the major topoi and philosophical preoccupations that epitomized his lifelong fixation with the Bard, namely, the negation of personal identity by conceiving Shakespeare as a ghost in life, a spectral, elusive figure whose 'nothingness', by extension, paradoxically implies 'everything' – following the pantheistic system proposed by the Dutch philosopher Baruch Spinoza. On a metaphorical level, moreover, Shakespeare functions as a haunting cultural construct whose omnipresent shadow has exerted a pervasive influence across the centuries, a legacy that Borges seeks to renegotiate from his particular standpoint as an Argentine writer. In this way, the ghostliness of Shakespeare emerges as an intricate interweaving of critical sources and philosophical doctrines which, rather than solving 'the enigma of Shakespeare' (to borrow the title of a guest lecture Borges delivered in Buenos Aires to mark the quatercentenary celebrations), instead plunge the reader into further uncertainty, inevitably eliciting more gaps and a sense of eeriness and mystery.

Another strategy Borges deploys to underscore the elusiveness of Shakespeare is by stressing the striking (un)originality of his plots, most of which were borrowed, he writes in 'Shakespeare's Memory', from: 'Chaucer, Gower, Spenser, Christopher Marlowe, Holinshed's *Chronicles*, Florio's Montaigne, [and] North's Plutarch' (*CF* 512). As such, he claims that Shakespeare's towering genius resides precisely in his skilful reworking and recycling of pre-existent stories, an idea based on Borges's playful conceit that all stories can be reduced to one story and all authors to one author. As he puts it in 'Tlön, Uqbar, Orbis Tertius' – a seminal *ficción* that toys with an imaginary planet based on the idealist metaphysics of the Irish Bishop George Berkeley – 'all men who speak a line of Shakespeare are William Shakespeare' (*CF* 76). This principle coincides with another of Borges's distinctive pet themes: the cyclical conception of literature (a system of thought based, in turn, on the Pythagorean idea of the transmigration of the soul and Nietzsche's theory of eternal return) that intricately frames many of his Shakespearean fictions, particularly the vignette 'The Plot', included in *The Maker*, and the story 'Theme of the Traitor and the Hero', published in *Artifices* (1944), both of which transpose Shakespeare's dramatization of the murder of Julius Cesar to two 'peripheral' countries: Ireland and Argentina.

The Enigma of Shakespeare

The plot of 'Everything and Nothing' is structurally organized according to two central 'enigmas': first, Shakespeare's tortuous and obsessive search for a much yearned (and, ultimately, unattainable) sense of self, and, second, the readers' (and Borges's) own search for the haunting and culturally loaded global phenomenon known under the name of 'William Shakespeare'. Neither mystery is fully solved. Manifestly, the negation of its unnamed protagonist – who is referred to throughout the story with the impersonal pronoun 'nobody' – is closely linked to Shakespeare's deeply unsettling existence that is described as a 'guided and directed hallucination' and a 'dream someone had failed to dream' (*CF* 319; 320). Not even a full-blown love affair with an older woman, Anne Hathaway, who initiated him in the 'performance of an elemental ritual of humanity', enables him to cast off 'the hated taste of unreality', thus further intensifying his alienation and condition as a ghost in life (*CF* 319; 320).

However, Shakespeare's phantasmal void is temporarily alleviated by the dual roles of actor and playwright that allow him to create and impersonate multiple selves. Based on John Keats's oxymoronic category, 'negative capability'[3] and Shaw's conception of Shakespeare as someone 'devoid of a soul',[4] Borges appropriated both models to exploit Shakespeare's histrionic capacity to embody multiple selves by becoming all his *dramatis personae*: 'Caesar, who ignores the admonition of the sibyl, and Juliet, who hates the lark, and Macbeth, who speaks on the moor with the witches who are also the Fates, the Three Weird Sisters' (*CF* 319–320). Inevitably, though, Keats's 'negative capability' results in the denial of the self and the ensuing condition of 'nobodiness' that would plague Shakespeare when 'the last line was delivered and the last dead man applauded off the stage' (*CF* 319).

The crux of 'Everything and Nothing' lies in the closing, spine-tingling epiphany (wherein Shakespeare's long-deferred name is finally revealed to the reader) that stages an otherworldly dialogue between Shakespeare and God. In so doing, Borges offers an inversion of the biblical dialogue between God and Moses in the Book of Exodus, a subject matter he had previously discussed in an earlier essay entitled 'A History of the Echoes of a Name' published in *Other Inquisitions* (1952). Thus, if Moses asks God who HE is, Borges playfully inverts the biblical dialogue by allowing Shakespeare to redirect the question to God and enquire about his own elusive identity:

> Then Moses said to God, 'Indeed, when I come to the children of Israel and say to them, "The God of your fathers hath sent me to you", and they shall say to me, "What is *His* name?" what shall I say to them?'
> And God said to Moses, 'I AM WHO I AM.' (*Exodus* 3: 13–14)
> History adds that before or after he died, he discovered himself standing before God, and said to Him: *I, who have been so many men in vain, wish to be one, to be myself*. God's voice answered him out of a whirlwind: *I, too, am not I; I dreamed the world as you, [my] Shakespeare, dreamed your own work, and among the forms of my dream are you, who like me are many, yet no one* (*CF* 320).[5]

By asking God to reveal his identity, Shakespeare (like the wizard in 'The Circular Ruins') is confronted with a dizzying dream-within-a-dream revelation that further increases his condition as a ghost. This metafictional effect mirrors the illusory fabric of *The Tempest* (written 1610–1611), where Prospero famously declares 'we are such stuff/as dreams are made on, and our little life/is rounded with a sleep',[6] as well as simultaneously evoking Borges's great fondness for the Shakespearean meta-theatrical device of the play-within-the-play, a structure that generates an infinitely-receding series of illusions. Finally, the gist of the passage lies in God's use of the possessive pronoun 'my' to address Shakespeare from a whirlwind, implying his predilection for Shakespeare (the creator par excellence) among all his human creatures, thus fortifying the pantheistic notion (or deification) of Shakespeare as a God-like figure firmly espoused by the Romantics. Indeed, the Romantic authors in question: Coleridge, Hugo, and Hazlitt represent (once again) a complex intertextual tapestry that can be traced back to earlier essays such as 'From Someone to Nobody' (1952), published in *Other Inquisitions*: '[For Coleridge] Shakespeare is no longer a man but a literary variation of the infinite God of Spinoza [. . .]. [For Hazlitt] "he was nothing in himself, but he was all that others were, or that could become." Later, Hugo compared him to the ocean, which is the seedbed of all possible forms' (*SNF* 342).

Shakespeare's Ghost

Conceived as an otherworldly 'gift' that is supernaturally transmitted from person to person, 'Shakespeare's Memory' grapples with complex ideas of spectrality, canonicity, and the ubiquitous cultural legacy of Shakespeare. By choosing a German academic as its principal protagonist – Hermann Sörgel – Borges explicitly alludes to the notion of 'bardolatry' ardently professed by another Romantic writer, Goethe. In the story, a fleeting character named Daniel Thorpe preposterously offers Sörgel 'Shakespeare's memory, from his youngest boyhood to early April, 1616' (*CF* 510). Sörgel accepts, without hesitation. Yet, the magic gift, as in many Borgesian fictions turns from joy into terror. Initially, a deluded Sörgel erroneously assumes that by possessing the memory of Shakespeare he will become Shakespeare: 'Throughout the first stage of this adventure I felt the joy of being Shakespeare' (*CF* 514). Not only does the spectral memory impede the narrator from becoming Shakespeare, but it also threatens to annul his own personal identity, turning him into neither Shakespeare nor himself: 'At first, the waters of the two memories did not mix; in time, the great torrent of Shakespeare threatened to flood my own modest stream' (*CF* 514). Like the 'rubbish heap' memory of Ireneo Funes in the story 'Funes the Memorious', published in *Fictions* (1944), the spectral memory reveals a useless number of dates, facts, and proliferating details, but lacks the most important aspect of the playwright, his creative genius: 'Shakespeare's memory was able to reveal to me only the circumstances of the *man* Shakespeare. Clearly, these circumstances do not constitute the uniqueness of *the* poet; what matters is the literature the poet produced with that frail material' (*CF* 513).

Unlike his fictional counterpart, the minor French writer Pierre Menard in Borges's celebrated parable 'Pierre Menard, Author of the *Quixote*', published in *Fictions* – who similarly conjures up another omnipresent canonical ghost: Miguel de Cervantes – Sörgel fails to purposely engage in the more meaningful activity of appropriating Shakespeare. Compared to Menard's undeniably ambitious, though ultimately achievable, aim 'to produce a few pages [of *Don Quixote*] which coincided – word for word and line for line – with those of Miguel de Cervantes' (*CF* 91), Sörgel's megalomaniac impulse to become Shakespeare is both impossible and naive: 'I would possess Shakespeare and possess him as no one had ever possessed anyone before – not in love, or friendship, or even hatred. I, in some ways, would *be* Shakespeare' (*CF* 511). In this way, Menard's innovative technique of 'deliberate anachronism and fallacious attribution' (*CF* 95) proves successful and, in a typical Borgesian twist, even surpasses his Spanish predecessor: 'The Cervantes text and the Menard text are verbally identical, but the second is almost infinitely richer' (*CF* 93; 94). Consequently, Pierre Menard succeeds in his arduous enterprise not by trying to become the Golden Age Spanish writer Miguel de Cervantes Saavedra but by remaining the French twentieth-century symbolist, Pierre Menard. In his foolish attempt to possess, rather than to creatively negotiate, Shakespeare's genius, Sörgel inherits a vast repository of useless data, the countless memories that once belonged to the mortal man William Shakespeare and not, metaphorically, the memory as a ubiquitous cultural heritage that reawakens across different cultures, languages, and histories.

What the above examples make clear is that the shrewder Pierre Menard understood correctly the fundamental lesson in reading and interpretation that the deluded Sörgel could only intuit at the end of the story, though by this time he resignedly renounces the spectral 'gift'. Borges's ghostly rhetoric may, in turn, be read in parallel with Walter Benjamin's notion of the 'afterlife' of a text as articulated in his essay 'The Task of the Translator' (1923), where he dismantles the original/translation dichotomy by questioning the traditional belief in the superiority of the original, positing, instead, that the original owes its surviving life to the translation.[7] Benjamin's richly suggestive imagery includes the metaphor of the translation as a 'royal robe with ample folds' that may be interpreted as an endlessly expanding fabric that elegantly spreads its numerous folds across a multiplicity of languages.[8] By the same token, one may say that the multifarious folds, layers, scripts, and afterlives of Shakespeare are constitutive of the instability of the Western canon, implying a complex process of translatability and interpretation through which his legacy is updated, expanded, and renegotiated within different historical and geographical contexts.

Shakespeare Travels

The notion of translatability is also at the core of Borges's ultra-concise vignette 'The Plot'. Here, the murder of the historical Julius Caesar (particularly as it was recorded by Shakespeare and the Spanish Baroque writer Francisco de Quevedo) is equated with a knife-fight among a group of gauchos in the Argentine pampas. If in Shakespeare the betrayed Caesar utters the famous Latin words: '*Et tu, Bruté?*' (*Julius Caesar* 3.1.79) upon discovering his beloved Brutus among the conspirators, Borges proposes a parallel scene wherein a godson kills his godfather, who similarly exclaims (albeit in the Argentine colloquial speech): '*¡Pero, che!*' ('hey, you!'; *CF* 307). In order to emphasize the importance of the vernacular, Borges reinforces that these words must be heard, rather than simply read on the printed page. Therefore, the locution 'che' (characteristic of *rioplatense* Spanish) offered Borges the appropriate expression with which to translate the historical tragedy of *Julius Caesar* into a local tradition, albeit by ironically – and anachronistically – linking the historical scene in the Roman capitol with an isolated terrain in the southern part of the province of Buenos Aires. Moreover, after Caesar has been assassinated, Cassius, one of the assassins and the main conspirator, dramatically drenches his hands in Caesar's blood and exclaims:

> How many ages hence
> Shall this our lofty scene be acted over
> In states unborn and accents yet unknown!   (3.1.112–114)

On one level, Cassius disrupts the illusion of the theatrical performance by drawing attention to the play as an artifice and to his condition as an actor. On another, Cassius's speech may be read as an anticipation, or validation, of Borges's subsequent staging of the 'lofty scene' of *Julius Caesar* in rural Argentina, subscribing to the idea of the cyclicality of literature, as stories are constantly rewritten and reborn: 'He dies, but he does not know that he has died so that a scene can be played out again' (*CF* 307).

The conception of history as a series of 'repetitions, variations, [and] symmetries' (*CF* 307) reappears in 'Theme of the Traitor and the Hero', where the cyclical 'morphologies' proposed by 'Hegel, Spengler, and Vico' (*CF* 144) are deployed to construct a tightly woven labyrinthine plot that re-enacts the tragedy of *Julius Caesar* in Ireland. The story utilizes a twofold temporal framework encompassing 100 years: first, depicting the 1824 Irish revolution gloriously led by the Irish 'hero' Fergus Kilpatrick and, second, marking its centenary with the biographical enterprise of his descendant, Ryan, and his shocking discovery that Kilpatrick was, in fact, the 'traitor' to the cause. One of Borges's most politically engaged fictions, from the outset 'Theme of the Traitor and the Hero' is associated with 'oppressed' and 'stubborn' countries (*CF* 143), as the unreliable narrator identifies Ireland as a model of political rebellion under British rule. Ryan painstakingly unravels a tangled pattern of symmetries that revolve around the 'English enemy Will Shakespeare' (*CF* 145), the imperial author whose tragedy, *Julius Caesar*, is subversively 'plagiarized' for the sake of Irish independence. Ryan therefore grapples with the seemingly unbelievable paradox that 'the idea that history might have copied history is mind-boggling enough: that history should copy *literature* is inconceivable' (*CF* 145). In this way, the traitor/hero Kilpatrick becomes an avatar of Caesar while the streets of Dublin are turned into a vast stage where the meticulously planned assassination is performed. In short, Shakespeare's trademark metaphor: 'All the world's a stage' (*As You Like It* 2.7.138) solves the political tension and guarantees the cyclical repetition of the 'lofty scene' in what would eventually become the Irish Free State. Note, finally, the real historical parallel with Ireland's Easter Rising in April 1916.

Borges's intricately woven Shakespearean afterlives are complexly poised between the local and the canonical as he adjusts, compresses, and demystifies the Bard's sacrosanct status by compounding his legacy with other regional, vernacular voices that are afforded equal treatment in his fictions. For Borges, the so-called 'enigma of Shakespeare' is less about solving the authorship question or reaching conclusive interpretations of his oeuvre, but rather a more playful, revisionary exercise that seeks to rethink (and reinvigorate) the Western canon from the outsider positionality of a Latin American writer. With his usual irreverence and customary cheek, Borges would hold the belief that it was precisely his marginal status as an Argentine author (*SNF* 420–427) that gave him an even greater right to the Western canon, particularly to its most famous exponent: Shakespeare.

Notes

1. Victoria Ocampo (ed.), *Shakespeare: 1564–1964, Sur* (1964), pp. 289–290.
2. Jorge Luis Borges (ed.), *Antología de críticas famosas sobre Shakespeare, Sur*, 289–290 (1964).
3. John Keats, *Selected Letters*, ed. Robert Gittings (Oxford: Oxford University Press, 2002), pp. 41–42.
4. George Bernard Shaw, 'Credentials', in Frank Harris (ed.), *Bernard Shaw: An Unauthorised Biography Based on First-Hand Information with a Postscript by Mr Shaw* (London: Victor Gollancz, 1931), p. 11.
5. Disappointingly, the pronoun – which is crucial to understand the meaning of the parable – has been removed from Andrew Hurley's translation.

6. William Shakespeare, *The Norton Shakespeare*, ed. Stephen Greenblatt et al. (London: Norton, 1997), 4, 1. 156–158. Hereafter cited in parenthesis followed by line number.
7. Walter Benjamin, 'The Task of the Translator', trans. Harry Zohn, in *The Translation Studies Reader*, ed. Lawrence Venuti (New York: Routledge, 2000), pp. 15–23.
8. Benjamin, p. 19.

CHAPTER 19

Borges and the Dialectics of Idealism

Marina Martín

Attention to detail in Borges's writings ensures a rich and intensely fruitful experience. Packed with a subtle network of allusions, his manuscripts feature the display of an unusually small handwriting committed to conciseness and accuracy. The flow of knowledge and creativity emerging from his pages requires a *magnifying* lens, in order to glimpse its magnitude.[1] Since metaphysics was for him a lifelong interest, the implementation of a philosophical approach, charting debates and themes, can certainly serve well.

In the last 25 years Borges scholarship has turned to philosophy, shedding light on the author's erudition and creativity.[2] Although such an approach yields a wealth of information, the debate continues. Many will argue that Borges himself claimed not to be a philosopher. 'I suppose that my thinking has been done for me by Berkeley, by Hume, by Schopenhauer, by Mauthner perhaps', he once explained in interview, as if he had no intention of admitting any value in his own thinking.[3] He would rather portray himself as 'simply a man of letters who turns his own perplexities and that respected system of philosophy into the forms of literature'.[4] Yet, there is good reason to assume that in the same way Borges blends literary genres in an artful manner, he may also be blending disciplines with no less skill. It should be no surprise to find his literary production and essays turned into insightful metaphors, subtle ironies, and philosophical critiques. There is also good reason to assume that he shared with Tlön's fictitious inhabitants the belief that metaphysics is 'a branch of fantastic literature' (*Labyrinths*, 10). Borges fully confirms this view in the Epilogue to *Other Inquisitions* where he claims to have noticed in his writings the tendency to value both religious and philosophical ideas 'for their aesthetic worth, and even for their intrinsic singularity and wonder, which entails a fundamentally sceptical position' (*OC* II: 153).[5] A philosophical analysis is thus needed. Ignoring the epistemological sources of his scepticism makes no sense. In this case, the dialogue he maintains with the British empiricist tradition is fundamental, as both 'Tlön, Uqbar, Orbis Tertius' and 'A New Refutation of Time' illustrate.

Crafted with irony and wit, as is the case with 'Tlön . . . ', or with concise and penetrating arguments, as happens with 'A New Refutation of Time', these famous texts present a subtle and highly illuminating critique of idealism that goes well beyond 'the feeble artifice of an Argentine lost in the maze of metaphysics' (*Labyrinths*, 217). Being adrift on metaphysical oceans, after all, may also mirror our minds, bound by limitations and impossible missions. We should bear in mind that the former passage opens the essay, 'A New Refutation of Time', reflecting the spirit of its ironic title: a *contradictio in adjecto*. With this enticing hint, Borges ultimately points to what he considers to be the main tenet of idealism: the illusory character of reality. Two brief yet monumental essays in his earlier writings, 'The Perpetual Race of Achilles and the Tortoise' and 'Avatars of the Tortoise', prefigure some of the arguments elaborated later. In 'Avatars . . . ' Borges invites us to take idealism further and 'seek unrealities' that confirm the hallucinatory nature of our world, as portrayed in Kant's antinomies or in Zeno's dialectics (*Labyrinths*, 208). This is the purpose of 'A New Refutation of Time', reflected in 'Tlön . . . ' through both the proposed denial of time and the acceptance of Schopenhauer's idealist pantheism as the ultimate consequence evolving from the British empiricist tradition.[6]

Wholly immersed in philosophical analysis and rich in quotations from Berkeley and Hume, 'A New Refutation of Time' happens to be one of Borges's most original contributions. The same can be said of 'Tlön . . . '. Composed with an intricate network of allusions, this fiction becomes a cognitive artefact that reads deep into contemporary debates on language.[7] A thread of consistent ideas can be traced throughout Borges's works, carrying the wish to pursue them further. Based on research and discussions with his father and friends, he thus publishes 'Berkeley's Crossroads' and 'The Nothingness of Personality' in 1925, endorsing refutations of the external world and the self. In the 1940s, he moves on to present an explicit refutation of time.

Borges's interest in the British cultural tradition is inseparable from his family upbringing. He himself admits that despite being raised in the urban life of his residential area in Buenos Aires, he grew up in the shelter of 'a library of unlimited English books' (*OC* I: 101). Questioning personal identity appeared early in life as part of 'endless discussions with Father' on idealism, and 'Georgie's own reading of Hume, Berkeley and Schopenhauer'.[8] We also know that his much admired Macedonio

Fernández held strong affinities with those philosophers and made him
'read sceptically' ('An Autobiographical Essay', 230). From the outset then,
Borges adopts a distinctive philosophical orientation that is fed from
various sources. A major one is British empiricism, and Hume's impact
happens to be remarkable, especially in the making of 'Tlön ... '. His
influence reveals this fiction's intellectual accomplishments, helping us
understand both the humour and the nature of the scepticism that perme-
ates its pages. Likewise, the story functions as a powerful critique since it
incorporates Hume's doctrine by efficiently illuminating its implications.
'Tlön ... ' carries the disintegrated, atomized, and anonymous world
revealed by Hume's analysis of sense-experience beyond the limits prescribed in his *Treatise*, helping us approach his theory of the external world
with a lens that prefigures debates in the heart of contemporary philosophy. Parodic mirrors and inverted images in 'Tlön ... ' portray metaphorically the inexorable boundaries of our world through the limits of our
minds and languages.

   Once the external world and personal identity become inventions,
Hume sinks into deep awareness of the limits of reason and admits to
being trapped in a maze: 'I find myself involved in such a labyrinth, that,
I must confess, I neither know how to correct my former opinions, nor
how to render them consistent.'[9] The conclusion of Book I also registers
a similar reflection: 'When I turn my eye inward, I find nothing but doubt
and ignorance' (*Treatise*, 172). He also accepts his fate for having exposed
himself to the contempt of metaphysicians, logicians, mathematicians, and
theologians in declaring disapproval of their systems: 'Can I wonder at the
insults I must suffer?' (*Ibid.*). Berkeley's doctrine encountered a similar
reaction, since it was not understood. The same happened with the scandal
brought about by Tlön's heresiarch in his defence of materialism,
a character who tacitly appears in the story as Berkeley's inverted image.
With humour, Borges registers debates and historical events through
a network of allusions, insights, and reflections that ultimately enable
philosophical discernment. His inquisitive and sympathetic interest in
heresies reappears, disclosing a type of scepticism that might be 'the most
enlightened of gnoseological postures'.[10]

   Despite the depressing tone that can at times be detected in Hume, the
sceptical outlook of his doctrine hardly ever gives way to dark and gloomy
melancholy. The spirit of this enlightened philosopher is balanced with
subtle humour and a taste for moderation. Driven by his interest in
encyclopaedias and learning, Borges's production is also far from presenting a world of anguished metaphors. For a 'sceptical pluralist' like Borges –

Mark Frisch remarks – the labyrinth 'does not automatically imply pessimism, chaos, and despair, but may suggest hope and affirmation' for, although inexplicable, it may be a coherent cosmos.[11] In this case, Borges's theological fantasy and affinity with Judaism, for instance, could be as relevant as his admiration for Schopenhauer.

Words echo other voices, other times, in this our infinite Library of Babel. Additionally, they evoke the Upanishad's ancient belief that views the universe as *mâya*, a mental construct. The inspiration found in Asian doctrines is also important. Borges connects Mahayana's absolute idealism to Berkeley and Schopenhauer; yet ... how far are these affinities to be extended? Does his reading of the Berkeleyan doctrine fit the limitations prescribed by Berkeley himself, or is it rather a reading process performed through Hume's eyes? How is his scepticism related to Berkeley? Are the imaginary Tlönians, for instance, a faithful depiction of the Berkeleyan doctrine, or rather a Humean extension of it? We need to understand not only Borges's scepticism but his whole philosophical position, as when he claims to have arrived at Schopenhauer's dictum '[v]ia the dialectics of Berkeley and Hume' (*Labyrinths*, 233).

Borges's acceptance of the premise *esse est percipi* is genuine and remained so throughout his life. This was also Hume's case. The mark imprinted by the Berkeleyan doctrine on Borges is no less relevant than it is on Hume.[12] Unlike both, however, Berkeley was far from adopting a sceptical position: '[W]e are not deprived of any one thing in nature. Whatever we see, feel, hear, or anywise conceive or understand, remains as secure as ever.'[13] He named his own doctrine 'immaterialism' and used all his skill and effort to show that it was the ally, not the opponent, of common sense. Formulated in a direct and clear language, his doctrine was intended as a fatal weapon against sceptics and atheists, but Hume and Borges think it fails despite its brilliant despite its greatness.

Hume did admire Berkeley; the concluding section of his first *Enquiry,* 'Of the Academical or Sceptical Philosophy', underscores this. But he also claimed that Berkeley's ingenious writings 'form the best lessons of scepticism' since '*they admit of no answer and produce no conviction*'.[14] Critics have often overlooked this objection, perhaps because it appears discreetly in a footnote, but the emphasis added by Hume himself is not irrelevant at all. Aware of this, Borges praises Hume's objection as being 'both polite and deadly' (*OC* I: 217). Most importantly, he incorporates it with meticulous accuracy in 'Tlön . . . ', turning fiction into a cognitive tool that not only questions knowledge of the external world and the self but also hints at the need to revise canonical versions of idealism.[15] Using numerous

allusions to *Treatise* 1.4.2, Borges illustrates Hume's approach to the
external world through a mind subject to common sense beliefs diame-
trically opposed to ours. A mirror of contrasts is created. Whatever we hold
as empirically true or real is either false or unthinkable in Tlön. The
existence of an external world persisting independently of its being perceived is inconceivable for Tlön's idealist nations. Such a belief is also for
Hume – the sceptic – a 'gross illusion' (*Treatise*, 144). Common sense
defenders in Tlön could not understand assumptions that our own cogni-
tion is compelled to take for granted. Borges portrays Hume's twofold
doctrine by showing through fiction the question-begging nature of our
common sense, as mirrored in our languages through the existence of
nouns and personal pronouns. Scepticism and naturalism are then intertwined, creating parodic images that illustrate imaginatively one of the
main tenets of idealism: our world is mind-dependent.

Once we question our faculties, reason ends up in 'a total extinction of
belief and evidence' (*Treatise*, 122). However, the road to Pyrrhonism is
limited: 'Nature, by an absolute and uncontrollable necessity has deter-
min'd us to judge as well as to breath and feel' (123). Hume's reply to
Berkeley, and by the same token to his own scepticism, bears the mark –
and the irony – of his positive doctrine. Naturalism plays a major role in
Kemp Smith's reading of Hume, implicitly shared in both 'Tlön . . . ' and
'A New Refutation of Time'. This critic's interpretation marks a turning
point in Hume's scholarship. The reference to Kemp Smith in the opening
paragraph of that essay is not arbitrary nor is Borges's own reading of
Hume's doctrine, extended into Schopenhauer's. In fact, 'A New
Refutation of Time' provides a compelling and profound vision that
opens the controversy of idealism and the need to evaluate its demarcation.
In this sense, *fiction* is not necessarily restricted to the category of *illusion*
since it extends to language, to a system built on rules that convey
a provisional yet a much-needed worldview.

Borges presents a concise and inspiring formulation of a subject that he
views as the central question in philosophy: time. Evolving from an
extension of Berkeley's doctrine on the one hand and a lifelong fascination
for Zeno's paradoxes on the other, 'A New Refutation of Time' expounds,
defends, and carries immaterialism to its ultimate consequences. Portrayed
as 'apologists of idealism', Berkeley and Hume stand at the heart of this
essay. Extensive quotes from their writings, together with conclusions
drawn from them, feature the instability of a world utterly made of time
and devoid of support: 'I have accumulated transcriptions from the apologists of idealism, I have abounded in their canonical passages, I have been

reiterative and explicit . . . so that my reader may begin to penetrate into this unstable world of the mind. A world of evanescent impressions; a world without matter or spirit, neither objective nor subjective; a world without the ideal architecture of space; a world made of time' (*Labyrinths*, 221). As if it were an unshakable postulate, these two philosophers leave time *untouched*. Conceived as a chain of fleeting perceptions, time is the only entity resisting Hume's refutations. For Berkeley, it is 'the succession of ideas in the mind'; for Hume 'a succession of indivisible moments' (221). In either case, time is unquestionable. Borges, however, challenges that assumption on the basis that once we admit the idealist argument it is inevitable to go further: 'I deny, with the arguments of idealism, the vast temporal series which idealism admits' (*Labyrinths*, 222).

The goal is to bring the epistemological quest to its end. If we assume that time has a beginning, as well as an end, we must assume that it is formed of indivisible moments succeeding each other. But how can we determine where or when exactly a given moment begins or ends? Does division stop? Once matter and spirit, which are continuities, are refuted, what right do we have to assume the alleged continuity of time? The beginning of a series is as inconceivable as its end. Time is then a delusion: the inseparability of one moment from another is sufficient to disintegrate it. Either conceived as succession or as eternity, its unintelligible nature blinds reason. Achilles and the unreachable tortoise re-enter the scenario. We thus encounter a distinctive feature in Borges's writings, the meeting point of art and metaphysics: paradoxes.

The beginning and the end of 'A New Refutation of Time' bear a resemblance. First, we learn that we should not expect a novel conclusion due to the author's 'rudimentary dialectics' (217). In fact, through the contradiction delivered in the title Borges intends to share his own perplexities: We may refute time . . . in vain, for it constitutes our being, and our languages. Our refutation may admit of no answer but certainly produces no conviction. The conclusion of the essay confronts us with a sound refutation of time and a necessary acceptance of its existence: '*And yet, and yet* . . . Time is a river which sweeps me along, but I am the river; it is a tiger that destroys me, but I am the tiger; it is the fire which consumes me, but I am the fire' (234). Like Escher's works, we come to the depiction of impossible symmetries. Borges's portrayal of time highlights human life rooted in contradiction. Indeed, God's splendid irony grants us books and blindness at one touch. Being and nothingness are mutually inclusive. We cling to time, our substance, to disappear in the magic shadow of a dream.

Notes

1. Daniel Balderston studies Borges's creative process through numerous manuscripts and notebooks. See *How Borges Wrote* (Charlottesville/London: University of Virginia Press, 2018).

2. See Silvia Dapía, *Die Rezeption der Sprachkritic Fritz Mauthners im Werk von Jorge Luis Borges* (Vienna: Böhlau, 1993) and *Jorge Luis Borges, Post-analytic Philosophy and Representation* (New York/London: Routledge, 2016).

3. 'An Interview with Jorge Luis Borges', *Philosophy and Literature* 3 (1977), pp. 337–341 (p. 339).

4. Reproduced by Ronald Christ in the 'Foreword' to *The Narrow Act. Borges' Art of Allusion* (New York: New York University Press, 1969), pp. ix–x.

5. Throughout this chapter, a handful of unattributed translations from Borges are mine. I am grateful to the Editor, Robin Fiddian, for his suggestions.

6. In 'An Autobiographical Essay', Borges confirms his admiration for Schopenhauer: 'If the riddle of the universe can be stated in words, I think these words would be in his writings'. Included in *The Aleph and Other Stories, 1933–1969* (New York: Dutton, 1970), pp. 203–260 (pp. 216–217).

7. See Alejandro Riberi, *Fictions as Cognitive Artefacts: The Case of Jorge Luis Borges' 'Tlön, Uqbar, Orbis Tertius'* (Auckland: Magnolia Press, 2004).

8. Emir Rodríguez Monegal, *Jorge Luis Borges. A Literary Biography* (New York: Dutton, 1978), p. 170.

9. David Hume, *A Treatise on Human Nature*, ed. David F. Norton and Mary J. Norton (Oxford: Oxford University Press, 2004), p. 399.

10. Floyd Merrell, *Unthinking Thinking: Jorge Luis Borges, Mathematics, and the New Physics* (West Lafayette: Purdue University Press, 1991), p. 9.

11. M. Frisch, *You Might Be Able to Get There from Here: Reconsidering Borges and the Postmodern* (Florham, NJ: Fairleigh Dickinson University Press, 2004), p. 16.

12. For Schopenhauer the world is 'akin to a dream' (*The World as Will and Representation*, 2 vols., trans. E.F.J Payne (New York: Dover, 1969), II, p. 4). No truth is more certain: everything that exists for knowledge is only object in relation to the subject, perception of the perceiver, or 'representation' (I, 3). Likewise, for Hume, perceptions are 'the first foundation of all our conclusions' (*Treatise*, 212). Existence – conceived neither as *cogito* nor as *res cogitans*, but rather as *cogitatio* – derives from the immediacy of impressions, giving them an ontological priority over mind constructions. Berkeley shares the same foundation, but he denies the illusory character of the world.

13. George Berkeley, *A Treatise Concerning the Principles of Human Knowledge*, in *Philosophical Writings*, ed. T.E. Jessop (New York: Greenwood Press, 1969), pp. 33–114 (p. 66).

14. David Hume, *Enquiries Concerning the Human Understanding and Concerning the Principles of Morals*, ed. L.A. Selby-Bigge. Revised and notes by P.H. Nidditch (Oxford: Clarendon Press, 2002), p. 155.

15. 'A New Refutation of Time' also incorporates Hume's reply to Berkeley: 'To understand it [his doctrine] is easy; what is difficult is to think within its limits' (*Labyrinths*, 220). Borges quotes Hume's words not just in 'Tlön . . .' but also in 'The Postulation of Reality': 'Hume noted once and for all that Berkeley's arguments admit of no answer and produce no conviction' (O C I: 435).

CHAPTER 20

The English Romantics and Borges

Jason Wilson

Jorge Luis Borges had an English grandmother from Staffordshire and spoke English with his father. He was bilingual, even a polyglot, for he also spoke and read German and French and knew Latin extremely well and later, Old English and Norse. Yet despite his mastery of different languages, he decided to write his poems and 'fictions' in his native language, Spanish. Nevertheless, he was drawn to English and what he called in the epilogue to *The Maker*, 1960, 'the verbal music of England' (156).[1] For Borges, English literature was the richest in the world. He was also tempted to write two poems in English in 1934, despite the convention that you wrote poetry in your native tongue, in his case, Spanish. English literature was there right from the start of his writer's career when he first read the English Romantics Keats, Shelley, Byron, and other poets, and from his teenage years with De Quincey, Coleridge, and Lamb. Of the authors he re-read throughout his life, De Quincey (160) stands out. He read around the Romantics too with biographies, letters, and studies on them. What arose from reading English so early and thoroughly was his precise use of words in his sentences, induced by English diction.

He may have told Norman Thomas di Giovanni that he came across the English Romantics as poets while still a boy, but his first published poems were 'ultraist' poems written during his year in Spain, turning his back on the Romantics as did all the avant-garde poets of the time. He later in life wrote poems and quirky essays on Keats and Coleridge, and constantly quoted De Quincey in his prose texts. But what is crucial is that he was never a historical reader, establishing careful categories, dealing with literary history. Instead, he read for pleasure and was a literary hedonist. Though made a professor of English Literature in 1956 and knowing about scholarly conventions, he always showed the enthusiasm of the autodidact he was and did not bother to fill in the gaps if he was not moved by the poets. For example, there is hardly a reference to William Wordsworth anywhere in his work, and he did not repair that oversight. The same treatment holds for Byron, though he named a cat 'Beppo' after him and Shelley was reduced to just his dates of birth and death in his *Introduction to English Literature*, 1965, written with his later biographer María Esther Vázquez. Only with this introduction did he bother with dates and history as the book's format, a history of literature, demanded. Today's most glaring omission is women Romantics, and this strange 'machismo' can only be excused by the period he was writing in, where he was not alone.

It was not until 1972 that Borges published a sonnet 'To John Keats (1795–1821)' on Keats. Some years before, in 1965, Keats was 'the greatest lyrical poet in English'.[2] Borges's sonnet, a literary form he used once he was blind to help him shape his poems, which he repeated to himself until he could dictate them, has some awkward rhymes and does not add much to Keats's reputation except to say that he survives in collective memory thanks to his nightingale and urn. In a later book of 1975, *La rosa profunda*, he wrote a longer poem 'To a nightingale' where he admits he has never heard an actual nightingale sing, but the bird's song is 'charged with mythologies'. In this poem he alludes to Homer, to the story of Ruth in the *Bible*, Shakespeare, Heine, FitzGerald's *Rubaiyat of Omar Khayyam* (which Borges's father had translated into Spanish), and finally to Keats, who heard the birdsong 'for everybody and for ever'. Borges insists that he is writing from his 'empty afternoon' this 'exercise' (not poem), which, in his memory of having read Keats, burns in love and dies 'melodious'.[3] That last word 'melodious' comes from Keats's 'melodious plot' in his 'Ode to a Nightingale' where he conveys the thrill of that bird's 'full-throated ease'. Unlike Borges, Keats had heard a nightingale sing.

In 1952 Borges published 'Keats's Nightingale', one of his quirky essays, on Keats. He had accompanied his poetry throughout his career with on-going essays and a biography of a local Argentine poet Evaristo Carriego, 1930. He titled his sixth critical book, *Otras inquisiciones (Other Inquisitions)*. He added the 'other' because he had already published *Inquisiciones* in 1925. It is a telling title, as the Inquisition was founded to get to the 'truth' in Spain's Counter Reformation. These essays take a small point in an aggressive way, to surprise a reader. Borges dispensed with the poem's 'inexhaustible and insatiable beauty' and jumped to its penultimate stanza about 'the voice I heard this passing night was heard / in ancient days by emperor and clown'. He delved into the meaning, and dismissed Sidney Colvin, a Keats biographer of 1887, who found a flaw in Keats's poem that separated an individual nightingale from the songbird's 'type'. Borges turned instead to Amy Lowell's intuition that Keats's bird was not a specific bird, but the species singing through an individual. Borges's erudition about Keats is self-evident, even boastful, as he is writing from the fringes, from Argentina, daring to criticize a tradition of Anglo-American interpretations. His point is that the English mind is wary of Platonism and that the nightingale reoccurs in poems throughout history. Much of Borges's thinking is based on 'archetypes', a notion which denies history as linear events by going deeper to recurring patterns. The English mind was born Aristotelian, and Borges includes Keats's critics up to F.R. Leavis who take this Lockean, empirical position. He concluded provocatively, that nobody in England had really understood this poem. Writing about archetypes, it should be said in passing that Borges frequently quoted Coleridge's dictum that all men are born either Platonists or Aristotelians, throughout history.

From Keats we move to Samuel Taylor Coleridge and Borges's ambiguous relationship with him. Like Coleridge, Borges did not have a university degree, tried to combine metaphysics with poetry, and made the mind itself the subject of his enquiry. Borges wrote two essays and many notes and asides on Coleridge. The first, 'Coleridge's Flower' was published in *Other Inquisitions*. This title refers to Coleridge's short parable about a man who crosses paradise in a dream, is given a flower and wakes up with the flower in his hand. Borges included this parable in his anthology on dreams and dreams are the key to literary composition, as was the case for all Romantic poets. But in this critical essay he veers off into his view that authorship has little to do with personality as literature is written by the spirit, and cites Paul Valéry, Emerson, and Shelley to back up his idea. He cites H.G. Wells's *The Time Machine* and a tradition of predicting the future with a character who arrives with a 'withered' flower. The article ends with Borges's attack on authorial individuality. He adds a list of names that is all the same one man and it ends with De Quincey. Words take over from what they represent and create their own verbal reality, for everything is written and there is no such thing as originality. Being original was one of the Romantic obsessions.

The second piece was titled 'Coleridge's Dream', also from *Other Inquisitions*. Borges retold the famous anecdote about the writing of 'Kubla Khan' in the summer of 1797, which began as a dream. Perhaps stimulated by laudunum, Coleridge woke up with the poem ready and wrote it down in a trance, but he was interrupted by a visitor and forgot the rest. Borges quotes the poet Swinburne about this poem being the supreme example of lyric poetry in English, and that to analyse it would be like trying to unpick a rainbow. Then he veered into dreams, and once again offered literary examples from Robert Louis Stevenson and the Venerable

Bede. Coleridge dreamed his poem, itself based on a dream a Persian had had about building a palace. The Persian entered Coleridge's dream. In his dream, Coleridge heard a voice and knew that music was building the palace. Borges closed with another interpretation that this dream was in *The Road to Xanadu* (an essay of 1927 by the American scholar, John Livingston Lowes), and speculated that this dream was slowly, over generations, entering reality. In this playful way he is repeating his story 'Tlön, Uqbar, Orbis Tertius' about the invasion of idealist objects in our world.

For Borges, Coleridge was the author of three great poems and reams of prose. He did finish his treatise on poetry and philosophy *Biographia Literaria*, but had difficulty in controlling his mania for digressions. We can see that Borges also digresses at whim, never sticking to the point. His critique is based on sudden insights, similar to what he calls Coleridge's 'luminous intuitions'. He is annoyed at the mix in Coleridge of platitudes, plagiarism, and ingenuous morals. There is something unreadable in his prose. Coleridge is one of those writers who could not find a form for his mental world, for the outpourings of what Borges called his 'very rich mind'.[4]

Here Borges, following up a biographer in a review written in the late 1930s who had called Coleridge the Socrates of his generation, tapped into his own work and it was as a 'conversationalist'. He decided that Coleridge's work was the decipherable echo of a vast conversation, and from this on-going conversation there developed the Romantic Movement in England. Coleridge's never-ending talking led Borges to extend his written work considerably by agreeing to be taped as he talked. Numerous books of conversations in Spanish, English, and French have appeared and have in common Borges's willingness to discuss literary matters, almost to the point of it being one, long conversation in different books and with different authors. The taped or video-based dialogue has become a sub-'genre' in his work and it derives from Coleridge. Coleridge was read as Borges's contemporary. He would instigate a conversation about Coleridge and argue with him to another as if he was still alive.

Adolfo Bioy Casares, Borges's close friend, took down notes for the often daily dinner chats he had with Borges and published his enormous book posthumously as *Borges* where he said that they would talk for hours about De Quincey, even if Borges does not much more than allude to him by name. In an interview published by *The Paris Review* in 1967 with Ronald Christ,[5] Borges touched on De Quincey's influence on his writing. And it was at the general level of speculation. De Quincey's idea about superstition, that there is a kinship between everything, however far off it

might seem, was based on a Stoic idea. Borges shared De Quincey's view
that everything in the world was a secret mirror of the universe, or a set of
symbols meaning something else.

De Quincey was the English Romantic writer who came closest to
Borges's own aesthetics. In 1965 Borges summarized De Quincey's reputation as disciple of Coleridge and fellow opium addict. He wrote prose, but
a prose that was as poetic as any verse. His main work, *Confessions of an
English Opium-Eater,* partially translated by Charles Baudelaire, as Borges
noted, is less central to Borges because he was not an opium taker, than the
fourteen volumes of De Quincey's articles that accompanied Borges
throughout his life. De Quincey was Borges's mentor, but he hardly
wrote about him. He defined his way of writing as: 'His delicate and
intricate paragraphs open like cathedrals of music' (833). He names De
Quincey constantly, and his sudden digressions, his choice of surprising,
yet odd adjectives, his intricate syntax, his odd erudition, and his fascination with dreams and nightmares are reflected in his own stories and
poems. You could say that De Quincey was a mirror in which Borges
saw himself. There was nothing objective about De Quincey's literary
passions, which emerge as unsystematic, even chaotic intuitions, based
on an 'antagonistic' mind where in a sentence you can switch to the
opposite side and not worry about contradictions. John Jordan in his
1973 *De Quincey as Critic* wrote that De Quincey wanted to 'impress
with his erudition and overwhelm with his polemics',[6] as did Borges.
What intrigued Borges most was De Quincey's view that reality was
structured both like a labyrinth and like a palimpsest, and both De
Quincey and Borges shared a passion for alternative forms of knowledge.

The power of the dream penetrates Borges's literary universe. In his
lecture on dreams and nightmares, published posthumously as *Seven
Nights,* 1980, Borges argued that the dream is an aesthetic activity, against
Freud's scientific view and psychologists like Havelock Ellis. Borges always
held, like Nabokov, anti-Freudian interpretations and dismissed any explanation of the surprising surface of a dream experience. As an aesthetic act,
the memory of a dream that we recall on waking is based on the categories
of a work of art with the predominant elements of surprise and oddity. And
this is even more the case with nightmares. Borges related his own recurring dreams of labyrinths and of mirrors, his realization that the place of his
dreams was always a street corner of Buenos Aires. He turned to Addison to
explain that the dreamer was the stage, the actors, the author, and the plot
all in one. André Breton held similar views. Borges loved the surface reality
and did not look for 'deeper' meanings. Then, in this lecture, he returned

to Coleridge and the impression created by the dream's effects that force an explanation on the dreamer. He recalled that it was De Quincey who described one of Wordsworth's dreams where the dreamer was in a cave by the sea, reading the Quijote and then he found himself in a desert as an Arab approached and handed him a shell which was also a book and a stone, then a flash of light and Wordsworth woke up. This account by Borges repeats De Quincey, who repeats Wordsworth, and is now repeated by me. Borges knew, but does not confirm it, that the Arab was Cervantes's invented author, or heteronym, Cide Hamete Benengeli. He concluded that it is 'one of the most beautiful dreams in literature'.[7] The Dream is then an ancient genre, based on the supernatural. All of Borges's views on the dream arose from reading Coleridge and De Quincey. Borges affirms that the dream is the source of all art, and this insight comes straight from Romanticism in general as described in Albert Béguin's *L'âme romantique et le rêve*, 1939, that explores German Romanticism using Novalis and the French poet Nerval as sources, in combination with Carl Jung's theories about dreams as revealing archetypal patterns.

However, for Borges the dream is his explanation of the creative process. Not only were many of Borges's stories 'given' by a dream, but the dream described the way he actually wrote a story. He claimed that he had no control over the content, that it arose like a dream from his unconscious, and all he had to do was edit it. This dream basis of his work is further evidence of his debt to Romantic theory about creativity.

Borges's knowledge of the English Romantics was profound. He knew much more than his critical essays convey, and read around them with critical studies and biographies, like Livingston Lowe's long study of the sources to Coleridge's *Ancient Mariner*. There are many isolated references to the English Romantics. Borges has a poem dedicated to William Blake called 'Blake', answering Blake's 'Oh rose, thou art sick' in his collection *La cifra / The Limit*, 1981. Byron left a 'great echo' in him, as he said in another poem 'Browning decides to be a poet' (92). He also knew and often cited the German and French Romantics like Novalis and Hugo, but, above all, he refused to systematize his vast reading. From the Romantics, he developed his ideas about the 'nothingness of personality', that literature was not written by individuals but that individuals tapped into a greater consciousness that had little relation to their surface selves. He upended chronology and linear history and based his readings of the Romantics on pleasure and identification, with De Quincey as his thinking writer. His image of De Quincey is akin to his own projected image and survives as a work of fiction, not of reality. For Borges, the English Romantics are part of 'world' literature where reading and writing are based on previous reading and writing, a palimpsest that has become now a common-place, a Borgesian insight attacking literary originality. This idea has entered the critical mainstream, but was once surprising and provocative. Borges could take this universalist stand because he was from the margins of the great national literatures such as the English or the German or the French literary traditions; an Argentine, his literary culture was based on reading random English, French, German, and Castilian Spanish literature from his towering position within the Argentine tradition.

Notes

1. Unless indicated otherwise, page references in this chapter are to the single-volume *Obras completas* (Buenos Aires: Emecé, 1974). All translations into English are the author's.
2. Jorge Luis Borges, 'Introducción a la literatura inglesa', co-authored with María Esther Vázquez (Buenos Aires: Editorial Columba, 1965) and included in *Obras completas en colaboración* (Buenos Aires: Emecé, 1979).
3. 'Al ruiseñor' is reproduced in *Obras completas*, 3 vols. (Barcelona: María Kodama & Emecé Editores, 1989), III, p. 88.
4. See Jorge Luis Borges, *Textos cautivos. Ensayos y reseñas en 'El Hogar'* (Barcelona: Tusquets, 1986), p. 302.
5. The interview, which was conducted in Buenos Aires in 1966, was published in *The Paris Review*, 40 (Winter–Spring 1967). It can be read online.
6. John E. Jordan, ed. *De Quincey as Critic* (London: Routledge & Kegan Paul, 1973), p. 40.
7. Jorge Luis Borges, *Obras completas* (Buenos Aires: Emecé, 2007), III, 252–253.

CHAPTER 21

Borges and the First Spanish Avant-Garde

Xon de Ros

The viaduct mentioned in Borges's poetic homage to Rafael Cansinos Assens, written on the eve of his return to America and published in Buenos Aires in 1924 (see *Textos recobrados 1919–1929*, 52–53) is an early example of the architectural structures – library, labyrinth, tower – used by Borges to conjure up and explore other dimensions, whether cultural, psychological, or metaphysical. Cansinos, who had been Borges's mentor during the months he spent in Madrid in 1920, was known among his contemporaries as 'the poet of the viaduct' not only because he lived close by the Segovia viaduct in Madrid but also because in his writings the site acquired an iconic status as the scenario for bohemian revellers returning home from their nocturnal gatherings in Café Colonial, the literary *tertulia* presided over by Cansinos himself. The 130 m-tall iron bridge inaugurated in 1874 was a landmark of modern technology and engineering, and had become emblematic of the first wave of avant-gardism in Spain. In the words of Juan Manuel Bonet, it was 'a distinctive symbol of Madrid Ultraism, a modest, more pedestrian version of what the Eiffel Tower represented for the Parisian avant-garde'.[1] In Cansinos's memoirs, the account of his first meeting with Borges in Café Colonial appears under the heading 'Blue Viaduct',[2] and Norah Borges's woodcut depicting the viaduct appeared on the cover of one of the issues of the magazine *Grecia*, a flagship of Ultraism, edited since 1920 by Cansinos. The latter's identification with the viaduct is underscored in his own spoof novel about the avant-garde scene in Madrid, *El Movimiento V.P.* (1921), where it is given prominence by its association with his fictional alter ego, the Poet of the Thousand Years, and becomes the setting for the novel's most lyrical passages.[3]

Later on, Borges would reminisce on the convivial atmosphere of the *tertulias*, and also about the squabbles between them, as one of the highlights of his time in Spain, whose cultural life had been invigorated with the arrival of foreign artists and writers taking shelter in the neutrality of Spain from the ravages of the European War.[4] Among them, the Chilean poet Vicente Huidobro, whose aesthetics of *creacionismo*, seminal for the emergence of the Ultraist movement, were introduced with the publication of Cansinos's translations of a number of poems from *Horizon Carré* in 1918.[5] Later in the same year, *Grecia* had featured a series of poems by Cansinos, under the pseudonym of Juan Las, with the heading: 'Poems of Ultra'. Among them there is one entitled 'The Still and Avid Viaduct' in which the poet adopts the aerial perspective and expansive vision favoured by *ultraísmo*. At the same time, the poem's Icarian allusions ('Airborne bridge / shaking like a body / jumping sideways') recall the reputation of Madrid's viaduct as a favourite spot for suicides. This notoriety is also recorded in Ramón del Valle-Inclán's *Luces de Bohemia*, when Max Estrella invites Don Latino to jump with him from the bridge. Later on, after a dismissive outburst – 'the Ultraists are fraudsters' – the protagonist formulates his own alternative 'dehumanized' aesthetics of the *esperpento*, informed by a social and political agenda. He links this aesthetic with a national tradition of the grotesque which resonates with German expressionism. Valle's conception of a radical poetics energized by a concern with ethical, moral, and social transformation' is closely akin to Borges's artistic ideology at the time he visited Spain, as reflected in the commentary to his own translations of German Expressionist poets. This aspiration for both aesthetic and social renewal sets Borges's own early poems apart from the more radical experiments of the first wave of avant-gardism in Spain, even if his translations as well as most of his own poems written in Spain, conform to the unpunctuated free verse characteristic of Ultraist poetry, and include avant-garde lexical signposts such as 'helix', 'plane', 'trolley', or 'isochronous', as well as the word 'viaduct' in two of his poems on the theme of the war.

If anyone among his contemporaries can be associated with the Expressionist style that Borges characterizes as 'Dostoyevskian, utopian, mystical, and maximalist', it should be Ramón del Valle-Inclán, whose chronicles from the French trenches were published in book form late in 1917.[6] Apart from the subject of the European war, traces of Expressionist influence detected in Borges's early poems – instances of an anthropomorphic nature, religious imagery, and sudden blasts of violence – can equally apply to Valle's prose. Even the phrasing is in places redolent of Valle's.[7] A gruesome passage, in Valle's account, of the soldiers' corpses being washed out to sea reappears in one of Borges's poems ('Russia') in a more restrained manner, the image swiftly covered by a reference to the burial fields of Europe.

It is yet more tempting to see in Borges's valedictory poem 'A Rafael Cansinos Assens' an echo of the two main characters' perambulations through old Madrid in *Luces de Bohemia*: the blind modern poet Max Estrella and his rogue agent and companion Don Latino de Hispalis. In all likelihood, Borges would have been acquainted with the play that had been serialized in the weekly review *España* from July to October of 1920 and shares with Borges's poem not just the nocturnal setting but also the elegiac mood. Borges's inherited eyesight problems and his youthful leanings towards revolutionary socialism can easily be projected onto the character of Max Estrella, and it is not hard to recognize the avuncular figure of the learned Cansinos, born in Seville, encoded in the name of Don Latino de Hispalis (the Latin name for Seville), a translator well acquainted with the literary scene, who displays a knowledge of the Kabbalah and esoterism. Cansinos was a prolific translator, his sources ranging from Dostoyevsky and Goethe to the Koran, the Talmud, and *Arabian Nights* – the latter highly commended by Borges. His philo-Semitism – he had converted to Judaism and published extensively on the subject – became a bond of kinship between the two that would be celebrated in a sonnet Borges dedicated to him, included in the collection *The Other, The Same* (1964). Cansinos was also a polymath generous with his knowledge, and there is gratitude and affection in Borges's memories as he declares that on saying goodbye to Cansinos he felt he was leaving behind all the libraries in Europe with all the knowledge held in them.[8]

For Borges, this image of Cansinos as a heterodox, iconoclastic, and erudite figure would soon supersede his role as the spearhead of *ultraísmo*. This view was not only a reflection of his own gradual estrangement from the movement but also an appraisal of Cansinos's contradictory stance, which is summed up by Gerardo Diego in his obituary: 'Because of the appreciation and gratitude we felt towards Cansinos – that Sevillian *maestro* –, it took us, the avant-gardists, a long time to realize that he did not have much faith in the new art. Deep down, Cansinos was a *modernista* and that explains why he has received so much attention from American poets, whereas in Spain he was soon, and unjustly, forgotten.'[9] Cansinos's reluctance to subscribe to any programmatic aesthetics was conspicuous in the belligerent atmosphere of the avant-garde where defections and allegiances were the subject of much debate among partisans of different tendencies, fostering a proliferation of manifestos and pronouncements. The rift between Huidobro and Guillermo de Torre in 1920 exposed the fissures caused by this indeterminacy and lack of cohesion among the members of the movement. Cansinos's subsequent falling-out with

Guillermo de Torre precipitated the former's abandonment of Ultraism in 1921.[10] In the course of that year, Borges would publish no fewer than six declarations in several literary magazines, showing an increasing preoccupation with defining the principles and norms of Ultraism. The last declaration was published in Buenos Aires in December and contained some examples of Ultraist poetry. However, the presence among those of Gerardo Diego's *creacionista* poem 'Mystical Rose' suggests that Borges was still sympathetic to Cansinos's early call to embrace all new tendencies, even if he felt compelled to qualify what he described as Cansinos's sweeping and cautious definition. This broad scope is reflected in the list of names mentioned by Borges in the text, from practitioners to sympathizers – among the latter Huidobro, and Valle-Inclán, as well as Ramón Gómez de la Serna, José Ortega y Gasset, and Juan Ramón Jiménez.

Unsurprisingly, the sample of poems in Borges's article also includes one of the short Ultraist poems or 'lirogramas' by Juan Las (also known as Cansinos Assens). In the article's final paragraph Borges lambasts the premises of confessional poetry and postulates for the Ultra poet a wandering poetic self in constant process of transformation. This notion, close to T.S. Eliot's theory of depersonalization, has its roots in Walt Whitman, for whom Borges would declare a life-long admiration. His influence was evident in Borges's first published poem 'Hymn to the Sea' which appeared in *Grecia* shortly after his arrival in Spain.[11] It is also present in his poetic homage to Cansinos which was penned just before leaving the country in 1921 and published together with two other poems under the general heading of 'Psalms'. Written in a series of long, self-contained, irregular lines in the manner of Whitman's poetry, the poem also displays instances of Whitmanesque oracular diction that Borges would cultivate in his late poetry. It is also an early example of a 'poetry of the vanishing' that would become one of his trademarks. As Harold Bloom points out, 'Borges sees himself as the celebrator of things in their farewell; his later poetry and stories frequently portray the experience of doing something for the last time, seeing someone or some place as a valediction.'[12]

Formally, the poem's 14 lines inevitably suggest a sonnet, a form that Borges had been practising in both the Shakespearian and the Petrarchan varieties before his visit to Spain.[13] It may seem a strangely conventional choice, as the sonnet, with its architectural conception and *modernista* resonances, was the avant-gardists' *bête-noire*. Predictably, it is the target of a diatribe in Cansinos's novel, where the practitioners of the form, deemed 'the very worst of all future aesthetics', are automatically disqualified from the avant-garde. Yet, the choice of an unrhymed free version of the traditional Petrarchan sonnet might have been dictated by the poem's subject: a promoter of the avant-garde who, just like his fictional incarnation, finds himself torn between the old and the new.[14] Moreover, the two-part division of the sonnet allows for the presentation of a dual identity, anticipating a pattern that Borges would later revisit in his poetry. Also, in a characteristic Borgesian manner, the nocturnal setting of the initial lines echoes the first expeditions of discovery to the viaduct of the Poet of the Thousand Years in the company of his acolytes. The poem's insistence on the collective pronoun 'nosotros' communicates the *esprit de corps* of the early avant-garde incursions before the in-fights and defections that would lead to the disintegration of the movement. The poem's proleptic structure, from past to present, is figured in the linearity of the viaduct which is perched at the end of the initial line that evokes the 'sublime exultation' of walking along the 'wing' of the viaduct. The positioning of the word reflects the idea of the Ultraist image in which, according to Borges's own formulation, the word is not a bridge for ideas but an end in itself.[15]

The concentric anaphoric pattern of the sestet suggests a more introspective voice, with a series of mirror constructions. The parallelism of the next two lines is followed by a set of chiasmic images that closely recall a reference to America within *El movimiento V.P.* where the two hemispheres are contrasted: 'just when people here are about to turn on the lamps, over there they are waking up' (Cansinos, *El movimiento*, 254).[16] In Borges's poem the idea of repetition with a difference conveyed in the chiasmus is further explored in the adverbial anaphora of 'aun/aún' [even/ still], two homonyms only distinguished by a graphic accent which provides the word with temporal elasticity. Whereas this play of reflections and repetitions suggests a merging of identities, it also implies a reversal. Cansinos's novel ends with the farewell of the Poet of the Thousand Years, leaving behind his former disciples and taking off for America, seen as a promised land for the new art. Borges's poem, written on the eve of his own departure, playfully assumes for himself the mantle of the Poet of the Thousand Years – a case of life imitating art imitating life, soon to become a familiar trope in his fiction.

In the course of time, Borges would disown his Ultraist origins and all things related to the movement. According to Guillermo de Torre, Borges's enthusiasm for that period – the years from 1919 to 1922 – soon turned into disdain, even animosity ('Para la prehistoria ultraísta de Borges', 457). This never applied to Cansinos, for whom Borges continued to profess admiration and affection throughout his life. Moreover, judging from his correspondence, the time Borges spent in Spain, not only in Madrid, but also in Majorca and Seville, was exciting and stimulating. It was certainly fruitful. The young writer was able to meet and collaborate with some of the major figures of Spain's literary scene, carving out for himself a reputation as a maverick writer. The experience was also seminal in that it allowed him to experiment with techniques and themes that he would develop later in his work. The bustling eclectic atmosphere of the first avant-gardist wave provided him with some lasting friendships, not just Cansinos but also Guillermo de Torre, Vicente Huidobro, and the Majorcan poet Jacobo Sureda, and with a first taste both for the literary life, and, as conveyed in his 'viaduct' poem, for an image of literary selfhood.

Notes

1. Juan Manuel Bonet, 'Baedeker del Ultraísmo', in Juan Manuel Bonet, ed. *El Ultraísmo y las artes plásticas* (Valencia: IVA and Centre Julio González, 1996), pp. 9–59 (p. 10).
2. Rafael Cansinos Assens, *La Novela de un literato*, 3 vols. (Madrid: Alianza, 2005), III, pp. 23–24. The two men were introduced by the poet Pedro Garfias who was an active member of Cansinos's Ultraist cohort and one of the signatories of their first manifesto in 1918; Garfias also introduced Guillermo de Torre who would marry Borges's sister, Norah.
3. Rafael Cansinos Assens, *El Movimiento V.P.* (Madrid: Hiperión, 1978), p. 103.
4. See 'La traducción de un accidente' (1925), in Jorge Luis Borges, *Inquisiciones* (Barcelona: Seix Barral/ Biblioteca Breve, 1994), pp. 17–21; see also in the same volume, 'Definición de Cansinos Assens', pp. 51–55.
5. Cansinos Assens, 'La modernísima poesía francesa (el creacionismo)', *Los Quijotes*, 4, 87 (October 1918).
6. Ramón del Valle-Inclán, *La media noche. Visión estelar de un momento de guerra* (Alicante: Biblioteca Virtual Miguel de Cervantes, 2017). Available online at www.cervantesvirtual.com/obra/la-media-noche-vision-estelar-de-un-momento-de-guerra-875777 (accessed 1 October 2018).
7. Some examples are: 'En el cuerno salvaje de un arco iris / clamaremos su gesta' ('Rusia'), and 'el silencio aulla en los horizontes hundidos' ('Trinchera'). For the influence of Expressionism in Borges's early poetry see Thorpe Running, 'Borges's Ultraist Poetry', in Harold Bloom, ed. *Jorge Luis Borges* (New York: Chelsea House Publishers, 1986).
8. Prologue to Rafael Cansinos Assens, *El candelabro de los siete brazos* (1914) (Madrid: Alianza, 1986), p. 3.
9. Gerardo Diego, 'Cansinos Assens', *Índice de Artes y Letras*, 186 (julio–agosto 1964), p. 15.
10. The estrangement between Cansinos and de Torre might have contributed to Borges's strained relationship with the latter. De Torre is mercilessly parodied

in *El Movimiento V.P.* as the 'Youngest Poet of All', speaking in neologisms and seemingly afflicted by logorrhea (III, p. 39 and passim); see also de Torre's remarks on Cansinos in *Literaturas europeas de vanguardia* (1925) (Sevilla: Renacimiento, 2001), pp. 76–78.

11. Guillermo de Torre refers to this influence as a 'Whitmanesque enthusiasm before the plurality of the universe', in 'Para la prehistoria ultraísta de Borges', *Hispania*, 473 (September 1964), pp. 457–463 (p. 458).

12. Harold Bloom, *The Western Canon* (New York: Riverhead Books, 1995), p. 443.

13. The other poem dedicated to Cansinos, 'Rafael Cansinos Assens', *The Other, The Same* (1964), is a Shakespearian sonnet.

14. In the prologue to his collection *La Moneda de Hierro* (Buenos Aires: Emecé, 1976) where he reiterates his indebtedness to Cansinos, Borges states that each subject, however occasional or minor requires a specific aesthetics, and, perhaps alluding to the poem discussed here, he claims that the possibilities of the 'Protean' sonnet and Whitmanesque free verse, are not yet exhausted.

15. 'Al margen de la moderna estética', published in *Grecia* (Sevilla, enero 1920), in *Textos Recobrados 1919–1929*, p. 31.

16. Cf. Borges's 'A Rafael Cansinos Assens': 'Cuando la tarde sea quietud en mi patio, de tus cuartillas surgirá la mañana. / Será sombra de mi verano tu invierno y tu luz será gloria de mi sombra'.

CHAPTER 22

Borges and James Joyce: Makers of Labyrinths

Patricia Novillo-Corvalán

The nexus between Borges and Joyce evokes a striking series of parallels: one thinks of their labyrinthine creations, cyclical conceptions of time, prodigious memories, fondness for encyclopaedias, eyesight afflictions, and the fact that both writers – for altogether different reasons – were denied the Nobel Prize. They are also interlinked by the geography of their native cities: Dublin and Buenos Aires, peripheral capitals they obsessively mapped out in their fiction as they grappled with the complex experience of modernity.

Despite these parallels, a fundamental difference lies at the core of their creative projects. This is exemplified by Joyce's gradual acquisition of an accretive style of composition that marked a shift from the 'scrupulous meanness' of *Dubliners* (1914) to the ballooning and totalizing novelistic gestures of his high modernist masterpieces: *Ulysses* (1922) and *Finnegans Wake* (1939). Borges, by contrast, crafted the metaphysical *ficción*, his own miniaturized form of writing, albeit no less complex or exhaustive, which he ascribed to a *multum in parvo* technique in which the notion of infinity is bound in a nutshell. As such, Borges has a unique, if not conflicted, relationship with Joyce. Throughout his career as a writer, Borges strategically strove to create an image of Joyce as the artificer of intricately woven labyrinths whose sheer size, encyclopaedic scope, and infinite nature both fascinated and horrified him. In this chapter, I will chart the twists and turns of Borges's ambivalent relationship with Joyce, from his 1925 review of *Ulysses* and fragmentary translation of 'Penelope', which were published in the second wave of the modernist review *Proa*[1] to the subsequent development of a more problematic attitude where he sought to reposition his art of brevity as the antithetical riposte to Joyce's epic legacy.

European Outsiders

Writing from the 'peripheral' urban spaces of late-colonial Ireland and postcolonial Argentina, Borges and Joyce responded ambivalently to the complex experience of modernity, whether that be the painstaking construction of a fragmented Dublin depicted as a 'centre of paralysis'[2] or the creation of an 'anti-modernity' space ambiguously located in the margins or *orillas* of the city. The youthful avant-gardist poet who returned to his native Buenos Aires from war-torn Europe in 1921 was inevitably drawn to Joyce's radical modernist vision and its provocative combination of unprecedented linguistic experimentation with a nuanced critique of British imperialism. Borges situated his equally innovative programme of aesthetic renovation within the political landscape of Argentina during the historical period marked by the *Centenario* of independence from Spanish rule. Inventing himself as a theorist and practitioner of the Ultraist movement (launched in Madrid in 1918), on the one hand, and as an ideologue boldly engaged with the idea of an Argentine tradition, on the other, Borges proposed an internationalist cultural agenda which, paradoxically, remained deeply Argentine. Intensely preoccupied with questions of language, tradition, and *criollismo*, the young Jorge Luis Borges would have been enthralled by Stephen Dedalus's memorable 'tundish' exchange with the Dean of Studies in *A Portrait of the Artist as a Young Man* (1916), an Irish-language political debate that lent a renewed impetus to his unceasing search for an Argentine idiom:

> The language in which we are speaking is his before it is mine. How different are the words *home, Christ, ale, master*, on his lips and on mine! I cannot speak or write these words without unrest of spirit. His language, so familiar and so foreign, will always be for me an acquired speech.[3]

Acutely aware of the tension between 'familiarity' and 'foreignness' also inherent in his River Plate Spanish, the question of the politics of language dominated Borges's early works, a subject matter that receives ample treatment in the essay collection suitably titled *The Language of the Argentines* (1928). Here, Borges shifts Stephen Dedalus's rhetorical scene to his local *rioplatense* vernacular, making a compelling case for the unique inflection of specific Argentine terms. The difference between the 'Spanish of the Spaniards and our Argentine conversation', says Borges, lies in 'the distinct environment of our voice':

> We haven't changed the intrinsic meaning of words, but we have altered their connotation. The word *súbdito* (subject) [. . .] is acceptable in Spain but denigrating in the New World. [. . .] Our greatest words in poetry, *arrabal* and *pampa*, are felt by no Spaniard. Our term *lindo* (beautiful) is a word that is total praise; among the Spaniards it is not so overwhelmingly approving. (*OA* 86)

Though like Joyce's decision to fly by the nets of 'nationality, language, and religion' (*A Portrait* ... 171), Borges despised entrenched forms of cultural nationalism. His search for an Argentine idiom manifested itself in a contradictory gesture that simultaneously intertwined national and international discourses, just as Joyce's complex historical circumstances necessitated a deeply personal and, likewise, contradictory engagement with Irish culture and politics by distancing himself from the Celtic revival while at the same time recognizing the importance of an Irish cultural tradition. In the case of Borges, this iconoclastic position was later expounded in 'The Argentine Writer and Tradition' (1951), where he urged Argentine (and Latin American) writers to take full advantage of their unassailable 'right' to the Western archive, a 'right', he suggested, 'greater than that which the inhabitants of one Western nation or another may have'. For Borges, the Irish are a case in point. By virtue of being 'different' and acting within a culture to which they feel no form of devotion, Irish writers were able to 'make innovations in English culture' (*SN-F* 426). These innovations owed to the fact that the Irish treated all the European subjects with 'irreverence', an outsider position he duly urged Latin Americans to follow (*Ibid.*). By foregrounding Joyce's subversive status as an Irish writer, Borges developed a cultural strategy that suited his own eccentric position as an Argentine, while construing both countries as alternative spaces defined by a form of marginality that greatly foments, rather than hinders, literary innovation.

Ulysses in Argentina

How did Borges get hold of a copy of the much-coveted first edition of *Ulysses* published under the imprint of Sylvia Beach's Shakespeare & Company bookshop? The Argentine writer Ricardo Güiraldes – author of the regionalist novel *Don Segundo Sombra* (1926) and co-founder of *Proa* – arrived in Paris at the precise moment that Beach was enlisting subscribers for the deluxe edition of *Ulysses* published in Dutch handmade paper and sold at 350 Francs each. Güiraldes, in turn, was a close friend of Joyce's official publicist, the influential French writer, critic, and translator Valéry Larbaud, who played a crucial role in championing the cultural value of Joyce's modernist masterpiece. According to the accounts where Beach methodically recorded the names of the subscribers to the first edition, Güiraldes purchased copy no. 47 of the 100 copies on sale.[4] Still, one might wonder, why did the Francophile Güiraldes purchase a copy of an overpriced book written in a language he could not read? Aware of the far-reaching potentiality of Joyce's revolutionary novel and eager to embrace the latest cultural innovations from abroad, Güiraldes decided to add his name to the list of subscribers. The investment paid off. For Güiraldes, Borges's twinning of youthful enthusiasm and polyglotism, avant-gardism and erudition, turned him into the ideal reader, reviewer, and translator of *Ulysses*. In short, the voyage of *Ulysses* from Paris to Buenos Aires would radically change the Argentine cultural landscape. From the crucial role played by Borges in its early reception to the first complete Spanish translation by J. Salas Subirat (1945) and the subsequent development of a distinctly Argentine tradition of 'Ulyssean' novels (to borrow Gerald Martin's term),[5] including Juan Filloy's *Caterva* (1937), Leopoldo Marechal's *Adán Buenosayres* (1948), and Julio Cortázar's *Rayuela* (1963; *Hopscotch*).

Borges's historic review of *Ulysses* opens with a boastful declaration: 'I am the first traveller from the Hispanic world to set foot upon the shores of *Ulysses*' (*SN-F* 12). The emphatic tone of Borges's rhetoric implies that he believed he was the first (Hispanic) critical explorer of Joyce's epic geography. As things stand, though, he was unknowingly competing for that honour with a Spanish critic, Antonio Marichalar, who in the end overtook Borges by a matter of two months, publishing his own review of *Ulysses* in the November 1924 edition of *Revista de Occidente* (founded in 1923 by José Ortega y Gasset).[6] Still, despite the grandiosity of Borges's opening claim, he soon laid bare his miniaturizing tendencies, describing his reading of the novel as 'transient', 'inattentive', and unashamedly confessing not to have tackled its 700 pages. By taking a strategic shortcut through the cityscape of Dublin, Borges endorses his own fragmentary exploration of the tangled Joycean labyrinth:

> I confess that I have not cleared a path through all seven hundred pages. I confess to having examined only bits and pieces, and yet I know what it is, with that bold and legitimate certainty with which we assert our knowledge of a city, without ever having been rewarded with the intimacy of all the many streets it includes. (*SN-F* 12)

Borges's enthusiastic, albeit deeply conflicted, response to *Ulysses* was followed by a translation of the last two pages of Molly Bloom's unpunctuated soliloquy, a passionate performance by a young man who, ironically, stands at odds with the mature writer later renowned for the asexual and metaphysical tone of his cerebral *ficciones*. Described by Joyce as, 'probably more obscene than any preceding episode',[7] 'Penelope' was notorious for its prolific allusions to male and female genitalia, bodily functions, and sexual practices, not least Molly Bloom's final, orgasmic reverie that closes the book with a capitalized 'Yes'.

Like the review that problematically foregrounds its own incompleteness, Borges's fragmentary translation of 'Penelope' remains an exercise in abridgement and rewriting, thus offering the reader a deeply mediated version of *Ulysses*. The Borgesian manoeuvre turned the translation into a self-contained performance in the variant of Spanish spoken in the River Plate area, a dialect that not only provided the appropriate idioms to convey the eroticism of the episode, but also added a distinctive linguistic significance to Molly's hallmark polyvalence. As a corroboration of his linguistic conviction to legitimize a primarily oral vernacular, Borges innovatively rendered Molly Bloom with the Argentine second person pronoun 'vos', thus challenging conventional practices that still employed the standard Spanish 'tú' as the customary norm in written texts:

> The sun shines for you he said[8]
> Para vos brilla el sol me dijo.

Among the other lexical choices and inflections from *rioplatense* Spanish that Borges deliberately included in his colloquial, yet ideologically laden, translation of 'Penelope' is the reiterated use of the adjective *lindo/a*, hence rendering Molly's 'a nice plant'[9] into 'una linda planta' and 'beautiful country'[10] into the superlative form 'un campo lindísimo' (*Textos recobrados* 1919–1929, p. 201). Again, these lexical choices must be read in conjunction with the distinctive linguistic agenda that Borges articulated in *The Language of the Argentines*. Finally, just as Joyce inserted Molly Bloom's contradictory identity within colonial Ireland and the disputed territory of Gibraltar (officially known as a British Crown colony), so Borges complemented and complicated Joyce's project by incorporating into the translation the politically charged context of his native Argentina.

Aesthetics of Expansion Vs Aesthetics of Compression

As Borges gradually shifted from the 'avant-garde *criollismo*' (in Beatriz Sarlo's phrase)[11] of his early writings to the stylistic canonicity of his mature prose, his creative antagonism towards Joyce became even more pronounced. This attitude can be summed up in Borges's tongue-in-cheek rebuff in the 'Foreword' to *The Garden of Forking Paths* (1941), where he utilized Joyce's accretionary novelistic impulses as a foil to endorse the aphoristic technique of his ultra-concise *ficciones*:

It is a laborious madness and an impoverishing one, the madness of composing vast books – setting out in five hundred pages an idea that can be perfectly related orally in five minutes. The better way to go about it is to pretend that those books already exist and offer a summary, a commentary of them. (*CF* 67)

In the same year, when writing his obituary of Joyce entitled 'Fragment on Joyce' (1941) – an early version of 'Funes the Memorious' (1942) – Borges took to further lengths his deep-seated aversion for the novelistic genre by arguing that the infallible memory of his fictional character Ireneo Funes mirrors the infinite expansiveness of Joyce's total novel. In his unyielding determination to stress the fallacies inherent in totalizing fictional gestures, Borges creates his hapless Fray Bentos *compadrito*, a character who has been equipped with an absolute memory and perception after a riding accident that left him paralysed. Therefore, Borges boldly juxtaposes the relentless memorizing habits of Funes with the sheer encyclopaedic scope of *Ulysses*. For Borges, then, *Ulysses* and Funes are united via their analogous mnemonic overload which, in turn, fashions them as monstrous creations:

I have evoked him because a consecutive, straightforward reading of the four hundred thousand words of *Ulysses* would require similar monsters. (*SN-F* 220)

As a literary character, Funes incarnates the ideal reader of *Ulysses* and, by extension, the 'ideal reader suffering from an ideal insomnia' prophesied by Joyce in *Finnegans Wake*.[12] Note, too, that Borges endows Funes with a persistent state of insomnia and, in the 'Foreword' to *Artifices* (1944), categorizes the story as 'one long metaphor for insomnia' (*CF* 129). Consequently, Borges constructs his dialogue with Joyce as a dialectic that reveals his fascination with Joyce's endeavour to contain infinity within fiction, on the one hand, and his repudiation of the colossal magnitude of the total novel, on the other. This creative tension, moreover, results in a possible synthesis between the two writers: Borges's aesthetic compromise lies in his portrayal of a character endowed with infinite powers of recollection (as a fictional equivalent of Joyce's total inclusion in *Ulysses*), albeit written in the most thoroughly concise narrative fashion. In other words, Borges's miniaturized version of *Ulysses* is intricately crafted as a satirical re-creation of Joyce's gargantuan tendencies. Thus, Borges teasingly emulates Joyce's ambitious endeavour to provide a painstakingly accurate reconstruction of the Dublin of 16 June 1904: 'I want to give a picture of Dublin so complete that if the city one day disappeared from the earth it could be reconstructed out of my book',[13] by conferring on Funes the equivalent totalizing gesture of providing a round-the-clock reconstruction of an entire day, which in turn demanded another whole day (*CF* 135). In this way, Borges cunningly transposes *Ulysses* into the tight confines of his quintessentially compact *ficción* and fulfils the precepts outlined in the 'Foreword' to *The Garden of Forking Paths* (cited above) by providing an irreverent 'summary' or 'commentary' of Joyce's 'vast book'.

Throughout the remainder of his literary career, Borges continued his non-apologetic disavowal of Joyce's unrestrained verbal profligacy (see, most notably, 'Joyce's Latest Novel', in *SN-F* 195), although his oppositional aesthetic stance was intermittently punctuated by interviews, lectures, and tribute poems that showed dazzling glimpses of the deep admiration he secretly held for Joyce. In a 1982 interview with Seamus Heaney and Richard Kearney that took place in Dublin (and on Bloomsday) during the centenary celebrations of Joyce's birth, Borges positively reminisced about his lifelong relationship with Joyce:

> Looking back at my own writings sixty years after my first encounter with Joyce, I must admit that I have always shared Joyce's fascination with words and have always worked at my language within an essentially poetic framework, savouring the multiple meanings of words, their etymological echoes and endless resonances.[14]

A similar conciliatory gesture can be found in his lecture 'Blindness', delivered in Buenos Aires in 1977, where an elderly Borges paid tribute to Joyce's unparalleled verbal artistry: 'He knew all the languages, and he wrote in a language invented by himself, difficult to understand but marked by a strange music. Joyce brought a new music to English' (*SN-F* 481). Alluding to *Finnegans Wake*, Borges expresses his admiration for Joyce's creation of an infinite book that sums up the history of the English language, a literary microcosm which, it may be argued, yields Joyce's own version of the Aleph. The looming shadow of the Irish artificer reappears in poems such as 'James Joyce' and 'Invocation to Joyce', both included in the poetry collection *In Praise of Darkness* (1969), the title, once again, alluding to their shared eye affliction, as well as to another blind bard, Homer. Foregrounded in both poems are the interchangeable symbols of their art: the infinite labyrinths and the boundless Alephs that encapsulate their dizzying fictional universes. If Borges – citing Hamlet's famous words in the epigraph to 'The Aleph': 'I could be bounded in a nutshell and count myself a King of infinite space' (*CF* 274) – describes the Aleph as: 'a small iridescent sphere of almost unbearable brightness' (*CF* 283), Joyce, in turn, offers his own cosmic version of infinity in the punning, dream-like idiom of *Finnegans Wake*: 'Putting Allspace in a Notshall'.[15]

Notes

1. *Proa* was founded by Borges and Macedonio Fernández and first launched in 1922. Borges re-founded the magazine with Ricardo Güiraldes, Pablo Rojas Paz, and Alfredo Brandán Caraffa in 1924.
2. James Joyce, *Letters of James Joyce II*, ed. Richard Ellmann (London: Faber, 1966), p. 134.
3. James Joyce, *A Portrait of the Artist as a Young Man*, ed. Jeri Johnson (Oxford: Oxford University Press, 2000), p. 159.
4. See Lawrence Rainey, *Institutions of Modernism: Literary Elites and Public Cultures* (New Haven, CT: Yale University Press, 1998), for a detailed account of the publishing history of *Ulysses*.
5. Gerald Martin, *Journeys Through the Labyrinth: Latin American Fiction in the Twentieth Century* (London: Verso, 1989), p. 148.
6. Antonio Marichalar, 'James Joyce in His Labyrinth', *Revista de Occidente*, 17 (1924), pp. 177–202.
7. Joyce, *Letters of James Joyce II*, p. 501.
8. James Joyce, *Ulysses*, ed. Hans Walter Gabler (London: The Bodley Head, 1986), 18, pp. 1571–1572.
9. *Ibid.*, p. 1556.
10. *Ibid.*, p. 1559.
11. Beatriz Sarlo, *Jorge Luis Borges: A Writer on the Edge*, ed. John King (London: Verso, 1993), p. 95.
12. James Joyce, *Finnegans Wake* (London: Penguin, 1992), 120, pp. 13–14.
13. Frank Budgen, *James Joyce and the Making of Ulysses* (London: Grayson & Grayson, 1934), p. 69.
14. Richard Kearney, *Transitions: Narratives in Modern Irish Culture* (Manchester: Manchester University Press, 1988), p. 49.
15. Joyce, *Finnegans Wake*, 455, 29.

CHAPTER 23

Borges and Kafka

Sarah Roger

It was while living in Switzerland as a teenager that Borges first encountered the writings of the Czech author Franz Kafka (1883–1924). About this experience, he remarked:

> I will never forget my first reading of Kafka in a certain professionally modern publication in 1917. Its editors – who didn't always lack talent – were dedicated to the abolition of punctuation, the abolition of capital letters, the abolition of rhyme, the alarming simulation of metaphor, the abuse of compounded words, and other tasks appropriate to youth at the time and perhaps to youth at any time. Amidst this clatter of type, an apologue signed by one Franz Kafka seemed to my young reader's docility inexplicably insipid. After all these years, I dare to confess my unpardonable literary insensibility: I saw a revelation and didn't notice it ('Franz Kafka, *The Vulture*', *TTL* 502).

Years later, Borges corrected his youthful misjudgement: he declared Kafka the greatest writer of the modern age.[1]

Reading Kafka

Borges read all three of Kafka's novels (*America*, 1927; *The Trial*, 1925; and *The Castle*, 1926), 41 of the 89 Kafka stories published in Borges's lifetime, and many of Kafka's fragmentary writings, including those published in *Reflections on Sin, Suffering, Hope, and the True Way* (1931) and *Wedding Preparations in the Country* (1953). Of these, Borges was partial to the short stories:

> I always read tales, stories, because a novel always has padding; but when one reads a story [...], everything is necessary [...]. In the case of Kafka, if I think of Kafka, I think of his shortest stories, 'The Great Wall of China', 'Odradek', 'Before the Law', and of his aphorisms as well. But I find his novels somewhat mechanical.[2]

The stories Borges read – largely the German originals – were in collections published by Kafka's best friend and literary executor, Max Brod. Kafka asked Brod to destroy his writings upon his death; instead, Brod edited them for publication. He made substantial changes, shaping the writings to present a polished version of his friend's works: he joined fragments into chapters, turning *The Trial* into a coherent novel; he retitled *The Man Who Disappeared* as *America* and restructured the text to give it a happy ending; he even gave titles to fragments and published them as complete stories.

Nowadays, many scholars view Brod's edited volumes with scepticism. Comparing them to the originals, they argue that Brod applied his own prophetic tendencies to give Kafka's writings a Messianic thrust. They also suggest that Brod's view shaped the version of Kafka that dominated throughout the twentieth century, including the one disseminated via the popular English translations by Willa and Edwin Muir. Borges read these translations alongside the German, and he also read Brod's 1937 biography of his friend, *Franz Kafka*.[3] It was not until the 1980s that editions of Kafka free of Brod's interventions were widely available, which was too late for Borges. Borges's Kafka, therefore, is Brod's Kafka, even if this is not the version of Kafka that scholars draw on today:

> The Brod version of [*The Trial*] is the one that was translated and read around the world, the one that influenced several generations of writers and readers, and indeed the one that changed the course of modern literary history. It is now an indisputable part of that history [. . .]. Literary historians will always have to use the Brod editions of this and other major texts as the basis on which to understand the Kafka of the twentieth century.[4]

Interpreting Kafka

Borges wrote 56 pieces (plus five in collaboration) mentioning Kafka, including a dozen that focused on him. In these texts, Borges put forth a view of Kafka that was, like Brod's interpretation, largely biographical and religious. For example,

> One could define [Kafka's] work as a parable or a series of parables whose theme is the moral relation of the individual with God and with His incomprehensible universe. Despite this contemporary ambience, Kafka is closer to the Book of Job than to what has been called 'modern literature'. His work is based on a religious, and particularly Jewish, consciousness; its imitation in other contexts becomes meaningless. Kafka saw his work as an

act of faith, and he did not want to be discouraging to mankind ('Franz Kafka, *The Vulture*', *TTL* 501).

Brod proposed a similar likeness between Kafka's writing and the Book of Job:

> Since the book of Job in the Bible, God has never been so savagely striven with as in Kafka's *The Trial* and *The Castle*, or in his *In the Penal Colony* [...]. Just the same in the Book of Job, God does what seems absurd and unjust to man. But it is *only* to man that this seems so, and the final conclusion arrived at in Job as in Kafka is the confirmation of the fact that the yardstick by which man works is not by that which measurements are taken in the world of the Absolute.[5]

Borges saw the Book of Job as about 'the enigma that is the universe', and he read Kafka's stories as modern-day versions of Job – stories about stoicism, suffering, and 'the inscrutability of God and the universe'.[6]

Borges's belief that Kafka's writing recalled the Book of Job was part of his view that Kafka drew on his own life to create works that were simultaneously personal and universal:

> 1883, 1924 – the two years that frame the life of Franz Kafka. Nobody can be unaware of the notable events contained within them: the First World War, the invasion of Belgium, the defeats and the victories [...]. They also include the personal events recorded in Max Brod's biography: Kafka's rift with his father, his loneliness, law studies, hours spent working in an office, the proliferation of manuscripts, and his tuberculosis. There were also the great baroque forays into literature: German expressionism and the verbal feats of Johannes Becher, Yeats and James Joyce.
>
> Kafka's destiny was to transform circumstances and agonies into fables ('Franz Kafka: *America*', 454).

Above all else, Borges believed that it was personal experience rather than the artistic or historical context that shaped Kafka's writing:

> He was sickly and sullen; his father never stopped secretly despising him and bullied him up until 1922. (Kafka himself has said that all of his work derived from this conflict and from his persistent meditations on the mysterious compassion and endless demands of the 'patria potestad' [parental authority]) ('Franz Kafka: *La metamorfosis*', 97).

Building on this interpretation, Borges proposed that Kafka's writing was essentially about the 'patria potestad' – a nested set of authorities that starts with the power exercised by a father over his son and extends to the control wielded by God over man. Contained within this hierarchy are what Borges believed to be Kafka's preoccupations: 'Two ideas – or more exactly, two obsessions – rule Kafka's work: subordination and the infinite' ('Franz Kafka, *La metamorfosis*', 97–98; 'Franz Kafka, *The Vulture*', *TTL* 502). For example,

> The hero of his second novel, Josef K., is increasingly oppressed by a senseless trial. He is unable to find out what crime he is accused of, nor can he even confront the invisible court that is supposed to be judging him and which, forgoing any trial, ultimately orders his execution. K., the protagonist of the third and final of Kafka's novels, is a land surveyor who is summoned to a castle to which he never manages to gain entry, and dies without being recognized by the authorities who govern it ('Franz Kafka, *La metamorfosis*': 98).

Kafka's writing conveys unending hierarchies in structure as well as in content. Borges noted that the novels 'have an infinite number of chapters, because their theme is the infinite number of possibilities', while the stories often imply Zeno's paradoxes – the intellectual puzzles that, for Borges, function as a literary representation of infinity ('Un sueño eterno', 238). Borges singled out Kafka's 'Before the Law', 'A Common Confusion', 'An Imperial Message', and his personal favourite 'The Great Wall of China' for containing infinite obstacles and authorities.

Zeno's paradoxes are central not only to Borges's interpretation of Kafka, but also to Kafka's place in Borges's work. 'Kafka and His Precursors' is perhaps the best-known of the texts that Borges wrote mentioning Kafka, and it is partly about the recurrence of the Kafkaesque motif of Zeno's paradoxes throughout literature. In the essay, Borges explores the concept of literary influence and suggests that Kafka's presence can be spotted in works as varied as those by Zeno of Elea, Søren Kierkegaard, and Robert Browning despite the fact that none read Kafka. The reader is the one who identifies Kafka's influence, retroactively importing it into the works of Kafka's precursors by virtue of the reader's familiarity with Kafka's writings. The idea that an author or reader can infuse a common meaning into otherwise unrelated texts reinforces the possibility that Borges's version of Kafka was rooted in Brod's interpretation, since it allows for the Kafka of Brod to generate the Kafka of Borges. This perspective is in accord with Borges's approach to reading and writing more broadly: he was famously flexible with meaning, interpretation, and rewriting, and his literary interactions with Kafka exemplify this.

Alongside reading and writing about Kafka, Borges authored (or co-authored) translations of 18 of Kafka's texts, among them 'Before the Law' and 'Josephine the Singer, or the Mouse Folk' (although who did some of these translations is a matter of contention).[7] Borges took liberties in these translations, changing titles to focus on aspects of the stories that interested him and cutting material to highlight his interpretation. For example, in his translation of 'Before the Law', Borges's subtle interventions remove any possibility that the man from the country will get past the doorkeeper – a change that emphasizes the power of the 'patria potestad'.

Emulating Kafka

Critics such as Efraín Kristal and Gene Bell-Villada have suggested that Borges's early work translating Kafka helped his development as a writer, and that he subsequently drew on Kafka's influence in his own stories.[8] Borges's own comments confirm this, as he cited Kafka as an influence on some of his key stories from the 1940s. For example, he said, 'When I wrote "The Library of Babel" and "The Lottery in Babylon", I tried to be Kafka.'[9] The latter of these stories even contains a sardonic reference to Kafka in the form of 'a sacred latrine called Qaphqa' (*CF* 104). With respect to Kafka's presence in these two texts, Borges may have been referring to any number of stylistic or thematic similarities: the unnamed narrators, the temporal and geographical vagueness, the yearning for meaning that goes unsatisfied, or the uncertain conclusions, to name a few. As in many of the Kafka stories that Borges admired, 'The Library of Babel' and 'The Lottery in Babylon' describe seemingly infinite systems of order or authority that are rooted in paradoxes and maintained by incomprehensible rules, to which their narrators are subordinate and from which they cannot escape. Both stories echo the Book of Job in their narrators' unfulfilled desire to have their circumstances – and their suffering – explained.

Borges also noted Kafka's influence on other works, among them 'Death and the Compass' (*Fictions*, 1944) and his late, long story 'The Congress' (*The Book of Sand*, 1975), both of which feature versions of Zeno's paradoxes. In addition, Kafka's presence can be identified in texts where Borges did not openly acknowledge his influence. Borges's poem 'A Dream' (titled by Borges in German as 'Ein Traum') from *The Iron Coin* (1976) is based on a Kafka story of the same name. In Kafka's version, a man dreams that another – whom he has dreamed into existence – is forcing him to climb into his own grave. In Borges's version, Kafka is in dialogue with two of his characters, a pair of lovers who are reluctant to consummate their relationship for fear that Kafka will wake up in order to kill them. Borges made use of the same idea in 'The Circular Ruins' (*Fictions*, 1944), a story that also plays with the concept of the 'patria potestad'.

Of Borges's stories, 'The Secret Miracle' (*Fictions*, 1944) is the one in which Kafka's concealed presence is strongest. The story contains references to the Czech throughout, including allusions to Zeno's paradoxes, subordination, and infinity. The protagonist, Jaromir Hladík, resides on the Zeltnergasse, the same Prague street where Kafka lived, first at 'Sixthaus' (number two) from 1888 to 1889 and at 'Zu den drei Königen' (number three) from 1896 to 1907.[10] As in Kafka's and Borges's versions of 'A Dream', the protagonist of 'The Secret Miracle' has a dream on which his life depends. He imagines that he is in the Clementinum (the Czech national library and the building where Kafka attended university lectures), where he hopes to secure salvation by finding the volume that holds the secret letter containing God.[11] This dream echoes 'The Library of Babel' with a Zenoesque search through an infinite library, and it also recalls the unending, impossible hierarchies of the 'patria potestad' with the officials who hold boundless power over Hladík. Rife with Kafkaesque authorities and unending labyrinths, the story's ambiguous conclusion offers up two possibilities: Hladík either is or is not granted the secret miracle he seeks.

On its surface, 'The Secret Miracle' may be about a mediocre author oppressed by authorities in Nazi Germany, but it is also the story of the relationship between man and God. Echoing the Book of Job, it interrogates man's place in an incomprehensible universe and his relationship with the unknowable, unreachable 'patria potestad'. Like the biographically inflected Kafka stories that Borges admired, 'The Secret Miracle' can be read as both specific and universal, rooted in a historical moment and timeless.

Borges believed that Kafka's writing grew out of his biography yet also surpassed it, and that it was about Kafka's relationship with his father yet also about the relationship between man and an incomprehensible God. Borges made use of this multi-tiered engagement in texts that he wrote – either openly or covertly – under Kafka's influence. Stories such as 'The Library of Babel', 'The Lottery in Babylon', and 'The Secret Miracle' can be read both as Borges's homage to Kafka and as part of his broader engagement with universal, Kafkaesque concepts such as Zeno's paradoxes and the Book of Job.

Notes

1. Jorge Luis Borges, 'Franz Kafka: *La metamorfosis*', *Prólogos con un prólogo de prólogos*, 1975, *Obras completas*, Vol. 4 (Buenos Aires: Emecé, 1996), pp. 97–99 (p. 97); Jorge Luis Borges, 'Franz Kafka: *América*', *Biblioteca personal: Prólogos*, 1988, *Obras completas*, Vol. 4 (Buenos Aires: Emecé, 1996), p. 454; Jorge Luis Borges, 'Un sueño eterno: palabras grabadas en el centenario de Kafka', *Textos recobrados, 1956–1986* (Buenos Aires: Emecé, 2003), pp. 237–239 (p. 238). Subsequent references to these materials are incorporated in parentheses, in the text.

2. Jorge Luis Borges, 'Kafka, la philosophie, la poésie', *Change International*, 3 (1985), 46; translations of citations from non-English texts are mine.

3. Michelle Woods, *Kafka Translated: How Translators Have Shaped Our Reading of Kafka* (New York: Bloomsbury, 2014), pp. 3, 72.

4. Clayton Koelb, 'Critical Editions II: Will the Real Franz Kafka Please Stand Up?', *A Companion to the Works of Franz Kafka*, ed. James Rolleston (Rochester: Camden House, 2002), pp. 27–33 (p. 30).

5. Max Brod, *Franz Kafka: A Biography*, 1937, trans. G. Humphreys Roberts and Richard Winston (New York: Da Capo, 1995), pp. 175–176, emphasis in the original.

6. Jorge Luis Borges, 'The Book of Job', *Borges and His Successors: The Borgesian Impact on Literature and the Arts*, trans. Edna Aizenberg (Columbia: University of Missouri Press, 1990), pp. 267–275 (p. 275).

7. Fernando Sorrentino, 'El kafkiano caso de la *Verwandlung* que Borges jamás tradujo', *Espéculo: Revista de estudios literarios* 10 (1998), np, Web, http://www.ucm.es/info/especulo/numero10/borg_tra.html (accessed 20 November 2009).

8. Gene Bell-Villada, *Borges and His Fiction: A Guide to His Mind and Art*, 2nd ed. (Austin: University of Texas Press, 1999), pp. 36–37; Efraín Kristal, *Invisible Work: Borges and Translation* (Nashville, TN: Vanderbilt University Press, 2002), p. 129.

9. Jorge Luis Borges, 'Borges sur Kafka', *Change International*, 3 (1985), 44–45 (p. 44).

10. Richard T. Gray et al., *A Franz Kafka Encyclopedia* (Westport, CT: Greenwood, 2005), pp. 263, 305, 303; Daniel Balderston, *Out of Context: Historical Reference and the Representation of Reality in Borges* (Durham, NC: Duke University Press, 1993), p. 58; Edna Aizenberg, 'Kafka, Borges and Contemporary Latin-American Fiction', *Newsletter of the Kafka Society of America* 6, 1–2 (1982), pp. 4–13 (p. 6); František Vrhel, 'Borges y Praga', *El siglo de Borges*, Vol. 1, ed. Alfonso de Toro and Fernando de Toro (Madrid: Iberoamericana; Frankfurt: Vervuert, 1999) I, pp. 439–449 (p. 445).

11. František Vrhel, 'Borges y Praga', p. 447.

CHAPTER 24

Borges and the Bible

Lucas Adur

The Bible is one of the most cited and reworked texts in Borges's output, whether in prose or verse. In recent years biblical characters and episodes recreated in the writings have been tracked, as well as the influence of the Bible in the conception of Borges's work.[1] Even theological interpretations of his fiction have been suggested.[2] However, few approaches have considered the context in which Borges did his reading of the Bible and its resulting implications. The aim of this chapter is to present a number of contextual elements that are key to understand Borges's particular interpretation of the Bible, and the consequent specific meanings derived from it.

The Argentine Context

Borges's most relevant literary work was originally produced and read within Argentina during the first half of the twentieth century. From a political and religious perspective, those were the years of the rise and consolidation of so-called *Catholic integralism*. This conception of Catholicism was characterized by intransigence and intolerance. Founded on the belief that Catholic doctrine provided the principle of absolute truth, it was thought to be the supreme rule that should govern society. The Borgesian approach to the Bible stands, to a large extent, in opposition to that adopted by Catholic integralism.

Catholic integralism emerged in the 1920s in a traditionally Catholic society yet strongly influenced by liberalism since the 1880s. In line with the rebirth of Catholicism in post-war Europe, in 1922 a sector of the traditional elite created the 'Courses of Catholic Culture' aimed at intervening decisively in Argentinian culture. To this end, the group sought to build a position in the artistic and cultural fields by taking part in various projects. Among the most important were the *Convivio*, an artistic group which emerged in 1927 as a part of the Courses, and the political and cultural magazine *Criterio*, founded in 1928.

In the following decade, the movement became highly relevant in Argentinian politics. On one hand, it established a strong presence among the masses, as evidenced by the creation of Argentinian Catholic Action in 1931 – with its tens of thousands of associates – as well as by the large processions on the occasion of the celebration of the Eucharistic Congress in 1934.[3] On the other hand, the expansion of Catholicism was substantiated by the 'ecclesiastic-military pact'. The aim of this project was to 'Catholicize' the military forces, since they were deemed to be a major instrument for the re-Christianization of society.

During its peak years – between the 1930s and the 1950s – Catholic integralism fostered what has come to be known as the 'Catholic nation myth', i.e. associating Catholicism with the Argentine Nation so as to insert religion at the very core of national identity.[4] From this standpoint, all of the non-Catholic religions – e.g. Judaism, Protestantism – were presented as threats to the Argentine identity, and hence were targets for persecution and public condemnation.

The hegemony of Catholic integralism extended approximately until the mid-twentieth century and is crucial for a proper understanding of Borges's literature. Towards the late 1920s, he was in close contact with intellectual members of the Catholic integralism circles. His sister Norah and some friends – like Leopoldo Marechal and Francisco L. Bernárdez – were part of the *Convivio* group. Moreover, in the same period, Borges himself attended some of the group's meetings and published poems and essays in *Criterio*. Even though his participation did not imply a personal commitment to the Catholic faith, there was still a relative closeness that made Catholic integralists think of him as a strategic ally. It is worth mentioning that, back then, Borges defined himself as a believer in 'God and immortality' ('A Sonnet by Francisco de Quevedo', collected in *The Language of the Argentines*, 1928), and an opponent of positivism, both of which were concepts he held in common with Catholic integralists.

In the following decade, as Catholicism became consolidated in the Argentine political sphere, Borges decided to disengage himself entirely from the group. The political context, both nationally – cf. the coups of 1930 and 1943, along with the emergence of Peronism – and internationally – the Spanish Civil War and the Second World War – placed the writer and most of the Catholic integralists on opposite sides of the fence. From 1930 on, Borges's statements regarding his scepticism began to proliferate in his work, and he situated himself as an adversary of Catholic integralists, with whom he would argue – in general, indirectly – in various texts.[5]

The Borgesian use of the Bible acquires a new meaning in the context of such controversy. While the singularity of Borges's approach to the Scriptures was already noticeable in the 1920s, it became more marked in the following decade, particularly when contrasted with the place given to the sacred writings by Catholic integralism. Thus, the Bible turned into a source of disagreement between Borges and Catholic integralists.

The Catholic Bible Vs the Borgesian Bible (1930–1950)

Within the literary field of the first half of the twentieth century in Argentina, the dominant ideological standpoints concerning the Bible were either the Catholic, orthodox and reverent approach – for example, as held by integralist writers who were part of the *Convivio* group – or the distant or indifferent outlook which characterized a considerable sector of the literary scene, both liberal and left-leaning. In this context, the importance that Borges attributed to the Scriptures, as well as his remarkable biblical knowledge, reveal singular traits. Quoting Borges's own words, it could be said that, unlike the sceptics, who neither pay attention to nor believe in the Bible, and the 'Argentine Catholics' who 'believe [. . .], but I have noticed that they are not actually interested', Borges defined himself as an *interested yet sceptical* individual (*TTL* 254–256).

Apropos the place of the Bible within pre-conciliar Catholicism, the Scriptures held a relevant yet less central place than, for example, in Protestantism. To Catholicism, the Divine Revelation was not only limited to the Bible, but it was also found in the Apostolic Tradition: a set of beliefs and customs that date as far back as the first Christian communities. Tradition indeed pre-exists writing; it provides a frame for its correct understanding. The Catholic Church was the institution that upheld and passed on this tradition through its Magisterium, which ensured the strict interpretation of the Bible. In this sense, and at least until the Second Vatican Council (1962–1965), individual readings by the faithful were frowned upon by the ecclesiastic hierarchy. The Bible had a limited place within Catholicism, and it was read using the Church's official text, the *Vulgata*, which was written in Latin, an inaccessible language for most of the faithful. Vernacular versions of the Bible had been restricted by Catholic Church after the Reformation. The first authorized version of the Bible in Spanish was a translation from the *Vulgata* and it appeared in 1793. The versions of the Scriptures translated directly from the original texts were finally authorized in 1943 by Pope Pius

XII. In fact, the Magisterium and the restricted circulation of translations can be understood as part of the means used to control and avoid unorthodox interpretations.

The position of the Argentine Church in this regard was clearly exemplified in the 'Collective Pastoral Letter about Protestant Propaganda' (1945), released by the Episcopate in one of the most critical moments of persecution for Protestantism in Argentina:

> The essential nature of the so-called Protestant Reformation was, and still is, 'the principle of free examination' in religious matters. [. . .] The original sin of every [Protestant denomination] resides precisely there, in the ignorance of the venerated Apostolic Tradition [. . .]. Leaving the Holy Gospels to free examination [. . .] is, in general, to carry the seeds of disintegration and of inevitable individual dissolution, which leads to pure laicism, thus committing complete heresy.[6]

As can be seen, at least until the mid-twentieth century, the ecclesiastical hierarchy considered individual readings of the Scriptures as a typically Protestant and potentially heretical practice. This may help explain why in the literature of Catholic authors linked to the *Convivio* group (Bernárdez, Marechal, Jacobo Fijman, Ricardo Molinari . . .), direct quotations from the Bible were relatively limited. They wrote poems and stories devoted to the Saints and the Virgin, and it is also possible to find variations on well-known Gospel episodes, or even theological quotes and references in their works. Nevertheless, strictly speaking, biblical intertextuality is very occasional.

In essence, Borges's use of the Bible seems to dispute the hegemony of Catholic integralism in terms of its claim to monopolize a sole legitimate interpretation. The Borgesian use of the Bible challenges that monopoly by means of at least three different arguments. First, Borges develops an approach which is agnostic – i.e. sceptical – yet interested in the Bible. In 'Three Versions of Judas', '*Biathanatos*', and 'The Mirror of Enigmas', for example, he contributes to the construction of a singular literary relation with the Scriptures within the realm of Argentinian literature; a relation which differs from the reverential status that confessional authors used to give them (barely quoting them in their works). His position, however, cannot be seen merely as a form of mockery or a dismissal of the mythical nature of biblical stories, as might be expected of a sceptic. The Borgesian approach could be said to be *profanatory*, in that it helps to return these sacred texts to an arena where writers can make 'free use' of them.[7] Rewritings of the Scriptures by later Argentinian writers – such as

Falsificaciones (1966) by Marco Denevi or *El otro Judas* (1961) by Abelardo Castillo – continue the profanatory line started by Borges.

Second, Borges questions the anti-Semitic speech of Catholic integralists – who considered Jews as enemies of the 'Catholic nation' – by underlining the Jewish origin of Christianity and its sacred book. References to the Bible as 'the work of Jewish visionaries' ('On Expressionism', *Inicial*, 1923) can be found in early texts. Still, it is especially from the 1930s and amid a rising anti-Semitic discourse in Argentina, that Borges starts to stress the contradiction entailed in the fact that Catholics were anti-Semitic since 'they profess a religion of Hebrew origin' ('A Comment on August 23, 1944', *TTL* 210), worship 'Hebrew texts' ('Prologue', *Mester de judería*, 1940), and venerate a Jewish Messiah ('Anti-Semitism', *Mundo Israelita*, 1932). Borges thereby deconstructs the discourse of Catholic integralism, pointing out both the ethical and logical absurdity of anti-Semitic Christianism. His acknowledgement of Semitic traits in the Scriptures does not limit itself to controversy; however, an account of this anti-Semitic context can enhance the understanding of Borges's insistence on the matter, and of the provocative way in which he refers to it.[8]

A third controversial dimension of the Borgesian use of the Bible has to do with its Protestant traits, which seems singular in the context of the 'Catholic nation'. Borges's position becomes clearly noticeable in his almost exclusive use of Protestant versions of the Scriptures. This is not a minor matter. Protestant and Catholic Bibles are significantly different. First, they diverge in their canon of the Old Testament: 46 books in the Catholic Bible, yet only 39 in the Protestant one, which excludes the so-called 'deuterocanonical' books. Furthermore, both Bibles conspicuously differ in their translation policies. Whereas the Catholic Church sought to restrict the circulation of vernacular versions, in contrast, one of the foundational actions of the Reformation was Luther's translation of the Bible into German, as Borges oftentimes notes (e.g. 'German Literature in the Age of Bach', *TTL* 432). In Spanish, the first Protestant Bible appeared in 1569 – centuries before Catholic versions – and it was translated directly from the Hebrew and Greek originals by Casiodoro Reina, a Spanish monk born in 1520 who became an adherent of the Protestant Reformation. After his death in 1590, his translation was revised and reedited in 1602 by Cipriano de Valera, another Spanish convert to Protestantism. This version, known as *Reina Valera*, despite undergoing various revisions, continued to be used among Spanish-speaking Protestants until the twentieth century.

When Borges incorporates quotes from the Bible in Spanish, he usually uses the *Reina Valera* version. In 'The Mirror of Enigmas', Borges expresses his preference for this translation over the one by Torres Amat, which was one of the most frequently used versions among Argentine Catholics, yet which he characterized as a 'wretched translation' (*OC* II: 98). It is also important to mention *King James* Bible, published in 1611 as an official translation for the Anglican Church, since Borges referred to this version as his favourite in several interviews. Regarding the canon, the writer follows the Protestant criterion: among the numerous biblical books that he quotes, there is no reference to the deuterocanonical books. Thus, in the light of the editions he uses and the canon he considers, it can be said that the Bible, to Borges, is the Protestant Bible.

On the other hand, his perspective is akin to bibliocentrism and to the principle of *free examination*, both characteristics of Reformed Christianity. This way of approaching the Bible can be contrasted with the importance given by Catholicism to tradition and its Magisterium. According to Protestantism, the Bible – the *Sola Scriptura* – is the sole source of Divine Revelation. The faithful can interpret this revelation applying the free examination principle – though this does not mean that it can be read in any given way. In fact, there is no Magisterium in Reformed Churches, since it is claimed that the Scriptures *per se* contain the necessary elements for their interpretation. In contrast with pre-conciliar Catholicism, direct reading of the Bible is a central plank in the religious practice of Protestants – as Borges underlines in his essay, 'German Literature in the Age . . . '.

The extensive Biblical intertextuality found in Borges's work – larger than that detectable in his Catholic compatriots – is indicative of his typically Protestant inclination towards Scriptures. In this sense, his approach to the Bible can be seen as a personal appropriation of the principle of *free examination*. A meaningful example is 'Three Versions of Judas' (*Sur*, 1944), an extreme case of *free interpretation* of the Scriptures, which are profusely quoted with heretical conclusions. It is not incidental that Nils Runenberg, the main character, is an Evangelical theologian. The short story triggered a hostile reaction among Catholics, with Jesuit Leonardo Castellani, one of the main intellectuals of the Catholic integralism, calling it 'blasphemous'.[9]

As shown here, the place Borges gives to the Bible, as well as the manner in which he uses it within his literature, is singular and controversial in a context ruled by Catholic hegemony. The writer challenges the monopoly claimed by the Church over the Bible: it does not only belong to the Catholics, but also to the Protestants, to the Jews, to all men. After all, it is the book that contains some of the essential stories, i.e. those which have been told by humankind over and over again 'throughout history' ('The Gospel according to Mark', *CF* 400).

After the 1960s: The Protestant Bible

A series of political and religious transformations linked to the radical renovations brought about by the Second Vatican Council displaced Catholic integralism from the central place it had held in Argentina. Borges, however, did not seem to notice this displacement. His representation of Catholicism always remained tied to the integralism that characterized the first half of the twentieth century – see the depiction of the Catholic faith in his 1970 short story, 'The Elderly Lady' (*CF* 377). Nevertheless, it is possible to detect a change in his relation with Christianity, which affects his way of presenting the Bible.

The international repercussion of Borges's work from the 1960s onward meant the writer was frequently invited to travel abroad. In those journeys, he was in contact with Protestant societies, especially in the United States, where he was welcomed as a visiting professor in various universities. After this experience, it is possible to detect a new emphasis in the way Borges conveys his preference for Reformed Christianity both in texts and interviews – e.g. *An Introduction to American Literature* (1967) and 'A Note on Argentinians' (1969).[10] In his *Autobiographical Essay* (1970) he would go as far as to define himself directly as an 'amateur Protestant'.

In his relation with the Bible, there seems to be in Borges a meaningful two-step approach. First, the writer starts insisting on the fact that the Bible is, essentially, the English Bible: 'When I talk of the Bible, for example, I am really talking of *King James* version.'[11] It is a Protestant and an English book ('Page on Shakespeare', *Sur*, 1964), which means that, in Argentina, the Bible can only be regarded as foreign literature – see the contrast between the Bible and *Don Segundo Sombra* in 'The Gospel . . . ' (*CF* 400).

Second, from the 1970s on, Borges spreads – both in poems and in interviews – an *autobiographeme* about his paternal grandmother, Fanny Haslam. She knew the Bible by heart – *King James*, of course. Here, Protestant bibliocentrism gets rewritten as a family tradition. Borges, her grandson, receives a rich inheritance through this 'foreign literature'. Completing Piglia's classic hypothesis about 'lineage fiction', it could be said that the writer not only gains access to Argentina's history through his maternal lineage, and to philosophy and an unlimited number of English books through his father, but also, that he gains access to the Bible through his grandmother.[12] It is from this standpoint that Borges himself highlights his interest in the Scriptures within a mainly Catholic context – i.e. 'not interested'. Borges seems to think of himself as a lonely reader, without valid interlocutors in Argentina, just like his grandmother Fanny – reading the Bible in the face of the desert ('Someone Dreams', *The Conspirators*, 1985).

Notes

1. See, for example, Gonzalo Salvador and Daniel Attala, *Borges y la Biblia* (Madrid: Iberoamericana, 2011); 'Jorge Luis Borges y la Biblia', in D. Attala and G. Fabry (eds.), *La Biblia en la literatura hispanoamericana* (Madrid: Trotta, 2016).
2. See Ignacio Navarro, *Últimas inquisiciones* (Buenos Aires: Agape/Bonum, 2009), and Richard Walsh and Jay Twomey (eds.), *Borges and the Bible* (Sheffield: Phoenix Press, 2015).
3. The 32nd International Eucharistic Congress was held in Buenos Aires between 10 and 14 October 1934. It was the first time that the Congress was celebrated in South America. During the main ceremony of the event, which took place in Plaza de Mayo, Argentine president Agustín Justo publicly consecrated the country to the Sacred Heart of Jesus. Borges refers critically to this massive manifestation of Catholicism in '1941' (*Sur*, 1941) and in 'Death and the Compass' (*Sur*, 1942).
4. The 'Catholic nation myth' played a key role in Argentine politics between the 1920s and the 1950s. See Loris Zanatta, *Del estado liberal a la nación católica* (Buenos Aires: Universidad Nacional de Quilmes, 1996).
5. About the indirect or *oblique* ways of Borges's style regarding political matters, see Annick Louis, *Borges face au fascisme* (París: Aux lieux d'être, 2006).
6. The full document can be found on the website of the Argentine Conference of Bishops. Available online at http://www.episcopado.org
7. We use *profanatory* in the sense of Giorgio Agamben, '*In Praise of Profanation*' (collected in *Profanations*. Brooklyn, NY: Zone Books, 2007).
8. For a study of Borges's reading of the Bible with special attention to its Semitic traits, see Edna Aizenberg's *The Aleph Weaver* (1984). Aizenberg asserts that, for Borges, the Bible is essentially a Hebrew book.
9. See Castellani's review of *Ficciones* in *Dinámica social*, 57 (1956).

10. 'Nota sobre los argentinos' is a brief essay included in *Argentina, análisis y autoanálisis* (1969), edited by H. Ernest Lewald. The book also contains contributions by Ernesto Sábato, José Ortega y Gasset, Eduardo Mallea, and others.

11. 'Borges on Borges', 1983, collected in Norman Di Giovanni, *In Memory of Borges* (London: Constable, 1988).

12. See Piglia's 'Ideology and Fiction in Borges", *Punto de vista*, 5 (1979).

CHAPTER 25

Borges and Judaism[*]

Corinna Deppner

Jorge Luis Borges's narrative prose is permeated by allusions to biblical contexts. Along with assimilations of the Christian tradition, references to the Hebrew Bible are readily demonstrable. What is more, both his literary work and his essays contain numerous citations of Jewish history, including experiences of the diaspora with the varied characteristics of its development since the second destruction of the Jerusalem Temple in AD 70.

Edna Aizenberg, a pioneer in deciphering traces of Judaism in Borges's work, sees the reason for his interest in *lo judío* in the fact that Borges did not merely, like many Jews in the diaspora, grow up bilingual, but he also sought to fashion his cultural identity on absolutely multicultural lines. Borges was Argentinian, but his education owed not a little to his upbringing in the English tradition. On the other hand, the assimilation of themes with a Jewish connotation in his work must be seen as an attempt to find points of contact between Jewish and Argentinian experiences. In his lecture 'The Argentine Writer and Tradition', he explains that in the attitude of Jews in the diaspora he actually saw a model for an Argentinian identity drawn from immigration and cultural overwriting. *Lo judío* is for him not just an image of the Strange and Other within Latin American culture; he also compares its special role with the (outsider) position of the Latin American author in Western culture.

Borges's references to the contents and intellectual approaches of Jewish culture are made in various different contexts of knowledge. They refer to historical events, biblical traditions, and mystical speculation, and are introduced both into his poetic and narrative work and into his essays. In the poem 'A Key in Salonica' (*El otro, el mismo*, 1964), Borges refers to a legend according to which the Sephardim, who, following their expulsion from Spain in 1492, settled in the territories of the old Ottoman Empire, kept the keys to their houses, in the hope that one day they would return.

---

[*] This chapter is dedicated to Evelyn Fishburn.

In his story 'The Aleph' (1949), Borges refers to the first letter of the Hebrew alphabet and the particular characteristic of this sign in Jewish religion and culture as the text-generating start of the alphabet. Essays such as 'The Cabbala' (*Seven Nights*, 1980) or 'A Defense of the Cabbala' (*Discussion*, 1932) point further to Borges's knowledge of Jewish mysticism and its reception in literary and philosophical contexts.

In search of an explanation for the murder of Rabbi Yarmolinski in Borges's story 'Death and the Compass' (*Sur* 1942; *Ficciones* 1944), detective Erik Lönnrot studies those books belonging to the Rabbi which he finds in his cupboard: 'a *Defense of the Cabbala*; a *Study of the Philosophy of Robert Fludd*; a literal translation of the *Sefer Yetsirah*; a *Biography of the Baal Shem*; a *History of the Hasidim*; a monograph in German on the Tetragrammaton; another on the divine nomenclature of the Pentateuch' (*CF* 148). All these references point to the Kabbalah, whose methods come to be applied in the course of the narrative with the aim of solving the riddle of Yarmolinski's murder. By including his own essay, 'Una vindicación de la cábala' in the Rabbi's collection of books, Borges makes himself a part of the Kabbalah reading. He explains that his interest is not in defending the doctrine, but in 'the hermeneutical or cryptographic procedures that led to it' (*SN-F* 83). These aim to construct secret meanings from the Bible, which is understood as an absolute.

In 'The Golem' (1964) Borges traces a many-faceted interpretation of perhaps the best-known figure in Jewish mysticism. The Golem is a creature of letters and clay. The combination of letters which will awaken the Golem to life has the innate property of accommodating the opposite outcome. Construction, design, as evinced by the world, turns out in fact to be destruction: the word *emeth* (אמת) marked on the Golem's forehead, signifies 'truth', however, by removing the first letter, the aleph, which is spoken like an aspirated 'e', it becomes meth (מת), i.e. death. The Golem, an ambivalent figure, provides suggestive potential for other writing, including both poems and stories.[1] Among these will also be found various forms of irony, as when Borges suggests that a crime could be solved by meditating on the secret nature of God and His tetragrammaton, JHWH, in 'Death and the Compass', or when in the story 'The Aleph' he calls the Hebrew letter of the same name a universe, but places it – a strange, image-generating being – in the cellar of a building.

From these examples it can be seen that Borges's primary aim is not simply to incorporate verifiable knowledge into his writing. Rather, his attention is directed to a potential which helps him to create aesthetic forms. Under this light, his interest in Jewish culture must be understood

as a training of the imagination in alien metaphor. Borges's poetic encap-
sulations of meaning in ironic twists and paradoxes indicate at the same
time that a basis for his writing cannot be found solely in a recourse to
Kabbalistic images such as the Golem as a humanoid figure or the Aleph as
a universe. Borges's interests are focused in particular on the conceptions of
a mobile language and textual structure derived therefrom. These conceptions revolve essentially around the function of letters as components in the
construction of an ambiguous speech and as a paradigm of the Creation
itself.

Paradigms of Jewish culture, such as the foundation upon letters and
writing of the Torah received on Mount Sinai, the Rabbinical exegesis of
the Hebrew Bible in the Talmud, the experience of the diaspora with the
hope of a return – with Messianic connotations – to Jerusalem, and
mysticism as a speculative absorption in the letters of the Hebrew alphabet
as a movable system with generative potential, each offer paths of their own
into ritual and academic knowledge. They coexist and have come to
acquire a different stamp in the varying traditions of the Ashkenazim,
the Chassidim, and the Sephardim. Borges, however, does not treat of
them in their singularities; he merges them.

The example of his story 'The Library of Babel' can show how Borges
interweaves motifs of varying provenance from the Jewish tradition:
Kabbalah and Rabbinical text exegesis are linked in every bit as diverse
a way as experiences from the diaspora, including an orientation to
a linking book. Genesis 11 of the Hebrew Bible conveys the tradition of
a semantically charged Babel. It portrays man's hubris, with the building of
the Tower of Babel as a visible sign with reference and a name. God's
intervention leads to the fragmentation of language and the dispersal of the
human race. As a consequence, the tower cannot be completed and the
reference dissolves. Furthermore, after the building of the Tower of Babel,
'the loss of language [. . .] coincides with the origin of Man's homelessness
on the earth', whereby human existence seems to be bound to a linguistic
phenomenon.[2] In Borges's work, the dispersal of people and languages is
translated into a dispersal of signs. The contents of the books contained in
the Library of Babel – reflecting the division of languages – turn out to be
an unpronounceable cacophony.

The view which sees in the Jewish diaspora not only a result of banish-
ment (Galut) but also a productive dimension, interprets the intervention
of God as positive. In Bernhard Greiner's account, 'The non-completion
of the Tower, the non-completed signifier, becomes a place of opening to
a multiplicity which cannot be referred back to any unity which preceded

it.'[3] At the same time, the dispersal becomes a common intellectual point of reference which is yet in itself subject to multiple ambiguities.[4] This consequence, too, is to be found in Borges's textual structure. His stories become a 'place of opening and multiplicity'– both in their referential power and with regard to an infinite reception (Greiner, 19). A literature has been created in which the signs continue to work with a dynamism of their own, evolving into a branching textual fabric, without abandoning a coalescence of thought as their perspective. This dynamism of writing signifies a 'transition' of the signs, which occur again and again in new constellations, including the association of numbers which Borges employs to calculate the library's holdings. Along with measurements to show the physical dimensions of the library, we are told the numerical characteristics of the books: 'each book contains four hundred [and] ten pages; each page, forty lines; each line, approximately eighty black letters' (*CF* 113). Letters and figures form a combinatory scheme of an apparently infinite kind, which Borges displays at the very start of the story: 'The universe (which others call the Library) is composed of an indefinite, perhaps infinite number of hexagonal galleries' (*CF* 112).

The method of interpreting text by combinations of letters was being cultivated by the Jewish Kabbalists as early as the eleventh century. Every letter in the Hebrew alphabet was allocated a numerical value in chronological order, i.e. aleph = 1, beth = 2, etc., which leads *inter alia* to the narrative enmeshment of numbers. Words whose numerical values produce the same total are read in a contextual sense. Using letters and number combinations, the early Kabbalists in Palestine searched in the Torah for concealed meanings. The polyvalences associated with the biblical Babel, which are related to knowledge of Kabbalistic letter and number manipulation and its further development into structural, spatial, figurative, geometric, and mathematical dimensions, and thus into secular terms, are characteristic of the complete output of Jorge Luis Borges. The fabric of different potentialities, stemming from biblical reception, mystical doctrine, and knowledge of both scientific and everyday phenomena, is formed into components of a multiform written meaning, which can be adduced both for modern literature and for poststructuralist philology. James Joyce supplies the comparison in the discourse of literature; Michel Foucault is the comparable poststructuralist thinker. So Borges's literary concatenations operate with displaced signifiers which have lost their connection to a referent, whose existence is concealed or displaced.

In 'The Library of Babel' the description of the library is reminiscent, along with other associations, of the structural plan of the biblical Ark –

thus creating a further drift of signs and meaning. This comparability can be seen on the one hand in the structural similarity of the building specifications: the 'hexagonal galleries' of which the library consists correspond to the chambers of the Ark; while encased air shafts are placed in the midst of the library's galleries, at the top of the Ark a porthole was to be installed. And Borges's enumeration of the sequential bookshelves is to be found analogously in the length, breadth, and height of the Ark as set out in the plan of its construction. What is called an entrance and exit to a gallery – 'a narrow sort of vestibule, which in turn opens onto another gallery'– would thus correspond to the door of the Ark (*CF* 112). The allusion to a winding staircase, which in Borges's work opens onto the infinite, makes the library into a multi-storey building, which also accommodates the layered floors of Noah's Ark (Genesis 6: 14–16).

The materials of which the Ark is built are wood and pitch. The material of the library is the letters themselves which acquire materiality in the (divine) building plan. At the same time, the equivalence of the library with Noah's Ark can be seen at a content-based level: the library appears as a possibility of collecting the world's knowledge in the form of letters and thus saving it. This would then be a response to the cultural catastrophe which followed Babel. In Borges, the rescue of speech is not effected only through conserving the 22 letters and 3 punctuation marks of Hebrew, but also by recollecting the damaged nature of the signs, which in this constellation are to be interpreted as a result of the Babylonian splintering of language. It is the damaged nature of the signs which gives them their mobility. This corresponds to a rabbinic conception which requires further work of interpretation by man. The broken tablets of the law in the Moses legend had already pointed towards this interpretation.[5] Thus Borges's story ends with a momentum towards sign-migration, which, through the 'eternal traveller', is to be transmuted into a principle of order. This thought, too, reflects the legend of Babel, according to which the multiplicity of languages gives rise to an identity-creating unity in the diaspora.

Borges's relationship with Jewish culture has been described on the one hand as a 'rhetoric of Jewishness', and on the other as an encounter with Jewish mysticism and the culture of memory.[6] If on the one hand his assimilation of attributes of 'Jewishness' appears to be a description of the 'Other', on the other hand those attributes function in his work as literary tropes with absent referents, which open the way to an exploded, constantly developing textual structure, which is peculiar not only to the Kabbalah but also to the Babylonian Talmud.

According to Graff Zivin, the exploitation of paradigms formed by Jewish culture leads, within the geopolitical and aesthetic frame of reference opened up within literature, to an empowerment or assimilation of Jewish experiences and cultural accruals. In *The Wandering Signifier*, Zivin uses the word 'Jewishness' to denote a mobile sign shifting between literary texts and socio-historical contexts and, in its apparently unaffiliated existence, offering itself for literary construction. This conception refers to the views of European and North American researchers who, under the term 'Jewish', have spotlighted a rhetorical flexibility and elasticity: 'I propose the idea of the wandering signifier both as a play on the hackneyed image of the "wandering Jew" and as a way to think about the mobility of the signifier "Jew" itself' (Zivin, 4). Thus at the same time these words draw our attention to the problem of classifying 'Jewishness', since endless opinions exist on what makes a community in the Jewish tradition. Zivin posits an ethical dimension, in order that the scope of action granted to Jewish culture may not be regarded as freely available. Using Borges's 'Emma Zunz' and '*Deutsches Requiem*' (both from *The Aleph*), she demonstrates that the Other, the Jew described, is not given his own voice. Borges, she says, uses Jewish topoi as ethical devices and wandering signifiers.

If we follow the interpretations of Jaime Alazraki, Saúl Sosnowski, Ruth Fine, and Evelyn Fishburn, for example, Borges takes his orientation from a Jewish culture of letters and language as the foundation of his narrative prose with signifiers that are different in themselves. If we supplement this interpretation with practices from Rabbinical text exegesis oriented towards the relation between verbal and written Torah, we may come to recognize something more. Borges's conception of a mobility of signifiers points to assimilation and continuation of a characteristic of Hebrew: since the written Hebrew alphabet contains no vowels, an understanding of the written form requires a knowledge of the pronunciation to start with. The spoken language, unlike writing, is a mobile factor and requires an interpretation of what is written. Consequently, the ascription of a *wandering signifier* to characterize Jewishness in Borges's work is not simply evidence for a construction of Jewishness 'from the outside'. On the contrary, the Argentinian author recognizes that it is Jewish culture itself which defines itself as constructive, by revealing itself on the basis of a mobile letter system, embracing language, text, and meaning. Thus a structure of mind cultivated in the Jewish tradition is peculiar to Borges's texts regardless of any explicit allusion, which distinguishes this particular frame of reference from others within his intertextual orientation. In their book *Jews and Words*, Amos Oz and Fania Oz-Salzberger take up the concluding sequence of Borges's story 'Pierre Menard, Author of the Quixote' (*Sur* 1939; *Ficciones*, 1944) to epitomize a specifically Jewish concept of textual exegesis: 'Menard does not *translate*, or *copy*, or *quote*, or *paraphrase*, or *review*, or *comment upon*, Cervantes's book. He *authors* it.'[7] What these commentators describe is a process of semiosis, which sees the reception of the text concurrently as its production.

The proximity which Borges sought to models of Rabbinical text interpretation comes accordingly in the form of literary constructions, based on a reciprocity of the verbal and the written – including the resulting differences and exegetical perspectives.[8] The one is concealed in the other and yet present. This principle applies to the understanding of Jewish discourses, including Talmud reading and alphabet mysticism; it applies to Borges's often cryptic and ambiguous texts – which, in their very cryptic construction and ambiguity, demand interpretation. Both paths lead to experiments, like the construction of models, which exceed existing knowledge.

Notes

1. Cf. Borges's essay 'La cábala', in *Obras completas* (Buenos Aires: Emecé, 1989), III, pp. 267–275.
2. Cf. Klaus Reichert, *Vielfacher Schriftsinn: Zu Finnegans Wake* (Frankfurt am Main: Suhrkamp, 1989), p. 204. All translations from German into English are mine.
3. Bernhard Greiner, *Beschneidung des Herzens. Konstellationen deutsch-jüdischer Literatur* (Munich: Fink, 2004), p. 19.
4. Christoph Schmidt, 'Zurück nach Babylon . . . Die Stellung des Berichts über den Turmbau zu Babel zwischen Sintflut und Sintbrand', in *Babylon. Beiträge zur jüdischen Gegenwart*, 18 (Frankfurt am Main: Neue Kritik, 1998), p. 91.
5. Cf. Bernd Witte, *Jüdische Tradition und literarische Moderne* (Munich: Hanser, 2007).
6. Erin Graff Zivin, *The Wandering Signifier. Rhetoric of Jewishness in the Latin American Imaginary* (Durham, NC: Duke University Press, 2008), pp. 88–91, 155–159, 160–193.
7. Amos Oz and Fania Oz-Salzberger, *Jews and Words* (New Haven, CT: Yale University Press, 2012), p. 203.
8. Cf. Arnold Goldberg, 'Der verschriftete Sprechakt als rabbinische Literatur', in Aleida Assmann et al. (eds.), *Schrift und Gedächtnis. Beiträge zur Archäologie der literarischen Kommunikation* (Munich: Fink, 1983), pp. 123–140.

CHAPTER 26

Borges and Buddhism

Evelyn Fishburn

The unified image suggested by the word 'Buddhism' is misleading in so far as it refers to a religion or belief system which is understood in multiple ways. The term, coined by Europeans in the eighteenth century, fails to take into account the imprecise nature of its history and different interpretations.[1] In this essay the focus is on Buddhism as defined, discussed, and re-imagined by Jorge Luis Borges.[2] His interest in Buddhism spanned most of his life, from when he read an epic poem on the life of Buddha at the age of seven to his journey as an octogenarian to Japan, where he was taken to several Buddhist temples and given the opportunity to converse with both a Buddhist nun and a monk.

Sir Edwin Arnold's *The Light of Asia* was one of 30 or so volumes on Buddhism in his father's library, which, it may be pertinent to recall, Borges once described as 'the chief event in my life'. These works, mostly in English, French, and German, formed the basis of his knowledge but not its full extent, evident from the bibliography that he quotes and discusses in some detail in his own writings.[3] Though most works referenced are by European writers, he also shows familiarity with original sources, Buddhist texts quoted in translation. However, as will become clear, Borges read from a European perspective filtered through Schopenhauer and other philosophers, and his interest in Buddhism was ultimately concerned with the extent to which it coincided with Western ways of thinking. Surprisingly, Borges's substantial engagement with Buddhism has not received the critical attention that it merits in that it is absent even in studies concerned specifically with Borges and religion. There are some insightful discussions included in general works on linked topics, but no systematic analysis. However, recent interest in Borges and the Orient may awaken a more focused critical response.

Borges's Appraisal of Buddhism and Its Values

Borges writes about Buddhism and his understanding of its main ideas in an introductory work, *What Is Buddhism* (1976, with Alicia Jurado),[4] a lecture published in *Seven Nights* in 1980 (*OC* III: 242–253), and in the essays: 'The Nothingness of Personality' (1922), 'A New Refutation of Time' (1944–1947), 'From Someone to Nobody' (1950), 'Personality and the Buddha' (1950), and 'Forms of a Legend' (1952). A self-proclaimed non-believer, he greatly admired a religion which not only does not postulate a God, but for which the existence of God is of no particular significance; what matters is the Doctrine, according to which doubt is a positive concept and a meditative obligation: 'to be a Buddhist is not to understand' (243). When Borges ends his address on Buddhism with a self-deprecating reference to 'this doctrine [. . .] of which I have understood so little' (253),[5] he may well be illustrating his keen comprehension of its essence.

What Is Buddhism, reputedly the only book on Buddhism by a major literary figure, offers a clear and informative introduction to the subject, seen from several angles. It begins by distinguishing the legendary Buddha from the historical figure before expanding on background information such as the antecedents of Buddhism, its branching out into different versions, and its spread to other regions in the East. It ends with a list of examples illustrating Buddhism's ethical position, summarized as the principle of non-harming. The doctrine and overall value system are analysed in greater detail in the above-mentioned lecture. There, Borges describes aspects of the religion that he finds most appealing such as its longevity, which he ascribes to its tolerance and the avoidance of extremes – it is sometimes referred to as the 'Middle Way' of moderation, standing in marked contrast with the Judeo-Christian aggressive and proselytizing tradition.

In both works Borges discusses what he considers to be the essence of the doctrine, preached by the Buddha in his first 'enlightened' sermon, in Benares, in the Park of the Gazelles, over 2,500 years ago. He alludes to the Four Noble Truths, which are about the truth of suffering and the way to overcome it. This is set out in the last Truth as the Eightfold Path and delineates the stages leading from suffering during a seemingly eternal cycle of birth and rebirth, to eventual salvation. The recurring cycle is referred to, in the Buddhist tradition, as *karma,* which Borges calls 'a cruel system' because it cannot be affected by any direct intervention but operates impersonally, like the law of gravity. He poetically likens it to 'an extremely fine mental structure' that transmigrates infinitely 'in a perpetual weaving and interweaving process' (*OC* III: 249). If *karma* is the process leading to salvation, *nirvana* is the desired outcome, which Borges, marrying style and content, defines at the end of his lecture as 'an extinction, a snuffing out' (253). While *nirvana* relates to the cessation of suffering, it is important to distinguish it from the ultimate bliss in Judeo-Christianity in that it does not promise any blissful identification or union with God, but rather an emptiness, a dissolution into nothingness.

The essays tend to concentrate on topics central to Buddhism, namely, a disbelief in the substantiality of things and of the self, and the unreliability of our perceptions. These preoccupations also permeate Borges's writings in so far as they seek to question all our accepted 'common-sense' beliefs in objective reality. Some parallels are noted in what follows.

Borges's pictorial image of *karma* has a striking affinity with the ever-forking *paths* of his eponymous story, 'The Garden of Forking Paths', in its structure, plot and, most relevantly, the concept of the garden itself. This is one of only two stories to mention Buddhism and, significantly, it is a Buddhist monk who saves the seemingly chaotic manuscripts about a garden whose paths fork in 'a growing, dizzying web of divergent, convergent and parallel times' (*CF* 127). The reference to *paths* in Buddhist doctrine and to *karma*'s endless cycles of transmigration becomes unmissable. A careful reading would reveal suggestions of transmigration at the level of character and of the quiet acceptance of one's fate. Another web-like karmic image is conjured by the endlessly proliferating, self-reflecting hexagons in the Library of Babel, suggesting that they are ultimately meaningless. Taking the library as a metaphor of the universe, as does the story, and read from a Buddhist perspective, this magnification into nothingness would indicate not only that the hexagons are empty and the world unknowable, but, more bleakly, that there is nothing to know.

'The Cult of the Phoenix' is about a secret transmitted from generation to generation whose association with the sexual act is made evident, perhaps misleadingly so. What is significant here is the symbolism of the title, suggesting transformation, death, and rebirth. Similarly, 'The Immortal' posits a literary-based cycle of transformation, at the level of text and author.

Many Borges stories include revelatory moments, some just before the death of the protagonist. These have mostly been understood in terms of ecstasy, but in some instances the Buddhist concept of *nirvana* may prove more appropriate. Funes, prostrate, immobile, unable to sleep would imagine himself 'at the bottom of a river, rocked (and *negated*) by the current' (*CF* 137, my italics).

In 'The Writing of the God', Tzinacán, an incarcerated Mayan priest, emerges after 'an indefatigable labyrinth of dreams' with a clear vision of the magic formula that mere utterance will allow him to free himself and his people from their colonizers' oppression. But it is no longer relevant: this enlightenment also reveals the illusoriness of the temporal world and of his individual self. All his consciousness longs for now is quiet oblivion. Without invalidating the many existing interpretations from different cultural perspectives, a Buddhist-based reading of this withdrawal from the world and self as the attainment of *nirvana* seems singularly convincing: '*I* no longer remember Tzinacán [...]. [N]ow *he* is no one [...]. *I* allow the days to forget me' (*CF* 253–254, my emphases). The intermingling of the first and third person pronouns supports this reading.

Legends appear in Buddhist texts as a favoured means to deal with the complexity of reality and its resistance to any defining depiction, and Borges, famously attracted to the aesthetic possibilities of religion, tends to refer to them in his essays to illustrate an argument. According to Alicia Jurado, in their joint reading of Buddhist texts he always showed greater enthusiasm for the fables and legends than for the spiritual truths of the doctrine (Borges nearly fell out with her over her Buddhist religious zeal).

The negation of the individual self (*anatman*) is arguably the notion that runs most contrary to our Western thought and it is addressed by Borges in 'The Nothingness of Personality', one of his most important early essays. In the legend from the Milinda Pañha, a well-known Pali text that Borges often cites, the non-existence of the self is argued by analogy with a chariot, which is 'not the wheels, nor the chassis, nor the axle, nor the shaft nor the yoke, neither is man matter nor form nor impressions [...] not the combination of these parts, nor does he exist outside them'. It is interesting to note that Borges chooses to dwell on a text that details what may be thought to define the self only to deny its validity, and then, paradoxically, personalizes the discussion on the non-self, first by mentioning a very intense emotional moment of friendship before disqualifying it as 'egotistical', and then, echoing the Milinda Pañha, proceeding to list extensively what he is, to say that he is not. I quote selectively: 'I am not the visual reality that my eyes encompass [...]. Nor am I the audible world that I hear [...]. That is, I am not my own activity of seeing, hearing, smelling, tasting, touching [...]' (*TTL* 8–9). In 'Personality and the Buddha' and elsewhere Borges quotes the Buddhist notion of impermanence, expressed in the Visuddhimagga (the Path to Purity) with a comparable simile arguing that as the wheel of a carriage can never touch the earth more than partially, and fleetingly, so does a being not exist other than in a flashing, self-erasing moment.

This type of negative enumeration also suggests the illusory quality of knowledge. It appears in a footnote to 'From Someone to Nobody' (strangely absent from the English translation (*TTL* 343)) and relates to the Buddha's legendary moment of enlightenment when, while sitting under a fig tree, he intuits all the effects and causes in the universe and all the past and future incarnations of every being. The point of the legend is to contend that this seeming vision of infinity and plenitude is 'as a grain of sand on the river Ganges, and then in as many Ganges as there are grains of sand in the new Ganges'. Buddhist texts, significantly, often refer to the grains of sand of the river Ganges as a metaphor for something incalculable, but what is notable here is that this all-knowing image of the Buddha is used to convey the magnitude of his ignorance.

Buddhist Concepts in Borges's Fiction

The wholeness of the self is a frequent preoccupation in Borges's fiction. Its illusory quality is skilfully dramatized in 'The Search for Averroes', where both the Arab philosopher and the Argentine author are shown to exist only in the narrator's imagination, each dissolving into nothingness. An indirect hint of the non-self may be found in the many transformations in the philosopher's name and then, more graphically, in the final dissolution of his defeated self and of all that surrounded him 'as though annihilated by a *fire*' (*CF* 241, my italics). The disappearance of Averroes through the failure of his attempt to understand another culture is replayed by the failure of the Borges-narrator to understand him and he too is dissolved, together with his story.

In 'The Theologians', the ideological differences in their interpretations of Plato's doctrine of cyclical time define two rival theologians, alternately, as orthodox or heretic. Both men die consumed by *fire*, one burnt at the stake, the other by lightning. In Heaven, one of them speaks to God, who took him for the other. Since no confusion can be imputed to the divine intelligence, the story concludes that the two theologians were undistinguishable, 'a single person' (*CF* 207). A similar confusion is the subject of 'Borges and I', where the self (the true 'live' author) and the persona (the author as implied by his oeuvre) are shown to exist oppositionally, in a hostile relationship similar to that of 'The Theologians', but with even greater complexity in that it is not God but the Borges-narrator who no longer knows 'which one of us is writing this page' (*OC* II: 186).

The self is problematized differently, in conjunction with a question of time in 'A New Refutation of Time', Borges's major theoretical consideration of the relationship between linear and cyclical times. Significantly, the Buddhist presence is made explicit in that both the Milinda Pañha and the Visuddhimagga are referenced. This meditative piece concludes, or seems to conclude, with a regretful affirmation of the existence of a time-bound self in a real world, asserting that it is irreversible and iron-bound; denials of this would be 'acts of desperation and secret consolations'. '*And yet, and yet* . . .', the traditional metaphor of time as a flowing river is linked to the subjectivity of the speaking self, with the caveat that 'Time is a river that sweeps me along, but I am the river; it is a tiger that mangles me, but I am the tiger; it is a fire that consumes me, but I am the fire' (*TTL* 332). The link to Buddhism is subtle: there we encounter the same concept about existence in time, expressed in similar words used by a Zen master who taught that 'Time is not separate from being: "You are time, the tiger is time, bamboo is time."'[6]

Borges's invented word *hrön* serves to designate ideas, dreams, and desires that are projected as solid poetic objects onto the world, taking it over; it encapsulates the notion of reality as a solidified product of our imaginations. It is the central conceit in 'Tlön, Uqbar, Orbis Tertius', one of the most analysed of Borges's fictions, but as far as ascertainable, the critical literature has failed to perceive any elements that it shares with Buddhist thought. Yet this becomes clear when read in the present context. From the geographical setting of Tlön, to its language without nouns, its fiction without external reference, and the objects that are found if believed in, nothing is grounded in reality. I suggest that a Buddhist-inflected reading would add many layers to the density of this story and many others not included in this survey.

'The Circular Ruins' (from *El jardín de senderos que se bifurcan* of 1941), is the story of a man, a wizard, who, coming from an undefined Southern region, arrives, unseen by anyone, at an abandoned temple. He sets himself the task of dreaming up a companion, a son, *and inserting him into reality*. He does so painstakingly, and eventually, after many years of dedicated dreaming, he succeeds. He is helped in this by the god of fire, whose condition is that he should instruct his son in the appropriate ritual and eventually give him independence by sending him downriver to worship at another temple. The wizard's main concern is that his son should not discover the humiliation of his dreamed existence. Having accomplished his life's goal, the wizard now lives in relative peace, but one night, after an undefined period of time, he senses the impending repetition of a fire destroying the remains of the temple. As he walks on the flames without feeling their bite, he comes to the self-realization that, like the son he engendered, he too is the product of another's dream.

The story has been interpreted variously, from the perspective of Western idealist philosophies, e.g. Berkeley's *esse est percipi*, Plato's thoughts on the cyclical nature of time, the story of Creation, and, most pointedly, the Kabbalistic legend of the Golem. The Oriental setting and reference to the language of the Zend has invited a Zoroastrian-based interpretation. Here, I draw on core aspects of Buddhism to construct an alternative frame of reference. A first consideration is the illusory nature of the self, and of all existence. The epigraph from *Alice Through the Looking Glass, 'And if he let off dreaming of you',* hints at the illusory quality of reality as being the nub of 'The Circular Ruins' and its constant underlying theme. The protagonist's unreality is established by all the references to 'no one' which acquire a literal meaning as the story unfolds, as does the information that he probably did not even feel the lacerations to his flesh. And, of course, the plot makes this plain.

In second place, the motifs of circularity and transmigration. The circularity referred to in the title is a literal reference to the 'ruins' but also acquires a metaphysical meaning as the plot evolves. The story is a re-writing of Carroll's novel, suggesting a transmigration of one text to another. Transmigration is also suggested by the many repetitions in the story: the destinies of the dreaming wizard and his dreamed creation, the identical temples and their devastation, notably by fire; all match the Buddhist belief that what extinguishes may be rekindled. And finally, the ending of the story is most insightfully understood as an example of *nirvana*. I refer again to the rekindling association with fire, to the wizard's enlightenment and acceptance of his gradual disintegration, within a structure of circularity. Read in this way, 'The Circular Ruins' stands out as Borges's consummate 'Buddhist' fiction.

Notes

1. Damien Keown, *Buddhism: A Very Short Introduction* (Oxford: Oxford University Press, 2013).
2. See, principally, William H. Bossart, *Borges and Philosophy: Self, Time and Metaphysics* (New York/Oxford: Peter Lang, 2003), and Didier Jaen, 'Borges's Allusions to Hinduism and Buddhism', *Journal of South Asian Literature*, 16 (Winter, Spring 1981), pp. 17–29.

3. The data is available at www.borges.pitt.edu (accessed 6 August 2019) via Finder's Guide.

4. *Qué es el budismo* (Buenos Aires: Columba & Emecé, 1976).

5. I quote from the English version, trans. Frank Thomas Smith. Available online at https://southerncrossreview.org/48/borges-buddhism.htm (accessed 6 August 2019).

6. Barbara O'Brien, 'About Time, from A Buddhist Perspective', ThoughtCo. 26 August 2018. Available online at thoughtco.com/about-time-449562 (accessed 5 August 2019).

CHAPTER 27

Borges and Persian Literature

Shaahin Pishbin

The writings of Jorge Luis Borges demonstrate a sporadic but sustained interest in Persian literature, with two figures who composed in verse eliciting a particularly strong response: these were Omar Khayyam (d.1131), the eleventh-century poet-astronomer, and Farīd al-Dīn 'Aṭṭār (d.1221), the Sufi poet and author of *The Conference of the Birds*. Not knowing Persian himself, Borges relied on the work of Western Orientalists for information about these individuals and the wider world of Persian letters and thought. It is not surprising, then, that issues of translation and transmission are central to his engagement with the topic. The aesthetic power of Persian images and figures – the nightingale, the Simurgh, the chessboard of life – clearly delight Borges too, however, and served to rhetorically embellish his own metaphysical explorations, as well as to confront and unsettle the centre-periphery dynamics he perceived at play among world literatures.

The Enigma of Omar Khayyam

Omar Khayyam (*'Umar Khayyām*), arguably still the most famous Persian poet in the Western world, probably did not write much – if any – of the poetry now ascribed to him. The earliest sources present Khayyam as a freethinking philosopher, astronomer, and mathematician, making conspicuously little record of any poetic activity or talent. The biographies produced by FitzGerald and other nineteenth-century Orientalists were largely based on Persian works written many centuries after Khayyam's death, 'whose object,' wrote the great British Persianist E.G. Browne, 'was rather to weave romantic tales than set forth historical facts'.[1] It was from this tradition of a quasi-mythical, romanticized Khayyam that Borges's *Omar* emerged.

Ever since the phenomenal success of FitzGerald's *The Rubaiyat of Omar Khayyam* (first published in 1859), Persian literary historians have laboured endlessly to identify Khayyam's authentic corpus. In the two centuries following Khayyam's death, extant manuscripts ascribe only 60 scattered quatrains to him; by the seventeenth century, collections appear with up to 1,000, and since then the number has continued to balloon. The Persian quatrain, known as a *rubāʿī* (pl. *rubāʿīyāt*), was one of the most simple poetic forms available to classical Persian poets. An epigrammatic genre, each quatrain (an isolated poetic unit, typically following the rhyme scheme: *aaba*) introduces a single proposition before cleverly and abruptly resolving it in the final line. The quatrains were often sung or recited socially, and could contain heterodox, even salacious content – both reasons why *rubāʿīs* were particularly prone to misattribution (accidentally in the social setting, or deliberately to deflect criticism in cases of improper content). Accordingly, scholars now tend to speak of the 'Khayyamian tradition', rather than the historic Khayyam when discussing the received quatrains.

Borges was thinking about Omar from early on in his career. His father, Jorge Guillermo, published translations of FitzGerald's *Rubaiyat* in the journal *Proa* in the 1920s; Borges Jr. edited this journal, which fostered a cosmopolitan ethos and sought to engage Argentinian intellectuals with global discourse and undermine nationalist parochialism. To accompany his father's translation, Borges wrote a short essay entitled 'Omar Khayyam and FitzGerald'.[2] This essay bears much in common with the more famous 'The Enigma of Edward FitzGerald', and both make clear that, for Borges, the historicity of Khayyam the poet was of little importance. Aside from a lack of suspicion regarding the authenticity of his *rubāʿīyāt*, Borges repeats some commonplace falsehoods about Khayyam, such as his alleged but unattested childhood friendship with Ḥasan al-Ṣabbāh (d.1124) and Niẓām al-Mulk (d.1092), and perpetrates other, more original distortions that scholars of Persian literature would quibble with. As already noted, some manuscripts attribute far more than 500 quatrains to Khayyam, and, contrary to Borges's claim that this 'paltry number' of poems 'will be unfavourable for his reputation for in Persia [. . .] the poet must be prolific,' (*SN-F* 367), some of the most celebrated poets in the Persian canon were hardly industrious writers (Hafiz (d.1390), for example, arguably the most celebrated Persian poet of all, produced less than 500 ghazals – short lyric poems no longer than 15 lines – in his entire career). Furthermore, the bald assertion that Khayyam was an atheist, though reflecting a popular strand of thinking among modern readers, is anachronistic. More inventively still, Borges's suggestion that Khayyam died around 1066 does not accord with scholarly consensus, which estimates 1123 to be his most plausible death

date. Robin Fiddian has noted how Borges obliquely observes the coincidence of Khayyam's death with the Battle of Hastings in order to unsettle
'Eurocentrism, and Anglocentrism in particular',[3] and this underscores
precisely how his primary interest in Khayyam was for discursive ends: as
both a figure who could disrupt twentieth-century cultural hierarchies, and
a vehicle through which to explore ideas about translation and literary
influence.

As is well known, Borges famously rejected the idea of a 'definitive text'
as corresponding 'only to religion or exhaustion' (*SN-F* 69). The lack of
a verifiable, single author in works like Homer's epics and *The Thousand
and One Nights*, and the profusion of translations they engendered, did not
impoverish but enriched his appreciation for them as monuments of world
literature, continually reborn and retold in new contexts, allowing for
different aspects of the works to shine through the prism of different
languages to different audiences. Proponents of more literal translation
and of translations which prioritize responsibly reproducing the cultural
terrain of a source language have long criticized FitzGerald for his excep-
tionally liberal, 'Orientalist' approach to rendering Khayyam's quatrains.
The original quatrains were isolated poems, organized alphabetically
according to the final rhyme, as is typical of collections of Persian verse.
FitzGerald was a very capable linguist, but speaks candidly about the non-
literal translation strategy he adopted in the preface to his *Rubaiyat*: he
reworked and reordered the quatrains into a quasi-narrative structure,
occasionally combining elements from different *rubāʿīs* into one quatrain,
and once or twice seeming to insert his own original compositions. Fully
aware of FitzGerald's approach, Borges heaps praise on his 'Anglicisation
of Omar, in which he can already glory for eternity' ('Omar Khayyam and
FitzGerald' 69). In his view, literal reproduction is an impossibility in
translation, and so one must embrace its productive possibilities.

Although known as a quatrain writer, Khayyam was a relatively obscure
poet in the Persian canon before FitzGerald's translation turbocharged
literary interest in him in his native land, as everywhere else. Borges's
reading of *The Rubaiyat* as 'an English poem with Persian allusions'
(*SNF* 368) therefore exemplifies how he saw translation, and indeed, all
writing, as an act of mysterious, generative, non-linear collaboration. The
inevitability of reading Khayyam in relation to FitzGerald today underscores this great Borgesian idea, namely, that writers create their own
precursors (and successful translators even more so). Khayyam's alleged
belief in metempsychosis works for Borges as an attractive metaphor for
this subversive notion of literary influence: FitzGerald is not merely

influenced by Khayyam, but, by dint of a successful translation, gives him new life. In reality, this is true in a more profound sense, too. For modern readers of Persian, Khayyam is not only read because of FitzGerald and as a precursor to FitzGerald, he is even read *as* FitzGerald, with Iranian bookstores often selling FitzGerald's renderings translated back into Persian alongside the originals.

Borges and the Simurgh

The other figure from Persian literary history with whom Borges repeat-edly engages is the Sufi poet Farīd al-Dīn ʿAṭṭār (1145/46–1221). Born just a couple of decades after Khayyam's death, ʿAṭṭār was also from Nishapur, then among the largest cities in the north-eastern Iranian province of Khorasan. He was a pharmacist by trade and, unlike Khayyam, his literary works are confidently attributed to him and have enjoyed prestige in the Persian canon for many centuries.

Like Khayyam, with whom he felt a personal connection thanks to his father's translation, in his later years we can detect in Borges a sense of kindredness with ʿAṭṭār. In the poem 'The unending rose', for example, Borges identifies a fellow intellectual and apocryphally attributes blindness to him, projecting his own ailments and temperament onto his favourite Persian mystic. Mostly, however, Borges mentions ʿAṭṭār in the context of his magnum opus, the *Manṭiq al-Tayr* ('The Conference of the Birds', 1177) and its central figure, the *Simurgh*.[4] Edward FitzGerald, again, was an important transmitter of this Persian figure, having translated sections of the *Manṭiq al-Tayr* under what Borges called 'the playful title' of *A Bird's Eye-View of Farid-uddin Attar's Bird-Parliament*. Other Orientalists, including Richard Burton, Edward Lane, Margret Smith, and Garcin de Tassy, are the prism through which Borges came to know ʿAṭṭār and his birds.

The Conference of the Birds is a long narrative poem (approximately 4,500 couplets) which depicts the birds of the world seeking out their king, the Simurgh, a Sufi allegory for worshippers seeking God. The Simurgh is said to live in the far-off, mythical mountains of Qāf, and so the birds set off on an arduous journey to find him. Only 30 birds endure the pilgrim-age, and upon arriving at the Simurgh's court, they reach a spiritual epiphany that hinges on the most famous pun in all of Persian literature: the '30 birds' realize that they themselves are the Simurgh, for *sī* in Persian means '30', and *murgh* means 'bird'.[5] This symbolizes the Sufi concept of God as emanating from all creation; the worshipper who endures hardship along the spiritual path becomes like a polished mirror, annihilating the self in order to reflect the beauty of the Divine.

The figure of the Simurgh was not invented by 'Aṭṭār, but is a magnificent bird from Persian mythology diversely imagined by various writers since pre-Islamic times. Firdawsi's Simurgh, in his epic poem the *Shāhnāmeh* ('Book of Kings', 1010), for example, lived among the peaks of the Alborz mountains in Iran, and became mother and protector to the great Iranian prince Zāl, who had been abandoned to the mountains as an infant on account of being born with white hair. Borges was familiar with Firdawsi's Simurgh, but kept returning to 'Aṭṭār's literarily superior representation. There are a number of reasons why he so enjoys 'Aṭṭār's allegory of the Simurgh in particular. 'The imaginative power of the legend of the Simurgh is apparent to all,' he writes, 'less pronounced, but no less real, is its rigour and economy'. He suggests that the challenge of a pilgrimage story is avoiding a banal, predictable ending and he praises 'Aṭṭār's masterful resolution: 'The author finds his way out of this difficulty with classical elegance; adroitly, the searchers are what they seek' (*SN-F* 297).

The Seeker and the Sought

Unity of the one with the many – pantheism by another name – is a concept Borges returns to again and again, particularly (but by no means exclusively) in his Islamic and Persian-inflected writings. It sometimes lurks in the background (Omar Khayyam, Borges imagines in 'The Enigma . . . ', was reading a treatise entitled *The One and the Many* on the day of his death), but very frequently Borges brings Persian-flavoured pantheism into direct comparison with items in the Western canon. One of his earliest mentions of 'Aṭṭār, in 'Note on Walt Whitman', includes him in a global canon of writers and texts that have explored and asserted the possibility that God is 'diverse, contradictory, or (better yet) miscellaneous things'– an eclectic canon that begins with the Bhagavad-Gita and Heraclitus, and continues with examples from Plotinus, Emerson, and Whitman. Borges's spiritual commitment to this philosophy is questionable, but as a writer, he recognized the conceit's endless potential: 'The rhetorical possibilities of that extension of the principle of identity seem infinite' (*OC* I: 251).

The rhetorical embodiment of pantheism receives further consideration in the essay 'The Simurgh and the Eagle', where Borges compares Dante and 'Aṭṭār's respective experiments with 'the notion of a being composed of other beings'. Although Borges concedes it may be a strange and off-putting concept in the abstract, he nevertheless declares that 'in incredible fashion, one of the most memorable figures of Western literature, and another of Eastern literature, correspond to it' (*SN-F* 294): Dante's eagle in Canto XVIII of the *Paradiso*, composed of 'thousands of just kings', is an 'unmistakeable symbol of Empire', and Attār's Simurgh, dreamed up a century later, is composed of 30 birds and 'implicitly encompasses and improves upon it' (295). Borges prefers the Persian image because the individual birds which make up the Simurgh entirely lose themselves in it; they *are* the Simurgh and the Simurgh is them. The noble kings that constitute the eagle, on the other hand, retain their individual identities: 'Behind the Eagle is the personal God of Israel and Rome; behind the magical Simurgh is pantheism' (297).

By highlighting the universalism of the *topos* of unity between the one and the many, and the superiority of the Eastern literary construction, Borges gestures towards an approach to literary history organized around ideas, not languages and borders. In doing so, he undermines dominant parochialisms that assert the centrality and supremacy of European (read: colonial) cultural canons whilst marginalizing and belittling the cultural achievements of the East.[6] The eagle is a limited symbol because it represents European civilization and domination, the boundaries of which Borges seeks to overcome; within the Simurgh, however, divisions, hierarchy, and personal identity (the self, in Sufi terminology) dissolve entirely. In this sense, 'Attār, like Khayyam and his quatrains, is an ally in the struggle for the literary voices of the 'Global South' to be heard on an equal footing with their Western counterparts, and the Simurgh is a vision, albeit an impossible one, of what an egoless model of world literature might look like.

Borges explores several of the 'rhetorical possibilities' of pantheism in his *ficciones*, too, in his story, 'The Zahir', for instance. Borges roots his literary invention in the Islamic world, telling us its first witness was the Persian dervish 'Lutf Ali Azur', as recorded in his biographical encyclopaedia, the 'Temple of Fire'.[7] In Arabic, *ẓāhir* means 'surface', 'visible', 'apparent', 'manifest', and in Islamic thought refers to the literal, exoteric meaning one can interpret from a Koranic verse, in contrast to the *bāṭin*, which is to say the hidden, inner, esoteric meaning. Sufis have historically valorized the *bāṭin* as equal or superior to the *ẓāhir*, believing that for every singular, exoteric meaning in the Koran, up to seven esoteric meanings can be determined, depending on one's level of spiritual insight, whilst advocates of strict literalism were known as *ẓāhirīs*.[8] Clearly, this hermeneutic principle does not correspond entirely to Borges's conception of the Zahir.

However, we might read his Zahir as the reification of obsessive literalism, the kind that perceives the totality of meaning as singular, eschews ambiguity and nuance, and, for Borges, constitutes a kind of madness.[9]

'The Approach to Al-Mu'tasim' is another significant example of Persian mystical thought's influence on Borges. Rather than write a story imitating the spiritual journey of 'Aṭṭār's birds, Borges writes a *ficción* disguised as a review of a novel which does just that. Mir Bahadur Ali's *The Approach to Al-Mu'tasim* describes an Indian law student who sets out on a spiritual journey to find the perfect man. The novel ends ambiguously, with the student on the verge of meeting Al-Mu'tasim, stepping into a light behind a curtain (this occurs shortly after the student encounters 'a Persian bookseller' (*CF* 85)). Borges's reviewer mentions the clear influence of *The Conference of the Birds* on the novel, and even summarizes the plot of 'Aṭṭār's poem in a lengthy endnote, in which he explains that 'ambiguous similarities' between the two narratives hint at the possibility that the lawyer and Al-Mu'tasim share the same identity – that the seeker and the sought are one and the same (*CF* 87). He omits mentioning the strongest clue pointing towards the same conclusion: just as the 30 birds (*sī murgh*) are homographic with the great Simurgh they seek, the word *al-mu'tasim* in the Arabic script, meaning 'the one seeking shelter', is graphically indistinguishable from *al-mu'taṣam*, literally meaning 'the shelter that is sought'.[10]

Conclusions – *Ustād Borges*[11]

From some of his earliest writings among the Argentinian avant-garde until the last years of his life, Borges sustained an interest in Persian literature that distinguishes him from the vast majority of his contemporaries. From a representational standpoint, it is fair to say that Borges's engagement is narrow and that he does not do justice to the great diversity of Persian thought. From a tradition that spans a millennium, he only repeatedly discusses the two poets Omar Khayyam and 'Aṭṭār, and cynics may justifiably complain that his discursive instrumentalization of these thinkers reproduces stereotypes of the Orient as essentially mystical and ancient.[12] We are inevitably left wondering what Borges might have made of the *Shāhnāmeh's* epic blending of history and legend, of the widespread bibliomancy of Hafiz's *Divan*, or of Nima Yushij and Persian literature's decisive turn towards modernism which occurred in his own lifetime. These questions should not detract, however, from what Borges does achieve. He seizes upon Khayyam and FitzGerald's curious relationship to remind us of the interconnectedness of all literary production and persuasively makes the case for the creative autonomy of translation, from a reader's perspective. His poetry and later essays make his personal sense of connection with 'Omar' clear – an affinity deriving from his own father's work translating *The Rubaiyat* and a certain sympathy towards other 'periphery' writers who unsettle Europe's colonial sense of cultural superiority. Similarly, by repeatedly centring 'Aṭṭār's Simurgh as the exemplary literary construction of the universal theme of the seeker being the sought, Borges emerges as an advocate for a postcolonial model of 'world' literature, a model that looks beyond petty regionalism towards an elusive 'autonomous sphere' of art.

Notes

1. Edward Granville Browne, *A Literary History of Persia*, Vol. 2 (Cambridge: Cambridge University Press, 1956), p. 248.
2. Jorge Luis Borges, 'Omar Jaiyam y FitzGerald,' *Proa*, enero 1925, pp. 69–70.
3. Robin W. Fiddian, *Postcolonial Borges: Argument and Artistry* (Oxford: Oxford University Press, 2017), pp. 122–123.
4. Borges mentions 'Aṭṭār and/or the Simurgh, in chronological order, in 'Nota sobre Walt Whitman' and a review entitled 'El Dr. Jekyll y Edward Hyde, transformados' (*Discusión*, 1932); 'El acercamiento a Almotásim' (*Historia de la eternidad*, 1936); 'El Zahir' (*El Aleph*, 1949); 'Sobre Chesterton' (*Otras inquisiciones*, 1952); 'El Simurg' (*El libro de seres imaginarios*, 1957); 'The unending rose' (*La rosa profunda*, 1975); finally (and most thoroughly) in the essay, 'El Simurg y el águila' (*Nueve ensayos dantescos*, 1982).
5. 'Aṭṭār writes at the climax of the poem (lines 4449, 4451): *When those thirty birds* [sī murgh] *looked on with haste / there was no doubt: these thirty birds were the Simurgh / . . . / they saw themselves as the complete Simurgh / the Simurgh itself was thirty complete birds.* (My literal translation.)
6. On British imperial anxiety towards Persian, for example, see Muzaffar Alam, 'The Culture and Politics of Persian in Precolonial Hindustan', *Literary Cultures in History: Reconstructions from South Asia*, ed. Sheldon Pollock (Berkeley: University of California Press, 2003), pp. 188–189.
7. Here Borges refers to a real eighteenth-century Persian writer, Luṭf 'Alī Āẕar Baygdilī (d.1781), who was indeed most famous for his biographical dictionary of poets entitled 'the Fire Temple' (*taẕkirah-yi Ātashkadah*). The anecdote he cites, however, is invented.
8. The Sufi principle was famously versified by the poet Jalāl al-Dīn Rūmī: *Don't consider the outward meaning* [ẕāhir] *of the Quran's words / Beneath the outward meaning is a powerful inward one* [bāṭin] */ Beneath this inward one there is another / thought and vision are beguiled therein / . . . / And so it goes for seven inner*

meanings, oh bounteous one! / From this saying, he provides the shelter you seek [muʿtaṣim]. (My translation.)

9. For more on the *ẓāhir/bāṭin* dichotomy in Borges, see López-Baralt, 'Islamic Themes', in *The Cambridge Companion to Jorge Luis Borges*, ed. E. H. Williamson (Cambridge: Cambridge University Press, 2013), pp. 68–80 (pp. 77–78).

10. In the Arabic and Persian, short vowels are not usually written. The words *muʿtaṣim* and *muʿtaṣam* are Arabic participles; the final short vowels ('i' and 'a') grammatically distinguish between the active and passive forms. The prefix 'al' (the definite article in Arabic) renders the participle a noun ('the one who seek shelter' and 'the shelter which is sought').

11. *Ustād* is a Persian term of respect for a person of great learning (simply meaning 'professor' in modern Persian). As an alternative to the derivation from "vuestra merced," some scholars have posited that the Spanish formal pronoun 'usted' could have derived from this word via Arabic.

12. Pantheism and metempsychosis, concepts Borges repeatedly attributes to ʿAṭṭār and Khayyam, are of course historically marginal views among writers and speakers of Persian.

CHAPTER 28

Borges and the 'Boom'

Dominic Moran

The fact that the author who, perhaps more than any other, inspired and helped shape the Spanish American 'new novel' of the 1950s and 1960s himself never wrote one, and even professed an abiding disregard for the genre (at least in its more orthodox realist guises), is the sort of irony which would doubtless have amused Borges and might easily have served as the germ for one of his more whimsical fictions. Yet few would dispute that it is the case. All the major novelists of the so-called 'Boom', regardless of their particular aesthetic sensibilities or ideological allegiances – and some of them, not least Gabriel García Márquez, publicly berated what they regarded as Borges's antediluvian political conservatism and aesthetic escapism – unhesitatingly acknowledged their profound indebtedness to a writer who famously quipped that, rather than taking the trouble to pen the sort of bulky, labyrinthine, formally experimental novels which would become the hallmark of the period, he preferred to imagine that such works already existed and offer a brief fictional précis of them instead.[1] That collective debt is both broadly cultural and more specifically literary and differs, sometimes significantly, from author to author. Nevertheless, there is a good deal of common ground.

Culturally speaking, perhaps Borges's most important contribution to twentieth-century Spanish American narrative was his unapologetic universalism. He was a consciously and conspicuously cosmopolitan writer, who drew freely on and incorporated into his own work an encyclopaedic and dazzlingly diverse range of literary traditions and allusions, often setting his stories in remote times and distant or even imaginary locations, from Ancient Rome to British India, early Christian Carthage to contemporary Cornwall, an oneirically transfigured Buenos Aires to a dreamed-up planet. An outspoken critic of all forms of literary nationalism, he insisted that for a writer to be authentically Spanish American (or Argentine, Mexican, Peruvian, etc.) there was no need to focus on narrowly American themes, just as Shakespeare had been no less English for having

228

set his plays in Ancient Greece or Italy.[2] He thus provided a vital antidote to the assiduously cultivated parochialism of much of the 'Regionalist' or *Indigenista* fiction which had dominated Spanish American narrative in the 1920s and 1930s, characterized by its cult of local colour, stagey folkloric tableaux, and exaggeratedly 'American' expression – what Mario Vargas Llosa subsequently referred to as 'primitive' literature.[3] The facility with which Borges adopted and adapted foreign literary sources and models helped subsequent writers overcome a long-standing cultural inferiority complex, particularly in relation to their European and North American counterparts, and thus break free from provincial bonds and accompanying stereotypes. And whilst many Boom novels are set wholly or partly in Spanish America, they remain unencumbered by the prolix documentation of autochthonous flora and fauna, amateur ethnology, and specialist glossaries which weigh heavy on the works of writers such as Peruvian Ciro Alegría or Venezuelan Rómulo Gallegos, whose *Doña Bárbara* (1929) was the flagship novel of the previous generation.

A key adjunct to Borges's creative eclecticism was his similarly wide-ranging work as a translator. Indeed, it was apparently on reading Borges's translation of Kafka's *Metamorphosis* (1938) that García Márquez stumbled upon a mode of narration which, when later combined with those of his maternal grandmother and of Borges himself, provided him with the unmistakeable tone of *One Hundred Years of Solitude* (1967).[4] Borges also translated in whole or in part several key works of Anglo-American Modernism which were to have a transformative effect on the Boom novelists who, as José Donoso remarks in his *Historia personal del Boom*, in what proved to be the ultimately liberating absence of home-grown literary forefathers, felt obliged to look elsewhere for inspiration.[5] As early as 1925, he published a translation of the final page of Joyce's *Ulysses* (1922), which subsequently became a template for many of the 'new novels', and later translated Virginia Woolf's *Orlando* (1937) and William Faulkner's *The Wild Palms* (1940). Faulkner would prove to be, if anything, an even more pervasive influence on the Boom writers than Joyce.[6] Again, the immediate beneficiary was García Márquez, the only one of the 'Big Four' Boom novelists who did not read English.[7]

If Borges broadened the literary horizons of the Boom novelists, he simultaneously helped hone and concentrate their expression by stripping Spanish American literary prose of the bombast, descriptive *longueurs*, lexical arcana, and rhetorical incontinence that had blighted it for a century or more, and endowing it with a clipped eloquence and razor-sharp concision. His own prose is by turns sinuous, suggestive, at once coolly precise and teasingly oblique. For Vargas Llosa, Borges rendered Spanish 'as lucid and logical as French and as nuanced and rigorous as English', to the extent that his work 'contains almost as many ideas as it does words.'⁸ García Márquez, meanwhile, his loathing of Borges the man and the 'unreality' of his work notwithstanding, confessed to reading him every day on account of his 'extraordinary capacity for verbal artifice' which taught the Colombian 'how to write . . . how to tune [my] instrument in order to be able to express [my]self' ('Diálogo', 70, 74). Despite their length, most Boom novels display an unprecedented and sustained concern with expressive rigour and linguistic inventiveness, so much so that Carlos Fuentes, who also identified Borges as the chief instigator of this thoroughgoing stylistic overhaul, dubbed them first and foremost 'novels of language'.⁹ Borges's fastidiousness with regard to expression is echoed in his obsessive striving for formal and structural perfection. Those attributes too may be more readily achievable within the modest confines of the short story, yet we find a similar preoccupation with craftsmanship and narrative organization on a grand scale in novels such as Carlos Fuentes's *The Death of Artemio Cruz* (1962) and Vargas Llosa's *The Green House* (1965). The latter in particular, whilst borrowing its basic narrative building blocks from Faulkner, is constructed with a quasi-mathematical exactitude entirely reminiscent of Borges.

Inseparable from Borges's terse, polished style is his refined, laconic, sometimes withering sense of humour and intellectual playfulness – qualities which, with a handful of notable exceptions, had been in decidedly short supply in earlier Spanish American fiction. Because of the long shadow cast by High Modernism over the Boom and the unremitting grimness of a number of its most emblematic works, it is easy to forget that several Boom novels – not least Julio Cortázar's *Hopscotch* (1963) and Guillermo Cabrera Infante's *Three Trapped Tigers* (1967) – are often very funny, and that perhaps the archetypal Boom narrative, *One Hundred Years of Solitude* is, *inter alia*, and despite critics' concerted attempts to transform it into a sombre existential tract, one of the twentieth century's comic masterpieces in any language. Its deadpan, devious, often outrageously nonchalant narrative voice is Borgesian through and through.¹⁰ Perhaps fittingly, *The Garden Next Door* (1981), José Donoso's tart fictional 'farewell' to the Boom, which does mischievous dirt on its grandiose, myth-making pretensions and megalomaniac cult of literary personality, is heavily reliant on Borges for its prickly literary satire and concluding narrative twist. And even those fiercely politically committed novelists such as Vargas Llosa who, while labouring under Sartre's influence throughout the 1960s, viewed the faintest whiff of humour in literature as an unpardonably frivolous bourgeois indulgence, later went on to write fine comic novels such as *Captain Pantoja and the Special Service* (1973) and *Aunt Julia and the Scriptwriter* (1977), in the latter of which in particular Borges's influence is manifest.

If I have begun with thematic and stylistic considerations, all of them crucial, it is because they have a perhaps understandable tendency to be side-lined or even overlooked entirely in the exegetical haste to address Borges's most distinctive and far-reaching legacy to modern prose fiction, namely his sustained, often mesmerizing undercutting and refinement of the core principles and practices of literary realism, a realism which, in his native South America, had too often taken the form of anachronistic and ungainly imitations or unwitting pastiches of European (particularly French) models. In tales which often foregrounded their own fictional status and tantalizingly exposed their inner workings, Borges blew apart this whole outmoded tradition by introducing unreliable narrators, sudden and surprising switches of narrative perspective, abrupt temporal shifts, and vertiginous metafictional jolts and *mises en abyme*. He also confused and conflated literary genres, casting stories in the form of obituaries, literary essays, 'notes', and book reviews and swathing them in a formidable veneer of sometimes bogus erudition. A common, indeed pivotal concern of the Boom novelists was to illustrate and explore the dauntingly complex, multi-layered socio-historical realities of their respective nations and of the continent as a whole, and Borges effectively equipped them with a set of techniques and devices which allowed them to do so with previously unimagined sophistication and sweep. Thus, the notion of time as a proliferating garden of forking paths adumbrated by Borges in his eponymous story furnished Carlos Fuentes with the means of re-imagining the roads not taken in Mexican history in *The Death of Artemio Cruz* and in the greater sweep of Western history in the mammoth *Terra Nostra* (1975). The deliberate withholding of the narrator's identity in tales such as 'The House of Asterion' or 'The Shape of the Sword', meanwhile, which results in the disconcerting blurring or inversion of identities of hero and villain or victim, may lie behind the famous revelation of the unnamed first-person narrator as the brutal college bully 'The Jaguar' on the final page of Vargas Llosa's *The Time of the Hero* (1962), a stratagem which obliges us radically to reassess both the character himself and our own, skewed ideological view of him. Above and beyond its stylistic debt, *One Hundred Years of Solitude* is full of mischievous nods and winks to Borges. Colonel Aureliano Buendía's experience before the firing squad is clearly modelled on 'The Secret Miracle', in which writer Jaromír Hladík, confronting precisely the same fate, seems *in extremis* to have God grant him a year to finish a play, only to be executed just minutes after the appointed hour in 'real' time. Aureliano, on the other hand, *is* granted a near miraculous reprieve – a thwarting of readerly expectations that is itself quintessentially Borgesian. The narration of his end, when it does finally come, is at least partly inspired by the protagonist's (anti) climactic vision of the Aleph in perhaps Borges's most celebrated tale. The unforgettable concluding *coup de théâtre* of the novel, which sees Aureliano Babilonia apparently deciphering a manuscript in which he himself is a character, triggers the sort of dizzying recursion which Borges explores in the essay 'Partial Magic in the Quixote' and stories such as 'The Circular Ruins'. The manuscript itself, meanwhile, penned in Sanskrit and subject to multiple outré encryptions, is taken straight from the shelves of Borges's Library of Babel. García Márquez also makes elaborate, often tongue-in-cheek use of the Borgesian ploy of combining 'real' and fictional characters, a number of whom are imported from other Boom novels. These figures or figments rub ghostly shoulders with, amongst others, a character named Gabriel who is himself an avatar of the author of the novel in which they all appear, further underlining the text's self-advertised status as a disorienting hall of mirrors or mirages. Borges's metaphysical obsessions and fondness for erudite textual citation and cross-referencing are also central to *Hopscotch*, even if Cortázar's unruly montage of a book is informed more by the mutinous spirit of Surrealism than by a fascination with equivocal footnotes to hoary incunabula. *Hopscotch* features, primarily in a series of ironically titled 'Dispensable Chapters', a running commentary on its own genesis, form and function, a commentary largely supplied by a fictitious author, Morelli, who also appears as a character and is himself attempting to write a book which, we infer, bears more than a passing resemblance to *Hopscotch* itself. Whilst Cortázar's extended experiment in literary game-playing and calculated narrative self-sabotage was underpinned by a fundamental seriousness of purpose (*Hopsotch*'s primary objective was to effect nothing less than a total spiritual purge of Western Man), Guillermo Cabrera Infante saw Borges's refined sense of fun, his puckish irreverence with respect to entrenched intellectual and aesthetic norms and orthodoxies, his suspicion of arbitrarily wielded authority, and his penchant for often wicked parody as constituting in and of themselves a salutary corrective to the escalating autocracy and dogmatism of a supposedly revolutionary regime which in practice quashed freedom of artistic expression and side-lined (or worse) those who, like himself, refused to bend to the new cultural exigencies. *Three Trapped Tigers* (for which he rejected the generic straitjacket of novel), originally written in 1964 and later significantly revised under Castro's darkening shadow, precisely so as to accentuate the playful over the dourly political, became a sort of bravura 500-page *boutade*, fizzing with puns, typographic puzzles, narratorial games of hide-and-seek and knowing literary allusion, whose centrepiece is an often hilarious series of parodies which involve recounting the assassination of Trotsky in the hyperbolized styles of seven of Cuba's most respected authors. The ludic spirit of Borges (bolstered by that of shared literary forebears such as Sterne and Lewis Carroll) is mobilized to pull tongues at State-sponsored socialist realism, nicely illustrating the Argentine writer's claim that an author, however firm his or her convictions, could never truly know what or for whom s/he might be writing.[11]

Cortázar and Cabrera Infante's kaleidoscopic novels also illustrate, perhaps better than any other Boom narrative, another of Borges's key aesthetic and indeed ethical precepts, namely his insistence that, rather than simply being handed textual meaning on a plate, the reader must be encouraged to play an active role in the decipherment and even the construction of the literary work. An inveterate reader of crime fiction, he cast the reader in the role of detective and took manifest delight in wrong-footing him and thereby exposing his unexamined presumptions and prejudices. In the figure of the 'reader-accomplice' whom Cortázar and Morelli imagine as a 'co-participant' in the composition and interpretation of the novel, left to make sense of a text that is fragmentary, discontinuous and, depending on the course we chart through it (various, sometimes mutually exclusive alternatives are put before the prospective reader at the outset), requires repeatedly jumping back and forth between chapters out of numerical sequence, we find a direct descendent of that uncommon reader alluded to at the start of 'Tlön, Uqbar, Orbis Tertius' (*OC* I: 431–443) who, behind the omissions, distortions and contradictions of a narrative might espy 'appalling or banal' hidden truths (431). Borges, like his mentor Cervantes, recoiled at facile moralizing and heavy-handed didacticism in literature, proclivities which had encumbered so much nineteenth- and early twentieth-century Spanish American narrative. He was similarly dismissive of the *littérature engagée* of his own day, repeatedly arguing that, rather than a means to some extra-literary end, the text should be an 'autonomous sphere', to be enjoyed and evaluated according to its artistry, artifice and power to beguile rather than in terms of any palpable design it might have on its readers.[12] All the Boom writers, even the most politically intransigent, took this lesson to heart, and in fact no novels of the period are more determinedly impersonal than those of Vargas Llosa, whose early espousal of the aesthetic diktats of the French thinker was fanatical enough to earn him the nickname 'The Bolshy Little Sartre'. Whilst he may have taken his initial aesthetic cue regarding narrative autonomy from Flaubert, Vargas Llosa later confessed that, even as in public he was noisily touting literature as a political weapon, in private he was devouring *Fictions* and *The Aleph* at least as greedily as he had *Qu'est-ce que la littérature?*[13] Indeed, if anything, the notable lack of explicit bias in novels such as *The Green House* is what renders them most politically compelling, since it falls to the reader to tease out and think through their ideological implications. Again, then, we see the aesthetic criteria of Borges the miniaturist assimilated and amplified within the far grander arena of the 'total' or 'totalizing' novel, a term used by many Boom writers to describe the capacious, multifaceted, seemingly free-standing narrative universes from which all traces of a controlling authorial hand had been painstakingly excised.

Given the forbidding complexity of most of the novels that it produced, along with its origins in the Modernism of 1920s and 1930s, the 'Boom' has perhaps inevitably come to be enveloped in a pall of intellectual solemnity and high-mindedness, not to mention a significant dose of pretentiousness and pomposity, particularly on the part of academic literary critics. Yet it may be worthwhile recalling that, after a juvenile and perhaps partly cosmetic flirtation with the poetic avant-garde – he was clearly anything but disconcerted to be seen as a Young Turk rattling the cage of the stuffy Hispanic literary establishment – Borges went on to cultivate literary tastes that, did we not know otherwise, might be viewed as those of a quirky, even reactionary *amateur* rather than a paradigm-shifting (for once the term is genuinely applicable) literary colossus. Turning his back on the more iconoclastic experiments in poetry and fiction of the day, he preferred the less strenuous pleasures of Poe, Twain, Conan Doyle, Stevenson, Wells, Chesterton, Priestley and detective fiction of the Golden Age. Indeed, many of his apparently more radical narrative innovations result from his subtle tweaking or filigree underscoring of techniques and conventions (partial narrators, the use of 'found', fragmentary or adulterated documents, the presence of characters acquainted with their own creators, etc.) which feature unselfconsciously in the works of those more traditional predecessors. He often professed, or more likely feigned bewilderment at the more extravagant formal or epistemological upheavals that had been proclaimed and perpetrated in his name, as well as his *ex post facto* consecration as a founding father of literary postmodernism and senescent poster-boy for the *nouvelle critique*. That somewhere within the forbidding narrative edifices of the new Spanish American novel lurked Huckleberry Finn, Father Brown, and the Master of Ballantrae is also, one suspects, an irony that Borges, more attuned to the vagaries of literary inheritance than many of his more theoretically minded commentators, would have relished.

Notes

1. Jorge Luis Borges, 'Prólogo' to *El jardín de los senderos que se bifurcan* (1944), in *Obras completas (henceforth OC)*, 4 vols. (Buenos Aires: Emecé, 2004–2005), I, 429; Gabriel García Márquez, in Mario Vargas Llosa and Gabriel García Márquez, *La novela en América Latina: Diálogo (henceforth 'Diálogo')*, 4th ed. (Lima: Petroperú, Departamento de Relaciones Corporativas, 2013 [1967]), pp. 69–71, p. 74. Unless otherwise indicated, all translations are my own.
2. Borges's most important pronouncement on the subject is the lecture 'El escritor argentino y la tradición', *OC* I, pp. 267–274 (p. 232).
3. Mario Vargas Llosa, 'Primitives and Creators', *Times Literary Supplement* (14 November 1968), pp. 1287–1288.
4. Gerald Martin, *Gabriel García Márquez: A Life* (London: Bloomsbury, 2008), pp. 98–99, 144.
5. José Donoso, *Historia personal del Boom* (Madrid: Alfaguara, 1998), pp. 21–24.
6. Borges also published an essay on the novel, 'El *Ulises* de Joyce', in *Proa* 2, 6 (January, 1925), later included in *Inquisiciones* (1925). For an extensive account of Joyce's influence on the modern Latin American novel see Gerald Martin, *Journeys Through The Labyrinth* (London: Verso, 1989), chapter 5.
7. Regarding the influence of *Orlando* in particular on *One Hundred Years of Solitude*, see Gene Bell-Vilada, *García Márquez: The Man and His Work* (Chapel Hill, NC: University of North Carolina Press, 2010 [rev. ed.]), p. 86.
8. Mario Vargas Llosa, 'An Invitation to Borges's Fiction', in *A Writer's Reality* (London: Faber and Faber, 1991), pp. 1–19 (pp. 8, 10) (translation amended).
9. Carlos Fuentes, *La nueva novela hispanoamericana* (Mexico: Joaquín Mortiz, 1969), pp. 23–26, pp. 30–35.
10. For a refreshing and itself highly amusing take on the humour of García Marquez's novel and Borges's influence on it, see Clive Griffin's 'The Humour of *One Hundred Years of Solitude*', in Bernard McGuirk and Richard Cardwell (eds.), *Gabriel García Márquez: New Readings* (Cambridge: Cambridge University Press, 1987), pp. 81–94.
11. See Jorge Luis Borges, 'Prólogo' to *La rosa profunda* (1975), *OC* III, pp. 87–88 (p. 87).
12. Jorge Luis Borges, 'El arte narrativo y la magia', *OC* I, pp. 226–232 (p. 232).
13. Mario Vargas Llosa, 'An Invitation to Borges's Fiction', pp. 1–2.

CHAPTER 29

Argentina and Cuba: The Politics of Reception[1]

Alfredo Alonso Estenoz

In an early essay, 'La fruición literaria' ('Literary Pleasure', *TTL* 28–31), Borges argued that certain non-literary factors influence – and sometimes determine – an author's fate. Borges agreed with the Spanish scholar Marcelino Menéndez y Pelayo that 'If we did not read poetry through history's eyes, very few lines would survive.'[2] Later, in the short story 'An Examination of the Works of Herbert Quain', Borges considered other factors besides literary history: the timing of a publication, the aesthetic fashions of a period, and the literary market. Quain's books met adverse circumstances at the time of their publication; for that reason, he was barely remembered at the time of his death.

It seems ironic that Borges, who tried to establish clear distinctions between a work's intrinsic qualities and the context of its reception, would fall victim to the same dynamic he condemned. In his case, politics – the politics of his time and his own political views – were of capital importance. Borges declared that a writer's political views were superficial and circumstantial and should not interfere with his or her literary creation and reputation. However, he was keenly aware of how impossible it is to isolate the purely aesthetic qualities of a text – if they can be objectively measured – from the context in which that text is read.

For quite some time, the prevailing critical view of Borges focused on his public statements and obscured a deeper understanding of the politics present in his writing. Along with his nationality and the distinctive local flavour of his literature – which was either erased or softened in many translations of his work – Borges's political positions were often simplified or reduced to colourful and – sometimes – outrageous anecdotes. More recent studies have challenged this interpretation and deepened our understanding of Borges's political evolution as well as his specific interventions in the public sphere.

The present chapter does not constitute an exploration of Borges's political views, but it offers an analysis of how specific cultural and political interests shaped his reception in different periods and countries. Through a comparative study of the reception of Borges in Argentina and Cuba, I intend to show differences and similarities that were largely determined by political considerations. For the purpose of this essay, I will focus on three periods: the mid-1940s, the mid-1950s, and the first decade after the Cuban Revolution of 1959.

When did politics begin to play an essential role in Borges's reception in Argentina and Cuba? In the latter country, it is easier to give precise dates; between 1968 and 1971 the revolutionary government's cultural policy declared that literary and artistic creation would be judged on ideological grounds. In Argentina, on the other hand, such defining moments are more difficult to establish: there was never a centralized cultural policy, even though Juan Domingo Perón tried to establish something of that nature. What can be said with certainty is that there was never a moment in which Borges's reception was free of political and ideological considerations. Questions about the relationship between literature and its context of production, how literature should reflect the national spirit, or what position a Latin American writer should adopt before his or her twofold European and American heritage, dominated the conversation around Borges's work and public figure.

A key moment in the politicization of Borges occurred in 1942, when he submitted his book *El jardín de senderos que se bifurcan* (1941) for the National Literary Award. The jury not only failed to award him any of the prizes, but it also issued a statement explaining their decision:

> [. . .] the jury did the right thing when it decided not to offer the Argentine people, at this hour of the world, an exotic and byzantine work that, under the influence of certain deviant trends that define contemporary British literature, fluctuates between the fantastic short story, an obscure and self-aggrandizing erudition, and detective fiction.[3]

At first glance, the statement seems to be based on the aesthetic qualities of Borges's book – it refers to the genres he employed and parodied. But it also claims to know what the 'Argentine people' needed at that historical moment. Were the members of the jury referring to the global context and, specifically, to the Second World War? Did they overlook the fact that *El jardín de senderos que se bifurcan* (the collection, *The Garden of Forking Paths*, included in the English-language compilation, 'Labyrinths') contains one of the most insightful (and earliest) reflections on the nature of Nazism, 'Tlön, Uqbar, Orbis Tertius', where the propensity to ignore facts and create mental realities is presented as a characteristic of totalitarian systems? Was the jury instead referring to the Argentine context, in which the increasing polarization of politics would lead to the 1943 coup d'état and, a few years later, to the rise of Peronism? In any case, Borges's work was perceived as disconnected from the immediate social context, a perception that took decades to overcome.

The first critical text on Borges written in Cuba appeared in 1944: a review by Cintio Vitier of *Poemas*, a compilation of Borges's poetry up to 1943. Vitier was a key member of Orígenes, the leading cultural and literary group in Cuba from the mid-1940s until the mid-1950s, and which edited the journal of the same name. Did the group's political views influence Vitier's reading of Borges? The absence of an explicit political definition has been interpreted as Orígenes's lack of interest in the most urgent social and political problems of the time. Nevertheless, the group aspired to participate in the construction of the Cuban nation by different means; culture, particularly poetry, offered a response to the question of national identity and political and cultural independence from the United States and Spain. According to Orígenes's leader, José Lezama Lima, 'A country which is frustrated in its political essence may attain other virtues and reasons by hunting on a higher ground,'[4] i.e. its culture. Faced with the frustration of the Cuban republican project, Orígenes responded with the idea of salvation through culture. How did this view influence the group's reading of Borges?

Vitier condemned those Argentine critics who examined Borges from either European or nationalistic positions, celebrating instead the writer's solution to this duality, which was a synthesis of his double heritage. Rejecting a stereotypical view of national identity, Vitier praised Borges's embrace of an invisible, essential Argentina, far from the exaltation of local colour.[5] María Zambrano, the exiled Spanish philosopher who offered her support to Orígenes, spoke of a 'secret Cuba' when referring to the group's work and vision.[6] A 'secret Cuba' meant an essence, a national character that lay beneath (and hidden from) the visible symbols and constructs of national identity, one that rejected local colour and stereotypes.

Around the same time in Argentina, Peronism was taking over the country's political life. Borges disavowed Perón's populism and turned his gaze inwards, a position criticized as a manifestation of bourgeois-elitist writers' desire to distance themselves from a social reality that escaped or scared them. David Viñas, for instance, referred to an 'invisible Argentina' towards which writers like Eduardo Mallea direct their attention as a reaction against the rise of populism. In his analysis of Borges, Viñas takes this idea further and argues that Borges's rejection of Peronism led him to occupy his thoughts with 'the invisible world',[7] a world in which culture becomes a disembodied essence. Thus, the same element – the less obvious aspects of national identity – can be read in opposite manners: in Cuba, it meant a rejection of the stereotypes that distorted the country's image (mainly in the eye of foreign tourism); in Argentina, an opposition to the masses' acquisition of political prominence.

The politicization of Borges's work and public persona became more radical during the Perón years. The writer's position was clear, but he maintained a critical distance and expressed his anti-Peronism in a highly philosophical and metaphorical fashion that was often overlooked. In an interview for the popular magazine *El Hogar*, he declared:

> My literature has never been at the service of what is called *ideas* in political and social jargon. My opinions became visible during the last decade [. . .] With respect to the [dictator] we suffered, I maintained an attitude consistent with my conscience, and I preferred to hide my disgust, so that I could live with the highest dignity [. . .] Some people see my position as one of coldness and indifference toward the problems that directly affect the Argentine people. They are ignoring my support for many national and international causes I considered just and honourable.[8]

After Perón was overthrown in 1955, Borges enjoyed widespread official recognition. He became the director of the National Library and a constant presence in the media. At the same time, several young Argentine writers voiced their indifference towards, or even their repudiation of, his work. The intellectuals who founded the journal *Contornos* took a position against Peronism's view of culture and education and against Borges, whom they saw as too removed from the country's realities. In 1954, Adolfo Prieto published *Borges y la nueva generación*, a book whose main argument was that Borges did not speak to their interests, and that his distinguished place in Argentine letters owed more to his public persona than to his work.

Meanwhile in Cuba, a new literary magazine sought a place of prominence in the country's cultural life. *Ciclón* emerged from the schism between Lezama Lima and José Rodríguez Feo, the former editors of *Orígenes*. Virgilio Piñera, an ex-member of Orígenes, became *Ciclón*'s editor, along with Rodríguez Feo. According to Piñera, *Orígenes* had failed to give culture an influential role in society. Cuba was under the dictatorship of Fulgencio Batista and the regime wanted to implement a new cultural policy. For this purpose, Batista founded in 1955 the National Institute of Culture, an institution that proclaimed artistic expression should remain neutral territory. *Ciclón* disagreed with this position; in an editorial, the journal maintained that the Institute's view was hypocritical, because there was one set of moral criteria for judging art and a different set for judging and conducting politics.

Ciclón, and the almost defunct *Orígenes* (it would cease publication the following year) expressed their support of Borges's work. The latter published an article by Roberto Fernández Retamar refuting Hector Murena's argument in his book *El pecado original de América* ('The Original Sin of America'). Murena claimed that, in order for Latin American intellectuals to create an authentic culture, they should break entirely with their European heritage. Retamar pointed out that Borges had already offered a solution to the cultural dilemmas faced by Latin American writers; in his 'The Argentine Writer and Tradition' (1951), Borges had claimed Western tradition as his own and the Latin American writer's right to treat that tradition with creative irreverence.

Ciclón, on the other hand, took part in the debate produced by Prieto's book. It reprinted an article published in the short-lived Argentine journal *Ciudad* that defended Borges's work and political positions. Even Piñera, who a decade earlier had criticized Borges for his supposed lack of concern with his immediate context, now took his side. He did it in the most indirect way, by publishing an article in which Borges attacked the Spanish philosopher José Ortega y Gasset, who had died recently. Major Latin American journals – including *Sur* – paid tribute to Ortega y Gasset, but Borges chose a Cuban journal to air his dissenting views. He decried Ortega's style; his metaphorical writing interfered with the clear communication of his ideas. For Piñera, the article became a denunciation of official culture both in Argentina and Cuba, the type of culture promoted by the Cuban National Institute of Culture.

The Cuban Revolution caused a redefinition of the intellectual's role and of literature's social function. In 1959 Borges was celebrated by the leading Cuban newspaper as the most important living writer of the Spanish language. Two years later, his views on the Revolution were well-known: he signed a declaration in support of the Cubans who took part in the failed Bay of Pigs invasion. Despite this open act of hostility towards the Revolution, Borges's name continued to appear in Cuban publications for most of the 1960s. The turning point came in 1968. A year earlier, the critic Rogelio Llopis, the main promoter of fantastic fiction on the island, called Borges a major influence on Cuban writers who practise that genre. A debate on whether revolutionary writers should adopt socialist realist precepts was taking place at the time, and Llopis turned to Borges to defend imaginative literature. The author was proof that realism did not necessarily capture reality more accurately; both realism and fantastic fiction could achieve this aim by different means. In 1968, Llopis included 'Las ruinas circulares' in his compilation *Cuentos fantásticos*; in a biographical note, he called Borges 'the master of an entire generation of Latin American writers', but also a man whose 'reactionary, shameful political positions' would secure him a place in the 'universal history of infamy'.[9] In spite of this, there was still room to print Borges's work. That would change soon, and Borges would be censored in the island for the next two decades.

In the late 1960s and early 1970s, important sectors of literary criticism in Cuba and Argentina coincided: a book such as *Borges y el juego trascendente* by Blas Matamoro (1971, dated in 1969), and the famous essay, 'Caliban', by Roberto Fernández Retamar (1971), set out to transcend the apparent dichotomy between Borges's literary genius and his outrageous political views. Several critics in both countries had tried to separate the man from his work, but Matamoro and Retamar sought to identify in Borges's fiction – not in his public statements – his real ideology. Retamar, for example, saw in Borges's symbols (mirrors that multiply the same image, labyrinths without exits, dark libraries) a reflection of the world from which he came: the world of the declining Latin American bourgeoisie.

This perspective, though, was not shared by everyone. The Argentine critic Beatriz Sarlo has written that in 1970 Borges was for her 'an exasperating love-hate object'.[10] She read with surprise and irritation 'El otro duelo' ('The Other Duel'), one of Borges's most violent short stories, published by the journal *Los Libros*. A few weeks earlier, the general who led the 1955 coup against Perón, Pedro Eugenio Aramburu, had been kidnapped and killed by the Montoneros, one of the guerrilla groups that emerged in the late 1960s following the example of the Cuban Revolution and Che Guevara's idea of bringing the revolution to all of Latin America. Sarlo recounts that the short story's brutality anticipated the violence that would dominate the decade and would find its culmination in the systematic repression organized by the military junta that took power in 1976.

In Cuba, a dark period for artistic freedom was beginning. The 1970s saw a prescribed method for producing literature, the censorship and punishment of Cuban writers, and the increasing division among Latin American intellectuals regarding literature's role in society. One would think that Borges had completely vanished from Cuban literary circles – and he had, but only publicly. He was still read, and his influence extended to many writers of the time. The first generation of writers educated within

the Revolution – the founders of the magazine *El Caimán Barbudo* – read
Borges in secret and considered him one their principal influences. Borges's
imaginative literature represented a refuge from the narrow aesthetic
criteria that had been imposed.

   Cuba had seen a social transformation that many writers in Argentina
and Latin America wanted for their countries. A revolution like Cuba's was
supposed to have created (or was in the process of creating) what David
Viñas described as a literary utopia under Socialism:

> In an authentic socialist society, dreams will become superfluous: every-
> thing will take place during the waking hours because there will not
> exist a boundary between dream and reality. Once this separation is
> eliminated, literature and art will be created just by living our everyday
> lives: not even the 'exceptionality' conferred today on literary expression
> will be necessary.[11]

   Borges's literature would be opposed to that dream because it embodied
a 'defence mechanism' against a changing society that had seen the rise of
Peronism. The emotions his work evoked (generosity, intensity, reconciliation) were only possible within the limited space his writings had
created. Nevertheless, the young Cuban writers who were supposedly
producing a new literature for a new society made Borges into
a fundamental figure. Their attitude questioned the possibility of ever
arriving at such a literary utopia.

   This comparison of the influence politics played on the reception of
Borges in Cuba and Argentina has aimed to show that literary interpretation is tied to particular reading contexts. On numerous occasions,
a writer's work becomes significant for what it means in a specific place
and time. Furthermore, writers and critics, particularly those connected to
a larger national and cultural project, tend to read other writers in relation
with their own personal or collective enterprises. In a way, these two
approaches represent a distortion of what the work is, and they may hinder
an accurate reading. But, is it ever possible to separate a work from the
context in which it is read? Borges himself taught us that 'a book [. . .] is
a relationship, an axis of innumerable relationships,'[12] and therefore we
cannot predict how his literature will be read in the future.

Notes

1. A version of this essay was presented at the International Symposium, 'The
   Future of Borges Studies', University of Pittsburgh, 21–23 March 2018. I want

to thank my colleague Nancy Gates-Madsen for her comments and suggestions.

2. Jorge Luis Borges, *El idioma de los argentinos* (Buenos Aires: M. Gleizer Editor, 1928), p. 89. All translations from Spanish sources are my own.

3. Martín Lafforgue, ed., *Antiborges* (Buenos Aires: Javier Vergara Editor, 1999), p. 45.

4. José Lezama Lima, *Imagen y posibilidad* (La Habana: Editorial Letras Cubanas, 1981), p. 196.

5. Cintio Vitier, 'En torno a la poesía de Jorge Luis Borges', *Orígenes* 1, 6 (1945), pp. 311–320.

6. María Zambrano, 'La Cuba secreta', *Islas* (Madrid: Verbum, 2007), pp. 92–100.

7. David Viñas, *Literatura argentina y política: de Sarmiento a Cortázar* (Buenos Aires: Ediciones Siglo Veinte, 1974), p. 89.

8. 'Dice Borges, 'El conocimiento del idioma en que se expresa crea un sentimiento pudoroso y casi reverencial en el escritor.' Entrevista de Jotabea, *El Hogar*, 2433 (1956), p. 107.

9. Rogelio Llopis, ed., *Cuentos fantásticos* (La Habana: Instituto del Libro, 1968), p. 407.

10. Beatriz Sarlo, *La pasión y la excepción* (Buenos Aires: Siglo XXI Editores Argentina, 2003), p. 10.

11. Viñas, *Literatura argentina y política*, p. 88.

12. Jorge Luis Borges, 'A Note on (Toward) Bernard Shaw', in *Labyrinths* (New York: New Directions, 2007), p. 214.

CHAPTER 30

Borges and Coetzee

Fernando Galván

There are reasons to regard Borges and J.M. Coetzee as very different writers, even if both share common views on metafiction and what some readers consider a difficult and obscure style characterized by philosophical and esoteric concerns, the pervading use of fantasy and allegory, and the distance between their fictions and the world of reality. Certainly, a basic fact that separates them is that Borges was no novelist, whereas Coetzee is mainly defined as such; there is a great contrast between Borges's numerous collections of short fictions, and only two minor books of short stories (but 17 novels!) in the case of Coetzee.[1] The development of characters and the depiction of society, so characteristic of the novel as a genre, that define Coetzee's contribution to literature, definitely cannot be called 'Borgesian'. Moreover, some of Borges's more peculiar literary preferences, like his love for Anglo-Saxon and Old Icelandic texts, or for Stevenson, Chesterton, Wells, and Kipling, seem worlds apart from Coetzee's literary treatment of apartheid, or his ethical interest in the rights of animals.

What, then, are the contexts in which both writers can be read together, and how can their writings and ideological and aesthetic positions help in interpreting their respective works? Detailed critical attention to their parallels has so far been scarce, despite Coetzee's professed admiration for Borges. In 1998, he reviewed *Collected Fictions* for the *New York Review of Books*,[2] demonstrating a great familiarity with Borges's works and his role in Latin American and international literature: 'He more than anyone renovated the language of fiction and thus opened the way to a remarkable generation of Spanish-American novelists' (*Stranger Shores,* 140). He also commended Borges for sharing with Samuel Beckett (one of his favourite writers) the International Publishers' Prize of 1961 (139). Curiously enough, Borges and Coetzee have consistently written literary criticism throughout their careers, and there are similar views on specific writers, philosophers, works, and a variety of topics, showing as well a common interest in some geographical areas, historical periods, and other issues: central Europe (particularly the Austro-Hungarian empire), the United States, Jewishness, mathematics, national literatures *vs* international literature, the process of writing, etc.[3] Kafka, Dostoevsky, Nietzsche, Kierkegaard, Whitman, Faulkner, Defoe and Cervantes are among their most cited authors.[4]

Coetzee's profound knowledge of Borges seems uncommon for a writer who is not especially associated with Hispanic literatures,[5] because he does not simply mention Borges's best-known fictions, but also alludes to the great variety of writings he produced, including his numerous non-fiction pieces and poetry. Coetzee is clearly aware of Borges's evolution, as well as of some biographical details that throw light on his oeuvre: 'Englishness was one part of Borges's self-fashioning, Jewishness another [. . .]. The young Borges also taught himself German and read Schopenhauer, who came to exert a lasting influence on his thought'. That familiarity includes, for instance, references to the very young Borges, citing his 'youthful radicalism', as when 'he dreams up a language in which one word will stand simultaneously for sunset and the sound of cattle bells' (*Stranger Shores*, 142), thus evoking Borges's declaration in his *ultraísta* period in favour of new and refreshing metaphors (see his 1926 'Verbiage for Poems', *TTL* 20–22).

The explanation for this is a shared view about writing, and Coetzee's own reflections on language and style are akin to Borges's mature considerations about precision, concision, and economy in the use of language, as well as in the avoidance of dialect and regional vocabulary. Robin Fiddian has emphasized the young Borges's anti-colonial position vis à vis the Royal Spanish Academy and metropolitan Spanish; but also how he later became more open to a universal focus ('We cannot confine ourselves to what is Argentine in order to be Argentine', Borges said).[6] Coetzee has recently echoed Borges's defence of Western culture in 'The Argentine Writer and Tradition' in his review of another Argentine writer, Antonio di Benedetto (*Late Essays*, 138). Although he did not go through a similar phase regarding language, it is true that his claim to a European tradition took place, as J.C. Kannemeyer has put it, 'not by negating his colonial background, but by conscious, nuanced reflection on its cultural crisis'; also, David Attwell focuses on the 'unlocatable' English spoken and written by Coetzee, 'a function of his cosmopolitanism and his election of world culture over regional or national culture', to the extent that even though he was born into the language, his English looks like Beckett's French: 'naturalness was gradually lost . . . [his English being] shorn of the identity markers of Englishness'.[7]

When discussing the diversity of options and translations into English for Borges's Spanish texts, Coetzee manifests himself fully conscious of how much the Argentine was a stylist: 'Borges's prose is controlled, precise, and economical to a degree uncommon in Spanish America. It avoids (as Borges notes with some pride) "Hispanicisms, Argentinisms, archaisms, and neologisms; [it uses] everyday words rather than shocking ones"' (*Stranger Shores*, 148). It is as if Coetzee were talking about his own compressed and extremely concise style, and on his attempt to write in an English that bears no trace of the South-African (or any other) variety. His knowledge of Spanish in the period spent in the United States (1965–1971) was, according to his own words, 'weak' (Kannemeyer, 145, 175): it seems he taught himself the language, as he did with French (Kannemeyer, 96). But that knowledge must certainly have improved with time, as his detailed comments on the different English translations of Borges's fictions show (*Stranger Shores*, 148–150). No wonder, given his interest in translation, which for him is equivalent to 'reading' or 'criticism': 'all reading is translation, just as all translation is criticism' (*Doubling the Point*, 90). In fact, most of Coetzee's criticism of foreign works (originally in Dutch, German, French, Italian, and Spanish) abounds in discussion of their respective translations.[8] Borges is an obvious parallel in this respect, as shown by his own translations (from English, French, German, Anglo-Saxon, or Old Icelandic), and his reflections on some of them (see, for instance, his discussion of the title of Kafka's *Die Verwandlung*, *OC* IV: 102–104; or 'The Translators of *The Thousand and One Nights*', *TTL* 92–109).[9]

Perhaps their condition of bilingual speakers from an early age (Spanish/ English and Afrikaans/English) may account for that special linguistic awareness, but also their self-teaching of other languages, including German, Anglo-Saxon, and Old Icelandic in the case of Borges, or French, Spanish, and Russian in the case of Coetzee. That bilingualism has occasionally made both of them utter puzzling declarations, such as Borges's words in 'An Autobiographical Essay', when he listed the first books he had read as a child, all of them in English (due to the influence of his English grandmother), and added that 'When later I read *Don Quixote* in the original, it sounded like a bad translation to me'.[10] Similarly, Coetzee in response to a letter from Paul Auster, wrote that he felt English for him was just a 'first language' in which he did not 'feel at home', so it was rather a 'primary tongue', not a 'mother tongue' (*Here and Now*, 72).[11]

These similarities about language are also paralleled in their respective (international) education, family background (colonial ancestors), and admiration towards Western or European culture. Recent scholarly work on their postcolonial agendas, such as Fiddian's and Attwell's books cited above, or the monumental biographies produced by Edwin Williamson (*Borges: A Life*, 2004) and Kannemeyer, bear witness to a depth and richness of allusions and common positions that would probably merit a full-length comparative study. These volumes have proved, for instance, that the widespread notion that presents Borges and Coetzee as Southern writers whose main ambition was to be considered Western (and even European), neglecting their own native cultures and countries of origin, is now a worn-out and false cliché. Borges's and Coetzee's aspirations were no doubt to become international writers, but they were equally involved in their national literatures and cultures, holding a critical position versus colonialism and neo-colonialism.

Another fundamental common tenet is their ultimate philosophical position, which can also account for some of their stylistic similarities. Jan Wilm has recently explained how Coetzee's oeuvre requires slow reading, a reading that is characteristically philosophical for its level of abstraction and its transformative power: 'the trembling aspects of an unceasing hovering between absolute clarity, sentences chiselled as into stone, like axioms, and total ambiguity, a positive openness through which allusion, poetry, and signification seep into the readers' minds'.[12] It is self-evident that this statement is applicable to the reading of Borges, and thus it is no surprise that Wilm (200) also points to 'Pierre Menard' *CF* 88–95 as one of the sources behind Coetzee's novel, *The Childhood of Jesus* (2013).

Since the publication of Coetzee's very first book, *Dusklands* (1974), critics have mentioned Borges's shadow upon him. In the case of that novel many of the allusions to Borges (though not all) were unfavourable, coming from some South-African Marxist critics who deplored that Coetzee, like Borges, was too 'cerebral' and 'cold', and did not engage himself with the demanding political circumstances of his country, as other white writers (e.g. Nadine Gordimer) did.[13] As a general rule, critical references to Borges's influence in other works, although not absolutely absent, are not frequent, and, when given, are mostly generic and lack detailed discussion. For instance, his third novel, *Waiting for the Barbarians* (1980) is, like others, Kafkaesque. Coetzee himself has mentioned Dino Buzzati's novel *Il deserto dei Tartari* as one of his references when writing it (Attwell, 113), but no connection has been made so far to Borges's comments on Buzzati's work and its relation with Kafka (*OC* IV: 467, in the preface to the edition of the novel in his 'A Personal Library').

The Czech writer is certainly a major influence for Coetzee, particularly in the novels of the 1970s and 1980s (*In the Heart of the Country*, 1977; *Waiting for the Barbarians*, 1980; *Life and Times of Michael K*, 1983; or *Foe*, 1986), but so was he for Borges,[14] who is present (even if indirectly) behind those novels. Borges seems to be always there, in the background at least: it cannot be a mere coincidence that Coetzee included him in the courses he taught in that period at the University of Cape Town (Kannemeyer, 228–230). Readers feel that there is a common mood in the mysterious environments, the allegorical worlds, and the transcendental fictions of these novels, not only common within Coetzee's oeuvre, but also in Borges's stories.

In the case of *Foe*, the presence of Borges is even more intense, with his celebrated games with the *doppelgänger* and the figure of the author, as well as the process of rewriting. The shadow of 'Pierre Menard' is evidently there again, and possibly that of 'The Writing of the God', too. After his Nobel Prize Lecture, 'He and His Man' (2003), there is no doubt that Coetzee was inspired by Borges and his narration 'Borges and I' in the writing of *Foe* and the Lecture itself (Attwell, 149).[15] In my view, the words that close that Lecture, redolent of the atmosphere of *Foe*, recall that Borgesian text, even if 'Borges' has been substituted here by 'Defoe' ('his man'):

> He yearns to meet the fellow in the flesh, shake his hand, take a stroll with him along the quayside and hearken as he tells of his visit to the dark north of the island, or of his adventures in the writing business. But he fears there will be no meeting, not in this life. If he must settle on a likeness for the pair of them, his man and he, he would write that they are like two ships sailing in contrary directions, one west, the other east. ('He and His Man', *Three Stories*, 71)

Behind that rewriting of *Robinson Crusoe* (and in other works published after *Foe*) lies the preoccupation with the identity and the construction of the 'I' of the author, probably a direct influence of French post-structuralism. In this respect, it is relevant to remember, as Coetzee does in his 1998 review of *CF*, that 'In the 1950s Borges was more highly regarded, and perhaps more widely read, in France than in Argentina' (*Stranger Shores*, 140). But we cannot fail to notice either that Borges had also written on *Robinson Crusoe* and on *Moll Flanders* (see *OC* IV: 510–511, and *TTL* 63, 143, 429), and that he dealt as well with the construction and self-masking of the author in other writers, such as Walt Whitman (*OC* IV: 163–166, notably 164–165; also, *TTL* 445–449, especially 447), an author equally reviewed by Coetzee (*Inner Workings,* 174–188). Coetzee discusses this question of the masking of the author in other critical reviews of writers such as Günter Grass (*Inner Workings,* 139–143) or W.G. Sebald (*Ibid.,* 145–154), mentioning Borges explicitly in the latter case in reference to his treatment of time and paradoxes, due – Coetzee says – 'to one of Borges's mentors, the neo-Platonist Sir Thomas Browne' (*Inner Workings,* 148).

The post-structuralist notion that language writes us, that language speaks through us, is of course ultimately Borgesian, no matter whether Coetzee might have taken it directly from Barthes or Derrida; and it dominates many of the recent novels published by Coetzee, not least the three autobiographical books (*Boyhood,* 1997; *Youth,* 2002, and *Summertime,* 2009), in which he prefers to use the pronoun 'he' instead of 'I' to refer to himself, as well as the present tense to narrate past actions.[16] Similarly, and again, the Borgesian self-masking of the author (how not to recall, for instance, Borges reviewing his own *Historia universal de la infamia* under the Cervantine guise of 'El Bachiller Carrasco'?)[17] pervades other books, like *Elizabeth Costello* (2003), *Slow Man* (2005), and *Diary of a Bad Year* (2007), where the author and his masks are extraordinarily powerful and disconcerting: how much of the old Australian writer Elizabeth Costello is really J.M. Coetzee in the first two novels, and how much of 'JC', 'Señor C', 'Mr. C', or 'Juan' is part of the real flesh-and-blood writer in *Diary of a Bad Year*? The figures of the author in those novels undoubtedly share many features with J.M. Coetzee, but none of them is really Coetzee himself (Attwell, 233–246).[18] As Borges wrote at the end of 'Borges and I' (*CF* 324), Coetzee might have also confided, 'I am not sure which of us it is that's writing this page'.

Notes

Page references to the Obras completas of Borges in this chapter are to the 4-volume edition published in Buenos Aires by Sudamericana (2011).

1. The two collections are recent: *Three Stories* (Melbourne: The Text Publishing Company, 2014) and *Siete cuentos morales* (Buenos Aires: El Hilo de Ariadna, 2018); the English original, *Moral Fables,* remains unpublished at the time of writing these pages.
2. Now in *Stranger Shores. Literary Essays 1986–1999* (New York/London: Penguin Books, 2002), pp. 139–150; hereafter cited in the text as *Stranger Shores.*
3. In addition to *Sranger Shores,* Coetzee's literary essays have been collected in *White Writing* (1988), *Doubling the Point* (1992), *Giving Offense* (1996), *Inner Workings* (2008), and *Late Essays* (2017). Other non-fiction titles

include two anthologies of texts translated from Afrikaans and Dutch: *A Land Apart*, with André Brink (1986) and *Landscape with Rowers: Poetry from the Netherlands* (2004); and three other collections: *The Lives of Animals* (1999), *Here and Now*, with Paul Auster (2013), and *The Good Story*, with Arabella Kurtz (2015).

4. Even when writing about other writers not discussed by Borges, like Philip Roth, Coetzee cannot avoid drawing the reader's attention to what Borges would have done instead; writing on *The Plot Against America*, he says: 'Borges would have made better use of the layer of solid historical research on which Roth has built his book ... What Borges knew is that the ways of history are more complex and more mysterious than that' (*Inner Workings*, 243).

5. He has also written on Juan Ramón Jiménez (*Late Essays*, 130–133), Gabriel García Márquez (*Inner Workings*, 257–271) and Antonio Di Benedetto (*Late Essays*, 134–151). However, in recent years Coetzee has become more attached to South America through the establishment, in 2015, at the Universidad Nacional de San Martín (Argentina), of the 'Cátedra Coetzee: Literaturas del Sur' ('Coetzee Chair: Literatures of the South') in which he participates very actively.

6. Robin Fiddian, *Postcolonial Borges, Argument and Artistry* (Oxford: Oxford University Press, 2017), pp. 55–65, and 112–115.

7. J.C. Kannemeyer, *J.M. Coetzee. A Life in Writing* (Melbourne/London: Scribe, 2012), p. 215; and David Attwell, *J.M. Coetzee and the Life of Writing* (Oxford: Oxford University Press, 2015), pp. 39, 41.

8. See, for instance, in *Stranger Shores,* in addition to Borges, Harry Mulisch, Cees Nooteboom, Rilke, Kafka, or Robert Musil; in *Inner Workings*, the cases of Italo Svevo, Robert Walser, Joseph Roth, Paul Celan, Günter Grass, or García Márquez; and in *Late Essays*, works by authors such as Goethe and Hölderlin.

9. See also Suzanne Jill Levine, 'Borges on Translation', in *The Cambridge Companion to Jorge Luis Borges*, ed. Edwin Williamson (Cambridge: Cambridge University Press, 2013), pp. 43–55.

10. Borges, with Norman Thomas di Giovanni, 'An Autobiographical Essay', *The Aleph and Other Stories 1933–1969* (London: Jonathan Cape, 1971), p. 209.

11. In the same letter (27 May 2009) Coetzee mentions his unease when he finds '*Traduit de l'anglais (Sud-Africaine)*' in the French translations of his works: 'I'd like someone to point to the moments when my *anglais* becomes *sud-africaine*. To me it reads like *anglais* purged of markers of national origin, and a little bloodless for that reason', (*Here and Now*, 72). On this issue, Attwell's discussion (pp. 35–48) is very interesting, alluding not only to this letter with Auster, but also to the voice of J.C. in Coetzee's novel *Diary of a Bad Year* and all the subtle negotiations with Afrikaans that Coetzee has made during his lifetime.

12. Jan Wilm, *The Slow Philosophy of J.M. Coetzee* (London: Bloomsbury, 2016), p. 19.

13. Favourable reactions to the Borgesian influence are those of Tony Morphet and Steven Watson cited by Kannemeyer (pp. 252, 256); the unfavourable ones include, among others, those of Paul Rich, and Sarah Christie, Geoffrey Hutchings, and Don Maclennan (cited by Sue Kossew ed., *Critical Essays on J. M. Coetzee* (New York: G.K. Hall & Co., 1998), pp. 3, 15).

14. Jane Poyner has pointed out some of the parallels between Coetzee and Kafka, quoting David I. Grossvogel's interpretation of *The Trial* as a 'Borgesian' misreading, which she connects with Coetzee (*J.M. Coetzee and the Paradox of Postcolonial Authorship*, Farnham, Surrey: Ashgate, 2009, 76). Attwell (145–146) mentions some of Kafka's texts that were an inspiration for *Michael K*, not surprisingly, in my view, old favourites of Borges: 'Report to an Academy' and 'A Hunger Artist', as well as Melville's *Bartleby the Scrivener* (see Borges, *varia*, in *TTL* 245–246, 501–502).

15. See also Martin Woessner, 'In the Heart of the Empire: Coetzee and America', Tim Mehigan and Christian Moser (eds.), *The Intellectual Landscape in the Works of J.M. Coetzee* (Rochester, New York: Camden House, 2018), pp. 109, 125 (n. 2).

16. For further details on the three autobiographical books and their ethical implications, see Fernando Galván, 'Cuando el "yo" es "él": la *autre*biografía de J.M. Coetzee', *Revista de Occidente*, 344 (January 2010), pp. 43–63.

17. J.L. Borges, *Textos recobrados, 1931–1955* (Buenos Aires: Emecé, 2001), pp. 382–384.

18. Particularly on Borges's presence in *Elizabeth Costello*, see Lucy Graham, 'Textual Transvestism. The Female Voices of J.M. Coetzee', in Jane Poyner (ed.), *J.M. Coetzee and the Idea of the Public Intellectual* (Athens, OH: Ohio University Press, 2006), pp. 219–220; and for further Borgesian details in these texts, as well as in *The Childhood of Jesus* (through a curious *alter ego* of Borges's character, Funes), Fernando Galván, 'Borges, Cervantes and Coetzee, or the Fictionalisation of the Author', *EJES*, 20, 2 (2016), pp. 179–191.

CHAPTER 31

Borges in Portugal

Phillip Rothwell

In the Arco do Cego, near Saldanha, one of the busiest districts of Portugal's capital city, a sculpture by the Argentinian artist Federico Brook depicts a golden hand crowned by a marble cloud. The sculpture is a dimensionally faithful copy of Jorge Luis Borges's hand, as it was in 1985, when its measurements were carefully taken, shortly after the ailing writer had visited Portugal for the last time. For the sculptor Brook, the memorial was meant to invoke Borges's Portuguese origins. It was inaugurated in 2008. The unveiling ceremony was led by one of Portugal's most celebrated contemporary authors, José Saramago, whose work is often read to channel Borges's style and literary (although rarely political) concerns.

The memorial includes verses (in the original Spanish accompanied by a Portuguese translation) from the Argentinian writer's poem 'Los Borges', in which the poetic voice of Jorge Luis begins by asserting that he knows next to nothing about his Lusitanian ancestors. Despite this, he claims their customs and fears persist in all that he does. For the poetic voice, they are an indecipherable part of his time, place, and his oblivion. He admits that his sparse knowledge about his ancestors enables him to project onto them the myths and deeds of a people. The Borges thus become, for the poet Jorge Luis, Portugal itself, a nation made famous because it forced open the walls of the Orient.

In the poem, Borges also equates his forebears with Dom Sebastian, the ill-fated king of Portugal, whose demise on a battlefield of North Africa in the latter half of the sixteenth century led to the Spanish take-over of the Portuguese throne, and 60 years of rule under the Habsburg dynasty (1516–1700). A recurring national myth to which Borges alludes in his poem is that Dom Sebastian had not, in fact, died on the sandy beaches of Alcácer Quibir by the Saracen's sword and would one day in the subsequent centuries return as Portugal's messiah.

The poem 'Los Borges' evidences the Argentinian's knowledge of Portuguese culture, and his willingness to use that knowledge to locate himself as part of European universalizing traditions. The myth of Dom Sebastian persists to this day in Portuguese literature and culture. It does not matter to Borges that he knows few of the specifics of his Portuguese ancestors. They provide him with material onto which to cast his imagination, and another culture to inflect in his writing.

There are various theories about Borges's ancestry on his paternal side. The surname Borges is not uncommon in Portuguese-speaking countries. One of Mozambique's most acclaimed contemporary writers, João Paulo Borges Coelho, is a famous example. Jorge Luis Borges's great grandfather was probably a lieutenant in the Portuguese navy, who married into a Creole family from Córdoba (Argentina) in 1829. Despite a number of references by Borges to his Portuguese origins, Daniel Balderston argues that the most likely provenance of his nineteenth-century ancestors who arrived in Argentina was Southern Brazil, speculating that Borges's representations of that border area may point to a family history of smuggling.[1]

Borges himself propagated a narrative that placed his great grandfather's home in Torre de Moncorvo, in the Trás-os-Montes region of the north of Portugal – not far from the border with Spain. Such a story is not incompatible with a genealogical interlude in Brazil. The municipality of Moncorvo proudly proclaims itself to be the writer's ancestral home, and has invested in researching and commemorating the Argentinian writer's northern Portuguese roots.

In 1984, the ageing writer arranged to visit that ancestral seat of the Borges clan on his trip to Portugal. Ill health and exhaustion led to a change of plans, and he remained in Lisbon, the city with which he had fallen in love on a visit 60 years earlier accompanied by his parents and sister, Norah, shortly before he turned 25.

In an interview in 1971, Borges recalled his first trip to Lisbon. The details of where his family stayed are sketchy. From his experience of Portugal, he remembers best an encounter with a young Modernist writer, with whom he became friends.[2] The writer was António Ferro. Within a decade, Ferro had become the propaganda chief of Portugal's authoritarian dictator, António Salazar, as well as an ardent supporter and publicist of Mussolini and European fascism.

Borges recalls Ferro as a charismatic youth with whom he discussed literature, Modernism, and the avant-garde most days while he was in Portugal's capital in the spring of 1924. Even by 1971, Borges claims he could not think of Portugal without associating it with Ferro who, by then, had fallen from Salazar's favour, been widely discredited, and died on the sidelines of Portugal's politics and culture.

Whether through Ferro's intervention or not, Borges became an avid reader of Portuguese literature. One of his favourite authors was the nineteenth-century realist novelist Eça de Queiroz, a passion for whom he shared with his mother.

One of the most revealing sources of the extent of Borges's knowledge of Portuguese literature is an encyclopaedia entry he wrote on the subject in the mid-twentieth century. It is 20 pages long and appears in the *Enciclopedia práctica Jackson: Conjunto de conocimientos para la formación autodidacta (Compendium of Knowledge for the Self-Taught).*[3] In it, Borges provides an overview of Portuguese literature beginning with its medieval poetry (including his own translations into Spanish). His discussion includes *Menina e moça,* a prototype pastoral novel from the Iberian Peninsula, attributed to Bernadim Ribeiro, narrated from a female perspective and first published in the mid-sixteenth century. Borges also discusses the eighteenth-century neo-classical libertine, Bocage. Other writers on whom he comments include Portugal's greatest Renaissance poet, Luís de Camões; the nineteenth-century playwright, novelist and politician Almeida Garrett; and the father of Portuguese historiography, Alexandre Herculano, whose historical novels influenced a generation of Romantics. Borges admires Antero de Quental, a nineteenth-century philosopher famous for his sonnets and his suicide; Guerra Junqueiro, whose work was part of a republican cultural backdrop that helped to bring an end to the Portuguese monarchy in 1910; and Camilo Castelo Branco, whose very public love life scandalized and enthralled nineteenth-century readers almost as much as his prolific, often melodramatic novels.

For Borges, Portuguese literature was, like the Portuguese people, characterized by 'its taste for marvels, its nostalgia, its fondness for melancholy and unhappiness'.[4] Through this pessimistic stereotype, the influence of one of Portugal's leading nineteenth-century historians and intellectuals, Oliveira Martins, can be detected in Borges's characterization of the Portuguese and their culture. He claimed the Portuguese did not have the same impact on other European literatures as their Iberian neighbour, despite having writers of the stature of Camões and Eça, and historians like Oliveira Martins. He also lamented that the Portuguese failed to pay much attention to their own writers, who were consequently rather solitary agents.

The Portuguese nation did, however, have the great distinction of centuries of maritime contact with Asian cultures, proof of which was manifest in the work of Camões (or Camoens as Borges refers to him), Mendes Pinto, and Wenceslão de Morães. For Borges, in Portuguese literature, like in Portuguese life, 'the ocean and remote adventures in Africa, China and Brazil are present'.[5] As Balderston points out, for Borges the merit of Portuguese literature was never in doubt. But, in contrast to its Iberian neighbour and fellow perpetrator of a world empire, Spain, Portugal was 'largely an importer' rather than a 'net exporter of literature' (Balderston, 'Borges and Portuguese Literature', 163–164). Part of Borges's project was to 'correct this evident injustice' (*Ibid.*, 164).

Borges wrote a poem dedicated to Camões, which reveals once again the influence of Oliveira Martins on the Argentinian's perception of Portugal. Oliveira Martins propagated various pessimistic currents of intellectual thought, one of which associated the end of Portugal's greatness with the death of Camões in 1580. Borges's sonnet tells of Camões's return to Portugal to die in his homeland. With his death, the doors were opened to the nation's rugged ('áspero') Spanish neighbours. The Portuguese bard's demise coincided with the year Philip II of Spain (who would be known as Philip I of Portugal) acceded to Portugal's throne, essentially because the foolhardy Dom Sebastian had died without issue.

Borges also published an essay entitled 'Destiny and the Work of Camões' [Destino e Obra de Camões] on Camões's life and poetry. It was the transcript of a talk he gave in 1972 for the Brazilian Studies Centre at the Brazilian Embassy in Buenos Aires after his sight was failing.[6] He reveals a passion for *The Lusiads*, Portugal's epic poem that both celebrates and critiques its sea-borne empire. For Borges, Camões's poem is about loss with multiple resonances with the classics of antiquity. In other words, he situates Camões as an inheritor of 'universal' European culture.

Around 1960, he wrote another survey article on Portuguese literature that was published in 2003, in his *Textos recobrados*. In it, he discusses the poets António Nobre and Mário de Sá-Carneiro, the philosopher and essayist António Sérgio, and Portugal's most famous twentieth-century writer Fernando Pessoa amongst others. He would return to Pessoa in a letter he penned to the now deceased and globally celebrated poet, dated 2 January 1985. In his anachronic epistle to posterity, he claimed his Portuguese lineage enabled him to grasp Pessoa's writing more thoroughly: 'the blood of the Borges line of Moncorvo and of the Acevedos (or Azevedos) without geographic origin can help me understand you, Pessoa'.[7]

Pessoa and Borges would be brought together by José Saramago in his 1984 novel, *The Year of the Death of Ricardo Reis*. Ricardo Reis is the name of one of Fernando Pessoa's most famous heteronyms – a complex web of fictional personae under which Pessoa wrote. In Saramago's novel, the protagonist is depicted as trying to read a work of detective fiction entitled *The God of the Labyrinth,* by the Irish writer Herbert Quain – the invented author of an imagined text created by Borges.

Saramago, whose communist sympathies were the polar opposite to Borges's political beliefs, confessed in 2000 to the Argentinian newspaper *La Nación,* 'You cannot but love Borges: in him, everything belongs to another universe, to a dreamed world' [no se puede no amar a Borges: en él todo pertenece a otro universo, a un mundo soñado].[8] For Saramago, Borges, like Pessoa, made everything up. The difference between the two was that Borges eschewed the personalities he invented while Pessoa was intermingled with his. Saramago saw Pessoa as the embodiment of the labyrinth to which Borges constantly referred. He admitted to *La Nación* that the manner in which he brought together the literary inventions of two deceased literary titans in *The Year of the Death of Ricardo Reis* was 'all very Borgean' [todo muy borgiano].[9]

Scholars of Portuguese literature including Adriana Martins and Patricia Vieira have pointed to allusions to Borges in multiple epigraphs of Saramago's novels.[10] In the words of Mark Sabine, *The Year of the Death of Ricardo Reis* is a novel that explores the 'politics of literary quotation'.[11] For Sabine, Saramago's protagonist Reis's smuggling of the imagined Irish writer Quain's novel into Portugal, and thus Saramago's 'insinuation of Borges into a novel ostensibly about Pessoa, mock the attempted "cultural policing" of national borders, whether literally, through censorship, or figuratively, through the strict delineation of a literary canon predicated on often blatantly ideological criteria' (*José Saramago: History, Utopia, and the Necessity of Error,* 121). Such strategies on Saramago's part owe much to Borges's influence on his writing. They also demonstrate how the Portuguese Nobel-prize-winning writer was capable of imbuing the tropes of his famously non-Nobel-prize-winning Argentinian muse with a decidedly progressive slant.

Borges has been repeatedly feted within Portuguese culture. Beyond the replica of his hand in the Arco do Cego, there is a mural in his honour in one of the exits to the metro station nearest the Portuguese National Library in Lisbon, Entrecampos. The artwork by one of Portugal's most prominent twentieth-century painters, Bartolomeu Cid dos Santos, fuses the Library, the Labyrinth, and the Aleph. It includes quotations and autographs by celebrated twentieth-century writers including José Cardoso Pires, João de Melo, António Lobo Antunes, Natália Correia, Manuel da Fonseca, and Augustina Bessa-Luís, intertextually linking them with Borges.

The art critic Edward Lucie-Smith claims that Borges had a decisive influence in liberating Cid dos Santos's artistic imagination.[12] In fact, another Portuguese artist, Paula Rego, claims to have recommended to Cid dos Santos that he read Borges, something he first did on a trip to the USA in 1969. Cid dos Santos associates Borges with the American film director Stanley Kubrick, whose work he discovered around the same time, and claims that both Kubrick and Borges became fundamental in shaping the trajectory of his subsequent work as a painter. He credits the way both played with ideas and concepts, mysteries, spaces, and ambiguities with completely changing the nature of his artistic expression (see Araújo Blanco, 101).

Borges's work was first published in Portugal in 1964, when Europa-América launched Francisco Lopes Cipriano's translation of *Historia universal de la infamia*. Another translation by José Bento of the same text was released by Quetzal in 2015, as part of the Lisbon-based publisher's systematic attempt to make available all Borges's principal works of fiction in peninsular Portuguese. His *Ficciones* is recommended by the national curriculum for use in secondary schools.

Borges's poetry and prose have been translated by leading Portuguese writers, including the poets Rui Belo and Pedro Tamen, and the novelist António Alçada Baptista. In 2007, the publisher Presença successfully began to market a series of texts 'chosen' by Borges, including prefaces he had written on writers ranging from Edgar Allen Poe and Oscar Wilde to G.K. Chesterton, Robert Louis Stevenson, and Herman Melville. Borges's 'endorsement' of these canonical, mainly Anglophone male writers played on his reputation within twenty-first century Portugal, over two decades after his death, as a gourmet of 'universal' culture. For Isabel Araújo Branco, the marketing value of Borges within Portugal continues to this day, and is deployed by publishers to increase the appeal of other writers with whom they tenuously seek to link the Borges name (Araújo Blanco, 98).

In a similar vein, Borges is the protagonist in the former Portuguese Secretary of State for Culture, Jorge Barreto Xavier's debut work of fiction *Alexandria* (2017). Barreto Xavier juxtaposes Borges with Alexander the Great, as the constructor of an empire of words that extends well beyond the horizon. In some ways, Barreto Xavier's fictional depiction of Borges plays into a very Portuguese narrative, popularized in the poetry of Fernando Pessoa, to whom the Argentinian Borges had once written. Pessoa had argued that Portugal embodied the Fifth Empire – an empire based on an expansive culture and linguistic spirituality, rather than territorial possession. As a result, this Fifth (Portuguese) Empire was glossed as truly 'universal' in its scope and influence. Clearly, the concept of universalism is fundamentally flawed and nearly always freighted with Eurocentric prejudices of taste and quality. That does not stop it impregnating much of Portuguese intellectual thought. Borges's multilingual appreciations of much of his European heritage, and his repeated framing as one of the leading 'universal' writers, together with his obvious interest in the literature of Europe's oldest nation-state, goes a long way towards explaining the affinities and affection so many of Portugal's cultural producers feel they share with someone they see as their Argentinian scion.

Notes

1. Daniel Balderston, 'Borges and Portuguese Literature', *Variaciones Borges*, 21 (2006), pp. 157–173 (p. 158).
2. Interview with Joaquim de Montezuma de Carvalho, 'Jorge Luís Borges Argentino Universal Recorda António Ferro', *A Tribuna*, Lourenço Marques (15 April 1971), p. 14, quoted in Patrício Ferrari, 'Pessoa and Borges: In the Margins of Milton', *Variaciones Borges*, 40 (2015), pp. 3–21 (p. 4).
3. Jorge Luis Borges, 'Portugal', *Enciclopedia práctica Jackson: conjunto de conocimientos para la formación autodidacta*, Vol. 9 (Mexico, D.F.: W.M. Jackson, 1963), pp. 321–331.
4. Quoted and translated by Balderston, 'Borges and Portuguese Literature', p. 163.
5. *Ibid.*, p. 163.
6. Isabel Araújo Branco, 'Borges: ¿uno de los argentinos preferidos por los portugueses? Sobre su recepción en Portugal', *Variaciones Borges*, 44 (2017), pp. 93–103 (p. 97).
7. Quoted and translated by Balderston, 'Borges and Portuguese Literature', p. 167.
8. Interviewed by *La Nación*, 24 March 2000. Available at (www.lanacion.com.ar /10257-no-se-puede-no-amar-a-borges (accessed 23 September 2018).
9. *Ibid.*
10. Adriana Alves de Paula Martins, *A construção da memória da nação em José Saramago e Gore Vidal* (Frankfurt: Peter Lang, 2006), p. 292; Patricia Vieira, *Seeing Politics Otherwise* (Toronto: Toronto University Press, 2011), p. 170.
11. Mark Sabine, *José Saramago: History, Utopia, and the Necessity of Error* (Oxford: Legenda, 2016), p. 120.
12. Quoted in Araújo Branco, 'Borges', p. 99.

CHAPTER 32

Borges and Italy

Robert S. C. Gordon

Borges Reads Italians

Across the vast terrain of Borges's personal library and the arcane corners of his erudite mind, Italian writers and Italian sources held a significant, if relatively minor place, with one signal exception as we shall see. Italian was certainly a presence in Borges's early Buenos Aires youth, growing up in the Palermo district surrounded by Italian immigrants, before his family moved to Europe in 1914. But he only learned Italian much later, through books. In fact, his Italian canon looks largely conventional, that of a European humanist or man of letters, although as ever with a twist of fantastical Borgesian digression and a web of connections to innumerable other literatures and languages, Western and Eastern. His essays, poems, and stories are peppered with allusions to, among others, the fantastical voyages of Marco Polo, the lyrics of Petrarch, the epic romances of Ariosto (often as a forerunner of Cervantes) and (less frequently) Tasso, the scientific imaginings of Galileo, the poetry of Baroque mannerist Giambattista Marino or eighteenth-century satirist Giuseppe Parini. From the generation preceding his own, Borges admired the august idealist philosopher Benedetto Croce, rather dismissed the Futurist Filippo Tommaso Marinetti and the bombastic decadent Gabriele D'Annunzio, faintly praised the great modernist playwright Luigi Pirandello, and displayed a surprising sympathy for Giovanni Papini, whose reputation as a story-writer he helped revive within Italy. A rare example of a contemporary Italian who interested Borges was Dino Buzzati, whose novel *The Tartar Steppe* (1940) was included in his 'Personal Library' series of 1985–1986 and who shared his own affinity with both Poe and Kafka.

The great exception to this rule of occasional, somewhat cursory glances towards Italian literature was Dante. His *Commedia* ([*Divine*] *Comedy*, ca. 1306–1321) sat at the very highest pinnacle in Borges's map of world literature, 'the greatest work in all of literature'.[1] Dante's poem of the

medieval Afterworld permeated Borges's own writing and imagination
from his epiphanic first encounter in the 1930s. (He claimed to have
learned Italian by reading the *Comedy*, like T. S. Eliot, and to have re-
read it a dozen times thereafter.) Dante is there in playful scholarly
allusions and elaborations, in repurposed Dantesque inventions and fantastical constructions (geometries and numerologies, roses and eagles,
monsters and shadows); but the *Comedy* was also a deeply personal text
for Borges, bound up with an idea of love that he intuited in the figure of
Beatrice.

   Perhaps the most concentrated illustration we have of the fragmentary,
eccentric but genuinely powerful fascination of Borges for Dante is found
in the series of essays he wrote between 1945 and 1951, published in 1982 as
Nueve ensayos dantescos (*Nine Dantesque Essays*). The essays, each only a few
pages long, pick out key moments from the *Comedy* – some very well
known, such as Paola and Francesca in Inferno V or Ulysses in Inferno
XXVI; others, single images or metaphors (the sapphire sky in Purgatory I,
13); or *cruxes* of interpretation (the 'false problem' of whether Count
Ugolino was a cannibal) – and weave around these an allusive dialogue
with the centuries-old scholarly commentary tradition (Pietro di Dante,
Francesco da Buti, Benvenuto de Imola); with contiguous or indeed
distant traditions (the Anglo-Saxon Bede; the Persian Sufi Farid al-Din
Attar); with translators and critics (Cary, Longfellow, but also Hugo,
Lamartine, Croce, Gioberti, Nietzsche) and obscure medievalists
(Ozanam, Torraca, Vitali); before typically ending with an enigma or
a final flourish of Borges's own intuition.

   Borges's Dante is above all an anti-realist, a volcanically creative magi-
cian and fantasist, his poem 'a magical work, a panel that is also
a microcosm' (*TTL* 267) of the medieval universe. It is less shaped by
traditional medieval allegory than by the 'precise traits' of Dante's language, by simile and metaphor, gesture and psychology. Further, the poem
is an extended 'union of the personal and the marvelous' (291), that stages
profoundly felt questions of morality, including the moral question of
theological judgement (why are these figures in Hell?), through extended
projections of Dante's own inner dilemmas. In one passage, Borges compares Dante's condemned souls to Dostoevksy's Raskolnikov. Above all,
for Borges, the *Comedy* is a dream, and also a nightmare, built around
Beatrice: 'I suspect that Dante constructed the best book literature has
achieved in order to interpolate into it a few encounters with the irrecuper-
able Beatrice' (303). All the more astonishing, then, that in the final
instance, in Paradiso XXXI, Dante has Beatrice smile – the final essay is

entitled 'Beatrice's Last Smile' – and turn away from him towards the godhead, for Borges 'the most moving lines literature has achieved' (302).

Borges in Italian

If Borges followed an idiosyncratic path through Italian literature, Italy took to Borges with intense enthusiasm, starting in the mid-1950s; earlier than in most countries, with the signal exception of France (and indeed word of this remarkable 'new' voice had reached Italy via France). *Ficciones* was translated as *La biblioteca di Babele* (*The Library of Babel*) in 1955, by Franco Lucentini, for the dynamic, left-leaning Turinese publisher Einaudi, in its influential book series 'I gettoni' ('Tokens') edited by writer Elio Vittorini. A few years later, Einaudi was a leading player in establishing the Prix International des Editeurs (sometimes known as the Prix Formentor), which was shared ex aequo in 1961 between Borges and Beckett, giving a significant fillip to the international reputation of both. Thereafter, Borges's renown spread rapidly; he was widely translated and he became a key reference-point for the intense literary debates of the 1960s–1970s – debates between a faded neo-realism and an experimentalist neo-avantgarde; between an emergent mass culture and the traditional literary élites; between and within new disciplines such as semiology and structuralism, and crucially also between left and right (with Borges often uncomfortably rejected by the dominant *marxisant* left as a 'reactionary').

This was increasingly accompanied, for good or ill, by the full para-literary panoply of the lionized writer: press and television interviews, a fêted visit to Italy (including a reception for a thousand guests), awards and honorary degrees, a biography, academic conferences and criticism, proliferating translations and reprints, including a Complete Works in the prestigious Meridiani series for Mondadori (1984–1985). One survey counts nearly 60 Italian volumes authored by Borges between 1955 and his death in 1986 (not including reprints), published by 20 different publishers, large and small.[2] At the peak of his renown, he was even the subject of a literary hoax, when in 1984 a frustrated rejected writer sent his short-story to a leading literary magazine, *Nuovi argomenti*, with Borges as its fake author: the story was published. His name was now a talisman.

One lively and not insignificant new editorial project in this period originated in Italy. Bibliophile and publisher Franco Maria Ricci commissioned Borges to select and edit a book series of fantastic literature: the 'Library of Babel' appeared in 33 elegant volumes between 1975 and 1985, offering an eclectic corpus from Poe to P'u Sung-ling, from Voltaire to *The Thousand and One Nights*, including work by Borges himself.

Following his death, a pivotal point of consolidation in his Italian reception came in 1998, just before his centenary in 1999, when the rights to his entire oeuvre were taken over by Adelphi, perhaps the 'purest' of literary publishing houses in Italy. This was a significant move: Adelphi is run by a writer and mythographer not without his own Borgesian affinities, Roberto Calasso, and has a reputation for publishing a cosmopolitan array of authors of the highest literary quality, many of them iconoclasts and visionaries, several with a penumbra of counter-Enlightenment or contrarian radicalism (Nietzsche was a prominent early Adelphi author). Nearly 30 Adelphi volumes of Borges have appeared to-date.

Italians Read Borges

The rapid and extensive dissemination of Borges's work in Italian from 1955, and particularly from the 1960s onwards, inspired an intense dialogue with many of the most creatively interesting and intellectually sophisticated writers of modern Italy. The depth of interaction has led one critic to talk of a 'Borges function' in modern Italian literature;[3] and whilst it is open to debate whether the Italian reception can be distinguished from his global impact on modern literature, we can certainly say that his influence in Italy was both deep and wide, pluriform and multi-dimensional. Many highly important writers absorbed Borgesian elements in many different ways, often mediated through other writers and models.

Three names stand out for the sheer extent and complexity of their engagement with Borges and for their own national and international prominence: Italo Calvino (1923–1985), Leonardo Sciascia (1921–1989), and Umberto Eco (1932–2016). These writers engaged with Borges from differing perspectives; one critic talks of a cosmological-epistemological strand for Calvino; a parodistic and pseudo-bibliographical strand for Eco; and a metaphysical strand for Sciascia.[4] It is striking that all three were tied to Borges's earliest 1955 Italian translation; Sciascia was one of the first to review him, Calvino worked for Einaudi who published him, Eco came to him through Lucentini's great mentor, Sergio Solmi who had himself brought *Ficciones* to Einaudi. All three absorbed him then and over the following 30 years (and more for Eco) into their reflections on literature and into their works of literature, regularly citing Borges, alluding to Borgesian motifs, developing and playing with ideas of literature, history, knowledge, and memory through Borgesian patterns of storytelling.

Calvino first did so in his remarkable 1962 essay 'The Challenge to the Labyrinth', a key moment in Italian literature's re-alignment from the politics of post-war realism to a complex model of response to late twentieth-century modernity. As the title suggests, the motif of the labyrinth is his organizing principle and symbol, and Borges is prominent amongst his reference-points, but alongside him, Calvino also cites the labyrinths of Robbe-Grillet, Butor, Gadda, and finally also his own, underlining a key pattern in the reception of Borges as one prominent vessel, one source within widely circulating conceptual currents of the era. Calvino was still drawing on and deeply admiring of Borges in his final, unfinished, sparkling lecture series, *Six Memos for the Next Millennium* (1988), where he speaks of Borges as having invented a new genre – 'literature squared' and the 'square root' of literature – through his fake texts, his *mise en abyme* commentaries, and the 'quickness', 'multiplicity', and 'exactitude' of his stories, every one of which contains 'a model of the universe' (echoing Borges on Dante). From the 1960s onwards, influenced not only by Borges, but also by Parisian interlocutors such as Raymond Queneau and Georges Perec (themselves of course in their own dialogue with Borges), Calvino built his own version of a modular, combinatory literature, from his elaborate rewriting of *The Count of Monte Cristo* in a story in the collection *t zero* (1967), which has clear echoes of 'Pierre Menard, Author of the Quixote' and is packed with motifs of labyrinths, castles, maps, and manuscripts; to his *Invisible Cities* (1972) recalling the fantastic lands in 'Tlön, Uqbar, Orbis Tertius'; to the embedded books-within-books and tricksy meta-fictions of *If on a Winter's Night a Traveller* . . . (1979).

The case of Eco as a Borges avatar is, if anything, even more compelling, both in his writings as a semiologist and essayist, and in his later career as a best-selling novelist, especially *The Name of the Rose* (1980). Eco was a voracious bibliophile and encyclopaedic reader, as well as a talented parodist, and it is in webs of intertextual play that he and Borges find their strongest affinities. Eco writes about these affinities in a typically lucid and lively essay, 'Borges and My Anxiety of Influence', itself a knowing gloss on Borges's own famous paradoxical piece 'Kafka and His Precursors', on the influence of Kafka on his precursors. Eco's essay proposes a three-way triangular model of literary influence, with author A (e.g. Borges) possibly influencing author B (e.g. Eco), directly or more likely via a third term, X, representing a consciously or unconsciously shared, mediating 'universe of the encyclopaedia'. Eco evokes his secret passion for Borges, even when he was politically and literarily suspect in the 1960s, but also elaborates on the many ways in which they shared common sources – from the arcana of medieval Europe to Joyce and Kafka – or indeed showed clear differences – e.g. between Eco's passion for serial fiction and 500-page novels, as opposed to Borges's legendary economy of form. And in this light, *The Name of the Rose*, a novel written as a medieval and crypto-modern encyclopaedia, looks among other things very much like a compendium of Borgesian motifs: a detective story and multiple murder mystery, a love story, a found manuscript and a secret book, mirrors and medieval scholasticism, a library, a castle, and a coded labyrinth, and, last but not least, the pivotal cameo role of the blind monk Jorge of Burgos. The hint was there in subtler and wittier form already in the 'Prologue', which evokes the chance discovery in an antiquarian bookshop on Corrientes in Buenos Aires of a Spanish translation of a book by Milo Temesvar entitled *On the Use of Mirrors in the Game of Chess*. As Giovannoli points out, Temesvar and his book had been invented by Eco as far back as 1963, where he was also presented as the imputed author of an erudite study of *The Bibliographical Sources of J.L. Borges.*[5]

Sciascia reads Borges through somewhat different eyes from Calvino and Eco, perhaps because filtered through other strong influences, not least Pirandello and the literature of his native Sicily. Sciascia was particularly alert to problems of history, memory, reason and illusion, the fragility of truth and identity, and the fragmentation of both. He made his name as a writer of detective fiction, the first literature directly to address the Sicilian mafia, and later as a writer of historical essay-enquiries, into heretics, absconded mathematicians, and most significantly, the kidnapped and mur-dered former Italian prime minister Aldo Moro, in *The Moro Affair* (1978). If the prime models for this work were classic enquiries into injustice by Voltaire or Zola, in Sciascia's remarkable conception of the public playing out of Moro's death as if it were 'already written . . . a completed work of literature', there are several explicit evocations of Borges; of Pierre Menard and the paradoxes of meaning; and of the Moro case as Borgesian detective story lost in a sequence of wrong solutions and misreadings of 'facts'. As a recent PhD by Clara Martínez Nistal has argued,[6] the Borgesian patterns in Sciascia's detective stories and in his enquiries converge in a third genre, his historical fiction, especially his 1963 novel *The Council of Egypt*, which probes the discursive mechanisms of history itself, in a narrative of forgery and imposture, and the power of language, the document and the archive. Sciascia, we might say following 'Kafka and His Precursors', draws out hidden political and historical aspects in Borges himself.

The catalogue of Italian writers working in Borges's shadow stretches far beyond Calvino, Sciascia, and Eco, into an extended series of figures perhaps less fêted abroad, but of major significance in post-war Italian literary history. Buzzati has already been mentioned and his work points to a particular influence of Borges on Italian fantastic literature, and possibly also science-fiction, both of which genres underwent a late flourishing in the 1950s–1960s, heavily influenced by the same figures (Lucentini and others) who first presented Borges. A brilliantly inventive exponent of literary experimentalism, with elements of the fantastic is Giorgio Manganelli, who had several oblique but strong Borgesian connections, e.g. in his compendium of 100 one-page 'novels', *Centuria* (1979), or in his highly original essay *Literature as Lie* (1967). Links have also been drawn from Borges to Tommaso Landolfi, who was already writing grotesque or 'magical realist' stories in the 1930s; Antonio Tabucchi was heavily influenced by Fernando Pessoa, but also by Sciascia and Borges; Borges's poetry was widely translated, read, and absorbed by major poets such as Mario Luzi; Luigi Serafini's baffling work of obscure design and imaginary language, the *Codex Seraphinianus*, published by Franco Maria Ricci in 1981, could hardly be conceived without Borges. Even Primo Levi, who professed to dislike Borges, was nevertheless fascinated as a scientist by the pseudo-science and mythology of his *Book of Imaginary Beings*.

The list could continue (Bufalino, Magris, Sofri), but there is a limit to the usefulness of such compilations. A more intriguing final moment to explore might be not a work of literature at all, but a film. Bernardo Bertolucci's *The Spider's Stratagem* (1970) is a loose adaptation of 'Theme of the Traitor and the Hero', the story of Kilpatrick, an early nineteenth-century Irish nationalist who dies a hero despite having betrayed his cause to the British. In Bertolucci's hands, the story becomes a complex meditation on Italian Fascism and anti-Fascism, memory and history, fathers and sons, truth, fiction, and identity. The film is also, appropriately given its source, a virtuoso experiment in narrative form and intertextuality, packed with allusions to Shakespeare, Verdi, Magritte, *Gone with the Wind*, Freud, Baroque architecture, and more. The very fertility of the exchange between Borges and Bertolucci (and so many others in between and around), the potential to probe via Borges the most urgent and unresolved faultline in modern Italian history (Fascism), speaks volumes about the fluid translatability of the Borgesian model and the astonishing, innovative energy he gave to two generations and more of Italian literature and culture.

Notes

1. Television interview. Available online at www.lafrusta.net/riv_Arbasino_Bor ges.html (accessed 11 September 2018).

2. Enrique Santos Unamuno, 'Borges en Italia: Perfil de una receptión [*sic*]'. Available online at www.club.it/culture/enrique.santos.unamuno/ (accessed 11 September 2018).
3. Stefano Lazzarin, 'Il cantiniere dell'Aga Khan: ovvero, Buzzati tra Kafka e Borges', *The Italianist*, 25, 1 (2005), pp. 55–71 (p. 55).
4. Renato Giovannoli, 'Manzoni e Pierre Menard. L'influenza di Borges sulla letteratura italiana intorno al 1960 e *Diario minimo*', in Rocco Capozzi, ed. *Tra Eco e Calvino. Relazioni rizomatiche* (Milan: EncycloMedia, 2013), pp. 221–250.
5. Giovannoli, pp. 234–235.
6. Clara Martínez Nistal, 'Rewriting the Limits Between History and Fiction: Jorge Luis Borges in the Work of Leonardo Sciascia', PhD dissertation, University of Edinburgh, 2017.

Further Reading

General

Aizenberg, Edna, ed. *Borges and His Successors. The Borgesian Impact on Literature and the Arts* (Columbia, MO: Missouri University Press, 1990).

Balderston, Daniel, *Out of Context: Historical Reference and the Representation of Reality in Borges* (Durham NC: Duke University Press, 1993).

The Literary Universe of Jorge Luis Borges (New York: Greenwood Press, 1986).

Boldy, Steven, *A Companion to Jorge Luis Borges* (Woodbridge: Tamesis, 2009).

Fiddian, Robin William, *Postcolonial Borges. Art and Artistry* (Oxford: Oxford University Press, 2017).

Louis, Annick, *Borges ante el fascismo* (Bern: Peter Lang, 2007).

Rodríguez Monegal, Emir, *Jorge Luis Borges. A Literary Biography* (New York: Dutton, 1978).

Sarlo, Beatriz, *Jorge Luis Borges: A Writer on the Edge* (London: Verso, 1993).

Shumway, Nicolas, *The Invention of Argentina* (Berkeley and Los Angeles: University of California Press, 1991).

Tabarovsky, Damián, *Fantasma de la vanguardia* (Buenos Aires: Mardulce, 2018).

Williamson, E.H., *Borges: A Life* (Harmondsworth: Viking Penguin, 2004).

ed. *The Cambridge Companion to Jorge Luis Borges* (Cambridge: Cambridge University Press, 2013).

The Penguin History of Latin America (London: Penguin, 1992).

Wilson, Jason, *Jorge Luis Borges* (London: Reaktion Books, 2006).

Relating to specific contexts

Chapter 1

Williamson, E.H, 'Borges against Perón', *Romanic Review*, 98 (2007), pp. 275–296.

Borges: A Life (Harmondsworth: Viking Penguin, 2004).

The Penguin History of Latin America (London: Penguin, 1992), pp. 288–293 and 459–484.

Chapter 2

El Uruguay de Borges: Borges y los uruguayos, 1925–1974. Ed. Pablo Rocca
(Montevideo: Universidad de la República; Fundación BankBoston;
Linardi y Risso, 2002).

Chapter 3

Williamson, E.H., *Borges: A Life* (Harmondsworth: Viking Penguin, 2004).
    'Borges in Context: The Autobiographical Dimension', in *The Cambridge
    Companion to Jorge Luis Borges* (Cambridge: Cambridge University Press,
    2013), pp. 201–225.

Chapter 6

Williamson, E.H., *Borges: A Life* (Harmondsworth: Viking Penguin, 2004).

Chapter 7

García, Diego F. and Mike Seear, eds., *Hors de combat. The Falklands-Malvinas
    Conflict in Retrospect* (Nottingham: CCCP, 2009).

Chapter 8

Contreras, Sandra, 'Intervenciones con Sarmiento. A propósito de "Historias de
    Jinetes"', in *Jorge Luis Borges: políticas de la literatura*. Ed. Juan Pablo Dabove
    (Pittsburgh: Instituto Internacional de Literatura Iberoamericana, 2008),
    pp. 77–99.
Monteleone, Jorge et al., in *Sarmiento en intersección: literatura, cultura y política*.
    Eds. Alejandra Laera and Graciela Batticuore (Buenos Aires: Libros del Rojas,
    2013).
Sarmiento, D.F. (1845), *Facundo. O civilización y barbarie*. Prólogo de Noé Jitrik.
    Notas de Nora Dottori y Susana Zanetti (Caracas: Biblioteca Ayacucho,
    [1977] 1993).
Sarmiento, D.F. (1850), *Recuerdos de provincia*. Prólogo y notas de Susana Zanetti
    y Margarita Pontieri (Buenos Aires: Centro Editor de América Latina, 1979).

Chapter 9

Borges, J.L., *On Argentina*. Ed. with an introduction and notes by Alfred
    MacAdam (New York: Penguin, 2010).
    Textos recobrados, 1919–1929 (Buenos Aires: Emecé, 1997).
    Textos recobrados, 1931–1955 (Buenos Aires: Emecé, 2001).
    Textos recobrados, 1956–1986 (Buenos Aires: Emecé, 2003).
Borges, J.L. and Adolfo Bioy Casares, *Poesía gauchesca* (Mexico, D.F.: Fondo de
    Cultura Económica, 1955).

Borges, J.L. and Betina Edelberg, *Leopoldo Lugones* (1955) (Buenos Aires: Emecé, 1998).

Borges, J.L. and Margarita Guerrero, *El Martín Fierro* (1953) (Buenos Aires: Emecé, 2005).

Shumway, Nicolas, *The Invention of Argentina* (Berkeley and Los Angeles: University of California Press, 1991).

Chapter 10

Gorelik, Adrián, 'Horacio Coppola, 1929. Borges, Le Corbusier and the "Casitas" of Buenos Aires', in *Horacio Coppola: fotografía*, ed. Jorge Schwartz (Madrid: Fundación Telefónica, 2008), pp. 349–353.

Kefala, Eleni, 'Borges and Nationalism: Urban Myth and Nation-Dreaming in the 1920s', *Journal of Iberian and Latin American Studies*, 7, 1 (2011), pp. 33–58.

Sarlo, Beatriz, *Jorge Luis Borges: A Writer on the Edge* (London: Verso, 1993).

Chapter 11

Artundo, Patricia, 'Buenos Aires 1921–1933: modernidad y vanguardia', *Capitales del arte moderno*. Ed. Fundación Cultural MAPFRE (Madrid: Fundación MAPFRE, 2007), pp. 241–275.

'Punto de convergencia: *Inicial* y *Proa* en 1924', *Bibliografía y antología crítica de las vanguardias literarias. Argentina, Uruguay, Paraguay*. Ed. Carlos García and Dieter Reichardt (Frankfurt: Vervuert, 2004), pp. 253–272.

Castillo, Jorge Luis, 'A Poetics of the Interstice: The Mundane and the Metaphysical in *Fervor de Buenos Aires*', *The Romanic Review*, 98, 2–3 (2007), pp. 153–168.

Gallone, Osvaldo, 'Revista *Martín Fierro*: el ingreso en el siglo XX', *Hispamérica*, 25: 74 (1996), pp. 121–226.

Lafleur, Horacio and Sergio Provenzano, *Las Revistas Literarias Argentinas (1893–1960)* (Buenos Aires: Ediciones Culturales Argentinas, Ministerio de Educación y Justicia, 1962).

Miceli, Sergio, *Ensayos porteños: Borges, el nacionalismo y las vanguardias* (Bernal: Universidad Nacional de Quilmes, 2012).

Montgomery, Harper, *The Mobility of Modernism: Art and Criticism in 1920s Latin America* (Austin: University of Texas Press, 2017).

Olea Franco, Rafael, *El otro Borges, el primer Borges* (Mexico, D.F.: El Colegio de Mexico, 1993).

Sarlo, Beatriz, 'Borges: Tradition and the Avant-Garde', in *Modernism and Its Margins. Reinscribing Cultural Modernity from Spain and Latin America*. Ed. Anthony L. Geist and José B. Monleón (New York and London: Taylor and Francis, 1999), pp. 228–241.

Una modernidad periférica: Buenos Aires 1920 y 1930 (Buenos Aires: Ediciones Nueva Visión, 1999) (1st ed. 1988).

Towne Leland, Christopher, *The Last Happy Men: The Generation of 1922, Fiction, and the Argentine Reality* (New York: Syracuse University Press, 1986).

Chapter 12

Aizenberg, Edna, 'Borges, Postcolonial Precursor', *World Literature Today*, 66, 1 (1992), pp. 21–26.

Barili, Amelia, *Jorge Luis Borges y Alfonso Reyes: la cuestión de la identidad del escritor latinoamericano* (Mexico, D.F.: Fondo de Cultura Económica, 1999).

Catelli, Nora, 'La cuestión americana en "El escritor argentino y la tradición"', in *L'écrivain argentin et la tradition*. Ed. Daniel Attala, Sergio Delgado and Rémi Le Marc' Hadour (Rennes: Presses Universitaires de Rennes, 2004), pp. 25–35.

Contreras, Sandra, 'Variaciones sobre el escritor argentino y la tradición', in *Borges. Ocho ensayos*. Ed. Sergio Cueto (Rosario: Beatriz Viterbo Editora, 1995).

Falcón, Alejandrina, 'Debates sobre las lenguas americanas en la revista *Sur* (1931–1945)', *Fragmentos*, 37 (2009), pp. 181–201.

Premat, Julio, 'Borges: Tradición, traición, transgresión', in *L'écrivain argentin et la tradition*. Ed. Daniel Attala, Sergio Delgado and Rémi Le Marc' Hadour, pp. 39–47.

Roger, Sarah, 'Critics and Their Precursors: Theories of Influence in T. S. Eliot, Jorge Luis Borges and Harold Bloom', in *Bloomsbury Influences*. Ed. E. H. Wright (Newcastle upon Tyne: Cambridge Scholars Publishing, 2014), pp. 2–15.

Siskind, Mariano, 'El cosmopolitismo como problema político: Borges y el desafío de la modernidad', *Variaciones Borges*, 24 (2007), pp. 75–92.

Chapter 13

Bioy Casares, Adolfo, *Borges*, edición al cuidado de Daniel Martino (Barcelona: Destino, 2006).

Blanco, Mariela, 'Borges y Bioy Casares, lectores de la fiesta populista', *Variaciones Borges*, 43 (2017), pp. 87–107.

Chapter 15

González, J.E., *Borges and the Politics of Form* (New York: Garland, 1998).

Irwin, J.T., *The Mystery to a Solution: Poe, Borges and the Analytic Detective Story* (Baltimore, MD: The Johns Hopkins University Press, 1994).

Lafforgue, J. and J.B. Rivera, *Asesinos de papel: ensayos sobre narrativa policial* (Buenos Aires: Colihue, 1996).

Oubiña, D., 'El espectador corto de vista: Borges y el cine', *Variaciones Borges*, 24 (2007), pp. 132–152.

Parodi, C., 'Una Argentina virtual: el universo intelectual de Honorio Bustos Domecq', *Variaciones Borges*, 6 (1998), pp. 53–143.

Shaw, D.L., *Borges' Narrative Strategy* (Liverpool: Francis Cairns, 1992).
Williamson, E.H., ed., *The Cambridge Companion to Jorge Luis Borges* (Cambridge: Cambridge University Press, 2013).

Chapter 16

Aira, César, 'Ars narrativa', *Criterion*, 8 (1994), pp. 70–72.
'La innovación', *Boletín del grupo de estudios de teoría literaria*, 4 (1995), pp. 27–33.
'La nueva escritura', *Boletín del centro de estudios de teoría y crítica literaria*, 8 (2000), pp. 165–170.
Contreras, Sandra, 'Aira con Borges', *La Biblioteca*, 13 (2013), pp. 184–198.
Las vueltas de César Aira (Rosario: Beatriz Viterbo, 2002).
Fernández, Nancy, 'Borges, Aira y el narrador en su tradición', *Revista Landa*, 2 (2014), pp. 206–216.
Geraghty, Niall H.D., *The Polyphonic Machine: Capitalism, Political Violence, and Resistance in Contemporary Argentine Literature* (Pittsburgh: Pittsburgh University Press, 2019).
Montaldo, Graciela, 'Borges, Aira y la literatura para multitudes', *Boletín del centro de estudios de teoría y crítica literaria*, 6 (1998), pp. 7–17.
'Un argumento contraborgiano en la literatura argentina de los años '80 (Sobre C. Aira, A. Laiseca y Copi)', *Hispamérica*, 19 (1990), pp. 105–112.
Piglia, Ricardo, *Nombre falso* (Buenos Aires: Seix Barral, 1994).
Premat, Julio, *Héroes sin atributos: figuras de autor en la literatura argentina* (Buenos Aires: Fondo de Cultura Económica, 2009).

Chapter 17

Agheana, Ion, 'Borges, "Creator" of Cervantes; Cervantes Precursor of Borges', *Revista de Estudios Hispánicos*, 9 (1982), pp. 17–22.
Balderston, Daniel, *The Literary Universe of Jorge Luis Borges: An Index to References and Allusions to Persons, Titles, and Places in His Writings* (Westport, CT: Greenwood Press, 1986).
Borges, Jorge Luis, 'Análisis del último capítulo del *Quijote*', *Revista de la Universidad de Buenos Aires*, 5a. época, tomo I (1956), pp. 28–36.
'El testigo', *La rosa profunda* (Buenos Aires: Emecé, 1975), p. 137.
'La conducta novelística de Cervantes', *Criterio* (Buenos Aires) 2 (15 March 1928), pp. 55–56.
'Las alarmas del Dr. Américo Castro', *Sur*, no. 86 (November 1941), pp. 66–70.
'Magias parciales del *Quijote*', *La Nación* (6 November 1949), 2da sección, p. 1.
'Nota preliminar', Miguel de Cervantes, *Novelas ejemplares* (Buenos Aires: Emecé, 1946), pp. 9–11.
'Nota sobre el *Quijote*', *Realidad. Revista de Ideas* (Buenos Aires), año 1, vol. 2, 5 (September–October 1947), pp. 234–236.
'Pierre Menard, autor del *Quijote*', *Sur*, no. 56 (May 1939), pp. 7–16.

'Sueña Alonso Quijano', *La rosa profunda* (Buenos Aires: Emecé, 1975), p. 65.

'Una sentencia del *Quijote*', *La Nación* (Buenos Aires) (6 March 2002), sección 6, pp. 1–2 (originally published in *Boletín de la Biblioteca Popular Azul*, 1933).

González Echevarría, Roberto, 'El Cervantes de Borges: fascismo y literatura', in *In Memoriam: Jorge Luis Borges*. Ed. Rafael Olea Franco (México, D.F.: El Colegio de México, 2008), pp. 79–100.

Louis, Annick, *Jorge Luis Borges: oeuvre et manoeuvres* (Paris: Harmattan, 1997).

Rabell, Carmen R., 'Cervantes y Borges. Relaciones intertextuales en "Pierre Menard, autor del *Quijote*"', *Revista Chilena de Literatura*, 42 (August 1993), pp. 201–207.

Rodríguez Monegal, Emir, *Jorge Luis Borges: a Literary Biography* (New York: Dutton, 1978).

Williamson, Edwin, *Borges: A Life* (Harmondsworth: Viking Penguin, 2004).

Chapter 18

Bate, Jonathan, ed., *The Romantics on Shakespeare* (London: Penguin, 1992).

Garber, Marjorie, *Shakespeare's Ghost Writers: Literature as Uncanny Causality* (London: Methuen, 1987).

Novillo-Corvalán, Patricia, *Borges and Joyce: An Infinite Conversation* (Oxford: Legenda, 2011).

Tiffany, Grace, 'Borges and Shakespeare, Shakespeare and Borges', in *Latin American Shakespeares*. Ed. Bernice W. Kliman and Rick J. Santos (Madison: Fairleigh Dickinson University Press, 2005), pp. 145–166.

Chapter 19

Dapía, Silvia G. *Jorge Luis Borges, Post-analytic Philosophy, and Representation* (New York and London: Routledge, 2016).

Martín, Marina, 'Borges, perplejo defensor del idealismo', *Variaciones Borges*, 13 (2002), pp. 7–21.

Chapter 20

Christ, Ronald J., *The Narrative Act: Borges' Art of Allusion* (New York: New York University Press, 1969).

Paoli, Roberto, 'Borges y la literatura inglesa', *Revista Iberoamericana*, LIII, num. 140 (1987), pp. 595–614.

Stephens, Cynthia, 'Borges, De Quincey and the Interpretation of Words', *Romance Quarterly*, XXXIX, 4 (1992), pp. 481–487.

Valverde, Estela, ed., *A Universal Argentine. Jorge Luis Borges, English Literature and Other Inquisitions* (Sydney: Berrima Southern Highlands, 2009).

Chapter 21

Bonet, Juan Manuel, ed., *El ultraísmo y las artes plásticas* (Valencia: IVA and Centre Julio González, 1996).

Borges, J.L., *Cartas del fervor. Correspondencia con Maurice Abramowicz y Jacobo Sureda (1919–1928)*. Ed. Cristóbal Pera (Barcelona: Galaxia Gutenberg/Círculo de Lectores, Emecé, 1999).

De Torre, Guillermo, *Literaturas europeas de vanguardia* (1925) (Sevilla: Renacimiento, 2001).

Meneses, Carlos, *El primer Borges* (Madrid: Fundamentos, 1999).

Running, Thorpe, 'Borges's Ultraist Poetry', in *Jorge Luis Borges*. Ed. Harold Bloom (New York: Chelsea House Publishers, 1986), pp. 199–225.

Schwartz, Jorge, 'Cansinos Assens y Borges: ¿un vínculo vanguardista?' Available online at www.cervantesvirtual.com/nd/ark:/59851/bmcdr4t8 (accessed 30 July 2019).

Silverman, Renée, 'Questioning the Territory of Modernism: Ultraísmo and the Aesthetics of the First Spanish Avant-Garde', *Romanic Review*, 97.1 (January 2006), pp. 51–71.

Chapter 22

Fiddian, Robin, *Postcolonial Borges: Argument and Artistry* (Oxford: Oxford University Press, 2017).

Levine, Suzanne Jill, 'Notes to Borges's Notes on Joyce: Infinite Affinities', *Comparative Literature*, 49, 4 (1997), pp. 344–358.

Novillo-Corvalán, Patricia, *Borges and Joyce: an Infinite Conversation* (Oxford: Legenda, 2011).

Modernism and Latin America: Transnational Networks of Literary Exchange (New York: Routledge, 2018).

Salgado, César A., 'Barroco Joyce: Jorge Luis Borges and José Lezama Lima's Antagonistic Readings', in *Transcultural Joyce*. Ed. Karen Lawrence (Cambridge: Cambridge University Press, 1998), pp. 63–92.

Venegas, José Luis, *James Joyce and the Development of Spanish American Fiction* (Oxford: Legenda, 2010).

Waisman, Sergio, *Borges and Translation: The Irreverence of the Periphery* (Lewisburgh, PA: Bucknell University Press, 2005).

Chapter 23

Balderston, Daniel, *Out of Context: Historical Reference and the Representation of Reality in Borges* (Durham, NC: Duke University Press, 1993).

Bell-Villada, Gene, *Borges and His Fiction: A Guide to His Mind and Art*, 2nd ed. (Austin: University of Texas Press, 1999).

Kristal, Efraín, *Invisible Work: Borges and Translation* (Nashville, TN: Vanderbilt University Press, 2002).

Roger, Sarah, *Borges and Kafka: Sons and Writers* (Oxford: Oxford University Press, 2017).

Chapter 24

Attala, Daniel, 'Borges y la Biblia', in *La Biblia en la literatura hispanoamericana*. Ed. D. Attala and G. Fabry (Madrid: Trotta, 2016).

Nahson, Daniel, *La crítica del mito* (Madrid: Vervuert/Iberoamericana, 2009).

Navarro, Ignacio, *Últimas inquisiciones* (Buenos Aires: Ágape/Bonum, 2009).

Walsh, Richard and Jay Twomey, eds., *Borges and the Bible* (Sheffield: Sheffield Phoenix Press, 2015).

Chapter 25

Aizenberg, Edna, *Religious Ideas/Eternal Metaphors. The Jewish Presence in Borges*. Doctoral dissertation, Columbia University, 1981.

Alazraki, Jaime, *Borges and the Kabbalah. And Other Essays on His Fiction and Poetry* (Cambridge and New York: Cambridge University Press, 1988).

Deppner, Corinna, *Wissentransformationen in fiktionalen Erzähltexten. Literarische Begegnungen mit jüdischer Erinnerungskultur im Werk von Jorge Luis Borges, Mario Vargas Llosa und Moacyr Scliar* (Frankfurt am Main: Peter Lang, 2016).

Fine, Ruth and Daniel Blaustein, eds., *La fe en el universo literario de Jorge Luis Borges* (Hildesheim: Georg Olms, 2012).

Fishburn, Evelyn, '"El Aleph": A Repeating Universe', *Variaciones Borges*, 33 (2012), pp. 25–31.

Sosnowski, Saúl, *Borges y la cábala. La búsqueda del verbo* (Buenos Aires: Ediciones Hispamérica, 1976).

Chapter 26

Betancort, Sonia, *Oriente no es una pieza de museo. Jorge Luis Borges, la clave orientalista y el manuscrito de 'Qué es el budismo'* (Salamanca: Ediciones Universidad de Salamanca, 2018).

Chapter 27

Almond, Ian, 'Borges the Post-Orientalist: Images of Islam from the Edge of the West', *Modern Fiction Studies*, 50 (2004), pp. 435–459.

Farīd al-Dīn 'Aṭṭār, Dick Davis, and Afkham Darbandi, *The Conference of the Birds* (Harmondsworth: Penguin Books, 1984).

Fouchécour, Charles-Henri and B.A. Rosenfeld, 'Umar Khayyam', in *Encyclopaedia of Islam*, 2nd ed. 24 April 2012. Available online at https://re ferenceworks.brillonline.com/entries/encyclopaedia-of-islam-2/umar-khayyam (accessed 30 July 2019).

Karimi-Hakka, Ahmad, 'Mythical Birds and the Mystical Discourse in Persian Poetry', *Iran Nameh*, 23 (Fall and Winter 2007). Electronic access.

López-Baralt, Luce, 'Islamic Themes', in *The Cambridge Companion to Jorge Luis Borges*. Ed. E.H. Williamson (Cambridge: Cambridge University Press, 2013).

Reinert, B., 'Aṭṭār, Farīd-Al-Dīn', *Encyclopaedia Iranica*, III/1, pp. 20–25. Available online at www.iranicaonline.org/articles/attar-farid-al-din-poet (accessed 10 August 2019).

Chapter 30

Coetzee, J.M., *Doubling the Point: Essays and Interviews*. Ed. David Attwell (Cambridge, MA and London: Harvard University Press, 1992).

Inner Workings. Literary Essays 2000–2005 (London: Vintage, 2008).

Late Essays 2006–2017 (New York: Viking, 2017).

Coetzee, J.M. and Paul Auster, *Here and Now. Letters 2008–2011* (New York and London: Viking Penguin/Faber and Faber, 2013).

Chapter 31

Araújo Branco, Isabel, 'Borges: ¿uno de los argentinos preferidos por los portugueses? Sobre su recepción en Portugal', *Variaciones Borges*, 44 (2017), pp. 93–103.

Balderston, Daniel, 'Borges and Portuguese Literature', *Variaciones Borges*, 21 (2006), pp. 157–173.

Barreto, Xavier, *Alexandria* (Lisbon: Imprenta Nacional-Casa de Moeda, 2017).

Ferrari, Patricio, 'Pessoa and Borges: In the Margins of Milton', *Variaciones Borges*, 40 (2015), pp. 3–21.

Saramago, José, *The Year of the Death of Ricardo Reis*, trans. Giovanni Pontiero (London: Harvill, 1992).

Sabine, Mark, *José Saramago: History, Utopia, and the Necessity of Error* (Oxford: Legenda, 2016).

Chapter 32

Calvino, Italo, 'Jorge Luis Borges', in *Why Read the Classics*, trans. Martin McLaughlin (London: Penguin, 2002), pp. 237–244.

Eco, Umberto, 'Borges and My Anxiety of Influence', in *On Literature*, trans. Martin McLaughlin (London: Secker and Warburg, 2004), pp. 118–135.

Núñez-Faraco, Humberto, *Borges and Dante. Echoes of a Literary Friendship* (Oxford: Peter Lang, 2006).

Index

Haedo, Esther, 22
Hafiz, 220, 225
Haslam, Fanny (Borges's grandmother), 166,
  201–202
Heraclitus, 129, 223
Hernández, José
  Borges's interpretation of *Martín Fierro* and,
    15, 46, 70–73, 76–77, 78–79
  Borges's use of *Martín Fierro* and, 67, 76–77,
    79–80, 125
  and Lugones on *Martín Fierro*, 12, 14, 15, 72, 79
  and *Martín Fierro* as gauchesque, 11, 76–77,
    78–79, 95
heroism. *See* cult of courage
history
  cyclical nature of, 154–155
  in fiction, 40–41, 231, 264
  relationship with present and, 39, 67, 236
  truth of, 5–6, 37–38, 143
'History of the Echoes of a Name, A' (essay), 152
History of the Night, The (poems), 43, 55
'History of the Tango, A' (essay), 108
Hitler, Adolf, 15, 35, 36, 41
Hogar, El (magazine), 51, 56, 239
Homer, 7, 99, 167, 186, 221
'House of Asterion, The' (story), 231
Hugo, Victor, 3, 4, 149, 152–153, 171, 260
Huidobro, Vicente, 174, 175–176, 178
Hume, David, 158, 159–163
'Hymn to the Sea' (poem), 176–177

idealism
  Borges's interest in, 7, 85, 158–163, 217
  Buenos Aires and, 85, 87
  'New Refutation of Time, A' (essay) and, 159,
    162–163
  'Tlön, Uqbar, Orbis Tertius' (story) and, 39,
    150, 159–162, 169
identity
  negation of in literature, 30, 150–154, 171, 225
  negation of in philosophy, 159–160
  negation of in religion, 214, 215–216, 224
  self and, 215–217, 224
immaterialism, 161, 162
immigration
  Argentina and, 12, 83–88, 109
  national identity and, 13–14, 80, 100, 120,
    144–145, 204
'Immortal, The' (story), 213
In Praise of Darkness (poems), 186
infinity
  Joyce and, 180, 186–187
  Kafka and, 191–193
  religion and, 207, 213, 215
Inquisitions (essays), 85, 167

'Inscription on Any Tomb' (poem), 87
'Interloper, The' (story), 54
International Publishers' Prize, 1, 244, 261
interpretation
  context of, 242
  flexibility of, 38, 101, 191, 198, 209–210
*Introduction to American Literature,
  An* (anthology), 201
Invasión (film script with Bioy Casares), 117
'Invocation to Joyce' (poem), 186
Ipuche, Pedro Leandro, 22, 76
Ireland
  'Argentine Writer and Tradition, The' (essay)
    and, 103, 132
  Joyce and, 180–181, 184
  'Theme of the Traitor and the Hero' (story)
    and, 2–5, 151, 155–156
Irigoyen, Hipólito, 14–15, 16, 109
Iron Coin, The (stories), 43, 47, 55, 59, 192
Islam, 7, 222–224
'Israel, 1969', 60
Italy, 1, 6, 7, 83, 259–265

'James Joyce' (poem), 186
Japan, 55, 211
Jitrik, Noé, 59, 64
Job (biblical book), 189–190, 192–193
Joyce, James
  overview of, 6, 103, 180–187, 207
  influence of, 264
  Ulysses and, 180, 182–186, 229
  in writing of other authors, 190
'Juan López and John Ward' (poem), 48, 61–65
Judaism
  'Argentine Writer and Tradition, The' (essay)
    and, 103, 132
  Borges's engagement with, 7, 161, 204–210, 245
  Cansinos Assens and, 175
  Catholicism and, 196, 199, 201
  'Fiesta del monstruo, La' (story) and, 120
  Kafka and, 189
  See also anti-Semitism
Junín, Battle of, 4, 6
Jurado, Alicia, 149, 212, 214

'Kafka and His Precursors' (essay), 132, 134, 191,
  263, 264
Kafka, Franz, 6, 188–193, 229, 245, 247, 259. *See
  also* 'Kafka and His Precursors' (essay)
karma, 212–213
Keats, John, 151, 166–168
'Key in Salonica, A' (poem), 204
Khayyam, Omar, 219–222, 223–224, 225
Kierkegaard, Søren, 191, 245
Kipling, Rudyard, 77, 99, 244

Spain (cont.)
  Borges in, 27–28, 173–178
  imperialism of, 4–5, 14, 18, 26, 103, 238
  inquisition and, 204
  politics of, 11, 145, 196
  Portugal and, 252, 255
Spinoza, Baruch, 150, 152
Stevenson, Robert Louis, 69, 99, 168, 234,
  244, 257
stoicism, 22–24, 64, 170, 190
'Stories of Horsemen' (essay), 73
'Story from Rosendo Juárez, The' (story), 31–32
'Story of the Warrior and the Captive Maiden'
  (story), 76, 79
'Streets, The' (poem), 92
Suárez Haedo, Leonor (Borges's great-
  grandmother), 20
Suárez, Manuel Isidoro (Borges's great-
  grandfather), 5, 26, 87
'Sueña Alonso Quijano' (poem), 148
Sufism, 222, 224
Sur (magazine), 106, 116, 145, 147, 149, 240
Sureda, Jacobo, 85, 178
'Survey of the Works of Herbert Quain,
  A' (story), 236, 256
Switzerland, 16–17, 42, 55, 65, 188. *See also* Geneva

Talmud, the, 175, 206, 208, 210
tango, 13, 20, 45–46, 106–113, 123–126. *See also*
  milonga
'Tango, The' (poem), 125–126
'Testigo, El' (poem), 148
'Testigo, El' (story with Bioy Casares), 116
Textos cautivos (essays), 51
Textos recobrados (essays), 79, 255
'Theme of the Traitor and the Hero' (story), 1–4,
  128, 151, 155–156, 265
'Theologians, The' (story), 215–216
'Three Versions of Judas' (story), 198, 200
Tigres azules (stories), 51, 54
time
  anachronism and, 143
  Buddhism and, 212, 215–217
  concept of, 1–2, 30, 67, 87, 88–89, 180
  cyclical nature of, 129, 154–155, 168
  idealism and, 159, 162–163
  in literature, 180, 231–232, 249
  See also history; 'New Refutation of Time, A'
    (essay)
'Tlön, Uqbar, Orbis Tertius' (story)
  Buddhism and, 216
  idealism and, 150, 159–162, 169
  influence of, 118, 233, 263
  Nazism and, 39, 237
'To John Keats' (poem), 167

'To the Nightingale' (poem), 167
Torah, the, 206, 207, 209
tradition, 15, 99–104, 181, 197, 228, 237. *See also*
  'Argentine Writer and Tradition, The'
    (essay)
translation
  Borges's reading of, 246
  Borges's works of, 174, 183–184, 192, 229
  of Borges's writing, 1, 123, 246, 257
  in *Don Quixote*, 142
  interpretation and, 154, 219, 221–222,
    246
  religion and, 197–198, 199–200
transmigration, 134–135, 151, 213, 217
'Truco' (poem), 108
truth
  concept of, 5–6, 37–38, 143, 162
  literature and, 233, 264, 265
  religion and, 167, 195, 205, 212, 214
Twain, Mark, 77, 234–235
'Twelve Figures of the World, The' (story with
  Bioy Casares), 116
Two Memorable Fantasies (stories with Bioy
  Casares), 116

'Ulrikke' (story), 32
Ultra (magazine), 92
ultraísmo
  Argentine, 54, 85, 92–93, 94, 245
  Spanish, 92, 101, 166, 173–178, 181
Un modelo para la muerte (novella with Bioy
  Casares), 116, 127
'Unending Rose, The' (poem), 222
unitarios, 19, 79, 120. *See also* Sarmiento,
  Domingo Faustino
United States
  Borges and, 1, 45, 201, 245
  culture of, 11, 168
  politics of, 59, 145
  Spanish American culture and, 106–107,
    229, 238
Universal History of Iniquity, A (stories), 124,
  128, 249
Upanishads, the, 161
Uruguay, 6, 15, 18–24, 119. *See also* Montevideo
Úveda de Robledo, Epifanía (Fani), 32–33, 55

Valéry, Paul, 143, 168
Valle-Inclán, Ramón del, 174, 176
Vargas Llosa, Mario, 229, 230–231, 234
Vázquez, María Esther, 31, 53, 167
Venticinco de agosto de 1983 y otros cuentos
  (stories), 43
'Versos de catorce' (poem), 108
Virgil, 99, 143

For EU product safety concerns, contact us at Calle de José Abascal, 56–1°,
28003 Madrid, Spain or eugpsr@cambridge.org.

www.ingramcontent.com/pod-product-compliance
Ingram Content Group UK Ltd.
Pitfield, Milton Keynes, MK11 3LW, UK
UKHW020358140625
459647UK00020B/2532